PASS TRAK

SERIES 7

Workbook

(handwritten) Tien-Ping Ging, 1993

General
Securities
Representative

7th Edition

Dearborn
Financial Publishing, Inc.

The Series 7 Qualification Exam is copyrighted by the New York Stock Exchange. Each page of the examination contains the following notice:

> "The contents of this examination are confidential. Neither the whole nor any part of this examination may be reproduced in any form or quoted or used in any way without the written consent of the New York Stock Exchange, Inc."

Dearborn Financial Publishing, Inc. and its employees and agents honor the copyrights of the New York Stock Exchange. We specifically urge each of our students to refrain from any attempts to remove a copy of the exam; or to copy or record any of the questions on the exam.

At press time, this 7th edition of PassTrak Series 7 contains the most complete and accurate information currently available for the NASD Series 7 license examination. Owing to the nature of securities license examinations, however, information may have been added recently to the actual test that does not appear in this edition.

While a great deal of care has been taken to provide accurate and current information, the ideas, suggestions, general principles and conclusions presented in this text are subject to local, state and federal laws and regulations, court cases and any revisions of same. The reader is thus urged to consult legal counsel regarding any points of law—this publication should not be used as a substitute for competent legal advice.

Executive Editor: Kimberly K. Walker-Daniels
Development Editor: Nicola Bell
Cover Design: Vito dePinto

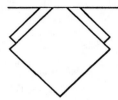

Contents

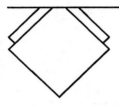

Introduction to PassTrak Series 7

Welcome to PassTrak Series 7. Because you probably have a lot of questions about the course and the exam, we have tried to anticipate some of them and provide you with answers to help you on your way.

The Course

How is the course structured?

PassTrak Series 7 is divided into three books: a textbook, a workbook and an exam book. The textbook, titled *Principles & Practices,* consists of 19 chapters, each devoted to a particular area of general securities sales and regulation that you will need to know in order to pass the General Securities Registered Representative Exam (the Series 7). Each chapter is subdivided into study sections devoted to more specific areas with which you need to become familiar.

The *Workbook* contains 20 chapters. The first 19 chapters provide additional hands-on learning exercises that complement the 19 chapters in *Principles & Practices.* Chapter 20 contains mnemonics and study aids designed to help you review some of the important facts you need for the exam.

The exam book, titled *Questions & Answers,* contains review exams that test the topics covered in *Principles & Practices,* and concludes with two final exams composed of questions similar to those you will encounter on the Series 7 exam.

What topics are covered in this course?

The information needed to pass the Series 7 exam is covered in PassTrak Series 7 through the following chapters:

Chapter 1: Equity Securities
Chapter 2: Debt Securities
Chapter 3: Corporate Special Securities
Chapter 4: U.S. Government and Agency Securities
Chapter 5: Money-market Securities and Interest Rates
Chapter 6: Issuing Securities
Chapter 7: Trading Securities
Chapter 8: Client Accounts
Chapter 9: Brokerage Office Procedures

How much time should I spend studying?

You should plan to spend approximately 90 to 120 hours reading the material and working through the questions. Your actual time, of course, may vary from this figure depending on your reading rate, comprehension, professional background and study environment.

Spread your study time over the six to eight weeks prior to the date on which you are scheduled to take the Series 7 exam. Select a time and place for studying that will allow you to concentrate your full attention on the material at hand. You have a lot of information to learn and a lot of ground to cover. Be sure to give yourself enough time to learn the material.

What is the best way to approach the exams?

Approach each review and final exam as if you were preparing to take the actual Series 7 test. Read each question carefully and write down your answer. Then check your answers against the key and read the accompanying rationale. Making yourself go through all of these steps (rather than simply reading each question and skipping directly to the rationale) will greatly increase your comprehension and retention of the information in the book.

Do I need to take the final exams?

The final exams test the same knowledge you will need in order to answer the questions on the Series 7 exam. By completing these exams and checking your answers against the rationale, you should be able to pinpoint any areas with which you are still having difficulty. Review any questions you miss, paying particular attention to the rationale for those questions. If any subjects still seem troublesome, go back and review those topics in *Principles & Practices*. At the end of each rationale, you will find a page reference that directs you to the page in *Principles & Practices* where the information is covered.

The Exam

Why do I need to pass the Series 7 exam?

Your employer is a member of the New York Stock Exchange (NYSE) or another self-regulatory organization that requires its members and employees of its members to pass a qualification exam in order to become registered. To be registered as a representative qualified to sell all types of securities (except commodities), you must pass the Series 7 exam.

What is the Series 7 exam like?

The Series 7 is a two-part, six-hour, 250-question exam administered by the National Association of Securities Dealers (NASD). The exam is given in two three-hour sessions, each covering different areas of general securities sales and regulation. It is offered as a computer-based test at various testing sites around the country. A paper-and-pencil exam is available to those candidates who apply to and obtain permission from the NASD to take a written exam.

What topics will I see covered on the exam?

This course covers the wide range of topics that the NASD has outlined as being essential to the general securities registered representative. The NYSE exam is divided into six broad topic areas:

	No. of Questions	Percentage of Exam
Advertising, Qualifying Customers, Industry Regulations	31	12%
Securities Instruments	84	33%
Handling Customer Accounts, Taxation, Margins	34	14%
Securities Markets, Order Handling, Confirmations	34	14%
Economics, Securities Analysis, Sources of Financial Information	29	12%
Portfolio Analysis, Investment Strategies, Retirement Plans	38	15%
	250	100%

What score must I achieve in order to pass?

You must answer correctly at least 70% of the questions on the Series 7 exam in order to pass and become eligible for NYSE registration as a general securities representative.

How long does the exam take?

You will be allowed six hours, in two three-hour sessions, in which to finish the exam. If you are taking the computerized version of the exam, you will be given additional time before the test to become familiar with the PLATO® terminal.

Are there any prerequisites I have to meet before taking the exam?

There are no prerequisite exams you must pass before sitting for the Series 7.

How do I enroll for the exam?

To obtain an admission ticket to the Series 7 exam, your firm must file the proper application form with the NASD, along with the appropriate processing fees. The

NASD will then send you an admission ticket that is valid for 90 days and a directory of Professional Development Centers. To take the exam during this 90-day period, you must make an appointment with a Professional Development Center at least two weeks before the date on which you would like to sit for the test.

What should I take to the exam?

Take one form of personal identification that bears your signature and your photograph. You are not allowed to take reference materials or anything else into the testing area except a calculator. Your calculator must run silently and have an independent power source, no alphanumeric keys or programmable memory and no print device.

Scratch paper and pencils will be provided by the testing center, although you will not be permitted to take them with you when you leave.

What is PLATO® ?

The Series 7 exam, like many professional licensing examinations, is administered on the PLATO® computerized testing system. PLATO® is an interactive computer network developed by Control Data as an educational and testing service. Included with your notice of enrollment from the NASD, you will receive a brochure describing how the exam is formatted and how to use the computer terminal to answer the questions.

When you have completed the exam, the PLATO® System promptly scores your answers and within minutes displays your grade for the exam on the terminal screen.

How well can I expect to do on the exam?

The examinations administered by the NASD are not easy. You will be required to display considerable understanding and knowledge of the topics presented in this course in order to pass the Series 7 exam and qualify for registration. If you study and complete all of the sections of this course, and consistently score at least 80% on the review and final exams, you should be well prepared to pass the Series 7 exam.

1   Equity Securities

Corporate Ownership and Common Stock

What Is Stock?

Ownership

Shares of stock represent ownership (equity) in a corporation. Companies issue stock to raise business capital. The property a business owns (its assets) less the claims of its creditors (its liabilities) belongs to the stockholders.

Diversified Ownership, Centralized Management

Each share of stock represents ownership of a company and gives its holder one vote in the company's management. A person who owns ten shares of stock would have 10 votes. Each share carries with it the same rights and privileges of every other share.

In most corporations the holders of the common stock vote for and elect a limited number of people to a board of directors to manage the company's business.

Different Types, Different Rights

Preferred stockholders acquire equity in the corporation, but usually do not have the same voting rights as the holders of common stock.

Classifying Stock by Its Holder

Authorized stock. As part of its original charter, a corporation receives authorization from the state to issue a specific number of shares of stock.

Issued stock. A corporation may issue fewer than the total number of shares authorized by the state and reserve the unissued stock for future needs.

Treasury stock. Treasury stock is stock a corporation has issued and subsequently repurchased from the public in the secondary market. The corporation has the privilege of holding this stock indefinitely, reissuing it or retiring it.

Treasury stock does *not* carry the rights of other common shares, including voting rights and the right to receive dividends.

Outstanding stock. Outstanding stock includes any shares that have been issued by the corporation and that have not subsequently been repurchased by the company.

Putting a Value on Common Stock

Par Value

A stock's par value is an arbitrary dollar value. The par value of a share of stock may change in the event of a stock split.

When stock is sold, the amount of money received in excess of the par value is capital in excess of par (also called *paid-in surplus*, *capital surplus* or *paid-in capital*).

The following illustrates a portion of a balance sheet reflecting stock that was assigned a par value of $1.00 and was initially sold for $5.50 per share:

TCBS Balance Sheet
December 31, 1994

Net Worth

Capital stock	$ 2,000,000
TCBS was authorized to sell 2,500,000 shares. It issued 2 million of those shares with a par value of $1 per share.	
Paid-in surplus *(Capital surplus)*	$ 9,000,000
The company received $4.50 per share in excess of the $1 par value.	
Total	$11,000,000

Book Value

Book value per share is a measure of how much a holder of common stock could expect to receive for each share if the corporation were to be liquidated. Book value is the difference between the value of a corporation's assets and its liabilities divided by the number of shares outstanding.

Market Value

Market value is influenced by supply and demand. There is no direct relationship between the market value and the book value of a stock.

The market value of a stock is quoted in whole dollars plus fractions of a dollar (3/4 point = 3/4 of a dollar, or $.75; 1/8 point = 1/8 of a dollar, or $.125). In the brokerage world, however, the term "dollars" is not used; brokers quote stocks in points. If a stock is quoted at 35 (35 points), this means that the market price for that stock is $35 per share. A stock quoted at 42 1/2 is selling for $42.50 per share.

Normally, stock prices are quoted in 1/8ths of a point. Some low-priced stocks (known as **penny stocks** are quoted in fractions as small as 1/256th. You should become familiar with these fractions and their decimal conversions. You can do this

either by memorizing the conversions or using your calculator.

Think of 1/8 as the "bit" in "two bits," and it will help make conversions from fractions into dollars and cents easier. Because "two bits" is 25 cents, one bit equals 12 1/2 cents. A quote of 5 1/8 equals $5 plus 12.5 cents, or $5.125 per share of stock, and a round lot of 100 shares would cost $512.50.

Fraction Conversion Table

1/8 = 12.5 cents ($.125)

2/8 = 1/4 = 25 cents ($.25)

3/8 = 37.5 cents ($.375)

4/8 = 1/2 = 50 cents ($.50)

5/8 = 62.5 cents ($.625)

6/8 = 3/4 = 75 cents ($.75)

7/8 = 87.5 cents ($.875)

8/8 = 1 = 100 cents ($1.00)

The Rights of Corporate Ownership

Voting Rights

Holders of common stock elect a board of directors and vote on corporate policy at annual meetings. Stockholders are entitled to vote on matters involving:

- issuance of senior securities;
- stock splits; and
- substantial changes in the corporation's business.

Stockholders do not have the right to vote on either the timing or the amount of cash or stock dividends.

Calculating the Number of Votes

A stockholder is entitled to cast one vote for each share of stock she owns. Two ways of voting are known as *statutory voting* and *cumulative voting*.

Statutory voting. Under the statutory voting system, a stockholder may cast

- one vote,
- per share owned,
- for each position.

If four directors are to be elected, the stockholder with 500 shares may cast from 0 to 500 votes for each of the four positions. In the event that the stockholder casts fewer than 500 votes for a candidate for one of the available seats, the remainder of those 500 votes may not be cast for another candidate for the same seat.

Statutory voting tends to put majority stockholders at an advantage over investors who own smaller amounts of stock.

Cumulative voting. Cumulative voting entitles the stockholder to cast

- one vote,
- per share owned,
- times the number of seats to be filled,
- to be cast in any manner the stockholder chooses.

In the example above, the stockholder has a total of 2,000 votes (one vote per share times the number of candidates). Under a cumulative voting system, those 2,000 votes could be cast in any manner the stockholder chooses. The stockholder could cast all 2,000 votes for a single candidate or split them between two or more candidates.

In companies with cumulative voting rights, minority stockholders have a better chance of electing directors.

Voting Trust Certificates _to replace stock_

In some instances management responsibilities may be temporarily transferred to an outside trustee for the company. Stockholders' voting rights may be relinquished to this trustee and the trustee issues voting trust certificates to stockholders in place of their stock certificates.

All of the benefits of ownership except the power to vote are retained by the stockholders.

Nonvoting Common Stock

Companies that choose to issue both voting and nonvoting common stock normally differentiate the issues as Class A (voting) and Class B (nonvoting). Issuing nonvoting stock provides a company with a means to raise additional capital while maintaining control and continuity of management.

Preemptive Rights

When a corporation raises capital through the sale of common stock it may be required by law or by its corporate charter to offer the securities to its common stockholders before it offers them directly to the public. Stockholders then have what is known as a preemptive right to purchase enough newly issued shares to protect their proportionate ownership in the corporation.

To illustrate, a person who owns 4% of the stock of Datawaq Corporation (DWAQ) will have a preemptive right to purchase 4% of any new stock issue. Preemptive rights ensure that stockholders' rights are not diluted at the issuance of new stock.

Other Stockholder Rights

Limited Liability

Stockholders cannot lose more than they have invested in the stock of a particular corporation.

Inspection of Corporate Books

Stockholders have the right to obtain lists of stockholders, receive annual reports, and so on.

Protection of the Corporation

Stockholders may take the company's management to court if they believe that it has committed wrongful acts that could harm the corporation.

Restraint of Illegal Acts

Stockholders may take action against the board of directors of a corporation to restrain it from acting in a manner inconsistent with the corporate charter.

Residual Claims to Assets

When a corporation ceases to exist, the stockholder has a right to corporate assets. A common stockholder may make a claim only after all debts and other security holders have been satisfied.

Benefits and Risks of Owning Common Stock

Benefits of Owning Stock

Growth. Historically, owning common stock has provided investors with greater real returns than any other investment.

Income. Many corporations distribute a portion of their profits in the form of dividends, a major reason many people invest in corporate stock.

Risks of Owning Stock

Decreased or no income. Common stockholders must assume certain risks, including the possibility of dividend income decreasing or ceasing entirely during periods of corporate unprofitability.

Low priority at dissolution. In the event of a company's bankruptcy, owners of common stock have the lowest priority in claims against corporate earnings and assets.

Fall in price. Other investors in the marketplace may not value as highly as the investor does the shares she holds.

Questions

1. TCBS just issued 100,000 shares of common stock. If a pension plan manager purchased 3,000 shares of TCBS for the plan's portfolio, to how many votes would he be entitled?

   _____

2. What percentage of TCBS would its holdings represent?

   _____

3. At its next annual meeting, TCBS will be electing five directors to its board. One of your clients owns 200 shares of TCBS common stock and intends to cast his votes at the meeting. Under the statutory voting system, what is the maximum number of votes he is entitled to cast for each director?

   _____

4. Under the statutory voting system, what is the minimum number of votes he is entitled to cast for each director?

   _____

5. Under the statutory voting system, how many votes can he cast in total for all directors?

   _____

6. If TCBS was using the cumulative voting system, what is the maximum number of votes he is entitled to cast for each director?

   _____

7. What is the minimum number of votes he is entitled to cast for each director?

_____

8. How many votes can he cast in total for all directors?

_____

9. Which of the following represent ownership (equity) in a company?

   I.   Corporate bonds
   II. Common stock
   III. Preferred stock
   IV. Mortgage bonds

   A. I and IV only
   B. II only
   C. II and III only
   D. I, II, III and IV

10. Which of the following statements about treasury stock are true?

   I.   It has voting rights and is entitled to a dividend when declared.
   II. It has no voting rights and no dividend entitlement.
   III. It has been issued and repurchased by the company.
   IV. It is authorized but unissued stock.

   A. I and III
   B. I and IV
   C. II and III
   D. II and IV

11. Hybrid Technologies is authorized to issue 1 million shares of common stock. It has issued 600,000 shares. Of this amount, 40,000 shares are treasury shares. Hybrid Technologies declares a dividend of $2 per share. How many shares of common stock does Hybrid Technologies have outstanding?

   A. 40,000
   B. 560,000
   C. 600,000
   D. 1,000,000

12. Limited liability regarding ownership in a large, publicly held U.S. corporation means all of the following EXCEPT

   A. investors might lose the amount of their investment
   B. investors might lose their investment plus the difference between their investment and par value
   C. investors' shares are nonassessable
   D. investors are not liable to the full extent of their personal property

13. In a corporation with cumulative voting rights, minority stockholders have which one of the following advantages?

   A. More power
   B. Opportunity to form a block and have more power
   C. Chance to maintain voting privileges for a period of years
   D. Better opportunity to gain representation on the board

14. If a stockholder owns 100 shares of stock and five directors are to be elected to the board of directors, under the cumulative voting system the stockholder can cast a total of how many votes?

   A. 100 votes divided in any way among the candidates
   B. 500 votes divided in any way among the candidates
   C. 100 votes for any one candidate
   D. 500 votes divided evenly among the candidates

Answers

1.   If the plan manager purchased 3,000 shares of TCBS common stock, each of those shares would entitle the plan (the owner of the shares) to one vote, for a total of 3,000 votes.

2.   The plan's 3,000 votes represent a 3% ownership of TCBS (3,000 ÷ 100,000 = .03, or 3%).

3.   The stockholder with 200 shares may cast from zero to 200 votes for each of the five positions under the statutory voting system. In the event that your client elects not to cast all 200 votes for a particular director, he cannot carry them over and cast them for one of the others.

4.   Zero votes, because he doesn't have to cast any votes in the election if he so chooses.

5.   Under the statutory voting system, he can cast from zero up to 1,000 votes in this director election (five positions times 200 votes each).

6.   If he were allocating his votes for director at the TCBS annual meeting under the cumulative voting system, the client who owns 200 shares would have a total of 1,000 votes (one vote per share times the number of positions on which he will be casting his votes). Under the cumulative voting system, those 1,000 votes could be cast in any manner he chooses. He could cast all 1,000 votes for a single candidate and none for the others. He could cast 400 votes for his two top choices, 100 for each of two others and none for the last. Or he could choose to cast no votes at all.

7.   Under any voting system, the stockholder is entitled to not vote for any candidate.

8.   He is entitled to cast 1,000 votes, and can allocate them in any manner he desires.

9.   **C.**   Common and preferred stock represent ownership in a corporation; corporate and mortgage bonds are debt securities.

10.   **C.**   Treasury stock has no voting rights and no dividend entitlement, having been originally issued by the company and subsequently repurchased by the company.

11.   **B.**   Treasury stock is stock that has been reacquired by the corporation. Stock issued minus stock reacquired equals the amount of stock outstanding.

12.   **B.**   Investors never lose more than their investment.

13.   **D.**   In companies that allow cumulative voting, the stockholder multiplies the number of shares owned by the number of board vacancies to be filled. In cumulative voting, the stockholder can vote those shares as he pleases, including voting all 300 shares for one position to fill a board vacancy. This enables minority stockholders to maximize their impact by forming an alliance and casting all votes for a candidate who favors their views and interests.

14.   **B.**   In companies that allow cumulative voting, the stockholder multiplies the number of shares owned by the number of board vacancies to be filled. For instance, the stockholder who owns 100 shares and who has the opportunity to vote for directors to fill five board vacancies will have 500 votes. In cumulative voting, the stockholder can vote those shares as he pleases, including voting all 500 shares for one position to fill a board vacancy.

Preferred Stock

What Is Preferred Stock?

Preferred stock is an equity security and represents ownership in the issuing corporation. Preferred stock is often issued as a fixed income security with a stated dividend. Its price fluctuations tend to be affected more by changes in interest rates than by supply and demand. Most preferred stock is issued as nonvoting stock.

The owners of preferred stock have the following advantages over common stockholders:

- when dividends are declared by the board of directors, owners of preferred stock receive their dividends (plus any dividends in arrears) first; and
- if a corporation goes bankrupt after paying off creditors, preferred stockholders have a prior claim on the remaining assets.

Dividend Preference over Common Stock

Dividends must be paid to preferred stockholders before they can be paid to common stockholders.

Stated (Fixed) Rate of Return

An issuer of preferred stock will often state the annual dividend payments in terms of percentage of par value. A preferred stock with a par value of $100 that pays $4.50 in annual dividends would be known as a 4.5% preferred.

Adjustable-rate Preferred

The dividend on an adjustable-rate preferred is tied to the rate of some other interest rate and can be adjusted as often as quarterly.

Prior Claim over Assets at Dissolution

Holders of preferred stock can make a claim against the assets of the corporation before common stockholders can.

Limited Ownership Privileges

Preferred stocks usually do not carry either voting rights or preemptive rights.

No Maturity Date or Set Maturity Value

Preferred stock has no preset date at which it matures or is scheduled for redemption by the corporation.

Classes of Preferred Stock

Prior Preferred

Prior preferred stock has a prior claim over other preferred stock in receiving dividends, as well as in the distribution of assets in the event of liquidation.

Cumulative Preferred

An investor who has purchased cumulative preferred stock will be entitled to any and all dividends due that accumulate on the company's books until such time as the corporation is able to pay them.

To illustrate the advantage of owning cumulative preferred stock, suppose that one of your investors owns 100 shares of $100 par Nitco 8% Cumulative Preferred. Two years ago, the company paid out only $4 per share in dividends (a $100 par value 8% preferred should have paid a total of $8 in dividends for the year). Last year, payment of the dividend was suspended entirely.

This year, the board of directors finally believes that the corporation has enough cash to pay dividends to both preferred stockholders (including all dividends in arrears) and common stockholders. Before dividends are paid to the common stockholders, however, the holders of the 8% cumulative preferred must be paid a total of $20 ($8 for this year, plus $8 for last year, plus $4 for the first year of suspended payments).

Participating Preferred

The holders of participating preferred stock receive a share of any corporate profits that remain after all dividends due other securities are paid.

Owners of participating preferred stock do not participate in a corporation's profits until the company has paid:

- interest to bondholders
- dividends to other preferred stockholders
- the basic dividend rate
- dividends to common stockholders

Convertible Preferred

A preferred stock is convertible if the holder has the right to convert its shares into shares of common stock at some future point in time. To illustrate, a convertible preferred stock with a $100 par value might be convertible into common stock at $40 per share. For each share of $100 par value preferred an investor owns, she can exchange it for two and one half shares of common stock.

The conversion of preferred stock into shares of common increases the total number of common shares outstanding, thereby decreasing total earnings per common share.

Callable Preferred

Companies often issue preferred stock with a call feature during periods of high interest rates. The right to call back the stock allows them to eliminate a relatively high fixed dividend obligation sometime in the future and sell in its stead an issue of preferred stock with a lower dividend.

Combinations

A single preferred issue can include participating, cumulative, convertible and/or callable features.

Guaranteed Stock

When payment of dividends is guaranteed by a corporation other than the issuing corporation, the stock is known as *guaranteed stock*.

dual Security

Questions

1. All of the following statements concerning convertible callable preferred stock are true EXCEPT

    A. after the call date, dividends will cease
    B. upon conversion, earnings per common share will be diluted
    C. the dividend rate is less than a nonconvertible preferred stock
    D. if called, the owners have the option of retaining the preferred and will continue to receive dividends

2. All of the following statements are true of a callable convertible preferred issue EXCEPT that

    A. the convertible is issued with a lower stated dividend rate than a nonconvertible preferred
    B. the convertible preferred can increase in price because of the underlying security
    C. the stockholder must surrender the preferred when called or lose the right to par value
    D. dividend payments stop after the preferred is called

3. Brunswick issues a Series A $2.40 cumulative convertible preferred voting stock. This stock

    I. is convertible into common stock
    II. pays back dividends
    III. receives excess dividends on a pro rata basis with common stock

    A. I only
    B. I and II only
    C. I and III only
    D. I, II and III

4. In a period of stable interest rates, which of the following securities is MOST likely to fluctuate in value?

    A. Cumulative preferred stock
    B. Participating preferred stock
    C. Senior preferred stock
    D. Convertible preferred stock

5. Which of the following is NOT a typical variation of preferred stock?

    A. Callable and convertible
    B. Voting and nonvoting
    C. Cumulative and convertible
    D. Convertible and participating

6. A corporation has 7% $100 par cumulative convertible preferred stock outstanding. The preferred dividend was paid until two years ago, when 6% was paid. Last year, 5% was paid. This year, the corporation wishes to declare a common dividend. How much in preferred dividends must first be paid on each preferred share outstanding?

    A. $3
    B. $7
    C. $10
    D. $15

7. Amalgamated Widget has outstanding an issue of 6% callable preferred stock. Which of the following situations would induce Amalgamated to call the stock?

    A. Earnings increase by 6% or more.
    B. Dividends are withheld on common stock.
    C. Interest rates increase to 9%.
    D. Interest rates drop to 5%.

8. Guaranteed stock can be considered a

    A. senior security
    B. dual security
    C. collateral security
    D. preferred security

9. Preferred stockholders are entitled to certain rights, including

    A. receiving dividends after common stockholders
    B. receiving dividends based on a specified percentage of the current market value of the stock
    C. having a claim on corporate assets before common stockholders if the corporation is dissolved
    D. all of the above

Answers

1. **D.** When convertible preferred stock is called and the owner does not redeem it, dividend payments cease. The conversion feature is a "sweetener" that allows the preferred to be issued at a lower rate of return. Conversion results in a dilution of earnings per share of the common because more common shares are outstanding.

2. **C.** Owners of callable preferred don't have to surrender the shares if called. The par value doesn't change, but the conversion privilege and the right to dividends end. Investors want convertibles because they participate in increased value of the common. The dividend rate on convertibles will be less than on nonconvertibles.

3. **B.** Cumulative convertible preferred stock can be converted into common stock and will pay any back dividends. Only participating preferred can pay excess dividends.

4. **D.** Because interest rate movement affects the price of preferred stock, preferred stocks will not fluctuate as much in value during stable interest rates. Convertible preferred stocks will fluctuate with movements in the price of the common stock.

5. **B.** Holders of preferred stock generally exchange voting rights for a fixed rate of dividend return and seniority over common stockholders.

6. **C.** In order to pay this year's common dividend, the corporation must pay preferred stockholders the 1% dividend not paid two years ago, the 2% from last year and this year's 7% dividend. Therefore, 10%, or $10, must be paid.

7. **D.** When interest rates drop below the stock's stated dividend rate, the company will want to issue stock at the lower rate.

8. **B.** Guaranteed stock is a dual security, in that dividend payments are guaranteed by a corporation different from the one issuing the dividend.

Guaranteed stock can be either common or preferred stock.

9.   C.   Preferred stockholders are entitled to receive dividends before common stockholders. The dividend is usually fixed at a certain percentage of par value (not market value) or at a certain dollar amount for no-par preferred. Preferred stocks are senior securities; that is, preferred stockholders may make a claim against corporate assets before common stockholders in a dissolution.

Return on Investment

Dividends

Stockholders are entitled to dividend distributions only if the company board of directors votes to make such a distribution.

Cash Dividends

Cash dividends are normally distributed by corporations to stockholders in the form of quarterly checks representing the stockholders' share of the companies' profits.

Stock Dividends

With a stock dividend, the company issues shares of its common stock as a dividend to its current stockholders.

Property Dividends

A corporation that owns securities in other companies may distribute some of those securities as a property dividend. Property dividends may also take the form of the distribution of a company product.

Calculating Return on Investment

To determine the current yield, divide the yearly dividend (four times the quarterly dividend) by the current market price of the stock.

If, for example, the yearly dividend paid by TCBS on its common stock is $2.60 (a quarterly dividend of $.65) and the market price of the stock is $37, the current yield for TCBS would be 7%. If TCBS paid $.65 for the first quarter of the year and then raised its dividend to $.85 for each of the last three quarters, at a current market value of $37, TCBS's current yield would be 8.6% ($3.20 ÷ $37 = .08648, which is approximately 8.6%).

Stock Splits and Reverse Splits

Stock Split

The board of directors of ICBS has decided that ICBS common stock is selling for too much at $100 per share, so the companyt declares a 4-for-1 stock split. Each share of stock currently worth $100 will be replaced by four shares worth $25 each. Every stockholder will receive three new shares of ICBS for each share held before the split. The original outstanding shares have been split into four shares, each valued at one-fourth as much as before. A client who owned 100 shares before the split worth $10,000 (100 shares × $100 dollars = $10,000) will own 400 shares worth $25 each after the split.

To calculate the effect of a 4:1 split (4:1 is shorthand for "4-for-1"), multiply the number of shares by 4/1 and the price by 1/4. The stockholder's position doesn't change because he will hold stock of the same value both before and after the split.

Let's look at other possible splits. If DWAQ Corporation decides that its stock is overpriced when it reaches $90 per share and splits the stock 3-for-2 (shorthand: "3:2"), an investor with 100 shares before the split has 150 shares worth $60 per share after the split. To calculate the effect of a 3:2 split, multiply the number of shares by 3/2 and the price by 2/3. You can check your arithmetic because you know that the dollar value of the position will remain the same before and after the split.

If DWAQ Corporation decides that its stock is overpriced when it reaches $100 per share and splits the stock 5:4, an investor with 100 shares before the split has 125 shares worth $80 per share after the split. To calculate the effect of a 5:4 split, you multiply the number of shares by 5/4 and the price by 4/5. Check your arithmetic, and you will find that the dollar value of the position is the same before and after the split.

Reverse Split

After a reverse split, investors own fewer shares that are now worth more per share. After a 1:4 reverse split, for example, a stockholder who owned 500 shares with a market value of $17 per share now owns 125 shares worth $68 per share.

Questions

1. Datawaq has 10,000 shares outstanding and declares a 30% stock dividend. One of your clients owns 100 shares of DWAQ, and another owns 1,200. How many shares will the client who owns 100 shares receive as a dividend?

   _____

2. How many shares will the client who owns 1,200 shares receive as a dividend?

   _____

3. What proportion of the company does the owner of the 100 shares have before the dividend?

   _____

4. What proportion of the company does the owner of the 1,200 shares have after the dividend?

   _____

5. Common stock of ICBS, Inc. (I Can't Believe It's Sushi, a top competitor of TCBS) has a current market price of $30 per share and pays a yearly dividend of $3 (a quarterly dividend of $.75). An investor in ICBS's common stock would realize a current yield for that stock of 10% ($3 ÷ $30 = .10, or 10%). If ICBS stock rose to $40 and the company declared a $6 annual dividend, how much would an owner of 100 shares receive each quarter?

   _____

6. What would that investor's current yield be on her ICBS stock?

   _____

7. In which of the following ways may a company declare dividends?

   I. Cash
   II. Stock
   III. Stock of another company

   A. I only
   B. I and II only
   C. I and III only
   D. I, II and III

8. ABC Company currently has earnings of $4 and pays a $.50 quarterly dividend. The market price of ABC is $40. What is the current yield?

   A. 1.25%
   B. 5%
   C. 10%
   D. 15%

9. XYZ Corporation is currently paying an $.80 quarterly dividend. The stock is $10 par value and is selling in the market for $50 per share. What is its current yield?

   A. 1.6%
   B. 6.4%
   C. 8%
   D. 32%

In questions 10 through 13, write T (True) or F (False) next to each statement.

10. ____ Common stockholders receive dividends automatically each quarter a corporation shows a profit.

11. ____ The market value of a stock is determined by the board of directors.

12. ____ A common stockholder receives a fixed proportion of the corporation profits in cash.

13. ____ A stock dividend increases a stockholder's proportionate interest in a company.

14. If the ICBS board of directors voted a 5:1 split, how many shares would your client, who owns 150 shares at $100 each, own after the split?

_____

15. What would each of those shares be worth after the split?

_____

16. ICBS has declared a 4:5 reverse split. A stockholder who previously held 100 shares worth $25 per share will own how many shares after the split?

_____

17. How much will each of these new shares be worth?

_____

18. How much will the total value of the investor's shares change after the split?

_____

Answers

1. An investor who owns 100 shares will receive 30 additional shares of Datawaq stock.

2. An investor who owns 1,200 shares would receive 360 new shares as a dividend.

3. The owner of the 100 shares originally owned 1% of the company

4. The holder of the 1,200 shares owned 12% of the company. Because all common stockholders would receive the same percentage of stock as a dividend, a stock dividend does not increase any single investor's proportionate share of ownership in the company. The two stockholders still own 1% and 12% respectively.

5. An annual dividend of $6 would equal four $1.50 quarterly dividends. The owner of 100 shares of ICBS would be entitled to $150 each quarter, or $600 per year.

6. Her current yield would be 15% ($6 + $40 = .15, or 15%).

7. **D.** A company may pay a dividend that it has declared in any of the three ways shown: cash, stock or stock in another company such as a subsidiary. The last method is also known as a *property dividend*.

8. **B.** The quarterly dividend is $.50 as stated, paying $2 annually. $2 annually divided by $40 equals a 5% current yield.

9. **B.** The quarterly dividend is $.80; therefore, the annual dividend is $3.20. $3.20 + $50 = 6.4% current yield.

10. False. They receive dividends only when declared by the board of directors.

11. False. Price is subject to market demand—what someone is willing to pay.

12. False. The amount received depends on the dividends that are declared.

13. False. Stock dividends do not change proportionate interest—the investor has a larger slice of a larger pie.

14. To calculate the effect of this split, multiply the number of shares your client owns by 5/1. You should get 750.

15. Multiply the dollar value of the original shares by 1/5 (the same as dividing by 5). $100 times 1/5 (or divided by 5) equals $20. Your client owned $15,000 worth of ICBS before the split (150 × $100), and still owns $15,000 worth after the split (750 × $20).

16. A stockholder who previously held 100 shares worth $25 per share will own 80 shares after the 4:5 reverse split (100 shares × 4/5 = 80).

17. Each of these new shares will be worth $31.25 per share ($25 × 5/4 = $31.25).

18. The investor's shares are worth $2,500 both before and after the split.

Transferability of Ownership

The Stock Certificate

A stock certificate is physical evidence of a person's share in the ownership of a corporation, and individual stock certificates may be issued for any number of shares. Information printed on the face of a certificate includes the:

- company's name
- names of some of its officers and directors
- name of the transfer agent
- number of shares the certificate represents
- name of the investor
- CUSIP number

CUSIP Numbers

A CUSIP number is a universal security identification number used in trade confirmations and correspondence regarding specific securities.

Negotiability

Negotiability is the stockholder's right to assign, give, transfer or sell securities to another person without a third party's permission. To transfer ownership of any stock, the registered owner must either sign the stock certificate on the back in the place designated for the owner's signature or sign a stock power and an authorized person of a broker-dealer or an officer of a national bank must guarantee the signature.

Transfer Procedures

Transfer agent

The transfer agent for a corporation:

- sees that stock and bond certificates are issued in the correct owner's name;

- cancels and issues certificates;
- maintains records of ownership for the corporation;
- handles problems relating to lost, stolen or destroyed certificates;
- has the certificates signed by the appropriate officer(s);
- affixes the corporate seal;
- delivers them to the new owner (or transferee); and
- destroys the original certificates registered in the seller's name.

For each registered stockholder, the transfer agent records his:

- name
- full address
- Social Security number
- total number of shares he owns

The transfer agent distributes additional shares in the event of a stock split, or new certificates in the event of a reverse split.

Registrar   *must be independent of issuer co.*

The responsibilities of the registrar include:

- maintaining various stock records;
- keeping track of the names of the owners of the issuer's securities;
- ensuring that a corporation does not have more stock outstanding than can be accounted for on the company's books; and
- certifying that a bond represents a legal debt of the issuer.

Questions

1. Who is responsible for issuing new certificates for a publicly held corporation?

    A. Registrar
    B. Trader
    C. Transfer agent
    D. Broker-dealer

2. Who is responsible for handling problems relating to lost, stolen or missing coupons or certificates?

    A. Registrar
    B. Trader
    C. Transfer agent
    D. Broker-dealer

3. Who is responsible for ensuring that a corporation does not have more stock outstanding than it has been authorized to issue?

    A. Registrar
    B. Trader
    C. Transfer agent
    D. Broker-dealer

4. Who is responsible for certifying that a bond represents a legal debt of the issuer?

    A. Registrar
    B. Trader
    C. Transfer agent
    D. Broker-dealer

Answers

1.   **C.**   The transfer agent is responsible for issuing certificates and for recording the number of shares owned, and the stockholder's name, address and Social Security number.

2.   **C.**   The transfer agent is responsible for all matters relating to the physical certificates, their safekeeping and their transfer.

3.   **A.**   The registrar is responsible for keeping careful accounts of the number of shares a company is authorized to issue and the number it has outstanding.

4.   **A.**   As an independent agent of the company, the registrar is responsible for certifying that a bond represents a legal debt of the issuing corporation.

2 Debt Securities

Characteristics of Bonds

Bondholders do not have ownership interest in the issuing corporation. Bondholders receive interest on the debt as creditors of the corporation.

Issuers

The following entities issue bonds:

- municipalities
- corporations
- U.S. government and government agencies

Interest

The bond issuer promises to pay investors interest for that loan at a fixed rate and on particular dates. Interest accrues daily and is paid semiannually. An investor who owns a $20,000 bond that pays 4 1/2% interest will receive $900 ($20,000 × 4 1/2% = $900) in income each year in the form of two $450 semiannual installments. On the date the bond is scheduled to mature, the bondholder will receive a check for $20,450.

An investor who owns $50,000 of a 4 5/8% bond receives $2,312.50 ($50,000 × 4 5/8% = $2,312.50) each year in two $1,156.25 payments. On the date the bond is scheduled to mature, the bondholder will receive a check for $51,156.25.

Maturities

There are three basic bond maturity structures:

1. **Term** bonds mature all at once.
2. **Serial** bonds mature at set intervals over a period of time.
3. **Balloon** bonds mature at intervals, but most of the issue matures at the same time.

A bond issuer that spreads its bond sales over several years is issuing them in separate **series**.

Registration of Bonds

Coupon (Bearer) Bonds

No records are kept of the purchasers by the issuer of a coupon (bearer) bond and the securities are issued without an investor's name printed on the certificates. The person in possession of the bearer bond can collect interest by clipping the appropriate coupon and delivering it to the issuer's paying agent.

Registered Bonds

When a registered bond is issued, the issuer's transfer agent keeps a record of the bondholder's name. The name of the person who purchased the bond (the owner) will appear on the face of the bond certificate. Bonds can be registered in two forms:

- **Fully registered.** The bonds are registered as to both principal and interest

- **Registered as to principal only**. The bonds only have the owner's name printed on the front, and the coupons are in bearer form.

Book-entry Bonds

The owner of a book-entry bond does not receive a certificate.

Debt Service

Level debt service. In a level debt service arrangement, each payment will be for the same dollar amount, but the portion of the payment that represents principal and the portion that represents interest will change over time. The net result will be equal (level) payments over the life of the bond.

Decreasing debt service. In a decreasing debt service arrangement, the principal due to the bondholders is paid in installments of equal size. Principal repayments stay level and the interest paid bondholders goes down, so the total payment becomes smaller over time. The net effect is decreasing payments.

Pricing

Bonds can be sold at issuance and in the secondary market for any price the market (active buyers and sellers) sets.

- A bond sold for less than its face value is being sold at a **discount**.
- A bond sold for the same dollar amount as its face value is being sold **at par**.
- A bond sold for more than its face value is being sold at a **premium**.

Rating and Analyzing Bonds

Standard & Poor's, Moody's and Fitch's evaluate and publish their ratings of bond issues. They base their bond ratings primarily on the issuer's creditworthiness.

- Standard & Poor's and Moody's rate corporate and municipal bonds.
- Fitch's rates corporate bonds municipal bonds and commercial paper.

Investment grade. A municipal bond must be investment grade (a rating of BBB/Baa or higher) to be suitable for purchase by banks. Investment grade bonds are the same as **bank grade bonds**.

A plus sign or minus sign in a Standard & Poor's rating would indicate that the bond falls within the top or bottom of that particular category.

A1 and Baa1 are used by Moody's to indicate the highest quality bonds within those two categories. Moody's also provides ratings for short-term municipal notes, designating MIG 1 as the highest quality and MIG 4 as the lowest quality.

Criteria used to rate corporate and municipal bonds include:

- amount and composition of existing debt;
- stability of issuer's cash flows;
- ability of issuer to meet scheduled payments of interest and principal on its debt obligations;
- asset protection; and
- management ability.

Relationship of Rating to Yield

Generally, the higher the bond rating, the lower the yield. Investors are willing to accept a lower return on their investment if they expect their principal to be safe and annual interest payments more predictable.

Comparative Safety of Securities

U.S. government securities. The *highest safety* is found in securities backed by the U.S. government. These securities include:

- U.S. Treasury bills, notes and bonds (Series EE and HH bonds);
- Government National Mortgage Association bonds (Ginnie Maes or GNMAs); and
- Public Housing Authority bonds (PHAs).

The *second highest degree of safety* is found in securities that are issued by government agencies and government-sponsored corporations. These include:

- Federal Farm Credit Banks;
- Federal Home Loan Bank (FHLB);
- Federal National Mortgage Association (FNMA);
- Inter-American Development Bank (IADB); and
- International Bank for Reconstruction and Development (IB).

Municipal issues. Generally, the next highest degree of safety is found in securities issued by municipalities.

Corporate issues. The next highest category of safety is found in corporate debt securities, ranked as follows:

1. equipment trust certificates
2. first mortgage bonds
3. debentures
4. income bonds

Debt Retirement

Redemption

Sinking fund. To facilitate the early retirement of bonds, many issuers establish a *sinking fund*. A sinking fund may be used to call bonds, pay bonds off at maturity or buy back bonds from investors in the open market. A sinking fund aids a bond's stability due to the fact that the fund itself may be an active buyer of the bonds in the secondary market.

Extraordinary redemptions (calls). An extraordinary redemption occurs when the issuer is required to redeem all or part of an issue of bonds at the occurrence of certain events. If an issuer is required to call bonds, the call is known as an *extraordinary call*. Extraordinary calls may be either mandatory or optional.

Calling Bonds

An issuer may reserve the right to redeem (call) a bond issue before its final maturity date. Interest

rates on callable bonds tend to be higher than on comparable noncallable bonds.

A call feature in a bond's trust indenture allows the issuing company to call the bonds from investors. The issuer notifies bondholders that it is willing to buy the bonds back from them at a specified price on a particular date.

Call premium. In return for the call privilege, the issuer usually pays the bondholder a *call premium* over the bond's par value at the time of the call.

Advantages of a call option. Callable bonds can be advantageous to the issuer for the following reasons:

- The issuer can call in bonds on which it must pay a high rate of interest and replace them with a new issue with a lower coupon.
- The issuer can call in bonds to reduce its debt.
- The issuer can replace short-term debt issues with long-term issues, and vice versa.
- The issuer can call bonds as a means of forcing the conversion of convertible corporate securities.

Mandatory calls. A mandatory call would require the issuer to call specified bonds under particular circumstances.

Call protection. An initial noncallable period following the issuance of the bonds is known as call protection.

Risks to bondholders. Callable bonds subject their holders to **call risk**, the risk that the investor may be unable to obtain a similar yield.

Effects of a call on trading. After a call notice is issued and before the specified call date has arrived, bonds that are called continue to trade in the open market. Once bonds have been called, the bondholder can turn the bonds in to the caller immediately, or he can sell them in the open market. The bonds will trade at a slight discount to the call price during this period.

Refunding Bonds

Refunding an issue means retiring an outstanding issue of bonds using the money generated by the sale of a new offering. Like redemption, refunding can be done in full or in part. Generally, an entire issue will be refunded at once.

Prerefunding

In a prerefunding (**advance refunding**), a new issue is sold at a lower coupon than the original bond issue prior to the first call date on the original issue. The proceeds from the new issue are placed in an escrow account and invested in U.S. government securities or are held in cash equivalents, with the interest received from the investment used to pay the interest on the outstanding prerefunded bonds. The original bonds are then called at the first call date, and the escrowed securities are used to redeem them.

Put Bonds

Some bonds are issued with a put option and are known as put (or **puttable**) bonds. In return for accepting a slightly lower interest rate, the investor receives the right to put the bond back to the issuer at some point before the ultimate maturity for the full face value of the bond.

Questions

1. What is the face value of most bonds?

   _____

2. How much would an investor pay (excluding commissions and fees) for a bond being sold at par?

   _____

3. How much annual interest will the owner of a $1,000 5% bond receive?

   _____

4. How much will the semiannual interest payments be on a $1,000 9% bond?

   _____

5. A trust indenture is a contract between the

   A. issuer and investor
   B. issuer and trustee
   C. trustee and underwriter
   D. issuer and underwriter

6. Bonds that mature with a smaller amount in the earlier years and a greater amount in later years are called

   A. series bonds
   B. term bonds
   C. balloon bonds
   D. callable bonds

7. Which of the following statements are true of bonds?

   I. Bonds represent a loan to the issuer.
   II. Bonds give the bondholder ownership in the entity.
   III. Bonds are issued to finance capital expenditures or to raise working capital.
   IV. Bonds are junior securities.

   A. I and II only
   B. I and III only
   C. II and III only
   D. I, II, III and IV

8. Which of these bond features is the most attractive to a corporate issuer?

   A. Low call premium
   B. High interest rate
   C. Nonrefundable
   D. High sinking fund requirement

9. An investor purchased a 5 1/2% bond to yield 6 1/2%. If the company calls the bond at par before maturity, the effective yield would be

   A. less than 5 1/2%
   B. 5 1/2%
   C. 6 1/2%
   D. greater than 6 1/2%

10. A new convertible bond contains a provision that it cannot be called for five years after the date of issuance. This call protection would be most valuable to a recent purchaser of the bond if interest rates are

   A. falling
   B. rising
   C. stable
   D. fluctuating

11. A bond with a high coupon rate is selling at a premium and is called at par. The party that benefits from the call provision is the

   A. bondholder
   B. issuer
   C. trustee
   D. broker-dealer

12. 30-year term bonds have an average life of 21 years and 6 months to maturity. This probably means that the

   A. buyer has the option to redeem the bonds early
   B. issuer has the option to redeem the bonds in 21 years and 6 months
   C. bonds are callable in part at a future date
   D. bonds are sinking fund instruments

13. Which of the following are characteristics of bearer bonds?

   A. They come in registered form.
   B. They pay interest quarterly.
   C. They have interest coupons attached.
   D. They do not have interest coupons attached.

Answers

1. The face value of most bonds sold is $1,000. An issue is made up of many hundreds to thousands of these $1,000 bonds.

2. A bond sold at par, whether as part of an initial offering or in the secondary market, is being sold for $1,000.

3. The annual interest payment per $1,000 on a 5% bond is $50.

4. A $1,000 9% bond pays $90 per year in interest in two $45 semiannual payments.

5. **B.** A trust indenture is an agreement between the issuer and a trustee appointed to protect the interests of the bondholders.

6. **C.** A balloon maturity is one in which bonds mature serially with the vast majority of the issue maturing in the later years.

7. **B.** Bonds are debt securities; as such, they represent loans to the issuer. They are senior securities, taking precedence over common and preferred stock in claims against an issuer.

8. **A.** A low call rate means that the bond may be *called* or redeemed at a low premium before maturity. This feature is attractive to corporations because it increases the flexibility of their capital structure. For example, it allows a corporation to discontinue debt financing or to replace it with equity financing. The other answers would place burdens on a corporation and, therefore, are not attractive.

9. **D.** The bond with a 5 1/2% coupon is priced to yield 6 1/2% and is selling at a discount. If the bond is called before maturity, the discount will be earned in a shorter period of time, increasing the yield to greater than 6 1/2%.

10. **A.** Call protection is most valuable to a purchaser when interest rates are falling because the attractive coupon will increase the market price of the bond. In the meantime, the holder is assured the higher return even though interest rates generally fall below the bond interest rate.

11. **B.** When a bond is called, the party that benefits is the issuer. The call provisions are established for the benefit of the issuer, not for the benefit of the holder.

12. **C.** The fact that 30-year bonds have an average life of 21 years and 6 months indicates that the bonds have a sinking fund that allows the issuer to call bonds before their maturity.

13. **C.** Bearer bonds, also known as *unregistered bonds*, must have interest coupons attached.

Bond Yields

Comparing Yields

Bonds frequently are quoted and traded by their yields rather than by dollar amounts.

Nominal Yield

A bond's nominal yield is a fixed percentage of the bond's par value. It is set at issuance and printed on the face of the bond. A coupon of 3 1/4%, for instance, means the issuer will pay $32.50 interest per $1,000 of par value every year until the bond matures.

Current Yield

Current yield is a measure of the return an investor receives compared to the current price of the security:

$$\frac{\text{Annual interest}}{\text{Current market price}} = \text{Current yield}$$

Relationship of yield to price. A bond traded at par will have identical nominal and current yields. An investor who pays $10,000 for ten 5 1/8% bonds will receive a 5 1/8% return on investment, or $512.50 per year.

A bond purchased at a discount will have a current yield that is higher than its nominal yield. For example, a 5 1/8% coupon bond trading at a discounted price of $800 has an annual interest payment of $51.25 and a current yield of 6.4% ($51.25 ÷ $800 = 6.4%).

A bond purchased at a premium will have a current yield that is lower than its nominal yield. An investor who buys a 5 1/8% coupon bond trading at a premium of $1,100 receives an annual interest payment of $51.25 and a current yield of 4.7% ($51.25 ÷ $1,100 = 4.68%).

Current yield does not take into account a gain or loss on the sale of the bond or whether the bond is held to maturity.

Summary of current yield. As a rule, when a bond is traded:

- at **par**, the current yield equals the nominal yield;
- at a **premium**, the current yield is less than the nominal yield; and
- at a **discount**, the current yield is greater than the nominal yield.

Yield to Maturity

A bond's yield to maturity (YTM) is a measure of the annual return on investment from purchase until maturity and accounts for the difference between the amount an investor pays for the bond and the amount the investor receives at the time the bond matures.

Premium bonds. YTM on a premium bond will always be lower than the nominal yield, as illustrated by the following equations:

$$\frac{\text{Annual ROI}}{\text{Average price}} = \text{YTM}$$

$$\text{Annual interest} \begin{array}{c} + \text{ Prorated discount} \\ \text{or} \\ - \text{ Prorated premium} \end{array} = \text{Annual ROI}$$

$$\frac{\text{Purchase price} + \text{Par value}}{2} = \text{Average price}$$

$$\frac{\text{Annual ROI}}{\text{Average price}} = \text{YTM}$$

YTM calculations for premium bonds. The following formulas can be used to approximate the yield to maturity of a bond investment.

1. Calculate the **prorated premium**:

$$\frac{\text{Premium paid}}{\text{Years to maturity}} = \text{Prorated premium}$$

2. Calculate the **annual ROI**:

Annual interest − Prorated premium
= Annual ROI

3. Calculate the **average price**:

$$\frac{\text{Purchase price} + \text{Maturity price}}{2} = \text{Avg. price}$$

4. Calculate the **YTM:**

$$\frac{\text{Annual ROI}}{\text{Average price}} = \text{YTM}$$

The yield to maturity on a 6% bond purchased at 115 ($1,150 per bond, a $150 premium) and maturing in 20 years would be calculated as follows:

1. Calculate the **prorated premium**.

    $150 premium paid ÷ 20 years = $7.50

2. Calculate the **annual ROI**.

    $60 annual interest − $7.50 prorated premium = $52.50

3. Calculate the **average price**.

    $$\frac{\$1,150 \text{ purchase price} + \$1,000 \text{ maturity price}}{2}$$

    = $2,150 ÷ 2 = $1,075

4. Calculate the **YTM.**

    52.50 ÷ $1,075 = .0488
    (a 4.88% yield to maturity)

YTM calculations for par bonds. The yield to maturity of a bond bought at par will be the same as its current and coupon yields. Yield to maturity will differ from current yield whenever the price paid for the security differs from par value.

YTM calculations for discount bonds. The YTM of discount bonds is higher than the coupon rate because the investor realizes a capital gain when the bond is redeemed at par. Suppose an investor purchases a bond with a 12% coupon at a discounted price of 90 ($900 per $1,000 face value bond). She will receive $120 a year in interest plus a gain of $100 (the difference between the $1,000 value at redemption and the $900 purchase price) if she holds the bond to maturity.

Two discount bonds with the same current yields may have different yields to maturity. As an exam-

ple, two investors purchase two different 6% bonds, one maturing in ten years, one maturing in 20. Each pays 80 for his bond. The bonds will have different YTMs because they have a different number of years remaining until maturity. The investor with the 20-year bond has to wait a longer time to recoup the value of the $200 discount. Prorating the $200 discount over 20 years is the equivalent of an additional $10 per year in income (a 1% increase in return). Prorating the same $200 discount over ten years means an additional yield of $20 per year (a 2% increase in return).

Yield to Call

A bond may be called any time after a **call date** set at the time of issuance. A bond is said to have **call protection** before that date.

Discount bonds. When a bond bought at a discount is called before its maturity date, the discount will accrue faster and result in a higher yield.

Suppose an investor bought a 6% bond for 64 that is scheduled to mature in ten years but is callable at any time (that is, it has passed its call protection date). If the bond is not called and is redeemed by the issuer in ten years at $1,000, the investor realizes a gain of $360 ($1,000 minus the $640 paid). Prorating that $360 over the ten years the investor held the bond gives an extra $36 per year—the equivalent of an additional 3.6% in yield. The investor received an annual yield of 9.6% for the time he held that bond (6% coupon plus 3.6% prorated discount).

Now suppose that the issuer called the bonds back in only three years at $1,000. The investor would prorate the $360 gain over three years, which would be an extra $120 per year—an additional 12% in yield. The investor's annual yield would be 18% (6% coupon plus 12% in prorated discount). An investor who buys a callable bond at a discount profits when the bond is called.

Par bonds. The yield of a bond bought at par and called away before its maturity date will remain unchanged. An investor who buys a 7% bond for $1,000 receives a 7% return on the bond for however long it is held. That fact is not changed when the issuer calls the bond and repays the $1,000 original investment.

Premium bonds. An investor who buys a callable bond at a premium stands to lose money if the bond is called at par before maturity. The yield to call will be lower than the nominal yield, current yield or yield to maturity if the bond is called at par.

Calculating yield to call. Prorate the discount or premium over the time remaining to the **first call date**. The call price is used instead of the par value:

$$\text{Annual interest} + \frac{\text{Discount from call price}}{\text{Years to call}}$$
$$= \text{Annual ROI}$$

$$\frac{\text{Purchase price} + \text{Call price}}{2} = \text{Average price}$$

$$\frac{\text{Annual return on investment}}{\text{Average price}} = \text{Yield to call}$$

Summary of yield to call. As a rule, for a bond purchased:

- **at a discount**, yield to call will always be greater than yield to maturity;
- **at a premium**, yield to call may be greater or less than the yield to maturity depending on the relationship between the purchase price and the call price. If the purchase price of the bond is lower than the call price, the yield to maturity will be lowest; if the purchase price is higher than the call price, the yield to call will be the lowest;
- **at par**, the yield to call will be the same as the yield to maturity.

Yield vs. Price

Bond prices and yields have an inverse relationship. As bond prices go up, yields go down (and vice versa). If a bond is trading at a discount, the current yield increases; if a bond is trading at a premium, the current yield decreases.

As a rule of thumb, when comparing two premium or two discount bonds, the bond with the interest rate that is farther away from the current market rates will be more volatile in price.

Short-term vs. Long-term Yields

A positive yield curve is referred to as a *normal curve* due to the fact that most investors are willing to pay a higher price for the benefits of liquidity.

Changing interest rates have a greater effect on bonds with long maturities than on those with short maturities. As interest rates rise, the price of long-term bonds drops more quickly than the price of short-term bonds.

When a yield curve is inverted it is said to have a *negative* (or downward) slope. An inverted curve is one in which bonds with shorter maturities have higher yields than bonds of longer terms.

When the yields of bonds with short maturities are the same as those of bonds with long maturities the yield curve is said to be *flat* or *even*.

Bond Tables

Bond points. One bond point equals $10 (1% of the par value of $1,000). The price of a bond that is trading at 82 on Monday and 80 on Friday has decreased by two points (a dollar change of $20).

Basis points. One basis point equals 10 cents (1/100th of a percentage point or .01% of $1,000). The yield of a bond that has increased from 6.65% to 7.25% has increased 60 basis points (0.6%). Each basis point represents 1/100th of a percentage point—60/100ths of 1% equals .6%.

Using bond tables. Use the bond table shown in Figure 1 to find the YTM of a 9 1/2% coupon bond purchased at 87.34 and due to mature in 16 years and 6 months. Locate the column headed "**16-6.**" Go down the column until you find 87.34 (87.34% of $1,000). Follow this line left to find the YTM—11.20%.

Interpolation

You have just purchased a 9 1/2% bond at 91 that matures in exactly 15 years and want to calculate the bond's true YTM. In Figure 1, scan down the column headed "**15-0.**" "91" does not appear, so you will have to calculate the true yield to maturity of this bond from the information given.

Figure 1   **Example of a Page In a *Bond Basis Book***

Yield	14- 6	15- 0	15- 6	16- 0	16- 6	17- 0	17- 6	18- 0
			Years and months				**9 1/2%**	
5.00	146.02	147.09	148.14	149.16	150.16	151.13	152.08	153.00
5.20	143.41	144.41	145.38	146.32	147.24	148.14	149.02	149.87
5.40	140.86	141.78	142.68	143.56	144.41	145.24	146.04	146.83
5.60	138.38	139.23	140.06	140.86	141.65	142.41	143.15	143.87
5.80	135.95	136.73	137.50	138.24	138.96	139.66	140.34	141.00
6.00	133.58	134.30	135.00	135.68	136.34	136.98	137.60	138.21
6.~~	134.~2	~32.~~	132.78	~35.~~	135.1~	~~5.67	~~6.26	136.81
9.30	~1.9~	~~1.80	~1.~~	1~.65	~~.~~	101.~~	10~.~	~~.~~
9.40	100.78	100.80	100.81	100.82	100.83	100.84	100.85	100.86
9.50	100.00	100.00	100.00	100.00	100.00	100.00	100.00	100.00
9.60	99.23	99.21	99.20	99.19	99.18	99.17	99.16	99.15
9.70	98.46	98.44	98.41	98.39	98.37	98.35	98.33	98.31
9.80	97.70	97.67	97.63	97.60	97.57	97.54	97.51	97.49
9.90	96.95	96.91	96.86	96.82	96.78	96.74	96.70	96.67
10.00	96.21	96.16	96.10	96.05	96.00	95.95	95.91	95.86
10.20	94.76	94.68	94.61	94.53	94.47	94.40	94.34	94.28
10.40	93.34	93.24	93.14	93.06	92.97	92.89	92.81	92.74
10.60	91.94	91.83	91.72	91.61	91.51	91.42	91.33	91.24
10.80	90.58	90.45	90.32	90.20	90.09	89.98	89.87	89.78
11.00	89.25	89.10	88.96	88.82	88.69	88.57	88.46	88.35
11.20	87.95	87.78	87.62	87.48	87.34	87.20	87.08	86.96
11.40	86.67	86.49	86.32	86.16	86.01	85.86	85.73	85.60
11.60	85.43	85.23	85.05	84.88	84.71	84.56	84.41	84.27
11.80	84.21	84.00	83.81	83.62	83.45	83.28	83.13	82.98
12.00	83.01	82.79	82.59	82.39	82.21	82.04	81.88	81.72

Figure 2

Yield		16-0
10.00	100%	96.05
10.14	30.9%	95.00
10.20		94.53

The yield for a bond at 91 will lie between 10.60 and 10.80, the yields for the prices on either side of 91. The yield will lie at the same relative position between 10.60 and 10.80 that 91 lies between 90.45 and 91.83.

The difference between the two prices in the bond table is 1.38 points (91.83 – 90.45 = 1.38). 91 points is .55 points more than the lower price (91 – 90.45 = .55). The price of 91 points is .55 points from 90.45 out of the total possible 1.38 points. To express this as a percentage, divide .55 points by 1.38 points: .55 ÷ 1.38 = .399. In other words, 91 is 39.9% of the way from 90.45 to 91.83.

Find the point that lies 39.9% of the way from 10.60 to 10.80. That will give you the yield for a bond priced at 91. Subtract 10.60 from 10.80 to get .20 basis points. Now find the point lying the same proportionate distance from 10.80 that 91 lies from 90.45. Multiply .20 by 39.9% (.399) to get .08 (rounded) basis points. Subtract .08 from 10.80 to get an interpolated yield for a bond priced at 91 of 10.72% (10.80 – .08 = 10.72%).

When interpolating yields based on data found in a *Bond Basis Book,* remember that both the price and the yield are a proportionate distance from either the top or bottom number (see Figure 2). In the last calculation, we moved from the bottom numbers up; choose one method and use it consistently.

Questions

1. What is the nominal yield of a bond paying $130 in interest every year?

2. What is the coupon rate of a bond paying $42.50 in interest semiannually?

3. What is the nominal rate of a bond paying $80 in interest annually that is currently being offered for $800?

4. What is the current yield of a bond paying $95 per year and trading at par?

5. What is the current yield of a bond paying $85 per year and trading at $700?

6. What is the current yield of a bond paying $110 per year and trading at $1,100?

7. A bond has a current yield of 12% and is trading at $1,000. What is its coupon rate?

8. A bond has a current yield of 12% and is trading at $800. What is its coupon rate?

9. A bond has a current yield of 12% and is trading at $1,600. What is its coupon rate?

10. An investor receives $37.50 in semiannual interest payments on a bond for which he paid $1,200. What is the bond's current yield?

11. An investor receives $37.50 in semiannual interest payments on a bond for which he paid $1,200. What is the bond's coupon rate?

12. An 8% bond is purchased at 120 and matures in ten years. What is the prorated premium?

13. An 8% bond is purchased at 110 and matures in 20 years. What is the prorated premium?

14. A bond at par has a coupon rate
    A. less than current yield
    B. less than yield to maturity
    C. the same as current yield
    D. greater than current yield

15. What is the calculation for determining the current yield on a bond?
    A. Annual interest ÷ Par value
    B. Annual interest ÷ Current market price
    C. Yield to maturity ÷ Par value
    D. Yield to maturity ÷ Current market price

16. A customer purchased a 5% U.S. government bond yielding 6%. A year before the bond matures, new U.S. government bonds are being issued at 4%, and the customer sells the 5% bond. The customer probably

    I. bought it at a discount
    II. bought it at a premium
    III. sold it at a discount
    IV. sold it at a premium

    A. I and III
    B. I and IV
    C. II and III
    D. II and IV

17. Which yield to maturity would be higher?

    A. 10% nominal yield bond with a premium price
    B. 10% nominal yield bond with a discount price
    C. 10% nominal yield bond with a price at par
    D. 10% nominal yield bond with a zero coupon

18. A corporation issues 9% Aaa rated debentures at par. Two years later, similar Aaa issues are being offered in the primary market at 9 1/2%. Which of the following statements are true regarding the outstanding 9% issue?

    I. The current yield on the issue will be higher.
    II. The current yield on the issue will be lower.
    III. The dollar price per bond will be higher than par.
    IV. The dollar price per bond will be lower than par.

    A. I and III
    B. I and IV
    C. II and III
    D. II and IV

19. Which of the following are included in the *Bond Basis Book?*

    I. Yield to maturity
    II. Percentage of $1,000 par value
    III. Taxable equivalent yield
    IV. Unit denominations

    A. I and II
    B. I, II and III
    C. II and III
    D. III and IV

20. A municipal bond dealer offers a 20-year, 6% bond at a basis of 5.3% to equal a price of 104.25. Another dealer offers the same bond at a basis of 5.2% to equal a price of 105.15. What would the basis quote be for a price quote of 104.80?

    A. 5.18%
    B. 5.24%
    C. 5.26%
    D. 5.32%

21. An investor has purchased three municipal issues quoted at 7% yield, with 5-, 10- and 15-year maturities, respectively. If municipal yields drop by ten basis points, which of the following will show the greatest dollar price movement?

    A. 5-year maturity
    B. 10-year maturity
    C. 15-year maturity
    D. All will move equally.

22. In a comparison of long-term bonds with short-term bonds, all of the following are characteristics of long-term bonds EXCEPT that they

    A. usually have higher yields than short-term bonds
    B. usually provide greater liquidity than short-term bonds
    C. are more likely to be callable
    D. will fluctuate in price more than short-term bonds in response to interest rate changes

23. When interest rates are falling or rising, the price fluctuations of which of the following will be the greatest?

    A. Short-term bonds
    B. Long-term bonds
    C. Money-market instruments
    D. Common stock

24. When interest rates decline, all of the following statements are true EXCEPT that

    A. bond prices in the secondary market increase
    B. prices of newly issued bonds remain the same
    C. prices of newly issued bonds rise as interest rates fall
    D. bond yields decrease

25. A 9 1/2% bond will mature in 15 years and 6 months and is issued at a 9.45% yield. Using the bond table in Figure 2.5, what will be the bond's price?

    A. 100.30
    B. 100.40
    C. 100.70
    D. 101.20

26. A 5% bond is being offered at 106.75 to yield a 4.2% return. Another 5% bond is offered at 105.50 to yield a 4.3% return. What would the quote be on a 5% bond yielding a 4.25% return?

    A. 104.75
    B. 105.75
    C. 106.125
    D. 107.75

27. Interest payments on a bond are based on the bond's

    A. par value
    B. discount value
    C. market value
    D. book value

28. A 5% bond is issued at par. It is now selling at 90 and is redeemable at par. What is its annual income?

    A. $20
    B. $50
    C. $500
    D. $5,000

Answers

1.   The nominal yield of a bond that pays an investor $130 in annual interest is $130 divided by $1,000, which is 13%.

2.   A bond that pays $42.50 every six months pays $85 per year. $85 ÷ $1,000 = 8.5%.

3.   The nominal rate is always calculated by using the par value. Even though the bond is currently selling for $800, to calculate its nominal yield you must divide $80 by $1,000. The bond has a nominal yield of 8%.

4.   To find the current yield of a bond paying $95 per year and trading at par, divide $95 by $1,000. The bond's current yield is 9.5%

5.   To find the current yield of a bond paying $85 per year and trading at $700, divide $85 by $700. The bond's current yield is 12.14%

6.   The current yield of a bond paying $110 per year and trading at $1,100 is 10%. $110 ÷ $1,100 = 10%.

7. $1,000 times 12% equals $120. A bond with a current yield of 12% trading at $1,000 is paying $120 in annual interest. This bond's current yield equals its coupon yield because the bond is trading at par ($1,000).

8.   A bond with a current yield of 12% that is trading at $800 is paying $96 in annual interest ($800 × 12% = $96). $96 in annual interest divided by $1,000 par value is a coupon rate of 9.6%.

9.   A bond trading for $1,600 with a current yield of 12% is paying $192 in interest annually to the investor ($1,600 × 12% = $192). To find its coupon rate, divide $192 by $1,000 to get 19.2%.

10. $37.50 in semiannual interest payments on a bond represents $75 in annual interest. $75 divided by the current price of $1,200 equals a current yield of 6.25%.

11. $75 in annual interest on a bond ($37.50 in semiannual interest payments times 2) divided by the bond's $1,000 par value represents a 7.5% coupon.

12.   The investor paid a $200 premium for the bond. $200 divided by ten years is a prorated $20 per year.

13.   The investor paid a $100 premium for the bond. $100 prorated over 20 years is $5 per year.

14.   **C.**   A bond at par has a coupon rate equal to current yield. All yields will be the same as the coupon yield when the bond is at par.

15.   **B.**

$$\frac{\text{Annual interest}}{\text{Current market price}} = \text{Current yield}$$

16.   **B.**   The customer purchased the 5% bond when it was yielding 6%, therefore at a discount. The customer sold the bond when other bonds of like kind, quality and maturity were yielding 4%. The bond is now at a premium because the 5% coupon is attractive to other investors. The customer, therefore, made a capital gain on the investment.

17.   **B.**   With the same nominal yield, the discount bonds will generate higher yields because the discount will be received in addition to coupon interest.

18.   **B.**   Because interest rates in general have risen since the issuance of the 9% bond, the bond's price will now be discounted to give a higher current yield on the bond—making it competitive with new issues now being sold at 9 1/2%.

19.   **A.**   The *Bond Basis Book* takes yield to maturity quotes and, based on the bond's coupon and maturity, converts the yield quote into a per-

centage of par quote. It has nothing to do with taxable equivalent yields or unit denominations.

20.   **B.**   The difference between 104.25 and 105.15 is .90. The number 104.80 is .55 away from 104.25, or 61.1% of the distance between the two prices. The difference between the two yields is .1 basis points (5.3% − 5.2%). 61.1% of .1 basis points is .06 (rounded). The yield to maturity is 5.24% (5.3% − .06 = 5.24%). Answers A and D are impossible because neither lies between 5.3% and 5.2%. Answer C is less than halfway from 5.3% to 5.2%. Answer B represents the yield that is the same relative distance from 5.3% that 104.80 is from 104.25.

21.   **C.**   For a given change in interest rates, bonds with the longest maturity will show the greatest change in dollar price.

22.   **B.**   Long-term bonds are not as liquid as short-term obligations.

23.   **B.**   Long-term debt prices will fluctuate more than short-term debt prices as interest rates rise and fall. Common stock prices are not directly affected by interest rates.

24.   **C.**   When interest rates decline, yields on outstanding issues decline; prices increase, but not in exact proportion to the loss in yield. Bonds are still issued at or near par value, but with different coupons.

25.   **B.**   The question asks for the dollar quote on a bond quoted at a 9.45% yield. The 9.4% price is 100.81 and the 9.5% price is 100.00. The difference is 0.81. The 9.45% quote is 50% of the difference between 9.4% and 9.5%: 50% × 0.81 = .41 (rounded); 100.81 − .41 = 100.40 (the bond price).

26.   **C.**   This question requires that the bond price be interpolated. The 4.25% yield is midway between the two yields given; therefore, the price must be midway between the two prices given. The difference between the two given prices is 1.25 points. Half of that difference is .625 points. The price of the bond is 106.125 (106.75 − .625, or 105.50 + .625).

27.   **A.**   Interest on bonds is always based on the bond's par value.

28.   **B.**   Regardless of current market price, the coupon is based on par value of $1,000. The bondholder receives 5% on $1,000, or $50, annually.

Characteristics of Corporate Bonds

Types of Bonds

There are two primary types of corporate bonds: secured and unsecured.

Secured Bonds

When the issuer has set aside certain identifiable assets as collateral for the prompt payment of interest and the repayment of principal the bond issue is known as *secured*. In a default, bondholders can lay claim to the assets.

Mortgage bonds. In reorganization or liquidation, mortgage bonds have absolute priority among claims on the assets pledged to secure them and are sometimes called **senior debt securities** (senior lien). First claim on the pledged property goes to first-mortgage bonds, second claim to second-mortgage bonds and so on.

Closed-end indentures. In a closed-end mortgage arrangement, a corporation issues the maximum number of bonds authorized in the trust indenture as first-mortgage bonds. Any subsequent issue will have subordinated claims on the property.

Open-end indentures. In an open-ended trust indenture, the corporation can issue more bonds of the same class later. Subsequent issues will be secured by the same collateral backing the initial issue and will have equal liens on the property.

Prior lien bonds. Mortgage bonds that take precedence over first-mortgage bonds are known as prior-lien bonds. Before issuing prior lien bonds, a corporation must have the consent of first-mortgage bondholders.

Collateral trust bonds. Collateral trust bonds are usually issued by corporations that own securities of other companies and issues bonds secured by a pledge of these investment securities as collateral.

Equipment trust certificates. Equipment trust certificates are used to finance the purchase of transportation equipment.

Unsecured Bonds

Unsecured bonds have no specific collateral backing and are classified into two primary types: debentures and subordinated debentures.

Debentures. Debentures are backed by the general credit of the issuing corporation. The owner of a debenture is considered a general creditor of the corporation.

Subordinated debentures. Subordinated debentures are so called because the claims of their owners are subordinated to the claims of other general creditors, including owners of ordinary debentures.

Guaranteed Bonds

With guaranteed bonds, a company other than the issuer has guaranteed payment of principal and interest.

Income Bonds

Income bonds pay interest on the bond only if the corporation's earnings are sufficient to meet the interest payment and if the payment is declared by the board of directors.

Income bonds are traded flat in the secondary market; that is, the bonds are bought and sold without any accrued interest paid by the buyer to the seller.

Zero-coupon Bonds

Issuing zero-coupon bonds. Zero-coupon bonds are debt obligations of the issuer. The issuers of zero-coupon bonds do not make interest payments to the owners of zeros. They sell these debt obligations to investors at a deep discount from the face value with a promise to redeem the bonds at face value when they mature. The difference between the deeply discounted purchase price and the

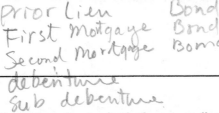

Prior Lien Bond
First Mortgage Bond
Second Mortgage Bond
debenture
sub debenture

full face value at maturity is the return (interest) the investor receives.

Zero-coupon bonds are issued by corporations, municipalities and the U.S. Treasury (e.g., Separate Trading of Registered Interest and Principal of Securities—STRIPS), and they may be created by broker-dealers from other types of securities, including those issued by the federal government.

Advantages and Disadvantages of Zero-coupon Bonds

An advantage of an investment in zero-coupon bonds is that there is *no reinvestment risk* (also known as *interest rate risk*) for the purchaser. A disadvantage of an investment in zeros is that they are *more subject to market risk* (also known as *price risk*) than are interest-paying debt obligations. Zero-coupon bond prices tend to be extremely volatile because of their deep discount and zero interest rate.

Taxation of Zero-coupon Bonds

The investor who owns corporate or government zeroes owes income tax each year on a portion of that amount, just as though it had been received in cash (interest from municipal obligations, including municipal zeros, is generally federally tax-exempt). The annual interest is not prorated on a straight-line basis and the investor is apportioned a different amount each year.

Liquidation Priority

In order of priority, liquidation occurs as follows:

1. unpaid wages
2. IRS (taxes)
3. secured claims (mortgages)
4. secured liabilities (bonds)
5. unsecured liabilities (debentures) and general creditors
6. subordinated debt
7. preferred stockholders
8. common stockholders

The Trust Indenture

The trust indenture is a legal contract between the bond issuer and a trustee that represents the bondholders. Within the trust indenture, covenants identify the bondholders' rights and name the entity that will act as trustee. The trustee ensures compliance with the covenants of the indenture and acts on behalf of the bondholders in the event of a default by the issuer.

The Trustee

The trustee helps prepare the issue. In the trust indenture the corporation agrees to abide by certain covenants.

Exemptions

Federal and municipal governments are exempt from the provisions of the Trust Indenture Act. The act also exempts securities not issued under an indenture, as long as the total dollar amount of securities issued by a single entity does not exceed $2 million in a twelve-month period.

Protective Covenants of the Indenture

The debtor corporation agrees to:

- pay the interest and principal of every bond;
- specify the places bonds or coupons can be presented for payment;
- defend the legal title to the property;
- maintain the property to ensure that business can be conducted profitably;
- do nothing that will diminish the claims of the bonds;
- insure the mortgaged property against fire and other losses;
- pay all taxes and assessments (property, income, franchises);
- maintain its corporate structure and the right to do business; and
- record the mortgage and pay any recording fees.

Remedies of Bondholders

If a corporation is judged to be bankrupt, liquidated or failing to meet its promises in the indenture, the trustee and bondholders have access to the following remedies:

- right of entry;
- right to sell property to the highest bidder;
- right to foreclose;
- right to bring suit; and
- right to declare the principal due prior to the maturity date.

Also included in the provisions of the indenture are:

- acceleration of maturity in cases of default;
- release of mortgaged property; and
- protection for bondholders in consolidations and mergers.

Unless the trust indenture specifies otherwise, changes in the indenture cannot be made without the unanimous consent of the bondholders.

Tracking Corporate Bonds

Quotes on corporate bonds are stated as percentages of the principal amount of the bond. For example, a bid of 103 1/2 means 103 1/2% of par, or $1,035. A bond point is equal to $10 (1% of $1,000). A bond quote of 92 1/4 means 92 and 1/4% (92.25%) of $1,000, which is $922.50. The minimum variation for corporate bond quotes is 1/8th (0.125%).

Questions

1. Ted Thompson bought five $1,000 corporate bonds. All of the following statements are true EXCEPT that

    A. Ted's bonds represent ownership in the corporation
    B. the bonds are debt securities
    C. Ted is a creditor of the corporation
    D. if the corporation goes bankrupt, Ted will receive company assets before corporate stockholders receive them

2. Which of the following is commonly referered to as funded debt?

    A. Corporate bonds
    B. Municipal bonds
    C. Preferred stock
    D. Government bonds

3. Equipment trust certificates would most commonly be issued by

    I. airline companies
    II. railroad companies
    III. farm equipment companies
    IV. automobile manufacturers

    A. I and II
    B. II
    C. III
    D. III and IV

4. Bonds that are secured by other securities placed with a trustee are called

    A. mortgage bonds
    B. collateral trust bonds
    C. debenture bonds
    D. guaranteed bonds

5. When a person owns a convertible bond, he is a(n)

    A. creditor of the issuer
    B. owner of the issuer
    C. neither A nor B
    D. both A and B

6. In case of bankruptcy, debentures rank on a par with

   A. first-mortgage bonds
   B. equipment trust certificates
   C. unsecured debts of private creditors
   D. collateral trust bonds

7. An indenture has a closed-end provision. This means that

   A. additional issues will have junior liens
   B. the bonds must be called before maturity
   C. a sinking fund must be established
   D. no additional bonds may be issued

8. An investor purchasing 2 GMAC ZR 12's at 53 1/2 would receive annual interest of

   A. $0
   B. $12
   C. $53.50
   D. $120

9. A customer who bought 10 Ogden 5's at 93 would receive annual interest of

   A. $50
   B. $93
   C. $500
   D. $930

10. A first-mortgage bond is issued by ABC Sewer Company. The bond is backed by the

   A. mortgages of cities serviced by the sewer company
   B. liens on the property of the sewer company
   C. customers' mortgages
   D. collateral of investments owned by the sewer company

11. A corporate bond valued at $1,012.50 is shown in the bond guide as

   A. 101.25
   B. 101 8/32
   C. 101 4/16
   D. 101 1/4

12. An investor buys $1 million of 10% corporate bonds at par. At the end of the day, the bonds close up 1/2 point. The investor has a gain of

   A. $2,500
   B. $5,000
   C. $25,000
   D. $50,000

Answers

1. **A.** Bonds, unlike stocks, do not represent ownership of the corporation. Instead, bonds represent corporate debt. The corporation owes money ($5,000 in Ted's case) to the bondholder, who is a creditor of the corporation. In bankruptcy, the corporation pays the debts (including bonds) before distributing assets to stockholders.

2. **A.** *Funded debt* is the term used to describe long-term corporate debt.

3. **A.** Equipment trust certificates can be issued only by companies that actually use the equipment (the equipment is collateral for the loan). Manufacturers do not issue equipment trust certificates.

4. **B.** Collateral bonds or collateral trust bonds are used frequently in railroad financing where securities owned by the parent are pledged as collateral for a loan. The pledged collateral for common stock is generally deposited in a trust, especially when money is raised publicly.

5. **A.** A bondholder is a creditor (whether or not the bond is convertible). Only after the bondholder converts is he considered an owner.

6. **C.** A debenture is an unsecured debt, backed only by the corporation's promise to pay. Therefore, of the answers offered, A, B and D are backed by specific assets and have preference before debentures.

7. **A.** The indenture may include a restriction on the sale of additional bonds—this is a "closed-end" provision. If any additional bonds are issued, their owners' claims on the mortgaged property will be subordinated to the claims of bondholders owning the original issue.

8. **A.** The GMAC bond is a zero-coupon bond (ZR) with no interest payments. These bonds sell at a deep discount, and the tax law requires annual accretion of the discount.

9. **C.** "Ogden 5's" means 5% bonds. 5% of $1,000 par equals $50 of interest per bond annually. For ten bonds, the annual interest is $500. The investor paid $930 for each bond.

10. **B.** A mortgage bond is evidence of indebtedness that is secured by a mortgage or other lien on some underlying real property of a corporation.

11. **D.** Corporates are quoted in fractions of 1/8th and 1/4th. The quote of 101 1/4th equals $1,012.50. This represents $1,010 (101% of par) plus $2.50 (1/4th of $10). Each point in a corporate bond is equal to $10.

12. **B.** The investor owns $1 million face value of bonds. An increase of 1/2 point is an increase of 1/2 of 1% of $1,000,000, or $5,000.

3   Corporate Special Securities

Convertible Securities

Why Corporations Issue Convertible Securities

A corporation will add a conversion feature to its bonds and preferred stock issues to make them more marketable. When the bond market is strong, convertible debentures are frequently issued as a means of raising equity capital on a postponed basis. When (and if) the debentures are converted, the corporation's capitalization changes from debt to equity.

Advantages to the Issuer

Corporations issue convertible securities for a number of reasons:

- Convertibles can be sold with a lower coupon rate than nonconvertibles.
- The company can eliminate a fixed interest charge as conversion takes place, thus reducing debt.
- A rapid increase in the number of shares in the market is unlikely because conversions take place over a longer period of time.
- The corporation avoids immediate dilution of primary earnings per share.

Disadvantages to the Issuer

Disadvantages of issuing convertibles include:

- Shareholders' equity is diluted at conversion.
- A substantial conversion could cause a shift in the control of the company.
- Reducing corporate debt through conversion means a loss of leverage.
- The corporation pays increased taxes as conversion takes place.
- There is uncertainty in the corporate capital structure.

The Market for Convertible Securities

Advantages of owning convertible securities include:

- A convertible debenture pays interest at a fixed rate and will be redeemable for its face value at maturity.
- The convertible bondholder has priority over common stockholders in the event of a corporate liquidation.
- The market price of a convertible debenture will tend to be more stable during market declines than the price of common stock.
- The market price of convertibles tends to move upward if the stock price moves up.

Conversion Price and Conversion Ratio

Conversion price. Conversion price is the amount of par value of the convertible bond that can be converted into one share of common stock. If a convertible debenture has a conversion price of

$125, each $125 worth of par value will be converted into one share of common stock. For every bond a holder converts, the bondholder would receive eight shares of stock (an 8-to-1 conversion ratio).

Conversion ratio. Conversion ratio expresses the number of shares of common stock obtainable by converting $1,000 par value of the bonds. A conversion price of $125 has a conversion ratio of 8 to 1 ($1,000 ÷ $125 = 8).

Fixed or Variable

Convertible debentures will be issued with a schedule of different conversion prices incorporated into the indenture agreement. The schedule usually calls for higher conversion prices as the debenture nears maturity. Factors that affect the initial conversion rate or price are the:

- price of the stock at the time the bonds are issued;
- earnings prospect of the issuing company and its effect on the stock price;
- market trend (convertibles become popular with investors in a rising market);
- conversion period (generally, the longer the time period, the less favorable the initial conversion rates need be); and
- amount of interest the corporation is willing to pay (a higher interest rate encourages investors to accept a higher conversion price at issuance).

Subscription Privileges for Stockholders

Because convertibles can dilute shareholder's equity, stockholders often have a preemptive right to purchase any new security issue that is convertible to stock, usually at a subscription price below the market value of the bond.

Protective Features

Stock splits and dividends. Conversion prices may be adjusted if stock splits and stock dividends are declared on the underlying common stock during the life of the debenture.

Changes in class of conversion securities. If outstanding common shares are converted into the same number of shares of another class, the conversion privilege would apply to an equal number of new shares.

Additional shares. The indenture fixes both the maximum number of additional shares the corporation can issue while convertible bonds are outstanding and the minimum price at which they can be issued.

Mergers, consolidations and dissolutions. If the corporation ceases to exist because of any of the previously described situations, holders of convertible bonds lose their conversion privileges.

Calculating Conversion Parity

Parity means that two securities are of equal dollar value. If a corporation issues a convertible preferred stock that has a par value of $100 and is convertible at $50, the conversion ratio is 2 to 1. The investor can receive two shares of common stock for one share of the preferred.

Suppose that a convertible preferred is selling in the market at $88 and is convertible into four shares of common stock. The market price of the common would have to be about $22 to be at parity with the convertible preferred. Four shares of common stock at $22 per share are equal in value to one share of the preferred at $88 per share.

If you know that the common is trading at $18 and that the convertible preferred has a conversion ratio of 5 to 1, you can multiply $18 by 5 to calculate that the preferred's parity price is $90.

Use the following formulas to calculate the parity prices of convertible securities and their underlying common shares:

$$\frac{\text{Market price of convertible}}{\text{Conversion ratio}} = \begin{array}{l}\text{Parity price}\\\text{of common}\end{array}$$

$$\begin{array}{l}\text{Market price of common} \times \text{Conversion ratio}\\ = \text{Parity price of convertible}\end{array}$$

Investment Value and Conversion Value

The estimated investment value of a convertible debenture is the market price at which the security would sell if it were not convertible into common stock. The conversion value of a debenture is the total market value of common stock into which the debenture is convertible.

Take the example of a convertible debenture selling at 110 that can be converted into 10 shares of common stock. If the market value of each share is $12, the conversion value of the debenture is $1,200 ($120 × 10).

Forced Conversion

A corporation can call convertible bonds when market conditions are such that bondholders will find it more profitable to convert the bonds than to submit them for redemption at the call price. This will happen when the parity price is above the call price.

Suppose, for example, that an issue of bonds is convertible into common stock at $50 (a conversion ratio of 20 to 1) and is called at 110. The stock is currently trading at $57 per share, so by converting a bond, an investor can become the owner of 20 shares of common worth $1,140. The parity price of the bond would be 114 ($1,140 for a $1,000 par value bond). The parity price, in other words, is above the call price. The bond owner is better off converting and selling the 20 shares of common for $1,140 than she is tendering the bond for redemption at $1,100.

Questions

1. Which of the following statements concerning convertible bonds is(are) true?

    I. Coupon rates are usually lower than nonconvertible bonds of the same issuer.
    II. Convertible bondholders are creditors of the corporation.
    III. If the underlying common stock should decline to the point where there is no advantage to convert the bonds into common stock, the bonds will sell at a price based on their inherent value as bonds, disregarding the convertible feature.

    A. I only
    B. I and III only
    C. III only
    D. I, II and III

Use the following tombstone to answer questions 2 and 3.

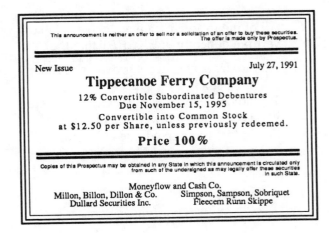

New Issue   July 27, 1991

Tippecanoe Ferry Company

12% Convertible Subordinated Debentures
Due November 15, 1995
Convertible into Common Stock
at $12.50 per Share, unless previously redeemed.

Price 100%

Moneyflow and Cash Co.

Millon, Billon, Dillon & Co.   Simpson, Sampson, Sobriquet
Dullard Securities Inc.   Fleecem Runn Skippe

2. The bonds are convertible into how many shares of common stock?

    A. 80
    B. 95
    C. 100
    D. 105

3. On December 3, 1994, the Tippecanoe debentures were trading at 102. Therefore, the parity price of the common stock on that date was approximately

A. 12 1/4
B. 12 1/2
C. 12 3/4
D. 13

4. A bond is convertible to common stock at $20 per share. If the market value of the bond falls to $800, what is the new parity price of the stock?

A. $12
B. $16
C. $25
D. $40

5. A convertible bond is purchased at its face value and convertible at $125.00. What is the conversion ratio?

A. 2
B. 8
C. 12
D. 20

6. All of the following are advantages of convertible debentures EXCEPT that the

A. holder shares in the growth of the common stock
B. holder receives a higher rate of interest
C. issuer pays a lower rate of interest
D. holder has a fixed rate of interest

Answers

1. **D.** All three choices are true of convertible bonds. Coupon rates are lower because of the value of the conversion feature; bondholders are creditors; and if the stock price falls, its value as an income and debt security will be maintained.

2. **A.** Because the debentures are convertible at $12.50, they are convertible into 80 shares ($1,000 ÷ 12.50).

3. **C.** $1,000 (par) ÷ $12.50 = 80 shares. $1,020 bond price ÷ 80 conversion ratio = $12.75 = 12 3/4.

4. **B.** The calculations are: $1,000 ÷ $20 = 50 shares for one bond. $800 bond price ÷ 50 shares = $16 parity price.

5. **B.** $1,000 par ÷ $125 conversion price = 8 shares per bond.

6. **B.** Because of the possibility of participating in the growth of the common stock through an increase in the market price of the common, the convertible can be issued with a lower rate of interest. This is an advantage to the issuing company.

Rights and Warrants

Issuance

Preemptive Right

"Preemptive right" refers to the right of an existing stockholder to purchase shares of a new issue of stock in proportion to the number of shares he already owns.

Rights are valued separately and trade in the secondary market during the subscription period. A stockholder who receives rights may:

- exercise the right to buy stock
- sell the right
- let the right expire

Approval by Vote of Stockholders

Decisions to issue additional stock must first be approved by the board of directors.

Characteristics of Rights

Subscription Right Certificate

One right is issued for each share of common stock the investor owns. Therefore, an investor with 1,200 shares of common stock receives a certificate representing 1,200 rights.

Significant Trading Dates and Prices of Rights Offerings

The following is an example of a rights offering. On September 1st, Amalgamated Featherbedders, Inc. declares a rights offering. Holders of the common stock as of October 1st will be able to subscribe to one new share at $30 for each ten shares already owned. The stock is currently trading at $41. The rights expire November 15th.

Assume Amalgamated Featherbedders, Inc. has 20 million shares outstanding and wants to issue another 2 million shares. Each existing share is entitled to one right, so there will be 20 million rights issued. Those rights entitle stockholders to only 2 million shares, so 20 million rights divided by 2 million new shares means that it will require ten rights to buy one new share. Between September 1st and November 15th, the stock tables in newspapers and other publications will show two different entries for Amalgamated:

- the price of the stock itself cum rights or ex-rights; and
- the price of the rights, on a when issued basis or at the current market price.

ex-date

The corporation will issue rights October 8th to any stockholder of record October 1st. Stock is traded cum rights until the ex-date. An investor who purchases the stock cum rights is also entitled to receive the right.

The Rights Agent

The rights agent does for rights what the transfer agent does for stocks. When a right is sold, the rights agent records the name of the new owner.

Standby Underwriting

If current stockholders do not subscribe to all the rights the unsold rights may be offered through a broker-dealer in a standby underwriting. This will be done on a firm commitment basis.

Value of Rights

Theoretical. The theoretical value of rights is based on the savings investors will be able to realize by exercising the subscription rights to purchase securities below market price.

Prior to ex-date. To compute the value of a right when the stock is trading cum rights, we will use the Amalgamated Featherbedders, Inc. example. The market price (M) of the stock cum rights is $41; the subscription price (S) is $30. The investor needs ten rights and $30 to buy one new share. The ten rights, therefore, earn the investor an $11 discount on a share of stock ($41 market price – $30 subscription price).

To determine the value of one right, divide the savings it represents (M – S) by the number of rights needed to purchase one share (N), plus one right (N + 1). ($41 – $30) ÷ 11 = $1.

After ex-date. On the day the stock first trades ex-rights, the market price typically drops by the value of the right. For the stock selling without rights, the divisor, in this case, is the same as the number of rights needed to purchase one share.

To determine the value of one right when the stock is ex-rights, divide the savings it represents (M – S) by the number of rights needed to purchase one share (N). In the previous example, the stock is now at $40. ($40 – $30) ÷ 10 = $1.

Warrants

A warrant gives the holder the right to purchase securities at a stipulated price from the issuer. A warrant is usually a long-term instrument.

Warrants may be detachable or nondetachable. If detachable, they trade in the market purely as speculation on the price of the underlying stock. The investor can (1) exercise the warrant or (2) sell the warrant in the market.

Origination of Warrants

Warrants are usually offered to the public as a sweetener in connection with issues of other securities. Warrants are occasionally bundled with other securities and offered as part of *units.* As an example, Amalgamated Featherbedders may make an offering of 4,000,000 shares of new preferred stock, bundling it into units of 4 shares of preferred and two warrants for 1/4 of a share of common stock exercisable at a specific price. An investor who purchases 100 units will receive 400 shares of preferred stock and warrants redeemable for 50 shares of common (100 units times two warrants for 1/4 of a share of common per unit).

Questions

1. A corporation issues new stock with a subscription price of $25. The stock is currently selling for $29. Under the terms of the offering, four rights are needed to subscribe to one new share. Using the ex-rights formula, what is the value of one right?

    A. $.80
    B. $1.00
    C. $4.00
    D. The value cannot be determined from the information given.

2. A corporation issuing stock has informed its stockholders that they can buy the newly issued stock for $21.50 per share with 20 rights. The outstanding stock is currently trading at $40. To purchase a share of the stock at the subscription price takes

    A. $21.50 with 20 rights
    B. $21.50 with 21 rights
    C. one right with $21.50
    D. one right with $40

Use the following information to answer questions 3 and 4.

An investor owns a stock with a current market value of $70. The company is issuing more common stock by way of a rights offering, with five rights required to buy one new share at $55 per share.

3. The value of the rights before the security trades ex-rights is

    A. $2.50
    B. $3.00
    C. $5.00
    D. $15.00

4. The stock is trading on the ex-rights day with a market value of $70. The rights now have a market value of

A. $2.50
B. $3.00
C. $5.00
D. $15.00

5. The DEF Company wishes to sell additional shares to its existing stockholders through a rights offering. The market price of DEF is currently $42 and the subscription price has been set at $28. The terms of the offering are that 20 rights are necessary to purchase one new share. If an investor wishes to buy the rights before the ex-date, the price per right will be approximately

A. $.67
B. $.70
C. $1.00
D. $1.12

Use the following information to answer questions 6 and 7.

Acme Corporation wants to raise $50,000,000 through a rights offering. The terms of the offering are 10 to 1. Your client receives 500 rights to subscribe to the new shares at $50. The current market price is $54.

6. While the stock is trading cum rights, what is the theoretical value of your client's rights?

A. $36.36
B. $40.00
C. $181.81
D. $200.00

7. How many shares of Acme common stock were outstanding before the issue of the subscription stock?

A. 1 million
B. 5 million
C. 10 million
D. 50 million

8. Which of the following instruments does NOT receive dividends?

A. Warrants
B. Common stock
C. Preferred stock
D. Convertible preferred stock

9. Which of the following statements is true of warrants?

A. Warrants give the holder a perpetual interest in the issuer's stock.
B. Warrants are shorter term than rights.
C. Warrants are issued to make a security offering more attractive.
D. Warrants are safer than corporate bonds.

10. Which of the following statements about rights is true?

A. Common stockholders do not have the right to subscribe to rights offerings.
B. Preferred stockholders do not have the right to subscribe to rights offerings.
C. Both A and B are true.
D. Neither A nor B is true.

Answers

1. **B.** Use the formula:

$$\frac{\text{Market value (M)} - \text{Subscription price (S)}}{\text{Number of rights (N)}}$$

$$\frac{\$29 - \$25}{4} = \$1$$

2. **A.** The subscription price of the new stock is $21.50 plus the 20 rights required to exercise. The 21 rights will be used only in calculating the theoretical value of the rights on a cum rights basis.

3. **A.** This is a cum rights problem. With the stock trading cum rights, the formula is:

$$\frac{M-S}{N+1} = \frac{15}{6} = \$2.50$$

4. **B.** This is an ex-rights question. The formula for the theoretical value of a right on and after the ex-date is the same as the above, except that the divisor is N (number of rights required).

5. **A.** Using the cum rights formula, the price per right is $.67.

$(M - S) \div (N + 1) = (42 - 28) \div (20 + 1)$

$= 14 \div 21 = \$.67$

6. **C.** Remember, the investor has 500 rights. The value of one right is $.3636 ($4 + 11). The value of 500 rights, therefore, is $181.81 ($.3636 × 500).

7. **C.** The information given has to be carefully dissected to find what is needed. Because Acme is raising $50,000,000 by selling shares at $50 each, it must be selling 1 million shares. If the terms of the offering are 10 to 1, that means there are 10 times as many shares already outstanding as there are being issued in the rights offering. There are 10,000,000 shares outstanding.

8. **A.** Warrants do not pay dividends under any circumstance. The other instruments listed will pay dividends when dividends are declared by the board of directors.

9. **C.** Warrants are issued with primary common stock or bond offerings as a "sweetener." Warrants are long-term options to buy common stock.

10. **B.** Preferred stockholders have a preference as to liquidation, distribution or income, but they have no right to maintain a percentage of ownership.

American Depositary Receipts

Trading in Foreign Securities

ADRs facilitate the trading of foreign securities in U.S. markets. An ADR is a negotiable security and represents a receipt for a given number of shares of stock (typically one to ten) in a non-U.S. corporation. The ADR itself is an instrument that can, like a stock, be bought and sold in the U.S. securities markets.

Registration Requirements

Foreign corporations often use ADRs as a means of generating U.S. investments without having to go through the entire SEC registration process.

Custodian Bank

ADRs are issued by foreign branches of large commercial U.S. banks. The shares of foreign stock that the ADR represents are held by a custodian. The stock must remain on deposit as long as the ADR is outstanding.

Registered in name of owner. ADRs are registered on the books of the U.S. bank responsible for them. The individual investors in the ADRs are not considered the registered owners.

Bank responsibilities. The depository bank holds securities and provides information to the ADR holders about any developments in the foreign corporation or the country of registry that could affect the ADR.

Rights of ADR Owners

ADR owners have voting rights and the right to receive dividends when declared, but do not have preemptive rights. Dividends are sent to the custo-dian bank as registered owner. The custodian bank collects any dividends paid, converts the payments into U.S. funds for U.S. owners and withholds any required payments of foreign taxes.

When the bank receives the rights or warrants from the issuer, it sells the rights and warrants in a market of the issuer's own country and distributes the sale proceeds in cash to the ADR owners.

Delivery of Foreign Security

Owners of ADRs have the right to exchange their ADR certificates for the foreign shares they represent.

Sponsored vs. Unsponsored ADRs

If the issuer creates the ADR by depositing shares with a custodian bank and agreeing to comply with SEC filing and reporting requirements, the ADR is considered *sponsored*. *Unsponsored* ADRs are created when a bank buys shares and keeps them on deposit overseas with a custodian.

Questions

1. ADRs are used to facilitate the

   A. foreign trading of domestic securities
   B. foreign trading of U.S. government securities
   C. domestic trading of U.S. government securities
   D. domestic trading of foreign securities

2. ADRs come in which two of the following forms?

   I. Open-end
   II. Closed-end
   III. Sponsored
   IV. Unsponsored

   A. I and II
   B. I and III
   C. II and IV
   D. III and IV

Answers

1. **D.** ADRs are tradable securities issued by banks, with the receipt's value based on the underlying foreign securities held by the bank.

2. **D.** ADRs are typically issued as either sponsored or unsponsored securities. Sponsored ADRs are similar in many ways to exchange-listed stocks, while unsponsored ADRs are similar to OTC stocks.

4

U.S. Government and Agency Securities

Marketable Government Securities

Treasury Bills ½ mil

Issuance and trading. T bills are issued at a discount from par in a **competitive bid** auction. Competitive bids are submitted for amounts of $500,000 and up.

T bills may also be purchased by **noncompetitive bid**. The investor who submits a noncompetitive bid pays the average of the competitive bids accepted at that auction and is guaranteed to have his order filled. Noncompetitive bids are limited to a maximum amount of $500,000.

T bills trade at a discount and do not pay interest.

Book entry. Treasury bills are issued in book-entry form.

Maturities and denominations. Treasury bills are short-term issues with maturities of one year or less. Issued in denominations of $10,000 to $1 million (in $5,000 increments), they mature in 13 weeks, 26 weeks or 52 weeks.

Pricing. Treasury bills are quoted at a discount from par. A quote of 3.50%, for example, means a T bill is selling at 3 1/2% less than its face value. For a $10,000 52-week Treasury bill, that would be a price of $9,650. A T bill quote might read as follows: Maturity April 6, bid 3.50%, asked 3.40%.

Treasury Notes 1—10 years (1000 → 1 mil)

Issuance and trading. T notes pay interest every six months. T note investors have a choice between receiving fully registered certificates and having a record of their ownership on computer in book-entry form.

Maturities and denominations. Issued in denominations of $1,000 to $1 million, T notes are intermediate-term bonds maturing in one to ten years.

Pricing. T notes and bonds are quoted in 1/32nds of a percent of par. A quote of 96.14 (which can also be expressed as 96-14 or 96:14) on a $1,000 note means that the note is selling for 96 and 14/32% of its par value of $1,000. A quote of 96.14 is equal to 96.4375% of $1,000, or $964.375.

Other examples are as follows:

A bid of:	Means:	In dollars:
98.1	98 + 1/32% of $1,000	$980.3125
98.2	98 + 2/32% of $1,000	$980.6250
98.3	98 + 3/32% of $1,000	$980.9375
.....	.....	.....
98.10	98 + 10/32% of $1,000	$983.1250
98.11	98 + 11/32% of $1,000	$983.4375
98.12	98 + 12/32% of $1,000	$983.7500

Redeemable at face value. At maturity, T notes can be redeemed for cash at par or they can be refunded.

Treasury Bonds   *10+ years*

Issuance and trading. T bonds constitute the smallest portion of the government's marketable debt. Interest is payable every six months. T bonds are sold only in registered or book-entry form.

Callable. Some Treasury bonds have optional call dates. U.S. government securities are always called at par and never at a premium.

Maturities. Issued in denominations of $1,000 to $1 million, Treasury bonds generally have maturities of ten years or more.

Pricing. T bonds, like T notes, are issued, quoted and traded in 1/32nds of a percent of par. A quote of 97.08 (97-08 or 97:08) on a $1,000 note means that the note is selling for 97 and 8/32% of its par value of $1,000. A quote of 97.08 is equal to 97.25% of $1,000, or $972.50.

Flower bonds. Prior to 1971, the Treasury department issued flower bonds with a special tax advantage. An investor could purchase these bonds at a discount from face value and, after the investor's death, her heirs could redeem the bonds at face value to pay federal estate taxes. The last issue matures in 1998.

Table 1 compares Treasury bills, notes and bonds.

Cash Management Bills

Cash management bills (CMBs) are used by the Treasury to meet short-term (10- to 20-day) borrowing needs. It takes a minimum bid of $10 million to purchase CMBs at auction.

Zero-coupon Securities

Broker-dealers buy Treasury securities, place them in trust at a bank, and then sell receipts against the principal and coupon payments separately to investors to create zero-coupon bonds (**Treasury receipts**). Treasury receipts are collateralized by Treasury securities held in escrow for the investor by a custodial bank. Treasury receipts are priced at a discount from face value. *no reinvest risk*

Investors are not subject to reinvestment risk with Treasury receipts.

STRIPS. The Treasury department entered the growing zero-coupon bond market by designating certain Treasury issues as suitable for stripping into interest and principal components. These special securities became known as *STRIPS,* which stands for "Separate Trading of Registered Interest and Principal of Securities." STRIPS are issued as book-entry securities.

While the securities underlying Treasury STRIPS are the direct obligation of the U.S. government, the actual separation and trading is performed by major banks and dealers.

Brokerage zero-coupon bonds. The original zero-coupon bonds were created by brokerage firms and include:

- TIGRs (Treasury Investment Growth Receipts);
- CATS (Certificates of Accrual on Treasury Securities);
- LIONs (Lehman Investment Opportunity Notes);
- ETRs (Easy-growth Treasury Receipts); and
- TBRs (Treasury Bond Receipts).

Table 1   Marketable Government Securities

Bond	Maturity	Denomination	Pricing	Form
Treasury bills	Ninety days to one year	$10,000 to $1,000,000	Priced on an *discounted* interest rate basis	Book entry
Treasury notes	One to ten years	$1,000 to $1,000,000	Priced at a percentage of par	Book entry
Treasury bonds	Ten to thirty years	$1,000 to $1,000,000	Priced at a percentage of par	Book entry /reg

Questions

1. Government bonds and notes are quoted

   A. in 1/8ths
   B. as a percentage of par
   C. on a yield to maturity
   D. as a percentage of par on a discounted annualized basis

2. The maximum maturity on a Treasury note is how many years?

   A. One
   B. Three
   C. Five
   D. Ten

3. Which of the following statements are true regarding T bills?

   I. T bills trade at a discount to par.
   II. T bills have one year or less maturity.
   III. Most T bill issues are callable.
   IV. T bills are a direct obligation of the U.S. government.

   A. I and II only
   B. I, II and III only
   C. I, II and IV only
   D. I, II, III and IV

4. Flower bonds are

   A. financing instruments for the Garden State Parkway
   B. original issue discount bonds
   C. used to pay estate tax liability
   D. used to pay real estate tax liability

5. Which of the following U.S. government securities states a rate of interest on its face?

   I. Treasury bond
   II. Treasury note
   III. Treasury bill

   A. I and II only
   B. I and III only
   C. II and III only
   D. I, II and III

6. Which of the following is an original issue discount obligation?

   A. GNMA certificate
   B. T bill
   C. Corporate bond
   D. FNMA bond

7. If you invest $10,000 in T bills over a period of years, which of the following statements are true?

   I. The principal is stable.
   II. The interest is volatile.
   III. The interest is stable.
   IV. The principal is volatile.

   A. I and II
   B. I and III
   C. II and IV
   D. III and IV

8. Consider the following T bills:

Maturity	Bid	Asked
8-2	6.36	6.20
8-16	6.42	6.26

   The T bills maturing August 2nd (8-2) are being offered at par

   A. plus a premium to yield 6.20%
   B. less a discount to yield 6.20%
   C. plus a premium to yield 6.36%
   D. less a discount to yield 6.36%

9. A U.S. Treasury bond is listed as "4's of 88/94." This means that the bond

   A. is callable at par between 1988 and 1994
   B. matures between 1988 and 1994
   C. stops paying interest between 1988 and 1994
   D. sells at a premium between 1988 and 1994

10. The bid price of a Treasury bond is $875. It would appear in *The Wall Street Journal* as

   A. 87:12
   B. 87:16
   C. 87:5
   D. 87:8

11. An investor wishing a short-term investment should choose

   A. T bills
   B. certificates issued by the U.S. government
   C. notes issued by the U.S. government
   D. bonds issued by the U.S. government

12. Which of the following statements is NOT true of T bills?

   A. They mature in a year or less.
   B. They are sold at a discount.
   C. They are noncallable.
   D. Investors receive principal and interest at maturity.

13. For the past ten years, Mary Smith has been investing in Treasury bills. What has MOST likely happened to Mary's investment during that period of time?

   A. The interest is stable, but principal has fluctuated.
   B. The principal is stable, but interest is volatile.
   C. Both principal and interest have fluctuated.
   D. Both principal and interest have been stable.

14. Which of the following securities are original issue discount obligations?

   I. Fannie Maes
   II. Ginnie Maes
   III. Treasury bills
   IV. Treasury notes

   A. I and II
   B. II and IV
   C. III
   D. III and IV

15. Auctions for twelve-month Treasury bills are held every

   A. day
   B. week
   C. 4 weeks (monthly)
   D. 13 weeks (quarterly)

16. You purchase ten 8% T notes at 101–16. What is the dollar amount of this purchase?

   A. $1,001.50
   B. $1,011.60
   C. $10,150.00
   D. $10,812.00

17. Treasury bills sold at a price that is the average of the auction yields are

   A. negotiated bids
   B. competitive bids
   C. auction bids
   D. noncompetitive tenders

Answers

1. **B.** The notes, bonds and certificates are all quoted at a percentage of par. Only bills are quoted on an annualized discount basis.

2. **D.** Treasury notes have maturities that run from one to ten years.

3. **C.** T bills trade at a discount to par, are one year or less to maturity and are a direct obligation of the U.S. government. T bills are noncallable.

4. **C.** Flower bonds are a series of U.S. government bonds acceptable at face value to pay estate taxes. Because interest rates on these bonds are typically low, the bonds sell at a deep discount.

5. **A.** Bonds and notes are long-term government securities and show a stated rate of interest on their face. Bills, on the other hand, are short-term securities that are sold at a discount from face and redeemed at face, with the difference being the interest. T bills, therefore, do not carry a coupon rate.

6. **B.** T bills are auctioned weekly and are issued at a discount from par. At maturity, the holder receives par value with the earned discount treated as interest income.

7. **A.** Because T bills have a fixed principal amount, a $10,000 T bill will always be worth $10,000 at maturity—the price will not fluctuate a great deal when the maturity is so near. Interest rates, however, may well fluctuate from auction to auction; therefore, the interest is volatile.

8. **B.** T bills are being offered at a discount of 6.20%. This will result in a yield somewhat higher than 6.20, but this is the closest answer.

9. **A.** A listing with two apparent maturities means that the bond is callable after the first date and reaches maturity on the second. Treasury bonds are callable at par, never at a premium.

10. **B.** A bond selling at 875 equals 870 plus 16/32 ($5 = a half a point, or 16/32). The quote is 87:16.

11. **A.** T bills represent the only short-term investment because they have maturities of three, six or twelve months.

12. **D.** T bills mature in one year or less, trade at a discount to par and are generally noncallable. However, T bills are not interest bearing; rather, the discount provides the income to the bill holder.

13. **B.** Because T bills represent a constant $10,000 principal amount, the principal is stable. However, interest rates will fluctuate over time; therefore, the interest is volatile.

14. **C.** Treasury bills are auctioned weekly and are issued at a discount from par. At maturity, the holder receives par value with the earned discount treated as interest income. Treasury notes are interest-bearing securities that are issued, quoted and traded as a percentage of par value. FNMA bonds and GNMA certificates are issued at par and pay interest periodically (either monthly for pass-through certificates or semiannually for regular bonds.)

15. **C.** Auctions for twelve-month T bills are held every 4 weeks; 3-month and 6-month T bill auctions are held weekly.

16. **C.** Government notes and bonds are quoted in 1/32nds. Therefore, a quote of 101–16 means 101 16/32nds. $101.5 \times 10 = \$1,015$; $\$1,015 \times 10$ bonds = $\$10,150$.

17. **D.** This statement defines noncompetitive bids in a Treasury bill auction. These tenders are filled first. The minimum is $10,000; bills can be purchased in increments of $5,000 over the $10,000 minimum. In such bids, the Federal Reserve Board acts as the fiscal agent.

Nonmarketable Government Securities

Savings Bonds

Savings bonds cannot be used as collateral and are not negotiable. They are *nonmarketable* securities because they are nontransferable. They are purchased from the Treasury department through various issuing agents, including commercial banks and post offices. They can be redeemed by only the purchaser or a beneficiary.

Series EE bonds. Series EE bonds are discount bonds: bondholders earn the discount over the 12-year life of the bond, and can continue to receive interest for up to thirty years. They can be redeemed for the face value at maturity. Series EE bonds are issued at 50% of their face value in denominations from $50 to $10,000. Series EE bonds can be redeemed before maturity, but will receive a lower rate of return. The tax on accrued interest on EE bonds can be paid annually or deferred until the bond matures. Tax can be deferred further by trading EE bonds for HH bonds.

Series HH bonds. Series HH bonds pay interest semiannually. Series HH bonds can be purchased only by trading in Series EE bonds at maturity. Series HH bonds come in denominations of $500 to $10,000 and mature in ten years.

Table 2 compares Series EE and HH bonds.

Table 2   Comparison of Series EE and HH Bonds

Bond Series	Maturity	Denomination	Pricing	Form
EE	12 years	$50 to $10,000	Discount	Registered
HH	10 years	$500 to $10,000	At par	Registered

Questions

1. All of the following are true of Series EE and Series HH bonds EXCEPT that

   I. EE bonds do not generate interest income whereas HH bonds have a fixed coupon
   II. HH bonds can be borrowed against
   III. EE bonds are registered whereas HH bonds are bearer bonds
   IV. EE bonds are sold at a discount whereas HH bonds are sold at par

   A. I and II
   B. I and IV
   C. II
   D. II and III

Answers

1. **D.** Series EE and HH bonds are nonnegotiable and cannot be borrowed against. Both are issued in registered form.

Agency Issues

Authorization. Certain agencies of the federal government issue marketable debt securities, including:

- Federal Farm Credit Banks;
- Federal Home Loan Mortgage Corporation (FHLMC or Freddie Mac);
- Government National Mortgage Association (GNMA or Ginnie Mae); and
- Inter-American Development Bank (IADB).

Other agency-like organizations that are operated by private corporations include:

- Federal Home Loan Banks (FHLBs); and
- Federal National Mortgage Association (FNMA or Fannie Mae).

While these entities are not technically government agencies, they do have ties to the government.

Yields and maturities. Agency issues sell at higher yields than do direct obligations of the federal government, but at lower yields than those available on corporate debt securities. The maturities of these issues vary from very short term to relatively long term. Agency issues are quoted at a percentage of par and are traded on the secondary market prior to their maturity.

Backing. Agency issues are backed in several ways: by collateral, such as cash, U.S. Treasury securities and the debt obligations; by a U.S. Treasury guarantee; by the right of the agency to borrow from the Treasury; or, in a few cases, by the full faith and credit of the government.

Taxation. Interest on government agency issues is sometimes exempt from state and local income taxes, but is always subject to federal income tax.

Federal Farm Credit Bank

Federal Farm Credit Bank Consolidated Systemwide Securities are not directly backed by the faith and credit of the U.S. government. The securities, issued to fund producers of crops and livestock and providing mortgages for farm property,

include discount notes, six- and nine-month notes and longer term bonds.

Taxation. Farm Credit Bank issues are federally taxed, but are exempt from local and state taxes.

Federal Intermediate Credit Banks

FICBs are private corporations and issue both common and preferred stock in themselves. They raise the funds they lend by issuing short-term debentures.

Taxation. Interest income from FICB securities is federally taxable, but exempt from local and state taxes.

Federal Home Loan Bank

The Federal Home Loan Bank issues three securities, all in book-entry form:

- short-term discount notes (with maturities of 30 to 270 days);
- interest-bearing notes (with maturities of less than one year); and
- bonds (with maturities of one to ten years).

These securities are available in denominations of $10,000, $25,000, $100,000 and $1 million. The minimum requirement for discount notes is $100,000. FHLB securities are backed by mortgages, cash and other bank assets.

Taxation. Interest income from FHLB securities is federally taxable, but exempt from local and state taxes.

Federal Home Loan Mortgage Corporation

The Federal Home Loan Mortgage Corporation purchases residential mortgages from financial institutions insured by an agency of the federal government and sells its interest in them through mortgage-backed securities.

Pass-through certificates. FHLMC sells certificates representing interests in the mortgages it pools: mortgage participation certificates (PCs) and guaranteed mortgage certificates (GMCs). Freddie Mac securities represent an undivided interest in the underlying pool of mortgages. The interest and principal payments from the mortgages pass through to the investors.

Taxation. All FHLMC securities are subject to full state and federal income taxation.

Federal National Mortgage Association

FNMA purchases conventional and insured mortgages from agencies such as the FHA and the VA. The securities are backed by FNMA's general credit.

Types of issues. FNMA issues debentures, short-term discount notes and mortgage-backed securities. The notes are issued in denominations of $5,000, $25,000, $100,000, $500,000 and $1 million. Debentures (3- to 25-year maturities) have denominations from $10,000 up in increments of $5,000. Interest is paid semiannually. They are issued in book-entry form only.

Taxation. Interest from FNMA securities is taxed at federal, state and local levels.

Government National Mortgage Association

GNMA is a wholly U.S. government-owned corporation that supports the Department of Housing and Urban Development. Ginnie Maes are backed by the full faith and credit of the government.

Types of issues. GNMA buys FHA and VA mortgages and auctions them to private lenders, which pool these mortgages and sell pass-through certificates based on them. Each month, principal and interest payments from the pool of mortgages pass through to investors. The amount of principal represented by a GNMA certificate is therefore constantly decreasing.

GNMA pay a higher rate of interest than comparable Treasury securities and they are guaranteed by the federal government. GNMA also guarantees timely payment of interest and principal. GNMAs are issued in minimum denominations of $25,000.

Taxation. Interest earned on GNMA certificates is fully taxable at federal, state and local levels.

Inter-American Development Bank

The Inter-American Development Bank finances capital projects. The IADB may borrow from all over the world, and its securities are denominated in various international currencies.

Student Loan Marketing Association

The Student Loan Marketing Association (also known as *SLMA* or *Sallie Mae*) is a publicly owned corporation that purchases student loans from the originating financial institutions and packages them for sale in the secondary market, guaranteeing the payment of principal and interest.

FHA/VA ⟶ FNMA Semi-annually
↓
GNMA
(min. $25,000)
monthly

Questions

1. The function of the Federal National Mortgage Association is to

    A. purchase FHA-insured, VA-guaranteed and conventional mortgages
    B. issue conventional mortgages
    C. provide financing for governmentassisted housing
    D. guarantee the timely payment of interest and principal on FHA and VA mortgages

2. How frequently do GNMA pass-through certificates pay interest?

    A. Monthly
    B. Quarterly
    C. Semiannually
    D. Annually

3. Federal Farm Credit Systemwide bonds are obligations of which of the following?

    I. Federal Land Banks
    II. Banks for Cooperatives
    III. Federal Intermediate Credit Banks

    A. I only
    B. I and II only
    C. I and III only
    D. I, II and III

4. Which of the following are characteristics of government agency issues?

    A. They are considered practically riskless by bank auditors.
    B. They are always in bearer form.
    C. They are always in registered form.
    D. They have been in a book-entry system for years.

5. The function of the FICB is to

    A. fund loans for farm expenses
    B. fund loans for international credit
    C. manage intermediate credit for the Federal Reserve Board
    D. insure commercial banks

6. All of the following are backed directly by the full faith and credit of the U.S. government EXCEPT

    A. Federal Intermediate Credit Bank issues
    B. Government National Mortgage Association issues
    C. Treasury notes
    D. New Housing Authority bonds

7. Which of the following statements are true regarding U.S. government agency obligations?

    I. They are direct obligations of the U.S. government.
    II. They generally have higher yields than yields of direct U.S. obligations.
    III. The Federal National Mortgage Association is a publicly traded corporation.
    IV. Securities issued by GNMA trade on the NYSE floor.

    A. I and II
    B. I and III
    C. II and III
    D. II and IV

8. All of the following debt instruments pay interest semiannually EXCEPT

    A. Ginnie Mae certificates
    B. municipal GO bonds
    C. municipal revenue bonds
    D. industrial development bonds

Answers

1. **A.** FNMA buys FHA, VA and conventional mortgages and uses these mortgages to back the issuance of debt securities. Currently, FNMA issues debentures, mortgage-backed securities and certificates.

2. **A.** Ginnie Mae pass-through certificates are backed by single-family home mortgages. The home owner making a mortgage payment pays both principal and interest monthly into the pool. The pass-through certificates, therefore, pay interest and principal monthly.

3. **D.** Federal Land Banks (FLBs), the Banks for Cooperatives (COOPs) and Federal Intermediate Credit Banks (FICBs) compose the Federal Farm Credit System.

4. **A.** Government agency issues are practically riskless. The new agency issues are in book entry, and some of the old agency issues may be in registered form.

5. **A.** Securities issued by the FICB are used to obtain funds to make short-term loans to farmers for farm expenses.

6. **A.** FICB issues are an obligation of a U.S. government-sponsored agency; the other answers are obligations of U.S. government, agencies or municipalities that are backed by the full faith and credit of the U.S. government.

7. **C.** U.S. government agency debt is an obligation of the issuing agency. This causes agency debt to trade at higher yields reflecting this greater risk. FNMA was created as a government agency but was spun off in 1968 and is now an NYSE-listed corporation. GNMA pass-through certificates trade OTC.

8. **A.** Almost all debt instruments, including the various types of municipal bonds, pay interest semiannually. Two exceptions are GNMA pass-through certificates (which pay interest monthly) and project notes where interest is payable only at maturity.

5 Money-market Securities and Interest Rates

The Money Market

Money-market instruments provide ways for businesses, financial institutions and governments to meet their short-term obligations and cash requirements yet avoid the time and expense of SEC registration of securities.

Moving money. The money market shifts funds from institutions with temporary excesses of money to institutions with temporary deficiencies. Borrowers in the money market include the U.S. Treasury, large commercial banks, corporations, dealers in money-market instruments and many states and municipalities. Lenders include large institutions such as banks, trust companies and insurance companies.

Liquidity and safety. Money-market instruments are fixed income securities with short-term maturities—typically one year or less. Money-market securities offer investors a highly liquid investment and a relatively high degree of safety.

Issuers. Money-market instruments issued by the U.S. government and its agencies include:

- Treasury bills trading in the secondary market;
- tax anticipation notes;
- Federal Farm Credit Bank notes and bonds maturing in one year;
- Federal Home Loan Bank discount notes and interest-bearing notes; and

- Federal National Mortgage Association discount notes.

Municipal tax-exempt money-market instruments include:

- bond anticipation notes (BANs)
- tax anticipation notes (TANs)
- revenue anticipation notes (RANs)
- construction loan notes (CLNs)
- tax and revenue anticipation notes (TRANs)

Corporation and bank money-market issues include:

- repurchase agreements (repos)
- reverse repurchase agreements   *re-repos*
- bankers' acceptances (time drafts)
- commercial paper (prime paper)
- negotiable certificates of deposit
- federal funds
- brokers' and dealers' loans

Money-market Instruments

Repurchase Agreements

A transaction in which a dealer raises cash by finding a temporary buyer for some of the securities it holds and then signing a contract with that party to buy the securities back at a later date is called a *repurchase agreement (repo)*. A repo is an agreement between a buyer and a seller to conduct a transaction (the purchase) and then to reverse that transaction (the repurchase) at some point in the future. A repo will include a repurchase price and maturity date in the contract.

A repo is very similar to a fully collateralized loan. The interest on the loan is the difference between the sale price and the repurchase price. The effective rate at which the loan is made is negotiated and generally is lower than the rate on a loan with similar terms from a bank.

Repos serve both as a way to raise short-term capital and as instruments of Federal Reserve monetary policy. Among the primary users of repos are:

- U.S. government and municipal securities dealers financing their inventories;
- commercial banks raising short-term funds; and
- the Federal Reserve effecting short-term changes in member bank reserves (fine tuning the monetary supply).

Reverse Repurchase Agreements

In a reverse repurchase agreement (**reverse repo**), a dealer agrees to buy securities from an investor and then sells them back to the investor later at a higher price. The difference between repos and reverse repos is that the dealer makes the initial sale in a repo and an investor makes the initial sale in a reverse repo.

Bankers' Acceptances

A banker's acceptance (BA) is a short-term time draft with a specified payment date drawn on a bank. Bankers' acceptances are used by U.S. corporations as a means of financing international trade.

Once a time draft is returned and accepted by the bank, the bank sells the new banker's acceptance in the money market at a discount from face value. When the acceptance matures, the U.S. firm makes good on the amount it borrowed and the current holder redeems the banker's acceptance for its face value at the accepting bank.

Bankers' acceptances are one of the few secured money-market instruments because the holder has a lien against the trade goods in the event the accepting bank fails. Bankers' acceptances frequently are used by banks as collateral against Federal Reserve Bank (FRB) loans.

Commercial Paper

Commercial paper is a less expensive alternative to borrowing from banks when a corporation needs short-term funds. Rates in the commercial paper market are usually lower than comparable bank loan rates, and securities with maturities of less than 270 days are exempt from registration under the 1933 act and are therefore less expensive to issue. Both the maturities and the rates of commercial paper are negotiable.

Commercial paper normally is issued in bearer form and at a discount from face value. Dealers in commercial paper generally consider $250,000 in face value as a minimum round lot, but issues of $1 million and more are not uncommon.

Direct paper. "Direct paper" is commercial paper sold directly to the public without the use of dealers. Direct paper is is also known as *finance company paper* when it is issued by finance companies. High-quality commercial paper is sometimes called *prime paper*.

Dealer paper. Dealer paper is commercial paper sold by the issuer through a dealer, rather than directly to the public.

Tax-exempt commercial paper. Municipal commercial paper is very similar to corporate paper, but the municipality usually has acquired the backing of a commercial bank for the issue.

Certificates of Deposit

Certificates with fixed interest rates and minimum face values of $100,000 are issued and guaranteed by banks and can be traded in the secondary market. Although they are not true money-market instruments, the following investments usually are included in discussions of them due to their short maturities:

Nonnegotiable CDs. CDs are time deposits offered by banks and savings and loans with set maturities and fixed interest rates. Banks offer maturities ranging from as short as 30 days to as long as ten years and more.

Negotiable CDs. Negotiable CDs are time deposits of funds with a bank at a specified rate of interest for a specified period of time. The issuer is required to redeem the CD at maturity for its face value (plus any interest due). In order to be negotiable, a CD must have a minimum face value of $100,000, but most are issued for $1 million or more.

A negotiable CD is an unsecured promissory note guaranteed by the issuing bank. Most negotiable CDs are issued with maturities of one year or less. These CDs are negotiable and can be bought and sold in the secondary market before their maturity. The price at which a CD is traded will depend on the prevailing interest rates at the time.

Commercial paper
{ Direct paper (finance company paper)
{ Dealer paper
{ Prime paper

Questions

1. All of the following are money-market instruments EXCEPT

   A. Treasury bills
   B. municipal notes
   C. commercial paper
   D. newly issued Treasury bonds

2. Which of the following is a money-market instrument?

   A. Short-term debt
   B. Long-term debt
   C. Short-term equity
   D. Long-term equity

3. The maximum maturity of commercial paper is how many days?

   A. 90
   B. 180
   C. 270
   D. 360

4. Which of the following statements are true of negotiable certificates of deposit?

   I. The issuing bank guarantees them.
   II. They are callable.
   III. Minimum denominations are $1,000.
   IV. They can be traded in the secondary market.

   A. I, II and III only
   B. I and IV only
   C. II and III only
   D. I, II, III and IV

5. Commercial paper is

   A. a secured note issued by a corporation
   B. a guaranteed note issued by a corporation
   C. a promissory note issued by a corporation
   D. none of the above

6. Which of the following money-market instruments finances imports and exports?

    A. Eurodollars
    B. Bankers' acceptances
    C. ADRs
    D. Commercial paper

V 7. A banker's acceptance is a

    A. promissory note
    B. capital-market instrument
    C. time draft
    D. means to facilitate the trading of foreign securities

8. Which of the following do NOT trade in the money market?

    I.   ADRs
    II. Series EE bonds
    III. Prime paper
    IV. Certificates of deposit

    A. I and II
    B. I and IV
    C. II and III
    D. II and IV

9. Which of the following money-market instruments is a time draft?

    A. Commercial paper
    B. CD
    C. Banker's acceptance
    D. Treasury bill

10. Which of the following trade with accrued interest?

    A. Zero-coupon Treasury obligations
    B. Treasury bills
    C. Certificates of deposit
    D. Bankers' acceptances

11. A U.S. government bond dealer sells bonds to another dealer with an agreement to buy back the securities in a specified period of time. This is a(n)

    A. repurchase agreement
    B. reverse repurchase agreement
    C. open market certificate
    D. open market note

12. A dealer buying debt securities from a customer with an agreement to sell the same securities back to the same customer at a later date is taking part in a

    A. repurchase agreement
    B. reverse repurchase agreement
    C. prearranged trade
    D. matched order

Answers

1. **D.** Newly issued Treasury bonds have a minimum maturity of ten years. Money-market instruments have a maximum maturity of one year.

2. **A.** A money-market instrument is short-term debt with one year or less to maturity.

3. **C.** Commercial paper is normally issued for a maximum period of 270 days.

4. **B.** Negotiable certificates of deposit are issued primarily by banks and are backed by (guaranteed by) the issuing bank.

5. **C.** Commercial paper is a short-term promissory note issued by a corporation.

6. **B.** Bankers' acceptances are used in international trade to finance imports and exports. Eurodollars are not money-market instruments.

7. **C.** A banker's acceptance is a time draft. It facilitates imports and exports, not the trading of foreign securities.

8. **A.** ADRs (American depositary receipts) are equities that trade on stock exchanges (capital markets) and do not have maturity dates. Series EE bonds have a maturity greater than one year and are nonnegotiable. Prime paper is another term for high-quality commercial paper. Negotiable certificates of deposit (CDs) are issued by banks in minimum denominations of $100,000 to $1 million. Prime paper and CDs are short-term instruments that trade in the money market.

9. **C.** A banker's acceptance is a time draft—that is, a check payable in the future.

10. **C.** Only securities with a stated rate of interest have accrued interest added to the transaction price. Zero-coupon securities, T bills and bankers' acceptances are all issued without a coupon at a discount and mature at face value. CDs are issued most often for their face amount (minimum of $100,000) with a stated coupon rate.

11. **A.** The question defines a repurchase agreement.

12. **B.** A sale with a contract to repurchase is a repurchase agreement. A purchase with a contract to sell is a reverse repurchase.

Interest Rates

The yields of money-market instruments and interest rates are as follows:

Prime rate. The base rate on corporate loans at large U.S. money center commercial banks. The prime rate is relatively stable and moves only when the major money center banks react to changes in the money supply.

Passbook rate. The rate established for bank and savings and loan passbook accounts. It is the most familiar and the least volatile of the commonly known interest rates.

Federal funds rate. Reserves traded among commercial banks for overnight use in amounts of $1 million or more. The federal funds rate is the most volatile of the interest rates, changing daily in response to the needs of the borrowing banks.

Discount rate. The charge on loans to depository institutions by the New York FRB.

Call money rate. The charge on loans to brokers on stock exchange collateral.

Commercial paper. The rate on commercial paper placed directly by GMAC or the rate on high-grade unsecured notes sold through dealers by major corporations.

Certificates of deposit. Average top rates paid by major New York banks on new issues of negotiable CDs, usually on amounts of $1 million or more. The minimum unit is $100,000.

Bankers' acceptances. Negotiable, bank-backed business credit instruments typically financing an import order.

London Interbank Offered Rate (LIBOR). The average of interbank-offered rates for dollar deposits in the London market based on quotations at five major banks.

Treasury bills. Results of the auction of short-term U.S. government bills sold at a discount from face value in units of $10,000 to $1 million.

Questions

1. The effective federal funds rate quoted in the business news represents the average rate for the previous

    A. hour
    B. day
    C. week
    D. two weeks

2. The federal funds rate is calculated from the

    A. daily average rate charged by the largest money center banks
    B. daily average rate charged by the national Federal Reserve member banks
    C. weekly average rate charged by the largest money center banks
    D. weekly average rate charged by the national Federal Reserve member banks

3. Which of the following interest rates is considered the MOST volatile?

    A. Discount rate
    B. Federal funds rate
    C. Prime rate
    D. Passbook savings rate

4. Which of the following interest rates is considered the LEAST volatile?

    A. Discount rate
    B. Federal funds rate
    C. Prime rate
    D. Passbook savings rate

5. The MOST volatile fluctuations in money-market rates would be found in the

    A. prime rate
    B. long-term interest rate
    C. federal funds rate
    D. discount rate

Answers

1. **B.** The effective federal funds rate as published is a daily average calculated from the rates negotiated between the various banks.

2. **B.** The federal funds rate reflects the rate charged by member banks lending funds to member banks that need to borrow funds overnight to meet reserve requirements.

3. **B.** The federal funds rate is the interest rate that banks with excess reserves charge other banks that are associated with the Federal Reserve System and that need overnight loans to meet reserve requirements. Because the federal funds rate is set daily, it is the most sensitive indicator of interest rate direction.

4. **D.** Until recently, passbook savings rates were regulated by the Federal Reserve Board. The interest rate remained stable for long periods of time and was not indicative of fluctuations in other interest rates. The prime rate is periodically changed by banks, and the discount rate is periodically changed by the Federal Reserve Board.

5. **C.** The federal funds rate is the rate at which banks lend money overnight to each other to maintain reserve requirements. It is the most volatile rate and can fluctuate widely even during a business day. The effective federal funds rate is considered to be the average rate each day throughout the country.

Eurodollars and the Foreign Currency Markets

Eurodollars   1 — 180 days

U.S. dollars deposited in banks in countries outside the United States in which the deposits remain denominated in U.S. dollars are known as *Eurodollars*. The term **"Eurocurrency"** is generally applied to non-U.S. dollar deposits.

Eurodollar time deposits tend to be short term, ranging from overnight to 180 days. European banks lend Eurodollars among themselves in much the same way that U.S. banks lend federal funds (to meet dollar deficits or to invest dollar surpluses).

Eurobonds

A Eurobond is any long-term debt instrument that is issued and sold outside the country of the currency in which it is denominated. U.S. dollar-denominated Eurobonds can be issued by foreign corporations, foreign governments, domestic corporations and domestic governments (including municipalities).

Because of the unregulated nature of the Eurobond market, interest rates paid by Eurobonds are typically higher than those paid by comparable domestic bonds.

Foreign Currencies and the Interbank Market

The **interbank market** handles, transacts business in, trades, lends and consolidates deposits of foreign currencies.

Regulation. The interbank market is an unregulated, decentralized international market that deals in the various major currencies of the world.

Trading. The interbank market for foreign currencies is a telephone/telex market conducting international monetary business and exchange from individual bank trading rooms around the world.

Most interbank trades occur to fulfill foreign currency contracts or commitments between two or more parties, each of which has negotiated the terms of the contract until all parties' needs are met. Banks and multinational corporations entering into multimillion dollar foreign currency contracts must negotiate price, delivery and settlement terms. Foreign currency transactions are usually settled in one of two ways: **spot trades** settle and are delivered in one or two business days (the **spot market**) and **forward trades** settle in more than two business days, with settlement dates normally set from 1 to 18 months out (the **forward market**).

Eurocurrency loans. The London Interbank Offered Rate (LIBOR) is the rate that most international banks dealing in Eurodollars charge each other for Eurodollar loans. LIBOR is the rate from which many other international interest rates are calculated.

Exchange Rates

An exchange rate is the rate at which one currency can be converted into another. Exchange rates change daily.

At one time, a fixed exchange rate set by international agreement existed between foreign currencies. This was changed in the 1970s to the current **floating exchange rate system**, in which foreign currency markets set the exchange rates. In a limited number of cases, the exchange rate of one currency to another is set by agreement between the countries involved, and in other cases, there is no exchange rate because the local government does not want its currency exchanged into that of another country.

Appreciation. A currency is said to be appreciating if it is rising in value compared to other securities on the foreign exchange market.

Depreciation. If currency falls in value on the foreign exchange market it is depreciating. Depreciation of the dollar tends to lead to improved balance of payments.

Valuation

Devaluation. Devaluation occurs when the value of a currency drops substantially in comparison to the value of gold or to the value of another country's currency. The devaluation of a currency is usually market driven and can be affected by that country's international trade balance, reserves of gold, rate of inflation and general economic health.

Revaluation. Revaluation is a change in the relative value of a country's currency and can represent either an increase or a decrease in that value. The revaluation of a currency usually occurs as the result of a decision by the government of that country and is implemented by its central bank.

Questions

1. Which of the following statements would constitute a valid reason for investing in Eurobonds?

   A. Eurobonds can provide diversification to a portfolio.
   B. Eurobonds can be purchased more inexpensively than comparable U.S. bonds.
   C. Eurobonds are traded in an unregulated market free from government intervention.
   D. Eurobonds can provide an exchange rate hedge against a fall in the U.S. dollar.

2. Interbank transactions in foreign currencies occur in which of the following markets?

   I. Spot
   II. Forward
   III. Pegged
   IV. Stabilized

   A. I and II only
   B. I and III only
   C. III and IV only
   D. I, II, III and IV

3. The interbank market was formed to trade which of the following?

   A. Foreign currencies
   B. American depositary receipts
   C. Commercial paper
   D. Foreign stocks

4. An international, unregulated, decentralized market for trading currencies as well as debt obligations, and in which prices are affected by economic policies and conditions, is the

   A. Federal Reserve Board
   B. interbank system
   C. London Stock Exchange
   D. International Monetary Fund

Answers

1.   **A.**   Eurobonds may provide a sophisticated investor with a means of adding diversification to her portfolio. All of the other answers are either untrue statements or represent disadvantages of investing in Eurobonds.

2.   **A.**   Foreign currency transactions occur in the spot market (same- or next-day settlement) or the forward market (1- to 18-month settlement).

3.   **A.**   The interbank market is a decentralized, unregulated market formed for the sole purpose of trading foreign currencies.

4.   **B.**   The interbank system is an international, unregulated, decentralized market involved in trading currencies and debt obligations. As with any market, changes in economic policies and conditions will influence prices.

6 Issuing Securities

The Regulation of New Issues

The Legislative Reaction

The Securities Act of 1933. The Securities Act of 1933 requires issuers of securities to provide sufficient information for investors to make fully informed buying decisions. This information must be registered with the federal government and published in a prospectus. The act outlaws fraud committed in connection with underwriting and issuing securities.

The Glass-Steagall Act (Banking Act) of 1933. The act forbids commercial banks to underwrite securities (except municipal general obligation bonds) and denies investment bankers the right to open deposit accounts or make commercial loans.

The Securities Exchange Act of 1934. The Securities Exchange Act of 1934 addresses secondary trading of securities, personnel involved in secondary trading and fraudulent trading practices. It also created the Securities and Exchange Commission (SEC), a government agency, to oversee the industry.

The **Maloney Act** provides for the establishment of a self-regulatory body to help police the industry. Under the provisions of the Maloney Act, the NASD regulates over-the-counter (OTC) trading in much the same way as the exchanges regulate their members.

Registration of Securities

The Legislation

The Securities Act of 1933 requires the registration of new issues of nonexempt securities if the mails or any other means of interstate commerce are used to offer or sell the security to the public. The main purpose of the act is to ensure that the investing public is fully informed about a security and its issuing company when the security is first sold to the public. The act also requires that a prospectus be given to buyers.

The 1933 act protects the investor by:

- requiring registration of new issues that are to be distributed interstate;
- requiring the issuer to provide full and fair disclosure about itself and the offering;
- requiring the issuer to make available all material information necessary for the investor to judge the merit of the issue;
- regulating the underwriting and distribution of primary and secondary issues; and
- providing criminal penalties for fraud in the issuance of new securities.

When a corporation wants to issue its securities to the public, the SEC requires it to:

- supply detailed information about itself and its securities to the SEC; and
- supply the relevant portion of that information to the general investing public.

A **registration statement** disclosing material information must be filed with the SEC by the issuer and must contain:

- a description of the issuer's business;
- the names and addresses of key people in the company, officers and directors, their salaries and a five-year business history of each;
- the amount of corporate securities owned by these key people and by owners of 10% or more of the company;
- the company's capitalization, including its equity and the amount of funded debt;
- a description of how the proceeds will be used; and
- whether the company is involved in any legal proceedings.

The Prospectus

Preliminary prospectus. After an issuer files a registration statement with the SEC, a **cooling-off** period begins. During the cooling-off period, a registered rep may discuss the new issue with clients and provide them with a preliminary prospectus (**red herring**) to gather **indications of interest**. A registered rep *may not send any other material* to potential customers with the preliminary prospectus.

A red herring must carry a legend to the effect that a registration statement has been filed with the SEC, but is not yet effective. By law, this disclaimer message must be printed in red ink.

SEC rules prohibit the sale of public offering securities other than by prospectus, which means that no sales are allowed unless and until the buyer is furnished with a final prospectus.

Final prospectus. When the registration statement does become effective, the issuer amends the preliminary prospectus. This revised report becomes the final prospectus. Registered representatives may then take orders from those customers who indicated an interest in buying during the cooling-off period.

A copy of the final prospectus must precede or accompany all sales confirmations. The prospectus should include:

- description of the offering;
- price of the offering;
- selling discounts;
- date of the offering;
- use of the proceeds;

- description of the underwriting, but not the actual contract;
- statement of the possibility that the issue's price may be stabilized;
- history of the business;
- risks to the purchasers;
- description of management;
- material financial information;
- legal opinion concerning the formation of the corporation; and
- SEC disclaimer.

SEC review. The SEC does not guarantee the accuracy of the disclosures, does not approve the issue, and does not pass judgment on the investment merit of the issue. The front of every prospectus must contain a clearly printed SEC disclaimer clause specifying the limits of the SEC's review procedures. The information supplied to the SEC becomes public information once a registration statement is filed.

Delivery of Prospectus by Dealers

Preliminary prospectus. This must be made available to any customer who expresses interest in the securities from the SEC registration filing date to the effective date.

Aftermarket sales by prospectus. All sales of public offering stock listed on an exchange or traded on NASDAQ must be accompanied by a prospectus during the period beginning with the public offering date through to a specified date following the public offering date. This restriction extends to:

- 90 days from the effective date (public offering date) for IPOs;
- 40 days from the effective date (public offering date) for additional issue securities; and
- 25 days from the effective date (public offering date) for an additional issue of listed stock.

If offering securities remain unsold beyond this end date, the sale-by-prospectus requirements continue.

Advertising a New Issue

The only advertising allowed during the cooling-off period is a **tombstone**. A tombstone announces a new issue, but does not offer the securities for sale. Advertising copy and other sales materials will qualify as tombstones and will not be deemed a prospectus if the body copy is limited to:

- the name of the issuer of the securities being offered;
- a description of the business of the person making the offer;
- the date, time and place of the meeting at which stockholders are to vote on or consent to the proposed transaction;
- a brief description of the planned transaction; and/or
- any legend or disclaimer statement required by state or federal law.

Any advertising copy in a tombstone *must* contain the following disclaimers:

- that the registration statement has been filed by the issuer but is not yet effective;
- that the communication does *not* represent an offer to sell the securities described—securities are *sold by prospectus only;*
- the name and address of the person (or firm) to contact for a prospectus; and
- that a response to this advertisement does not obligate the prospect to a buying commitment of any kind.

Underwriter and selling group member prohibitions. If a stock in registration is included in an underwriter's or selling group member's recommended list, the opinion given and quality rating assigned must not be upgraded or emphasized in any fashion.

Liability Under the Act of 1933

Willful omissions of facts (or those that can be attributed to gross negligence) or misstatements of material facts in any material related to a new issue are considered serious violations of the act of 1933. Only if the member can show that it did not know of the misstatement or omission and used reasonable care will that member not be held liable.

Questions

1. All of the following are prohibited during the cooling-off period EXCEPT

   A. promising a certain amount of the issue to a customer
   B. soliciting indications of interest
   C. taking an order
   D. accepting a check from a customer to purchase the issue

2. Which of the following can a registered representative do regarding an underwriting that is in the registration process?

   I. Take an order.
   II. Accept an indication of interest.
   III. Promise a specific number of shares.
   IV. Do a private transaction for a customer.

   A. I and II
   B. I and III
   C. II
   D. II and IV

3. Which of the following statements are true of the Securities Act of 1933?

   I. It requires the registration of exchanges.
   II. It is called the *Truth in Securities Act*.
   III. It requires full and fair disclosure.
   IV. It requires that debt securities be issued with a trust indenture.

   A. I and II
   B. I, II and IV
   C. I and III
   D. II and III

√ 4. Under the Securities Act of 1933, the SEC has authority to

   I. issue stop orders
   II. approve new issues   review
   III. review prospectuses

   A. I only
   B. I and III only
   C. II only
   D. I, II and III

√ 5. In the time before a registration statement becomes effective, which of the following statements is(are) true?

   I. No sales may be solicited.
   II. Sales literature may not be used.
   III. Unsolicited inquiries may be answered.

   A. I and II only
   B. I and III only
   C. III only
   D. I, II and III

6. Which of the following statements is(are) true?

   I. The SEC controls the release of new issues by approving or disapproving them.
   II. The prospectus contains all of the information that the registration statement contains, including all supporting documents.
   III. It is a criminal offense to imply that the SEC has approved a new issue.

   A. I and II
   B. I and III
   C. II and III
   D. III

7. Which of the following are considered to be nonexempt offerings according to the Securities Act of 1933?

   I. Government securities
   II. Private placement
   III. Public offering of $2,000,000 by a brokerage firm
   IV. Sale of corporate bonds of $5,000,000

   A. I and II
   B. I and III
   C. II, III and IV
   D. III and IV

8. Which of the following statements about the information in a registration statement is true?

   A. Names, addresses and past business histories of the corporate officers are considered irrelevant and need not be included.
   B. Amounts of securities owned by directors, officers and owners of 15% or more of the firm's securities must be revealed.
   C. The financing of a corporation must be included in the registration statement.
   D. Because most potential investors would know about the business a corporation was engaged in, information about the business itself is not necessary.

9. A registered representative prepares a summary of the preliminary prospectus, which contains no unverified claims or statements. The registered representative can send the summary to customers

   A. under no circumstances
   B. when approved by the manager, if a file is kept of the synopsis for three years
   C. when approved by both the manager and the supervisory analyst and kept on file for three years
   D. without restriction

Answers

1. **B.** During the cooling-off period for a new issue, a registration is not yet effective. During this period, no advertising of the issue is allowed, nor can the issue be sold, but the registered rep can send out the preliminary prospectus and take indications of interest.

2. **C.** When an issue is in the registration process (during the cooling-off period), sale of the security is prohibited. The registered representative may distribute red herrings (preliminary prospectuses) and take indications of interest. A registered rep may never do private securities transactions.

3. **D.** The Securities Act of 1933 provides for registration of new issues, not for the registration of exchanges. The reason for registering the new issues is to give full and fair disclosure of all material facts for new issues sold to the public.

4. **B.** The SEC reviews a prospectus to determine obvious ambiguities or omissions. If a prospectus does not have the proper disclosure of facts, the SEC can issue a stop order denying the effectiveness of a registration. The SEC does not approve (or disapprove) of any new issue.

5. **D.** During the cooling-off period, sales literature may not be used and sales may not be solicited. A red herring is not sales literature; it is a preliminary prospectus. If a customer enquires about the pending issue, those questions may certainly be answered.

6. **D.** The SEC neither approves nor disapproves the issue of any security. Any representation to the contrary is a criminal offense. The prospectus is very similar to the registration statement, but it does not contain the documentation that the registration statement has.

7. **D.** The Securities Act of 1933 exempts U.S. government bonds and private placements from registration. Public offerings of less than $1.5 million are also exempt (under Reg A), so choices III (an offering of $2.5 million) and IV (corporate)

are not exempt. They must be registered with the SEC before they are issued.

8.   **C.**   Read all four of these answers carefully, keeping in mind the fact that the main purpose of the act of 1933 is to protect the public investor. The information mentioned in answer A is, indeed, important and must be included. The percentage in answer B is wrong; it should be 10%. Answer D does not protect the public: financial statements about the corporations must be included in the registration statement.

9.   **A.**   The preliminary prospectus stands on its own; it cannot be accompanied by any material. Even if this were a final prospectus, any selling literature that accompanies that final prospectus must be filed with the SEC before it is used.

The Underwriting Process

Underwriting Corporate Securities

Investment Banking

An investment banker is a securities broker-dealer that specializes in underwriting new issues by helping to bring securities to market and sell them to investors. An investment banker's functions may include:

- advising corporations on the best ways to raise long-term capital;
- raising capital for issuers by distributing new securities;
- buying securities from an issuer and reselling them to the public; and
- distributing large blocks of stock to the public and to institutions.

Participants in a Corporate New Issue

Securities and Exchange Commission. When a corporation issues new securities, the SEC is responsible for the following:

- reviewing the registration statement filed for the offering;
- sending a deficiency letter to the issuer if the review uncovers problems; and
- declaring the registration statement effective.

The issuer. The issuer is the party selling the securities to raise money. The issuer's duties include:

- filing the registration statement with the SEC;
- filing a registration statement with the states in which it intends to sell securities (**blue-skying the issue**); and
- negotiating the price of the securities and the amount of the spread with the underwriter.

National Association of Securities Dealers. The NASD Committee on Corporate Financing reviews the underwriting spread to determine fairness and reasonableness of underwriting compensation.

The individual states. The issuer or investment banker may blue-sky an issue by one of the following three methods:

1. **Qualification.** The issue is registered with the state independent of federal registration, meeting all state requirements.
2. **Coordination.** The issuer registers simultaneously with the state and the SEC. Both registrations become effective on the same date.
3. **Notification.** Certain states allow some new issues to blue-sky by having the issuers notify the state of registration with the SEC. In this case, no registration statement is required by the state, although certain other information must be filed.

The underwriter. The underwriter assists with registration and advises the corporate issuer on the best way to raise capital, taking into consideration:

- whether to offer stock or bonds;
- the tax consequences of the offering; and
- whether to go to the money market for short-term funds or to the capital market for long-term funds.

Types of Offerings

Securities Markets

The **new issue market** consists of companies "going public"—privately owned businesses raising capital by selling common stock to the public for the very first time. New issue securities are also known as **initial public offering (IPO)** securities.

The **additional issue market** is made up of new securities issues from companies that are already publicly owned. This is accomplished when an underwriter either distributes the stock in a public offering or arranges for the shares to be sold in a private placement.

Primary Offering

A primary offering is one in which the proceeds of the underwriting go to the issuing corporation.

Secondary Offering

A secondary offering is one in which one or more major stockholders in the corporation are selling all or a major portion of their holdings.

Split Offering (or Combined Distribution)

A split offering is simply a combination of a primary and a secondary offering. Some of the stock offered will be issued by the corporation, and the rest represents shares held by present corporation stockholders.

Shelf Offering (Rule 415)

An issuer can register a new issue security without selling the entire issue at once through a **shelf offering**. The issuer can sell limited portions of a registered shelf offering over a two-year period without having to reregister the security or incurring penalties, but must file a supplemental prospectus prior to each sale.

Buying Groups

Present stockholders. Present stockholders of the issuing corporation may have a preemptive right to retain their current percentage of ownership of a new issue.

The general public. Securities that are not subscribed to in a rights offering by present stockholders are next offered to public investors. An investment banker will do this through a **standby offering**.

Public Offerings vs. Private Placements

Private placements occur when the institutional buyer, using an investment banker, purchases securities from the issuing corporation. Because private placements involve no sales to public investors, they are generally exempt from the registration requirements of the Securities Act of 1933.

Time Line for an Underwriting

Forming the Syndicate

In competitive bidding, the syndicate is assembled first and syndicate members work together to arrive at the bid. In a negotiated underwriting, the syndicate may be formed after the issuer and underwriting manager have negotiated the terms of the offering.

Preparing Documents

The underwriter may assist the issuer in preparing and filing the registration statement and prospectus.

Cooling-off Period

After the issuer files with the SEC for registration of the securities, a cooling-off period ensues before the registration becomes effective. If approved, the registration can become effective as soon as the 20th calendar day following the date the SEC receives it.

During the cooling-off period, underwriters may use the preliminary prospectus to tell investors about the new issue that will be available after the registration's effective date. The underwriter cannot sell the securities at this time, but can collect indications of interest and perform final due diligence.

Blue-Skying the Issue

The syndicate manager takes the preliminary registration packet to the various states in which it plans to offer the securities. If the issue meets the registration requirements of a particular state, the issue is blue-skyed and brokers within that state can sell the security to state residents.

Other state registration requirements. Each state has its own registration requirements, not only for securities but also for the registration of broker-dealers, investment advisers and registered reps. A person or broker-dealer must usually be registered in any state in which he sells or attempts to sell securities.

Due Diligence

The preliminary studies, investigations, research, meetings and compilation of information about a corporation and a proposed new issue that go on during an underwriting are known collectively as *due diligence*. The underwriter, primarily through the syndicate manager, is expected to exercise due diligence in obtaining all of the information it needs and in verifying its accuracy. As part of this process, the investment banker must:

- examine the use of the proceeds;
- perform financial analyses and fesibility studies;
- determine the stability of the company; and
- determine whether the risk is reasonable.

Due diligence includes a:

- preliminary study;
- letter of intent; and
- general examination of other factors, including the industry data, operational data, management and employee relations, financial stability and legal status of the issuer.

Pricing a New Issue

The price of an issue is determined by the effective date of the registration. It is based on such factors as:

- indications of interest from the underwriter's book;

- prevailing market conditions;
- price the syndicate members will accept;
- price-earnings ratios of similar companies; and
- company's dividend payment record and financial health.

The following factors are considered in determining a new issue's price:

- the company's present PE
- recent offerings

Hot issues

The POP for additional issue stock normally is priced off the open market price.

Effective Date

The effective date of an issue is the first date on which the securities can be sold to the public. The syndicate members can then contact clients who had indicated interest in the issue and confirm orders.

Final Prospectus

The final prospectus must be delivered with each sale of a newly issued security. It must contain all the information that is found in Part I of the registration statement.

Selling the Securities

After the final due diligence meeting and the passing of the cooling-off period, the syndicate sells the securities to the public.

Stabilizing Losses and Sticky Issues

The underwriter has the option of *stabilizing* a sticky issue by bidding for shares in the open market. The managing underwriter can enter stabilizing bids for the security until the end of the offering period. Stabilizing bids must *not* be made at a price higher than the public offering price.

Customer Settlement

Purchasers of public offering securities are expected to pay for the securities on the transaction settlement date, which is normally the fifth business day from the public offering date.

Disbursing Proceeds

When the offering has been completed, the underwriting manager allocates underwriting profits and commissions. A final accounting must be given to syndicate members for the disbursement of underwriting proceeds.

Questions

1. A standby underwriting is used

   A. for a company going public for the first time
   B. in a secondary offering
   C. in a best efforts underwriting
   D. in a rights offering

2. The XYZ Company has filed an offering of 425,000 shares of common stock. One-third of the shares are being sold by existing stockholders, and the balance are new shares. Which of the following statements are true?

   I. The XYZ Company will receive the proceeds from the entire sale.
   II. This offering is a combined distribution.
   III. The selling stockholders will receive some of the proceeds.
   IV. This offering is an exchange distribution.

   A. I and II
   B. I and IV
   C. II and III
   D. II, III and IV

3. The principal functions of an investment banker are to

   I. distribute securities to the public
   II. provide a secondary market
   III. provide financing for the individual
   IV. advise the issuer about alternatives in raising capital

   A. I and II
   B. I and IV
   C. II and III
   D. III and IV

4. The underwriting manager is the

   A. employee who supervises the underwriting activities of an investment banker
   B. broker-dealer that supervises the activity of the issuer on authority of the SEC
   C. broker-dealer that publishes the offering prospectus
   D. broker-dealer that supervises the activity of the underwriting syndicate and selling group

5. Which of the following are considered by an underwriter when establishing the offering price?

   I. Projected earnings for the company
   II. Likely dividends to be paid over the coming years
   III. Demand for the security by the investing public
   IV. Earnings multiples for other companies in the market in the same industry

   A. I and II only
   B. I, II and III only
   C. I, II and IV only
   D. I, II, III and IV

6. A new issue is offered at $21.00 per share. Which of the following are MOST likely to be stabilization bids?

   I. 18 7/8
   II. 20 7/8
   III. 21
   IV. 22

   A. I and II only
   B. I and III only
   C. II and III only
   D. I, II, III and IV

7. A dealer should consider all of the following factors when determining the spread on a new issue EXCEPT the

   A. prevailing amount
   B. amount bid on the issue
   C. type and size of the issue
   D. amount of the good faith check

Answers

1. **D.** The standby underwriter acts as a guarantor to the corporation, promising that the securities not purchased through a rights offering will be purchased by the underwriter. The underwriter then distributes the remaining shares on a firm commitment basis.

2. **C.** This is a combined primary and secondary distribution. The corporation receives the proceeds from the shares it sells and the selling stockholders receive the proceeds from the remainder.

3. **B.** The principal functions of the underwriter are to advise the issuer about the type of securities and the timing of the issue and to sell securities to the public.

4. **D.** The underwriting manager supervises the activity of the syndicate and selling group. The issuer publishes the prospectus.

5. **D.** The underwriter would consider all the factors listed when pricing a new issue.

6. **C.** An issue can never be stabilized above the market price. The issue would most likely be stabilized at, or slightly below, the market price.

7. **D.** The spread is the difference between the reoffering price and the amount bid on an issue in competitive bidding. Therefore, the dealer can take into account such factors as market conditions, the type and size of the issue, the dollar volume of the transaction and any extraordinary costs incurred by the syndicate.

The Underwriting Syndicate

Forming the Underwriting Syndicate

Underwriting manager. The investment banker that negotiates with the issuer is known as the *underwriting manager* or *manager of the syndicate*. The underwriting manager directs the entire underwriting process, signs the underwriting agreement with the issuer and directs the due diligence meeting and sales process.

Syndicate. The members of the underwriting syndicate make a commitment to the manager to help bring the securities to the public. Syndicate members sign a syndicate agreement that describes the responsibilities of the members and manager and allocates syndicate profits.

Selling group. The syndicate invites other broker-dealers to be members of the selling group. Selling group members act as agents with no commitment to buy securities.

Syndicate Structure

Corporate underwriting normally takes the form of a negotiated agreement between the issuer and investment banker. This negotiated agreement is known as the **syndicate letter** or **agreement among underwriters** and will be signed just prior to the effective date.

The syndicate manager oversees and manages the underwriting and makes decisions according to the underwriting agreement. The following are responsibilities of the syndicate manager:

- execute the underwriting agreement with the issuer;
- formulate the agreement among underwriters, establishing the underwriters' liability (Western/divided or Eastern/undivided) and compensation;
- obtain from each member of the syndicate a commitment to underwrite a specific amount of the issue (participation);

- determine how many shares from its bracket each firm will sell (retention);
- reallocate any securities not sold by a member of the syndicate to other syndicate members with excess demand or to members of the selling group;
- determine whether or not to establish a selling group; and
- form the selling group to assist in the distribution of the offering.

Selling Group Formation

The **selling group members** distribute the public offering stock to investors at the same time, same price and same terms as the underwriters. Selling group members have no financial responsibility to the issuer, nor to anyone else, because they are not underwriters. Selling group members do not make as much money on a public offering as the underwriters.

The **selling group agreement** contains the following terms:

- statement that the manager acts for all the underwriters;
- amount of securities each selling group member will be allotted and the tentative POP at which the securities will be sold (this price is firmed up just before the offering date);
- provisions as to how and when payment for shares allotted to each selling group member is to be made to the managing underwriter; and
- legal provisions limiting each selling group member's liability in conjunction with the underwriting.

Underwriting Compensation

The price to the issuer is referred to as the **underwriting proceeds**, and the price to the buying investors as the **public offering price**. The underwriting spread consists of:

1. manager's fee
2. underwriting fee
3. selling concession

Manager's fee. This is compensation for the manager's role in the underwriting. It is not shared with other members of the syndicate. The management fee is deposited in a fund pool called the *syndicate account,* and the managing underwriter takes its fee when the account is liquidated and the syndicate dissolved. The management fee may also be used to cover such underwriting expenses as advertising.

Underwriting fee. This fee compensates the syndicate members for the risk they assume in the underwriting. The underwriting fee is allocated to syndicate members based on their participation.

Takedown. The percentage of the spread that remains after subtracting the manager's and syndicate fees is called the *takedown.* The takedown is the discount at which a syndicate member buys bonds form the syndicate.

Selling concession or reallowance. The remaining portion of the spread (and the largest part) is the selling concession, the amount received by whoever actually sells the shares. The concession is the discount the selling group dealer receives from the syndicate. The concession can be considered a part of the total takedown. When the member does not sell the bonds directly to the public, it *concedes* a portion of the takedown to the selling dealer. The remainder is kept by the member and is called the **additional takedown.**

Factors that Affect the Underwriter's Compensation

An underwriter's compensation will be affected by the following:

- type of commitment
- marketability of the security
- issuer's business
- size of the offering

Reallowances

The underwriters may allow NASD member firms that are not members of the underwriting syndicate or the selling group to sell the public offering stock to customers and earn a sales commission called a *reallowance.*

Questions

1. The underwriter's spread in a competitive bid underwriting is the

   A. difference between the price paid to the issuer and the public offering price
   B. ratio of expenses to the offering price
   C. ratio of the bid price to the offering price
   D. difference between the bid price and the concession

2. The compensation that the selling group receives is called the

   A. concession
   B. allowance
   C. discount
   D. spread

3. In a public offering at $9 per share, the underwriting spread is $1. The issuer receives how much per share?

   A. $7
   B. $8
   C. $9
   D. $10

Use the following information to answer questions 4 through 6.

A corporation is offering 300,000 shares to the public at $15 per share. The manager's fee is $.15 per share, the underwriter's fee is $.20 per share, and the concession is $.65 per share. Participations are 100,000 shares for the manager and 200,000 shares for the underwriting syndicate. Retentions are 100% for the manager and 75% for the syndicate members.

4. How much does the public pay per share?

   A. $13.75
   B. $14.00
   C. $15.00
   D. $16.00

5. The total amount received by the issuer is

   A. $4,000,000
   B. $4,200,000
   C. $4,500,000
   D. $5,000,000

6. The manager's compensation for acting as manager and underwriter is

   A. $45,000
   B. $65,000
   C. $86,000
   D. $146,000

Answers

1. **A.** The spread is the difference between the price paid to the issuer and the reoffering price to the public.

2. **A.** The selling group receives a concession or reallowance. The underwriting spread or discount is the total amount due the syndicate.

3. **B.** If the offering is $9 per share and the underwriting spread is $1, the net to the issuer is $9 minus the $1, or $8 per share.

4. **C.** The corporation is issuing the stock at $15 per share, and that's the price the public pays.

5. **B.** The underwriting spread is composed of the $.15 management fee, the $.20 underwriting fee and the $.65 selling concession, for a total of $1. The issuer will receive $14 per share ($15 POP minus the $1 spread) times 300,000 shares, which is $4,200,000.

6. **B.** The manager receives the manager's fees for all 300,000 shares and underwriting fees on its 100,000-share participation. Total compensation for acting as manager and underwriter is $65,000: ($.15 × 300,000 = $45,000) plus ($.20 × 100,000 = $20,000). The manager will also receive a selling concession or reallowance for any shares it sells.

Types of Underwriting Commitments

Firm Commitment

In a firm commitment underwriting contract, the underwriter contracts with the issuing corporation (or selling stockholders, or both) to buy the securities described in the contract, within a defined price and quantity range, on or about a given date. The underwriter is committing to buying securities from the issuer and paying the underwriting proceeds to the company (or individual sellers). The underwriter does this without full assurance that the securities can be resold to the public. If part of an issue that is being distributed under a firm commitment contract goes unsold, any losses incurred are prorated among the underwriting firms according to their participation.

Negotiated underwritings. In a negotiated underwriting, the issuer and the investment banker *negotiate* the terms of the offering, including the amount of securities to be offered, the price at which they will be offered and the fees to be paid to the underwriters. Negotiated underwritings are standard in the corporate securities underwriting market.

Competitive bid underwritings. In a competitive bid (standard for municipal securities), a state or municipal government unit will announce its intention to issue debt securities and will invite investment bankers to bid for the bonds. The issuer then awards the securities to the underwriter(s) that submitted the highest bid price (which results in the lowest debt service cost to the issuer).

Best Efforts

The best efforts arrangement calls for the underwriter to buy securities as agent from the issuing corporation, contingent on the underwriter's ability to either sell them in a public offering or place them with select investors in a private placement.

All or None

In an all or none (AON) underwriting, the issuer reserves the right to cancel the offering if all of the securities are not sold.

Mini-max   → *Best effort with* $\uparrow$ *ceiling* $\downarrow$ *floor.*

A mini-max offering is a best efforts underwriting with a floor and a ceiling on the amount of securities the issuer is willing to sell.

Standby Underwritings

In a standby underwriting, a corporation may be obliged to protect the *proportional ownership interest* of the current stockholders and first offer any additional issue of the same class of stock to the existing stock owners before offering the securities to the general public. If any securites remain unsold, the issuing corporation needs an underwriter standing by to step in and buy up the unsold shares, and arrange for them to be sold to other investors.

Firm commitment. The standby underwriter *unconditionally agrees* to buy all shares not subscribed to by current stockholders at the subscription price.

Market price stabilizing. The standby underwriter normally agrees to *stabilize* the open market price of the shares already in the hands of the public, if necessary, for a period of 30 or 60 days.

Eastern and Western Underwritings

Eastern (undivided) account. In an Eastern (or undivided) underwriting, the underwriters act *severally and jointly*, with every firm sharing the risk that one or more underwriters will not be able to dispose of their full allotments of stock. The cost of the unsold stock is spread and assessed *pro rata* to all of the underwriters, based on the firm's original allotment (participation).

Western (divided) account. In a Western (or divided) underwriting, the underwriters act *severally but not jointly*. Unsold shares remain the responsibility of the firm that agreed to sell them. The cost of unsold shares is not prorated to those underwriters that sell out their allotments.

Questions

1. Which of the following are types of underwritings?

    I.   Firm commitment
    II. All or none
    III. Standby
    IV. Best efforts

    A. I and II only
    B. I, III and IV only
    C. II and III only
    D. I, II, III and IV

2. In a best efforts offering, an underwriter

    A. makes no guarantee that an offering will be sold
    B. makes a best efforts attempt to reduce the underwriting spread
    C. guarantees a minimum price and makes a best efforts attempt to increase that price
    D. makes a best efforts attempt to bring the security to market within the cooling-off period

3. When an underwriter is NOT responsible for unsold securities, it is engaged in which type of underwriting?

    A. Best efforts
    B. Firm commitment
    C. Negotiated
    D. Standby

4. An underwriting that is canceled by the issuing corporation if the issue is not 100% subscribed for is a(n)

    A. firm commitment
    B. best efforts
    C. all or none
    D. mini-max agreement

Answers

1. **D.** All of the choices listed are types of underwritings.

2. **A.** In a best efforts underwriting, the underwriter acts as an agent. It makes its best effort to sell the entire issue but is not responsible for unsold securities.

3. **A.** In a best efforts underwriting, the broker-dealer is an agent for the issuer and has no responsibility for purchasing unsold securities.

4. **C.** An all or none offering is a type of best efforts. If the securities are not 100% sold, the entire issue is aborted and the money returned to each prospective purchaser.

Exemptions from the Securities Act of 1933

Exempt Issuers and Securities

The Securities Act of 1933 requires the registration of new issues with the SEC. Certain securities are exempt from the registration statement and prospectus requirements of the Securities Act of 1933, either because of the issuer's creditworthiness or because another government regulatory agency has jurisdiction over the issuer. The following issuers and securities are not required to be registered with the SEC:

- U.S. government securities;
- state and municipal bonds;
- commercial paper and bankers' acceptances (maturities under 270 days);
- insurance policies and fixed annuity contracts (but not variable annuities);
- national and state bank securities (except bank holding companies);
- building and loan (S&L) securities;
- common carrier (e.g., motor and railroad) securities;
- farmers' cooperative securities;
- small business investment company (SBIC) securities; or
- charitable, religious, educational and non-profit association issues.

+ Any recognized foreign government securities.
+ Employee pension and profit sharing or saving plan.

Exempt Transactions

The manner of sale may qualify an offering for exemption. Securities offered by industrial, financial and other corporations may qualify for exemption from the registration statement and prospectus requirements of the 1933 act under one of the following exclusionary provisions:

- Regulation A: corporate offerings less than $1.5 million
- Regulation D: private placements

- Rule 144: control and restricted securities
- Rule 147: securities offered and sold exclusively intrastate

Regulation A: Small Offerings

The Regulation A (Reg A) exemption permits issuers to raise up to $1.5 million capital in a twelve-month period without full registration. Instead of filing a full registration statement with the SEC in Washington, the issuer files an abbreviated notice of sale (offering circular) with the regional office of the SEC. Purchasers are provided with an offering circular rather than a full prospectus.

Regulation D: Private Placements

Rule 506 under Regulation D specifically provides an exemption from registration if the issue is sold to no more than **35 nonaccredited** (nonqualified) investors. An unlimited number of sales may be made to accredited investors.

The SEC does not require registration of an offering privately placed with:

- officers or other insiders of the issuer;
- financial institutions or other similar investors that do not need SEC protection (accredited investors); or
- a maximum of 35 individual (nonaccredited) investors.

An **accredited** investor is generally accepted to be one who:

- has a net worth of $1 million or more; or
- has had an annual income of $200,000 or more in each of the two most recent years (or $300,000 jointly with a spouse) and who has a reasonable expectation of reaching the same income level in the current year.

The purchaser in a private placement must sign a letter stating that she intends to hold the stock for investment purposes only. Private placement stock is referred to as lettered stock (or **legended stock**) due to this investment letter. The certificate may bear a legend indicating that it cannot be transferred without registration or exemption.

apply to {restricted (not reg) securities, insider

Rule 144

Rule 144 regulates the sale of two types of securities: control and restricted. Stock that has not been registered is considered restricted stock. Control securities are owned by directors, officers or persons who own 10% or more of any type of outstanding securities of the company (or financially dependent relatives of such individuals). Persons who have a control relationship with an issuer are considered **affiliated persons**. Restricted securities are those acquired through some means other than a registered public offering. A security purchased in a private placement is a restricted security.

Under SEC Rule 144, control and restricted securities can be exempted from full registration before they are sold to the public. The requirements for a sale of restricted stock under Rule 144 are:

- The securities must have been owned fully paid for at least two years.
- Current financial information about the company must be made available to the buyer.
- The person selling the securities files notice with the SEC on Form 144 no later than the day of the first sale.
- The filing is effective for 90 days.
- The sale of these securities cannot be advertised, no special promotion is allowed and no extra commission can be paid.
- If the securities were owned for three years or more, there is no volume limitation on the amount of restricted securities sold under Rule 144.
- If the securities were owned between two and three years, the volume of securities that can be sold is limited to the greater of 1% of all of the outstanding shares of the company or the average weekly trading volume for the preceding four weeks.

Restricted stock certificates bear a legend stating that the sale of those particular shares is restricted. When restricted stock is sold to the public in a 144 offering, that legend is removed in the transfer process.

For sales by insiders or sale of control stock, Rule 144 applies as follows:

- Corporate insiders are officers, directors or anyone who owns 10% or more of the outstanding shares of the company (or financially dependent relatives).
- If the insiders' securities are restricted (i.e., purchased in a private placement), the minimum two-year holding period applies. If the securities are not restricted, the two-year holding period does not apply. (Securities may become control securities by being purchased in the open market by a control person.)
- The volume limitation is the same as for non-insider-owned restricted stock: the greater of 1% of the outstanding shares of the company or the average weekly trading volume for the preceding four weeks.

All other rules that apply to sales of restricted securities under Rule 144 apply to sales of securities by insiders.

Rule 147: Intrastate Offerings

SEC Rule 147 exempts offerings that take place entirely in one state from registration under the following conditions:

- The issuer of the securities has its principal office and receives at least 80% of its income within that state.
- At least 80% of its assets are located within that state.
- At least 80% of the proceeds of the offering are used within that state.
- The broker-dealer acting as underwriter is a resident of that state and has an office in the state.
- All of the purchasers are residents of that state. (100%)

Purchasers of an intrastate issue may not resell the stock to any resident of another state for at least nine months after the underwriting is completed.

Antifraud Regulations
of the Acts of 1933 and 1934

Although a security might be exempt from the registration requirement (and regulations regarding disclosure of information), *no offering is exempt from the antifraud provisions of the Securities Act of 1933*. The antifraud or antimanipulation provisions of the act of 1933 apply to all new securities offerings, whether exempt from registration or not. Issuers must provide accurate information regarding any securities offered to the public.

Exemptions from the act of 1934. Securities that are exempt from registration under the act of 1933 are not subject to most of the Securities Exchange Act of 1934's rules and regulations regarding trading, proxy solicitation, insider trading or margin requirements. As with the act of 1933, however, no security is exempt from the act of 1934's antifraud and market manipulation regulations.

Questions

1. A Regulation A exemption applies to

   A. the minimum margin requirements of $5,000 for an underwriter
   B. the minimum net capital of $5,000 for an underwriter
   C. a new issue of $1,500,000 or more
   D. a new issue of $1,500,000 or less

2. SEC Rule 147 provides exemption from registration for

   A. small issues
   B. securities issued by banks
   C. intrastate issues
   D. private placements

3. Under the intrastate offering rule, when may a resident purchaser of the securities resell them to a nonresident?

   A. Three months after the first sale made in that state
   B. Six months after the last sale made in that state
   C. Nine months after the first sale made in that state
   D. None of the above

4. The private placement rule states that the person to whom the offer of securities is made must be an informed person

   A. but the person need not have access to the same type of information contained in a registration statement
   B. who has a net worth of $2 million
   C. who either has access to the same type of information contained in a registration statement or is furnished such information
   D. or a person who signs a statement testifying that he will not hold the broker-dealer responsible for any losses

5. The fraud provisions of the act of 1934 do NOT apply to which of the following?

   A. Manipulation of the price of a municipal security
   B. Participation in an all or none offering and reporting the offering as firm to the client
   C. Short sale of municipal security serial bonds
   D. All of the above cases and all types of securities

Answers

1. **D.** Regulation A is the exemption for small issues with a maximum size of $1,500,000.

2. **C.** Rule 147 exempts intrastate issues from registration with the SEC. To qualify:

- The issuer must have its principal office and at least 80% of its assets in the state.
- At least 80% of the proceeds must be used within the state.
- The underwriter must be a state resident.
- All purchasers must be state residents.
- Purchasers may not resell the securities to a resident of another state for at least nine months.

3. **D.** If you chose answer C, you were close but not quite correct. Purchasers of an intrastate offering may sell their securities to residents of another state no sooner than nine months after the last sale of the issue. _Underwriting is complete._

4. **C.** In a private placement, securities can be offered to any number of accredited investors (net worth $1,000,000 or more; income of $200,000 per year). Any investor must have access to information about the issuing company and the issue.

5. **D.** All securities are subject to the anti-fraud provisions of the act of 1934, including such exempt securities as municipal and U.S. government issues.

Freeriding and Withholding: Hot Issues

NASD Rules of Fair Practice

Hot Issues

Hot issues are public offering securities that sell at an *immediate premium* over the public offering price (POP) in the secondary market.

Freeriding and Withholding

A member's failure to make a bona fide offering at the POP is considered *freeriding and withholding* under the NASD's Rules of Fair Practice (ROFP). Any NASD member firm engaged in the distribution of a stock that proves to be a hot issue must:

- make a bona fide public offering of the securities at the announced POP;
- not sell the stock to any officer or owner of the firm or to anyone in the firm's employ, under any circumstances;
- not sell the stock to any individual customer in the restricted account category unless such person can demonstrate that his normal investment practice and history include the purchase of similar public offering securities.

Restricted Accounts

It is a violation of NASD rules for any broker-dealer to sell any hot issue security to:

- the underwriters;
- any NASD member broker-dealer;
- any person associated with an NASD member;
- supported family members of a person associated with an NASD member; or
- any person financially dependent on a person associated with an NASD member.

Persons Associated with NASD Members

Under no circumstances may hot issues be sold to officers, directors, general partners, registered representatives, employees and agents of the member firm that is underwriting the hot issue, or any other member firm or persons associated with another member firm, such as officers, owners and employees.

Exceptions for Normal Investment Practice

Under certain circumstances, limited amounts of a hot issue may be sold to:

- nonsecurities persons associated with the underwriting;
- bank trust officers and similar senior officers of financial institutions; and
- family members of the above and nonsupported family members of any classified accounts.

Nonsecurities persons associated with the underwriting. Any person who acts in a business or professional capacity in connection with a public offering, such as finders, accountants, attorneys, financial consultants or others performing a fiduciary service for the managing underwriter as well as members of their immediate families should not be allowed to purchase hot issues unless it can be proved that they regularly and routinely buy public offering securities of the same type (normal investment practice).

Officers and certain employees of financial institutions. Any person who is a senior officer of a bank, savings and loan institution, insurance company, investment company, investment adviser or other types of institutional investors is restricted from purchasing hot issues.

Immediate family members. Any member of the immediate family of any person listed above as securities industry personnel may not buy a hot issue unless it can be proved that such person buys public offering securities or similar types of securities regularly and routinely.

Sales of hot issues to this group are permitted if it can be proved that the person's normal investment practice includes buying similar securities.

The circumstances under which hot issues may be sold to such customers are:

- the customer has a history of purchasing similar securities from the broker-dealer;
- the size of the purchase is consistent with the normal investment practice of the customer;
- each such sale is of an insubstantial amount compared to the total amount available to the customer; and
- the total of all sales of the security to all classified accounts is not disproportionate to the amount the dealer has available for sale.

Normal Investment Practice

A hot issue can be sold to a restricted individual if that type of security is consistent with the individual's investment patterns in terms of:

- the frequency with which similar securities have been purchased;
- the dollar amounts of these previous investments; and
- a clear history of buying new issue securities, provided that the normal investment practice includes buying new issues that are not considered hot.

Disproportionate Allocation

$< 10\%$

An underwriter or a selling group member will generally not be accused of a rule violation if no more than 10% of the firm's allotment of hot issues is sold to restricted accounts.

Insubstantiality

Sales may not be concentrated in only one or a few accounts. If there is no concentration, the NASD will most likely rule that no violation has occurred.

Hot Issues and Overallotments

The following rules govern overallotments:

15% maximum overallotment. Under SEC rules, overallotments of up to 15% of the amount of shares covered in the issuer's registration statement are allowed.

Green shoe. This overallotment provision is sometimes referred to as the *green shoe option,* named after the first corporate underwriting (the Green Shoe Manufacturing Company) to use this technique.

Prospectus disclosure. Prerequisite to an underwriter having the right to exercise an overallotment option, the SEC registration statement and the prospectus that must accompany all sales to customers must disclose the existence of any such options and the conditions under which they will be exercised.

Questions

1. "Freeriding and withholding" refers to

   A. distributing new issues valued at amounts exceeding the cost
   B. purchasing securities with the intent of selling them before the settlement date
   C. a member of an underwriting or selling group failing to make a public offering of a security at the public offering price
   D. none of the above

Answers

1. **C.** "Freeriding and withholding" is the failure of an NASD member to make a bona fide public offering at the public offering price of a hot issue. A hot issue, of course, is an issue that sells at a premium on its first trading day. An example would be when a securities firm sees that a new issue is selling at a premium and decides not to sell it to the public, but instead keeps a substantial portion of the shares in its own investment account to benefit the owners of the firm.

7

Trading Securities

The Regulation of Trading

The Securities Exchange Act of 1934

The intent of the Securities Exchange Act of 1934 is to maintain a fair and orderly market for the investing public. It seeks to attain this goal by regulating the securities exchanges and the OTC markets. The **Exchange Act** formed the SEC and gave the Commission authority to oversee the securities markets and to register and regulate the exchanges.

The Securities Exchange Act of 1934, which has much greater breadth than the act of 1933, addresses the:

- creation of the SEC;
- regulation of exchanges;
- regulation of credit by the FRB;
- registration of broker-dealers;
- regulation of insider transactions, short sales and proxies;
- regulation of trading activities;
- regulation of client accounts;
- customer protection rule;
- regulation of the OTC market; and
- net capital rule.

The Securities and Exchange Commission

The SEC, created by the act of 1934, was given responsibility and authority to regulate the securities markets. The SEC has established rules regarding net capital requirements for broker-dealers, hypothecation of customers' securities, commingling of broker-dealer securities with those of customers, the use of manipulative and deceptive devices and broker-dealer recordkeeping. The SEC enforces the Securities Exchange Act of 1934 (and others) by providing rules and prescribing penalties for violations.

Registration of Exchanges and Firms *& Exchange member + broker dealer*

Under the 1934 act, the national securities exchanges must file a registration statement and agree to comply with and help enforce the rules of this act. The exchange must also institute and enforce disciplinary procedures for members who do not use just and equitable practices.

The act of 1934 requires companies that list securities on those exchanges to register with the SEC. Each listed company must file quarterly and annual statements informing the SEC of its financial status.

Those firms with 500 or more stockholders and assets of $1 million or more must also register. Exchange members who do business with the public must register as well as broker-dealers that do business OTC or that use the mail to conduct OTC business.

The Maloney Act, an amendment to the Securities Exchange Act of 1934, permitted the establishment of a national securities association of broker-dealers transacting business in the OTC market.

Net Capital Rule

The act of 1934 states that broker-dealers must maintain a certain level of net capital. A firm must not let its debts exceed 15 times its net capital.

Financial Statements Sent to Customers

Every broker-dealer must furnish financial statements to customers. NASD rules require a broker-dealer to provide a copy of its current balance sheet to any active customer who makes a written request for one.

Audited financial statements. Audited financials must be furnished to customers. The audited financial statement must contain:

- a balance sheet;
- the amount of net capital computed under SEC Rule 15c3-1;
- a statement of changes in subordinated loans;
- whether the audit disclosed any material inadequacy in the broker-dealer's records; and
- a statement to the effect that the most recent audited full statement of financial condition is available for inspection either at the broker-dealer's office or at the SEC.

Regulation of Credit

The act of 1934 empowered the FRB to regulate margin accounts (that is, to regulate credit extended in the purchase of securities). Within FRB jurisdiction are:

- **Regulation T**—regulates the extension of credit by broker-dealers
- **Regulation U**—deals with the extension of credit by banks
- **Regulation G**—deals with the extension of credit by anyone else

Questions

1. The Securities Exchange Act of 1934 has some sections that deal with

   I. the regulation of investment companies
   II. trading activities such as short sales, stabilizing and the registration of over-the-counter brokers and dealers
   III. the form and content of the prospectus that must be given to all prospective purchasers of a security
   IV. the registration of persons engaged in the business of advising others about investment company transactions

   A. I and II only
   B. II only
   C. II and IV only
   D. I, II, III and IV

2. Under the Securities Exchange Act of 1934, the Securities and Exchange Commission does all of the following EXCEPT

   A. regulate the extension of credit by broker-dealers
   B. regulate the activities of members of national securities exchanges
   C. regulate the solicitation of proxies
   D. provide rules for the segregation of securities owned by clients

Answers

1.   **B.**   Choice II is the only correct answer. The others are dealt with under other securities legislation: choice I, the Investment Company Act of 1940; choice III, the Securities Act of 1933; choice IV, the Investment Advisers Act of 1940.

2.   **A.**   The Securities Exchange Act of 1934 does speak to the regulation of credit by broker-dealers—but it delegates this responsibility to the Federal Reserve Board, not the SEC.

Securities Markets and Broker-Dealers

Securities Markets

The market in which securities are bought and sold is also known as the *secondary* market. Securities transactions take place in one of four trading markets.

Exchange Market

The NYSE and other exchanges on which *listed* securities are traded compose the exchange market.

Over-the-counter Market

The dealer market in which *unlisted* securities are traded is called the *over-the-counter (OTC) market*.

Third Market (OTC-listed)

The third market is a trading market for institutional investors in which *exchange-listed* securities are bought and sold in the OTC market. All securities listed on the NYSE and AMEX are eligible for OTC trading, provided that trading information is reported for public display on the Consolidated Tape within 90 seconds after the execution of any transaction.

Fourth Market (INSTINET)

INSTINET is a market for institutional investors in which large blocks of stock (both listed and unlisted) change hands in privately negotiated transactions unassisted by a broker-dealer.

All INSTINET members are linked by computer terminals.

Trading Hours

Exchange business hours. Both the NYSE and AMEX begin trading at 9:30 am EST each business day and close trading at 4:00 pm EST.

OTC business hours. Normal hours for retail OTC trading are the same as those of the NYSE: 9:30 am to 4:00 pm EST, Monday through Friday.

Comparison of Listed and OTC Markets

Listed Markets

Location. A listed market has a central marketplace and trading floor facilities.

Pricing system. A listed market operates as a double-auction market.

Price dynamics. When a floor broker representing a buyer executes a trade by taking stock at a current offer price higher than the last sale, a plus tick occurs (market up); when a selling broker accepts a current bid price below the last sale price, a minus tick occurs (market down).

Major force in the market. The **specialist** is charged with maintaining an orderly market and providing price continuity.

Transactions away from the main market. Dealers do not maintain inventories in listed stocks and do little principal business in them. Customer orders are routed to an exchange trading floor for execution, and the originating firm charges a commission for services rendered.

OTC Markets

Location. There is no central marketplace for OTC trading. Trading takes place over the phone, over computer networks and in trading rooms across the country.

Pricing system. The OTC market works through an **interdealer network**. Registered market makers compete among themselves to post the best bid and ask prices.

Price dynamics. When a market maker raises its bid price to attract sellers and outpace other market makers, the price of the stock rises; when a market maker lowers its ask price to attract buyers and outpace other market makers, the price of the stock declines.

Major force in the market. The **market makers** post the best current bid and ask prices. The best price at which the public can buy (best ask) and the best price at which the public can sell (best bid) are called the **inside market**.

Transactions away from the main market. Unlike the situation in listed stocks, many dealers maintain inventories in OTC stocks (or stand ready to buy or sell for their own accounts). Such firms have the choice of filling customer orders either as principal trades (from inventory) or as agency trades (executed with a registered market), similar to the way listed stocks are handled.

- The broker may act as the client's agent by finding a seller of the securities and arranging a trade.
- The dealer may buy the securities from the market maker, mark up the price and resell them to the client on a dealer basis.
- If the dealer has the securities in its own inventory, it may sell the shares to the client from that inventory.

An easy way to remember these relationships is to memorize the letters **BAC/DPP**. The letters stand for "**B**rokers act as **A**gents for **C**ommissions/**D**ealers act as **P**rincipals for **P**rofits."

Broker-dealer role in transactions. A firm is prohibited from acting as both a broker and a dealer in the same transaction.

Trading Halts

In the event that a trading halt is called for a particular security in a particular market or exchange, all trading in that security stops. During the halt, however, open orders may be canceled and options may be exercised.

Role of the Broker-Dealer

Brokers. Brokers are agents that arrange trades for clients and charge them a commission.

Dealers. When firms act as dealers (or principals), they buy and sell securities for their own inventory. When selling from their inventory, dealers charge their clients a markup rather than a commission.

Filling an order. A broker-dealer may fill a customer's order to buy securities in any of the following ways:

Questions

1. The over-the-counter market is a(n)

   A. negotiated market
   B. auction market
   C. transfer market
   D. double-auction market

2. Which of the following statements are true regarding the OTC market?

   I. It facilitates the trading of stock not listed on an exchange.
   II. It is a connection of broker-dealers via computers and phones.
   III. Stocks of banks and insurance companies typically trade in the OTC market.

   A. I and II only
   B. I and III only
   C. II and III only
   D. I, II and III

3. Which of the following can make a market?

   I. Broker
   II. Dealer
   III. Floor broker
   IV. Principal

   A. I and II
   B. II and III
   C. II and IV
   D. III and IV

4. When a firm "position trades," it

   I. makes a market in securities
   II. trades for the firm's account
   III. sells short in all transactions
   IV. executes agency trades for customers

   A. I and II only
   B. I, II and IV only
   C. II and III only
   D. I, II, III and IV

Answers

1. **A.** The OTC is a *negotiated* market. The exchanges are *auction* markets. The new issue market is the *primary* market. There is no such thing as the "transfer market."

2. **D.** All of the statements are true regarding the OTC market.

3. **C.** Making markets involves buying and selling for one's own account, which are principal activities. Dealers act as principals in trades; brokers do not.

4. **A.** "Position trading" is simply trading as principal for the firm's inventory. Position trading may involve short or long positions.

The New York Stock Exchange

3/4 Volumm

The NYSE is located in New York City and handles roughly three-fourths of all exchange transactions. The primary objective of the NYSE is to provide a central location for the transaction of its members' business and to maintain high standards of integrity among its members, who are governed by a comprehensive set of rules that promote principles of fair trade. The Exchange itself does not buy and sell stocks, nor does it influence or determine prices. Its only active role is to monitor operations and to facilitate an orderly market and prevent fraudulent practices.

Exchange Listing Requirements

Listing. The NYSE's initial requirements for listed stock are as follows:

- The market value of publicly held shares must be at least $18 million.
- At least 1.1 million shares must be publicly held.
- Two thousand stockholders must each hold 100 shares or more.
- Corporate earnings before federal income tax must be at least $2.5 million for the latest fiscal year and at least $2 million for each of the two preceding years.

Consideration is also given to the following factors:

- whether there is national interest in the company;
- the market for the company's products;
- the strength and stability of the company;
- prospects for the company's maintaining its position in an expanding industry; and
- the company's prospective earnings.

Delisting. The NYSE reserves the right to delist companies. The Exchange may delist companies that engage in activities adverse to investors' inter-

ests, including failure to disclose financial statements or to solicit proxies for all meetings.

A company may also request that its stock be removed from the list, with the approval of its stockholders. The Exchange will not approve a security's removal from the list based solely on a decision by the board of directors.

Trading on the Floor of the Exchange

Only NYSE members can trade on the floor. The four types of traders are:

1. commission house brokers
2. two-dollar brokers
3. registered traders
4. specialists

Auction Market

Exchange securities are bought and sold in an auction market (or **double-auction market**).

Priority, precedence and parity. The specialist awards the trade in the following order:

1. priority—first order in
2. precedence—largest order of those submitted
3. parity—random drawing

Block Trades

The Exchange specifies procedures for trades involving large blocks of listed securities.

A trade judged to be a block trade must be processed according to the following regulations:

- All block trades must be approved by the NYSE.
- The originator of a block transaction pays all costs.
- A floor official has authority to grant permission for the specialist block.

Specialist block. The specialist block purchase is the smallest type of block trade. The trade is done after the market and is not shown on the Tape. It is reported weekly to the NYSE with the specialist's volume.

Exchange distribution or acquisition. A firm asks one or a few other members to help find offsetting offers for a large block of stock. The members take them to the crowd and cross the orders within the current quote. An announcement made on the Tape after the trade is completed identifies it as an acquisition or a distribution. An Exchange distribution takes place on the floor of the NYSE during market hours and involves only NYSE member firms.

Special offering or bid. A larger block will require a larger number of participants. An announcement is made before the transaction of a special offer or bid. The price stipulated is net to the buyer or seller, and the initiator pays transaction costs to sell or acquire the shares. As an incentive to complete the block trade, commissions to the selling agent are twice normal size. Partial completions are printed on the Tape at the close of business.

Secondary distribution. Secondary distribution procedures are suitable for the largest blocks of stock, those too large for other block procedures. An announcement is made after the market closes. The price is net to the buyer and is never higher than the closing price on the Exchange.

Nine Bond Rule

Orders for fewer than ten bonds must be shown on the floor of the Exchange before being traded OTC.

Arbitrage

Market arbitrage. An arbitrage trade that takes advantage of price differences between markets is known as *market arbitrage*.

Securities arbitrage. An arbitrage trade that takes advantage of price differences between equivalent securities is known as *securities arbitrage*.

Risk arbitrage. An arbitrage trade that takes advantage of price changes due to extraordinary events is known as *risk arbitrage*.

Questions

1. The New York Stock Exchange serves investors by

   A. offering securities for sale
   B. buying securities for members
   C. both A and B
   D. neither A nor B

2. Which of the following statements about the NYSE are true?

   I. The NYSE is a corporation operated by a board of directors.
   II. Membership on the Exchange is fixed at 1,000.
   III. Allied members can trade on the floor of the Exchange.
   IV. NYSE auction procedures are based on rules of priority, precedence and parity.

   A. I and II
   B. I and IV
   C. II and III
   D. III and IV

3. A company whose stock is listed on the NYSE may also have its stock listed on the

   A. American Stock Exchange
   B. Midwest Stock Exchange
   C. CBOE
   D. Chicago Board of Trade

4. Which of the following brokers would be allowed to trade on the NYSE?

   I. Registered representative
   II. Specialist
   III. Registered trader
   IV. Commission broker

   A. I and II only
   B. II and III only
   C. II, III and IV only
   D. I, II, III and IV

5. All of the following are used in awarding trades on the NYSE EXCEPT

   A. priority
   B. parity
   C. premium
   D. precedence

6. On the NYSE, specialists act as

   I. brokers for the public
   II. brokers for other brokers
   III. dealers

   A. I and III only
   B. II only
   C. II and III only
   D. I, II and III

7. Who is permitted to transact business on the floor of the Exchange?

   A. Members
   B. Allied members
   C. Floor clerks
   D. Floor officials

8. In order to be considered for listing on the NYSE, a corporation must meet which of the following requirements?

   I. At least 2,000 stockholders must each own at least 100 shares.
   II. At least 4,000 stockholders must each own at least 100 shares.
   III. A national interest in trading the stock must be present.
   IV. Voting by stockholders must be allowed through the solicitation of proxies.

   A. I, III and IV
   B. II and III
   C. II, III and IV
   D. II and IV

9. A company's stock is listed on the NYSE. Which of the following could result in the company's being delisted?

   I. The company files for bankruptcy under Chapter 11.
   II. The company issues nonvoting common stock.
   III. Public interest in the stock declines considerably.
   IV. The company does not mail out proxy statements.

   A. I and III only
   B. I and IV only
   C. II and IV only
   D. I, II, III and IV

Answers

1. **D.** The NYSE provides facilities for trading. The members, not the Exchange, buy and sell securities.

2. **B.** Membership is fixed at 1,366. Only members can trade on the Exchange floor.

3. **B.** Stock listed on the NYSE can also be listed on regional exchanges, but not on the American Stock Exchange. The Chicago Board of Trade is a commodities exchange, and CBOE is an options exchange.

4. **C.** Only members can trade on the floor of the Exchange. Registered reps may not.

5. **C.** Priority, precedence and parity are used for breaking ties on the floor of the NYSE. Priority goes to the first bid or offer. If priority cannot be established, the largest bid or offer takes precedence. If neither priority nor precedence can be established, parity exists and the trade is awarded by drawing straws or tossing a coin.

6. **C.** Specialists trade only with other members of the Exchange, not with the public. They act as dealers for their own accounts and as brokers for other members.

7. **A.** Only members of the Exchange are permitted to trade securities on the floor of the Exchange.

8. **A.** To be NYSE-listed, a corporation must have at least 2,000 stockholders; it must allow stockholders to vote; there must be a national interest in trading the stock; and minimum earnings and asset tests must be met.

9. **D.** The NYSE takes many factors into consideration when determining whether a company should be delisted. Among the factors are all the choices given: the company files for bankruptcy; the company issues nonvoting common stock; public interest in the company declines considerably; or the company does not mail out proxy statements. However, if the question said, "Which would definitely cause delisting?" answer C would be correct. Issuing nonvoting common stock or not mailing out proxy statements are more serious events than the other choices.

The Specialist

Role of the Specialist on the Exchange

Market maker. The specialist's primary function is to make a market or maintain a market in each assigned stock. He stands ready to buy or sell a round lot of the security (as well as give a quote on that security).

Agent and principal. On the floor of the Exchange, specialists can act in two capacities:

- As agents (or brokers' brokers), executing all orders left with them by other brokers.
- As dealers (principals), buying and selling for their own accounts.

Responsibilities of the specialist. Specialists are required to abide by certain NYSE floor rules in the daily conduct of their business:

- The specialist must work to maintain a fair and orderly market.
- The specialist must stand ready to buy and sell for his own account, if necessary, to maintain a fair and orderly market.
- The specialist is expected to transact business for his own account in such a way as to maintain price continuity and depth and to minimize temporary price disparities attributable to differences in supply and demand.
- The specialist must avoid transacting business for his own account at the opening or reopening of trading in a stock if this would upset the public balance of supply and demand.
- The specialist must file the reports and keep the books and records required by the Exchange.

→Limit & STOP

Limit Order Book

The specialist's book. A specialist's limit order book is a record of limit and stop orders the specialist holds for execution. The specialist must always get the best possible price for a limit order—at the limit or better.

Quotes. The current quotation always states the best (highest) bid and the best (lowest) offer.

Size. The specialist is allowed to reveal the number of shares available in a current quote, but is not allowed to reveal the number of shares or prices above or below the current quote. The quote and size (Q&S) are good only for the moment they are given; however, they provide some indication of the current price.

Stopping Stock

A specialist can guarantee that a market order will be filled at the current bid or offer by stopping stock with an out firm quotation. A specialist may stop stock only for the benefit of a public order and does not require the Exchange's permission to do so. In the event the price in the crowd moves beyond the stopped price, the specialist automatically executes the order.

Crossing Orders   ?

Before crossing orders, the member must offer the stock in the trading crowd surrounding the specialist's post at a price higher than the bid by the minimum variation, then go to the post at which the stock trades and ask the specialist for a quote. If there are no takers, the member can cross the two orders.

Questions

1. Stopping stock is permitted only if the specialist

   A. receives the permission of an NYSE floor governor
   B. is executing an order for another member
   C. has not guaranteed the price
   D. is executing a public order

Answers

1. **D.** A specialist may not stop stock for her own account, for the account of a competing specialist in the same stock or for the account of another member of the Exchange. The privilege of stopping stock is limited to public orders.

Types of Orders

Primary Types of Orders

Market (Unrestricted) Orders

An order that is sent immediately to the floor for execution without restrictions or limits is known as a market order. It is executed immediately at the current market price.

Limit Orders

An order on which a client has placed a limit on the acceptable purchase or selling price is called a limit order. Limit orders are usually not executed immediately.

Executing a limit order. Limit orders can be executed only at the specified price or better. If the order cannot be executed at the market, the commission house broker leaves the order with the specialist.

Risks and disadvantages of limit orders. Clients who enter limit orders risk missing the chance to buy or sell.

Stop Orders

A stop order is designed to protect a profit or prevent further loss if the stock begins to move in the wrong direction. The stop order becomes a market order once the stock trades at or moves through a certain price, known as the stop price. Stop orders are usually left with and executed by the specialist. A stop order takes two trades to execute:

1. trigger
2. execution

Buy stop order. A buy stop order is entered at a price above the current offering price and is triggered when the market price touches or goes through the buy stop price.

Sell stop order. Sell stop orders are made (1) to protect a profit; and (2) to stop losses. A sell stop order is entered at a price below the current offering price and is triggered when the market price touches or drops through the sell stop price.

Stop limit order. A stop limit order is a stop order that, after being triggered, becomes a limit order rather than a market order. First the stop is triggered. Then the trade is treated like any other limit order that must be executed at the limit price or better.

Restrictions on stop orders. In the OTC market, stop limit orders are not allowed unless the stop price and the limit price are the same.

Reducing Orders

Certain orders on the specialist's book are reduced when a stock goes ex-dividend.

All orders entered below the market are reduced on the ex-date. On the ex-date, the price of the stock drops by the amount of the distribution. Orders reduced include buy limits, sell stops and sell stop limits.

The stop or limit price is reduced by the next greatest increment of trading; that is, the amount of the dividend is rounded to the next highest 1/8th.

Do not reduce (DNR) orders. DNR orders may be entered by a customer. A DNR will not be reduced by an ordinary cash dividend only. It will be reduced for other distributions, such as after a stock dividend or when a stock trades ex-rights.

Up tick rule. The up tick for the short sale rule carries overnight. In the event of a reduction resulting from a distribution, the prior close is adjusted.

Reductions for stock splits (proportional reductions). To calculate the reduction in the price of an open buy order or an open stop order after a stock split, divide the market price by the fraction that represents the split.

Calculating Order Adjustments for Stock Splits

Order price: $100
Stock split: 5 for 4

    5/4 = 1.25
    $100 ÷ 5/4 = $80
    Adjusted order price = $80

Order price: $100
Stock split: 2 for 1

    2/1 = 2.00
    $100 ÷ 2/1 = $50
    Adjusted order price = $50

Order price: $100
Stock split: 3 for 2

    3/2 = 1.50
    $100 ÷ 3/2 = $66.67
    Adjusted order price = $66.67

If a calculation results in a price that cannot be converted exactly into 1/8ths, the order price is rounded *down* to the nearest 1/8th.

Other Types of Orders

Day orders. Unless marked to the contrary, an order is assumed to be a day order, valid only until the close of trading on the day it is entered by the client. If the order has not been filled, it will be canceled at the close of the day's trading.

Good till canceled (GTC) orders. GTC orders, or **open orders**, are valid until executed or canceled.

At-the-opening and market-on-close orders. At-the-opening orders are executed at the opening of the market. Partial executions are allowable. Market-on-close orders are executed at (or as near as possible to) the closing.

Not held (NH) orders. A market order coded "NH" gives the floor broker discretion as to the best time and price at which to execute the trade.

Fill or kill (FOK) orders. The commission house broker is instructed to fill the entire FOK order immediately at the limit price or better.

Immediate or cancel (IOC) orders. These limit orders are like FOK orders except that a partial execution is acceptable. The portion not executed is canceled.

All or none (AON) orders. These orders have to be executed in their entirety or not at all.

Alternative orders. An alternative order (also known as an **either/or order** or a **contingent order**) is an order to do either of two alternatives—for example, either sell a particular stock at a limit or sell on stop.

Questions

1. An order that instructs the specialist not to adjust the limit (or stop) price when a stock goes ex-dividend is designated

   A. DNA
   B. DNR
   C. FOK
   D. EX

2. Which of the following orders would NOT be reduced by the specialist on the ex-dividend date?

   I. Buy limit order
   II. Open sell stop order
   III. Buy stop order
   IV. Sell limit order

   A. I and II
   B. I and IV
   C. II, III and IV
   D. III and IV

3. An order to sell at 38 5/8 Stop, 38 5/8 Limit is entered before the opening. The subsequent trades are 38 7/8, 38 1/2, 38 3/8. The order

   A. was executed at 38 1/2
   B. was executed at 38 5/8
   C. was executed at 38 7/8
   D. has not yet been executed

4. A "not held" order means

   A. that the commission house broker will not be held responsible if he does not get an immediate execution of the market order
   B. the same as "stock ahead" and refers to an unexecuted limited order
   C. the order cannot be found by the member firm
   D. the order has expired

5. A sell stop order is entered

   A. above the current market price
   B. below the current market price
   C. either above or below the current market price
   D. at the current market price

6. A company is about to pay a dividend of $.70. On the ex-dividend date, an open order to sell at 46 stop would

   A. be automatically adjusted to 45 1/4 Stop
   B. be automatically adjusted to 45 3/8 Stop
   C. be automatically adjusted to 45 1/2 Stop
   D. remain 46 Stop

7. Which of the following statements are true concerning stop orders?

   I. They can limit a loss in a declining stock.
   II. They become market orders when there is a trade at, or the market passes through, a specific price.
   III. They are the same as limit orders.
   IV. They can affect the price of the stock when the specific stop price is reached.

   A. I and II
   B. I, II and IV
   C. I, III and IV
   D. II and III

8. A customer enters an order that must be effected at once, either in full or in part, and asks that any unfilled portion of the order be canceled. This is a(n)

   A. good till canceled order
   B. immediate or cancel order
   C. all or none order
   D. fill or kill order

9. A day order is entered to buy 500 XYZ at 24 3/8. By the close, the firm has 100 shares at 24 1/4 and 200 at 24 3/8. The remainder is unfilled. What is the outcome?

   A. The client may reject the incomplete order unless the broker can guarantee filling the remainder by the end of the day.
   B. The client may reject the incomplete order unless the remainder can be filled within five business days.
   C. The client may demand that the firm deliver the remaining shares at 24 3/8.
   D. The client must accept the execution for 300 shares, and the remainder of the order is canceled after the close.

10. A customer tells a broker to buy 1,500 shares of XYZ at 33 5/8 immediately or else to cancel the whole order. This is a(n)

    A. good till canceled order
    B. immediate or cancel order
    C. all or none order
    D. fill or kill order

11. The price range on a particular day for the stock of XYZ Company is shown below:

    XYZ Co. High 26 Low 24 1/4 Close 25 1/2

    If a client had placed a day order to buy 100 XYZ at 24 before the market opened, at what price would he buy the stock?

    A. 23 7/8
    B. 24
    C. 24 1/4
    D. The order was not filled.

Answers

1. **B.** The qualifying price on a do not re-duce (DNR) order will not be reduced by ordinary cash dividends on the ex-dividend date. DNRs do not apply to other distributions, such as rights or stock dividends.

2. **D.** When a stock goes ex-dividend, the specialist will reduce open buy limit orders and open sell stop orders because they are placed below the market price and could be triggered when the market price is reduced for the loss of dividend. The specialist will not reduce open sell limit orders and open buy stop orders.

3. **D.** A stop limit order is a stop order that becomes a limit order once the stop price has been triggered. When the limit price is the same as the stop price on a stop limit order, the order can be executed only at or better than the limit price. In this case, the order has not yet been executed be-cause no transaction has occurred at or above 38 5/8 since the stop was triggered at 38 1/2.

4. **A.** When a market order with an NH code is used, the client agrees not to hold the floor broker responsible for the time and price of execution.

5. **B.** Sell stop orders are always entered below the market price. A sell stop order is trig-gered when a transaction occurs at or below the price specified on the order. A buy stop order is always entered at a price above the current offering price.

6. **A.** When a stock goes ex-dividend, the price of the stock falls by the amount of the divi-dend. If the dividends are not equivalent to a round eighth, the dividend is rounded to the next highest fraction. A dividend of $.70 would reduce the stock price by $.75, or 3/4ths of a point. The specialist also reduces open buy limit orders and open sell stop limit orders by the amount of the dividend.

7. **B.** A stop order becomes a market order once the market price reaches or passes the specific stop price. An investor in a long position can use the sell stop order for protection against a market decline. When a large number of stop orders are triggered at a particular price, the advance or de-cline of the market at that point can be magnified. Stop orders are not the same as limit orders because there is no guarantee of a specific execution price or better for a stop order.

8. **B.** Under an immediate or cancel order, the commission house broker is instructed to fill immediately as much of the order as possible at the limit price or better. The remaining unexecuted part of the order is canceled. A fill or kill order must be executed in its entirety or it is canceled. An all or none order must be executed in its entirety, but does not have to be executed immediately.

9. **D.** A client must accept partial fulfillment of a limit order.

10. **D.** Under a fill or kill order, the commis-sion house broker is instructed to fill the entire order immediately at the limit price or better. If this cannot be done, he will cancel it and notify the originating branch office. An immediate or cancel order is similar except that partial execution is acceptable.

11. **D.** An order that can be executed only at a specified price or better is a limit order. A buy limit order can be executed only at or below the price specified on the order. Because the stock of XYZ Company never traded at or below 24, the order was not filled.

Long and Short Sale Rules

Long Sale

By purchasing shares in a company an investor is *going long*. The sale of those same shares would be a *long sale*.

Short Sale

The short-selling investor initially borrows stock from a broker-dealer, then sells the stock at the market. The seller is obligated to buy the stock and replace the borrowed shares in order to close the short position. The client takes a short position by selling shares of stock he does not own.

The following are points to remember about short sales:

- Short sales are always executed and accounted for in a customer's margin account and are subject to Reg T 50% initial margin requirements.
- Short sales always entail the delivery of borrowed stock to the buy side of the trade.
- Short sales are subject to higher NASD/ NYSE minimum margin maintenance requirements than long purchases in a margin account.

Exchange Short Sale Rules

plus tick or zero-plus tick.

Orders to sell a listed security short on an exchange may be executed only on a *plus tick* or *zero-plus tick*. A plus tick is a price higher than the last different price. A zero-plus tick occurs when the last trade for the security was made at the same price as the trade before, but that trade was higher than the previous trade.

Short Sale Regulations

No shorting by insiders. The Securities Exchange Act of 1934 prohibits directors, officers and principal stockholders (insiders) from selling short or selling short against the box stock in their own companies.

Sell Order Tickets

A person is considered to be long (own) a security if he (or his agent):

- has title to it;
- has purchased the security or has entered into an unconditional contract to purchase the security, but has not yet received it;
- owns a security convertible into (or exchangeable for) the security and has tendered such security for conversion or exchange; or
- has an option to purchase the security and has exercised that option.

Unless one or more of these conditions are met, the SEC will consider any sale of securities a short sale.

Identification of sell orders. The SEC requires that all sell orders be identified as either "long," "short" or "short-exempt."

exempt from uptick rule

Questions

1. Which of the following reasons is appropriate justification for selling a stock short?

   A. To cut losses on a long position.
   B. To benefit from a decline in the price of the stock.
   C. To benefit from a rise in the price of the stock.
   D. To seek a modest potential reward with limited risk.

2. XYZ Inc. stock was traded as shown below:

Open	251/4	25	251/4	251/8	251/4	251/4
		I	II	III	IV	V

   On which transactions can short sales be made?

   A. I, II, IV and V
   B. I, III, IV and V
   C. II, IV and V
   D. II and V

3. A customer is short against the box. He now sells the stock that he owned in the long position. The order will be marked

   A. long
   B. short
   C. round lot long exempt
   D. short exempt

Answers

1. **B.** Selling short does not reduce the risk of a long position: the investor is selling borrowed, not owned, stock. The appropriate time to sell short is when one suspects that the stock price is about to drop. The investor wants to sell at a high price, buy later at a lower price. Both the reward and risk potential of selling short are high. If the stock price moves down dramatically, the investor can reap a large gain. If it moves up dramatically, the investor can lose a great deal of money.

2. **C.** Short sales can be made only on upticks or zero upticks. An uptick occurs when the stock is traded at a price higher than the last different price. A zero uptick occurs when there is no change in price but the last time the price changed it was an uptick. Choices II and IV are upticks. Choice V is a zero uptick.

3. **B.** In the initial sale, to establish the short against the box, the order must be marked "short," and the security can be sold only on an uptick. The owner does not plan to deliver his own security. He is borrowing a certificate to complete the transaction. When the account is both long and short a security, it is said to be in a "zero net" position. Because he is selling long the securities he owns, the transaction is not exempt from the uptick rule. Only the short position will remain.

The Over-the-Counter Market

OTC trading is regulated by both the SEC and the NASD, the self-regulatory organization for the OTC market.

The computerized information system that keeps track of OTC trading is **NASDAQ**. Securities that can be traded in the OTC market include, but are not limited to:

- American depositary receipts (ADRs)
- bank stocks and insurance company stocks
- most corporate bonds
- municipal bonds
- U.S. government securities
- common and preferred stock
- equipment trust certificates
- closed-end investment companies

Mutual funds and other new issues are initially issued OTC.

Negotiated Market

The OTC market is a *negotiated* market in which market makers may bargain during a trade. A negotiated market is competitive.

OTC Market Makers

Some OTC dealers **make a market** in certain securities, buying and selling them for their own profit and at their own risk. A broker-dealer acting as a market maker acts as a principal and not an agent. The market maker takes a position in the security by purchasing it or selling it short. OTC securities listed with NASDAQ must be traded by at least two market makers.

Requirements for Market Makers

A market maker must:

- be registered as an NASD member
- meet minimum net capital requirements

When giving quotations on its securities, the NASD requires market makers to:

- provide continuous two-sided quotations for that security;
- be able and willing to execute a trade for at least a normal trading unit at its quote;
- ensure that its quotations are reasonably related to the current market for that security;
- adhere to the maximum allowable spread limits;
- file monthly trading data and other information as required by NASD rules;
- file daily volume reports for those securities in which it makes a market; and
- perform these functions during normal business hours.

If only one firm makes a market in a particular security, it cannot claim to be offering that security *at the market.*

Loss of Market-maker Status

Market makers may be prohibited from entering quotations in the NASDAQ system if they:

- are experiencing financial or operational difficulties to the point where investors might be jeopardized; or
- have been suspended or expelled from NASD membership or membership in a national securities exchange.

Pink Sheets

OTC market makers publish their interdealer quotations in the *Pink Sheets,* which have six key features:

1. They are devoted exclusively to OTC stocks.
2. The prices are quotes, not actual transaction prices.
3. The quotes are between dealers (*interdealer*—that is, not retail).

4. The quotes are subject, not firm.
5. For NASDAQ system stocks, the NASDAQ symbol appears right after the name of the stock.
6. An "M" preceding the stock's name means the stock is marginable.

Pink Sheet quotes are subject. A dealer that publishes a quote on a security in the *Pink Sheets* must be ready to quote a firm price for 100 shares of that security.

Questions

1. A firm that is making a market in a security is permitted to do which of the following?

    I.   Sell short without regard to the plus tick rule.
    II. Take either a long position or a short position in a stock.
    III. Charge a markup.
    IV. Charge both a markup and a commission on the same trade if both the markup and the commission are reasonable in size and related to the current market price of the stock.

    A. I, II and III
    B. I and III
    C. II, III and IV
    D. II and IV

2. When a broker-dealer maintains a firm market in a stock, that broker-dealer is committed to

    A. buying back any security it sells
    B. buying or selling the normal trading unit of that stock at the quoted price
    C. maintaining a continuous subject market
    D. working out the amount of the markup or commission on each OTC transaction

3. The *Pink Sheets* reflect

    A. retail securities prices
    B. quotes between dealers
    C. actual transactions between dealers
    D. firm quotes

4. A quote in the *Pink Sheets* indicates that a dealer is

    A. giving a firm quote for 100 shares
    B. prepared to make a firm quote for 100 shares
    C. quoting a firm market either way for 1,000 shares
    D. recommending the stock

Answers

1. **A.**   Market makers may take either a long position or a short position in a stock in which they make a market. They may also sell these securities short without regard to the plus tick rule. As a dealer, a market maker may charge a markup, but is prohibited from also acting as a broker (charging a commission) on the same transaction.

2. **B.**   When a broker-dealer maintains a firm market in the stock, that broker-dealer has issued a firm quote on that stock and, therefore, is committed to buying or selling one trading unit of that stock at the quoted price.

3. **B.**   Quotes listed on the *Pink Sheets* are quotes between dealers, not actual transaction prices. They are subject quotes.

4. **B.**   Although a *Pink Sheets* quote is subject, its inclusion signifies that the broker-dealer is willing to make a firm quote upon request. If a dealer places a quote in the *Pink Sheets* and then refuses to give a firm quote, the dealer is said to have *backed away*.

Quotations

Bids, Offers and Quotes

A quote (or quotation) is a dealer's current bid and offer on a security. The current bid represents the highest price at which any dealer will buy, and the current offer (or asked price) represents the lowest price at which any dealer will sell. The difference between the bid and ask is known as the **spread**.

Quotation Requirements

Firm Quote

A firm quotation is the price at which a market maker or broker-dealer stands ready to buy or sell at least one trading unit—100 shares of stock or five bonds—at the quoted price to other NASD member firms in the interdealer market. All quotes are firm quotes unless otherwise indicated.

Revising firm quotes. Firm quotes are good only at the moment they are given and are subject to revision.

Backing away. A market maker that revises a firm quote without apparent cause, or that otherwise refuses to do business at the price(s) quoted, is *backing away* from the quote, a practice inconsistent with the just and equitable principles of trade held by members of the NASD.

Recognized quotation. A recognized quotation under NYSE rules is any public bid or offer for one or more round lots.

Subject Quote

A subject quote is one in which the price is subject to reconfirmation by the market maker.

Qualified Quote

Workout quote. A workout quote is given in situations in which a market maker knows that special handling will be required to accommodate a particular trade. A workout quote is an approximate figure used to provide the buyer or seller with an indication of price.

Nominal quote. A nominal quote is someone's assessment of where a stock might trade if there were an active market.

Bid or offer wanted. Any statement to the fact that a member is entertaining quotes for a security from other members would be considered a quotation and must meet all of the requirements of quotations.

Quotation Spread and Size

Spread. The difference between the bid and the asked prices of a security is known as the quotation's *spread*. Factors influencing the size of a spread include the:

- size of the issue;
- financial condition of the issuer;
- amount of interest (market activity) in the issue; and
- market conditions.

Size. Unless otherwise specified, a firm quote is always good for one round lot or for the standard unit of trading for the security in question.

Reporting Quotes

Manipulative and deceptive quotes. The Rules of Fair Practice mandate that only bona fide transactions be reported. Any quote given must represent a real bid or offer.

Questions

1. An over-the-counter trader attempting to buy stock is given a quote of "16–17 work-out." This indicates that the quote is

   A. $16 with a suggested broker-dealer mark-up of $1
   B. firm
   C. bona fide
   D. approximate

2. If an over-the-counter trader gives the quote, "My market is 12 to 12 5/8," this is

   A. a firm quote, and the trader must be willing to trade 100 shares at that quote
   B. subject to approval
   C. subject to confirmation
   D. an unacceptable quote

3. Assume that ABC Corporation is quoted at 25–25 1/4 and XYZ Corporation is quoted at 24–27. Which of the following is MOST likely?

   A. ABC is more actively traded.
   B. XYZ is more actively traded.
   C. ABC is quoted on a work-out basis.
   D. XYZ has more market makers.

Answers

1. **D.** A *workout* quote is an approximate quote that is not firm. The trader giving the quote gives a range and will work out the final quote.

2. **A.** If a quote begins, "My market is ....," it is a firm quote and the trader must be willing to trade 100 shares at the specified price.

3. **A.** Dealers are very cautious about making a market in stocks that are traded inactively. A dealer may find it very difficult to liquidate a sizable position in such stocks. For protection, a dealer will open up or widen the spread on such stocks. If a stock is very actively traded, the spread will be relatively small.

NASD 5% Markup Policy

or
Markdown

The 5% markup policy is a *guideline* and is not a firm rule for markups and markdowns. The NASD 5% markup policy applies to all OTC transactions.

If the firm makes a market in the security, it can, as principal, buy from or sell to the customer, charging a markup or markdown. If the firm does not make a market in the security, its OTC trader will contact a broker-dealer that is making a market and, acting either as agent or as principal, fill the customer's order.

Markup Based on Representative Market Prices

In all OTC principal transactions, the base for computing the markup and testing for compliance with the 5% policy is the price *representative of prevailing (inside) market prices* at the time of the customer transaction.

Dealer's Inventory Costs

If a customer's buy order is filled from the broker-dealer's inventory, the net price to the customer is based on the prevailing market price. The price at which the broker-dealer might have acquired stock that is now being sold to the customer has no bearing on the net price to the customer; that price must be reasonably related to the current market.

Riskless and Simultaneous Transactions

A riskless and simultaneous transaction occurs when a broker-dealer holds an order to buy or sell stock that it does not carry in its trading inventory, and either:

- acts as **agent** for the customer, going to the market maker, buying or selling on the customer's behalf and charging a commission; or

- acts as **principal**, going to the market maker, buying or selling for its own account and then buying or selling to the customer and charging a markup or markdown.

total commission or MUP
< 5% of purchase

Proceeds Transactions

When a customer sells stock or other securities and uses the proceeds to pay for securities, the purchase is called a *proceeds transaction*. The NASD 5% markup policy limits the broker-dealer's commissions and markups to not more than 5% of the price of the securities. The buy and sell sides may each show a commission or markup, but *when combined*, they should not exceed 5% of the purchase amount.

Factors Relevant to the NASD 5% Markup Policy

In determining the fairness of a markup or markdown, the NASD considers the following factors:

- type of security
- actively traded vs. inactive stocks
- selling price of security
- dollar amount of transaction
- nature of the broker-dealer's business
- pattern of markups
- disclosure

Markups on inactive stocks (contemporaneous cost). For inactive stocks and situations where no prevailing market quotes are available, the broker-dealer may base the markup on its contemporaneous cost in the stock (acquisition cost plus inventory carrying charges).

Questions

1. A client wants to sell $10,000 worth of Barnett Banks and use those funds to buy $10,000 worth of Bay Banks. Assuming that your firm acts as a dealer in both transactions, which of the following statements is(are) true?

    I. This set of trades is called a *proceeds transaction*.
    II. Your firm must consider each transaction separately in determining a fair markup on the securities purchased.
    III. Your firm must consider the profit on the liquidated securities in determining a fair markup on the securities purchased.
    IV. Your firm has acted illegally: it may act as a broker in only one of the transactions.

    A. I
    B. I and II
    C. I and III
    D. IV

2. A broker-dealer holds in its inventory an OTC stock for which it paid an average price of $12 a share, and the stock is currently quoted at 9 3/8. The broker-dealer quotes its client a price of 12–12 1/2 for 100 shares. This price

    A. is reasonable because its markup is less than 5% of its original cost
    B. would violate the Rules of Fair Practice
    C. should reveal the amount of its commission
    D. would be justified only if the market were *thin*

Answers

1. **C.** A *proceeds transaction* occurs when a client sells securities to a dealer and uses the proceeds to buy other securities from the same dealer; for markup purposes, this is viewed as one transaction. The profit on the liquidated securities must be considered when computing the markup on the securities purchased by the client.

2. **B.** The stock is currently quoted at 9 3/8. If the broker-dealer quotes that stock to a client at 12–12 1/2, this price would violate the Rules of Fair Practice. Remember, markups must be based on the current market, not on the member's original cost.

NASD Automated Quotation System

Scope of NASDAQ Service

NASDAQ offers a variety of quotation services and market information display packages. In total, the NASDAQ system includes current price quotations from more than 500 market makers on more than 5,300 actively traded securities.

Levels of Quotation Service

The NASDAQ system provides three levels of stock quotation service to the securities industry.

- **Level 1**. NASDAQ Level 1 is available to registered reps through a variety of public vendors and displays the **inside** market only: the highest bid and the lowest ask for securities authorized for inclusion in the system.
- **Level 2**. NASDAQ Level 2 is available only to NASD approved subscribers and provides subscribers with the **current quote** and the **size of the quote** available from *each* market maker in that security.
- **Level 3**. NASDAQ Level 3 provides subscribers with all of the services of Levels 1 and 2 and allows registered market makers to **update** their quotes on any security in which they make a market. A selling broker-dealer must update its quotes within 90 seconds of any change.

Automated Confirmation Transaction Service

ACT's primary purpose is to make the reconciliation and matching of telephone-negotiated trades easier for member firms. Market makers are required to report transactions in securities eligible for ACT to the system within 90 seconds.

NASDAQ Market Maker Requirements

90-second Reporting

Registered market makers are required to transmit reports that include the security's NASDAQ symbol, the number of shares, the price of the transaction and whether the trade was a buy, a sell or a cross *within 90 seconds* after the execution of the transaction.

Definition of "Inside Market"

The inside market is the best bid price at which stock can be sold in the interdealer market and the best ask price at which the same stock can be bought.

The inside market quotation is critical because NASD rules require that customer transactions be based on the inside market quotation. This is true even though no business is actually transacted with the firm (or firms) making the inside market.

NASDAQ Authorized Securities

To qualify for NASDAQ listing, a company must meet minimum qualifications in:

- total assets;
- capital and surplus;
- outstanding principal value of convertible debt securities;
- publicly held shares;
- number of stockholders; and
- registered and active market makers.

Minimum of Two Market Makers

In order for a security to be listed on any NASDAQ quotation service, the security must have at least *two registered and active market makers* able and willing to enter firm quotations in the system.

NMS Issuer Qualifications

In order for its securities to be accepted as NMS securities, a company must meet minimum standards regarding:

- annual net income;
- number of market makers registered for its security;
- price per share; and
- market value of the outstanding shares.

Issuers of securities designated as NMS securities must meet higher minimum conditions than those listed only with NASDAQ for:

- number of publicly held shares
- available capital and surplus

Suspension or Termination of a Securities Listing

A security that has qualified for NASDAQ listing may have that privilege pulled if:

- the issuer of the security files for bankruptcy;
- the issuer's independent accountants issue a disclaimer opinion on the issuer's financial statements; or
- the NASD decides it is necessary to prevent fraud or to protect the public interest.

Questions

1. Level 2 of the NASDAQ system provides which of the following?

   I. Firm quotes
   II. Names of the firms making markets
   III. Actual prices of transactions
   IV. Cumulative, up-to-the-minute volume in the security

   A. I only
   B. I and II only
   C. II and III only
   D. I, II, III and IV

2. Level 1 of the NASDAQ system provides which of the following?

   A. Highest bid and lowest offer for each security
   B. Price of the last sale for each security
   C. Current bid and asked price of each market maker for each security
   D. Current representative bid and asked prices for each security

Answers

1.   **B.**   Level 2 on the NASDAQ system provides the current quote and the name of each market maker in each security.

2.   **A.**   Level 1 on the NASDAQ system is the inside quote—the highest bid and lowest offer on a stock.

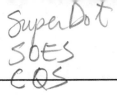

SuperDot
SOES
CQS

Computerized Order Routing

New York Stock Exchange SuperDot

Orders executed through SuperDot are often confirmed back to the broker in less than 60 seconds. All NYSE-listed stocks are eligible for trading on SuperDot, subject to the following limits:

- preopening market orders—up to 30,099 shares per order
- postopening market orders—up to 2,099 shares per order
- pre- and postopening limit orders—up to 99,999 shares per order

Chicago Board Options Exchange ORS and RAES

The **Order Routing System (ORS)** for market and limit orders handles up to 2,000 contracts. Market orders and executable limit orders of ten or fewer contracts received by ORS are sent to the **Retail Automatic Execution System (RAES)**. Customer orders sent through RAES receive instantaneous executions at the prevailing market quote and are confirmed almost immediately to the originating firm.

American Stock Exchange AUTOPER and AUTOAMOS

AUTOPER accepts both odd- and round-lot equity orders from brokers for up to 2,000 shares. AUTOAMOS automatically executes trades for the four to six most active stocks of the XMI index options. AUTOAMOS accepts options orders from brokers for up to 20 contracts.

Pacific Stock Exchange SCOREX

SCOREX is designed to accept all types of orders, including market, GTC and limit orders in both odd and round lots. The specialists at the SCOREX terminals will execute orders of up to the 10,099-share SCOREX limit and have the ability to waive that limit for larger orders.

Philadelphia Stock Exchange PACE

PACE is designed to handle market and limit orders of up to 3,099 shares for more than 1,100 actively traded stocks. PACE can provide electronic executions within approximately 15 seconds of order.

A special feature of PACE is its ability to check quotations on any of the seven U.S. exchanges and guarantee an execution at the best possible quote found on any of those markets.

National Association of Securities Dealers SOES

SOES is designed to facilitate the trading of small public market and executable limit orders (up to 1,000 NMS shares; up to 500 non-NMS shares). Any NASDAQ or NASDAQ-NMS security with at least one active SOES market maker is eligible for trading through SOES.

Clearance and settlement. Small orders may be aggregated if the total is less than the maximum 1,000-share limit, but broker-dealers may not split up large customer orders for the purpose of avoiding the 1,000-share limitation.

Restrictions. Institutions and broker-dealers may not use the system to trade for their own accounts or for other NASD members. Only public market and executable limit orders are acceptable.

Intermarket Trading System/ Computer Assisted Execution System

ITS/CAES market makers are responsible for maintaining a continuous, two-sided market. Once entered, an ITS/CAES quote is considered irrevocable for *two minutes*, unless the market maker specifically states that it will only honor the quote for one minute.

Consolidated Quotation System

The Consolidated Quotation System (CQS) is part of the NASDAQ market-making system. Quotation display service is available to all NASDAQ subscribers (at a fee), while quotation input service is available to only those members that are registered to do business in third market stocks. NASD members that are registered market makers may enter quotes into CQS through the NASDAQ system.

CQS securities. Securities eligible for quotation on CQS include all NYSE- and AMEX-listed securities, designated securities listed on regional exchanges and any securities registered for unlisted trading on the national exchanges.

Trading hours. CQS is open for quotations from 9:30 am to 4:00 pm EST, although a CQS market maker may designate a later closing time for a security (up to 6:30 pm EST).

Non-NASDAQ OTC Securities

If an equity security is not traded on a national exchange and is not included in the NASDAQ system, it is considered a *non-NASDAQ security*.

OTC Bulletin Board

The OTC Bulletin Board is an electronic quotation system for non-NASDAQ securities. Firms that participate in the Bulletin Board system can:

- enter quotations for securities in which they make a market;
- update those quotations almost instantaneously; and
- obtain information about bids and offers of other market makers.

INSTINET

The INSTINET Corporation is a privately operated computerized system to facilitate fourth market trades. Institutional investors subscribing to the service can enter bids and offers and trade directly with other institutions. Trades are reported to the Consolidated Tape.

The Consolidated Tape

How the Tape Works

The Consolidated Tape system delivers real-time reports of securities transactions to subscribers as they occur on the various exchanges.

Network A reports transactions in NYSE-listed securities wherever they are traded. **Network B** carries reports of AMEX-listed securities transactions as well as reports of transactions in regional exchange issues that *substantially meet* AMEX listing requirements. Transactions in these securities must be reported within 90 seconds for inclusion on the Consolidated Tape.

How to Read the Tape

Market Identifier

On the high-speed line, the transactions are reported with a market identifier, a letter identifying the exchange or market on which the transaction took place. Market identifiers are deleted for transactions sent over the low-speed line.

Quotations and Administrative Messages

Number of shares. The Tape reports a sale of a single round lot of stock by listing the trading symbol and the price at which the transaction occurred but with no quantity. Sales of multiples of a round lot are indicated by printing the number of round lots followed by the letter "s" and the price. If a transaction is executed for 10,000 shares or more, the entire amount will be printed. Odd-lot transactions are also reported in exact shares but the volume is followed by the letters "shrs." ← Odd lot

Stocks sold in 10-share units have their numbers abbreviated and are followed by the symbol (S/S) ← 10's (or Inactive stocks)

If two similar trades for the same security occur consecutively, the report prints them under the same trading symbol and separates them with a dot.

W/I ← When Issued

Error reports. The Tape will report any necessary corrections preceded by the letters "CORR." If the symbols "ERR" or "CXL" appear on the Tape, they indicate that a printed report is to be erased or disregarded.

Active markets. The following are some of the symbols used to indicate that information will be deleted:

- DIGITS & VOL DELETED. When this message appears, the first digit of the price and the volume will be dropped.
- REPEAT PRICES OMITTED. This message indicates that the Tape will be showing only transactions that differ in price from the previous report.
- MINIMUM PRICE CHANGES OMITTED. If necessary, the Tape will print only those trades that differ by more than 1/8th of a point from the last report printed.
- SLD indicates that the exchange did not report a sale on time, so it is out of sequence on the Tape.
- OPD announces the initial transaction in a security for which the opening has been delayed.
- HALT means that trading in that security has been halted.

INSTINET. INSTINET system (O) trades are included, as are trades involving NASD members.

Questions

✓ 1. Based on the following sample Tape, how many shares of Federal Paper Board (FBO) preferred were sold and at what price?

FBOpr	T	ADM
50 ⸾ 24 1/8	42 1/2	2s17 3/8

A. 5,000 at 24 1/8
B. 100 at 24 1/8
C. 500 at 24 1/8
D. 50 at 24 and 50 at 24 1/8

✓ 2. Because ABC Company split its stock 2 for 1, both old and new shares are trading on the floor of the NYSE. The old stock was priced at 70, the new stock at 35. If a client bought 300 of the new shares of ABC stock, how would this be reported on the Tape?

A. ABC 300s35
B. ABC 3s35
C. ABC 150s70
D. ABC 3s35 $_I^W$

3. A registered rep places an order for a client to buy 1,600 shares of RCA at 36 3/4 and sees the following trades on the Tape. Assuming he was the only bidder, how many shares did he buy and at what price(s)?

GE	RCA	TX	RCA
52 1/2	5s36 1/2	2s23 1/2	10s36 1/2.3/4

A. 500 at 36 1/2
B. 1,000 at 36 1/2
C. 100 at 36 3/4
D. 500 at 36 1/2, 1,000 at 36 1/2, 100 at 36 3/4

Answers

1. **C.** Inactive stocks that trade in round lots of 10 shares are recognizable on the Tape because they are reported this way: Volume $_S^S$ Price.

2. **D.** If a stock trades at a certain price and then splits and new shares are being issued, these new shares are traded "when issued," and they will be identified on the Tape by $_I^W$.

3. **D.** Two separate entries for RCA appear on the Tape. The first indicates that the registered rep was able to partially fill the order by picking up 500 shares at 36 1/2; he then filled the remainder of the order by buying 1,000 shares at 36 1/2 plus the final 100 shares at 36 3/4.

8 Client Accounts

New Accounts

Classification of Accounts

Account ownership. The principal types of ownership are:

- individual
- joint
- corporate
- partnership

Trading authorization. The principal types of trading authorization are:

- discretionary
- fiduciary 信託
- custodial

Payment method. In cash accounts, clients must pay the full purchase price of securities. In margin accounts, clients may borrow part of the purchase price of a security from the broker-dealer.

Securities traded. Clients must have special approval to make certain types of trades in their accounts, and additional special requirements exist for options accounts.

Opening New Accounts

Required information. According to NYSE Rule 405, exchange members must exercise due diligence to learn essential facts about every customer and account.

Payment and delivery instructions. For buy orders, the customer may give the firm any of the following instructions:

- transfer and ship _certificate_
- transfer and hold in safekeeping
- hold in street name
- delivery vs. payment

For sell orders, the customer gives one of two instructions: hold the cash at the broker-dealer, or forward the cash balance on the settlement date.

Approval and Acceptance of an Account

Each new account must be approved by a partner or a principal of the firm, in writing on the account form, before any trading can take place.

Documenting New Accounts

New Account Form

The registered rep must fill out a new account form and enter certain details regarding client identification and information concerning suitability. The firm must have a record of:

- full name;
- address and telephone number;
- Social Security or tax identification number;
- occupation, employer and type of business;
- citizenship;

- whether the client is of legal age;
- bank and brokerage references;
- whether the client is an employee of a member broker-dealer;
- how the account was acquired;
- name and occupation of the person with authority to make transactions in the account; and
- signatures of the representative opening the account and a principal of the firm.

Client information must be updated periodically as situations change. Transactions placed by the client but judged unsuitable by the registered rep may still be entered by the client.

Signature Cards

The client is not legally required to fill out a signature card for a cash account.

Mailing Instructions

Statements and confirms may be sent to someone other than the client if the client requests it in writing or if duplicate confirms are also sent to the client.

Cash vs. Margin Accounts

Cash Accounts

In a cash account, a customer is expected to pay in full for any securities purchased. Certain accounts may be opened *only* as cash accounts; among these are personal retirement accounts, corporate retirement accounts and custodial accounts.

Margin Accounts

"Margin" refers to the minimum amount of cash that a customer is required to deposit on the purchase of securities.

The Federal Reserve Board's Regulation T

The FRB established Regulation T, which sets forth the equity or margin required in a purchase of securities in a margin account. The board establishes the rules and regulations governing margin accounts, and then delegates the enforcement of them to the SEC.

Opening a Margin Account

The securities purchased in a margin account are held for the customer in the account in street name. The rate of interest on margin accounts is based on the broker call rate.

In a margin account the client can control investments while depositing into the margin account only a fraction of the investments' market value. A margin account can also serve as a potential source of cash (loans against fully paid securities).

Documenting a Margin Account

When opening a margin account, the client signs a margin agreement disclosing the terms under which credit will be extended. The margin agreement contains a credit agreement, a hypothecation agreement and an optional loan consent.

- The **credit agreement** discloses the terms under which credit is extended, including the annual rate and method of computing interest and the conditions under which interest rates and charges will be changed.

- The **hypothecation agreement** gives the firm permission to pledge (or hypothecate) securities held on margin.
- The **loan consent agreement** gives the firm permission to lend the customer's securities held in a margin account to other brokers (usually for delivery on short sales).

With a margin account, a firm extends credit to a client for a portion of the purchase price of securities, which allows the client to **leverage** investments.

Customer funds in a margin account. The firm may not pledge more of a customer's securities than are needed to cover the loan from the bank for the margin account, and may not pledge those securities for any purpose other than the customer's loan.

Customer Protection Rule

The customer protection rule (Rule 15c3-3) requires the following:

- A client's fully paid securities and excess margin securities must be segregated and kept safely.
- Each firm must keep a reserve bank account for clients' funds.
- Securities sold by a client must be delivered within ten business days after the settlement date.

ROP: registered Option principle

Options Accounts

When opening an options account, the customer signs a customer options agreement, which explains the risks and requirements of option trading. By signing the agreement, the client acknowledges having read the OCC Options Disclosure Document, which is published by the Options Clearing Corporation, and understanding the risks associated with trading options.

Initial approval for options accounts may come from the branch manager. If the manager is not a ROP, the manager's signature must be approved by either a ROP, Senior ROP (SROP) or Compliance ROP (CROP) within a reasonable time. When opening an options account, a registered rep must:

- ascertain the client's investment history and financial status;
- ascertain the client's investment objectives and needs;
- give or send the client the OCC Options Disclosure Document; and
- obtain the client's signature on a customer options agreement, which states that the investor will abide by OCC guidelines and option exchange regulations.

The client's account information must be updated within 15 days of a change in either the client's financial status or objectives.

Additional approval may be required if the client wishes to engage in writing options, naked option writing, ratio writing, spreads and straddles.

Retirement Account Agreements

When a registered rep opens a business account of any type, it is necessary to establish three items:

1. the business's legal right to open an investment account;
2. any limitations that the owners, stockholders, a court or any other entity has placed on the investments in which the business will be allowed to invest; and
3. who will be allowed to represent the business in transactions involving the account.

A copy of the legal documents that established the business will usually contain this information and must be kept on file together with all other account forms.

Trading Authorization/Power of Attorney

Any time a power of attorney or a discretionary power to the broker has been established for an investment account, a signed copy of that document must be kept on file with the rest of the account papers.

Special Account Situations

Numbered accounts. The client must sign a form certifying that she owns the account(s) identified by the number or symbol.

Multiple accounts. If a client wishes to open more than one individual account with a broker-dealer, the client must attest that no one else has any interest in the second and subsequent accounts and that each account unreservedly guarantees the others.

Account transfers. To transfer a client's account from one broker-dealer to another, the client must sign a transfer request form. If the account contains options, it may not be transferred during the last week prior to option expiration.

Account Records

All customer transactions are posted daily and are maintained at both the branch and the main office. The required information includes the following:

- client's name, address and phone number
- type of account and account number
- client's investment objective
- list of all securities deposited with the firm
- list of all transactions

Opening Accounts for Employees of Other Brokers

Broker-dealers must give special attention to accounts opened by certain individuals. Accounts opened by the following individuals fall within these rules:

- employee of a broker-dealer;
- the spouse or minor child of an employee of a broker-dealer; and
- (in certain cases) employees of non-NYSE member financial institutions.

NYSE requirements. The NYSE requires prior written approval from the employer broker-dealer before an employee of a member firm can open a cash or margin account with another firm. If the account is approved, duplicate statements and confirmations must be sent by the transacting firm to the employer broker-dealer. Employees of the NYSE also need the written permission of the employer. Duplicate confirmations need not be sent to the employer.

Employees of banks, insurance companies and NASD broker-dealers need prior approval to open a margin account. Duplicate confirmations do not need to be sent.

NASD requirements. NASD rules require the firm opening the account to notify the client's employer. The employee is responsible for disclosing that she is an NASD member when opening the account. Duplicate confirmations and statements must be sent to the employer broker-dealer only if the employer requests them.

MSRB requirements. The MSRB requires that the employer be notified in writing that the account is being opened and must be mailed duplicate confirmations, unless it requests in writing that it not receive them.

Questions

1. When a registered rep receives instructions from a customer to *transfer and ship*, the rep will instruct the margin department to transfer ownership into the

   A. customer's name and deliver the securities to the customer
   B. brokerage firm's name and deliver the securities to the customer
   C. brokerage firm's name and deliver the securities to the brokerage firm's commercial bank for safekeeping
   D. customer's name and deliver the securities to the customer's bank for safekeeping

2. A brokerage firm can open an account for all of the following EXCEPT a(n)

   A. pension fund
   B. insurance company
   C. estate
   D. third party without written authorization to do so

3. An employee of another broker-dealer would like to open an account with your firm. All of the following statements regarding the employee and the account are true EXCEPT that the

   A. employer must receive duplicate copies of all transactions made in the account if requested.
   B. employer must be notified of the opening of the account
   C. opening member must notify the employee, in writing, that the employer will be notified of the employee's intent to open the account
   D. broker-dealer holding the account must approve each transaction made by the person before entry of the order

4. A client wants her account designated by number, not by her name. The registered rep

   A. cannot open the account in this manner
   B. can open the account with a written statement of ownership from the client
   C. can open this account with a written statement of ownership and approval from an authorized delegate of the client
   D. can open this account without additional documentation

5. Which of the following must sign a new account form?

   I. Principal
   II. Registered representative
   III. Customer
   IV. Spouse of the customer

   A. I and II only
   B. I, II and III only
   C. II and III only
   D. I, II, III and IV

6. All of the following are required on a new account form EXCEPT the customer's

   A. name
   B. date of birth
   C. Social Security number
   D. occupation

7. All of the following need permission to open margin accounts with an NYSE member firm EXCEPT an employee of a(n)

   A. communications company
   B. bank
   C. broker-dealer
   D. insurance company

8. An NYSE member firm must notify or receive prior permission of the employer of a customer in all of the following situations EXCEPT when opening a

A. margin account for a bank teller
B. margin account for the president of an insurance firm
C. margin account for an employee of the NYSE
D. cash account for an employee of an NYSE firm

9. Confidential or numbered accounts may be opened provided that the client

A. has a regular account at the firm already
B. signs a power of attorney form
C. signs a form stating he is the owner of the numbered account
D. has/does none of the above

10. A client is going on a trip and wishes to have his brokerage firm stop sending mail. The firm can do all of the following EXCEPT

A. hold it for two months if he is traveling domestically
B. hold it for three months if he is traveling internationally
C. send the mail to a post office box
D. send the mail to his registered representative's office

Answers

1. **A.** "Transfer and ship" means to *transfer* the securities into the name of the customer and *ship* (deliver) the securities to the customer. *Hold in street name* would require the securities to be transferred into the name of the broker-dealer and held for safekeeping.

2. **D.** An account cannot be opened for a third party without proper authorization. For example, John Jones cannot open an account for his brother Fred. But Fred can open an account and authorize John to trade in it. Fred may also sign a power of attorney, which grants John the right to open an account and trade for Fred.

3. **D.** The NASD does not require prior approval of individual transactions by the broker-dealer at which the account has been opened.

4. **B.** For numbered accounts, the client must sign a document attesting to ownership.

5. **A.** To open a cash account, only the signatures of the registered rep introducing the account and the principal accepting the account are required. For margin accounts, the signature of the customer is required on the margin agreement. The signature of the spouse is required only for a joint account.

6. **B.** Although the date of birth is often obtained, it is not required. All that is required is information stating that the customer is of age.

7. **A.** Under NYSE rules, employees of other broker-dealers or employees of other financial institutions must have permission in hand to open a margin account. The rules do not apply to an employee or someone outside the financial industry. The communications company is outside the financial industry.

8. **B.** NYSE rules require that if an NYSE employee or an employee of a member firm opens either a cash or margin account at another member firm, the employer must be notified in writing. If

an employee of an institution wished to open a margin account (not a cash account), the employer must also be notified in writing. An officer of an institution is not an employee—no written notification is required for this individual to open a margin account.

9.   C.   A numbered account gives the client a degree of anonymity in the securities traded. The name of the client in a numbered account is not public knowledge, but someone in the member firm must know who owns the account. So, the client must sign a form attesting to the fact that he owns the account.

10.   D.   Client mail may not be sent to a client's registered representative's office. If this were done, there is no assurance that the mail would be forwarded to the client. It could also provide a way for a registered representative to withhold information from the client.

Types of Accounts

Single Account

In a single account, the account holder is the only person who can:

- control the investments within the account; or
- request distributions of cash or securities from the account.

Joint Account

If the names of two or more people appear on the account and each will be allowed some form of control over the account, it is called a *joint account*.

The account forms must be signed by all owners. Checks must be made payable to the name(s) in which the account is registered.

by %

Joint tenants in common. JTIC ownership provides that a deceased tenant's fractional interest in the account is retained by that tenant's estate and is not passed to the surviving tenant(s), if any.

Joint tenants with right of survivorship. JTWROS ownership stipulates that a deceased tenant's interest in the account passes to the surviving tenant(s).

Partnership Account

A partnership is an unincorporated association of two or more individuals. The partnership is required to provide a partnership agreement stating which of the partners can make transactions for the account.

When a partner dies, the partnership ceases to exist. The account must be frozen and no orders accepted until proper documentation is received from the deceased's estate.

Corporate Account

A corporate representative must complete a new account form and indicate which members of the corporation may trade in the account.

In addition to the documentation required for all margin accounts, corporate margin accounts require a certified copy of the corporate charter and bylaws authorizing a margin account.

Fiduciary and Custodial Accounts

In a fiduciary account, the custodian makes all of the investment, management and distribution decisions, and is required by law to manage the account in the best interests of the owner. Securities bought in a custodial account must be registered in such a way that the custodial relationship is evident. The *beneficial owner's Social Security number* would be used to open the account and would thereafter appear on the account statements.

Fiduciaries include:

- trustees
- executors
- administrators
- guardians
- custodians

The trust agreement will state whether there are restrictions or prohibitions that the fiduciary must abide by. Any trades that are entered by the fiduciary must be compatible with the trust's investment objectives.

Opening a fiduciary account. Opening a fiduciary account requires completion of a new account form for fiduciaries and acquisition of a court certificate or another acceptable document to certify the individual's appointment and authority. The registered rep for a fiduciary account must be aware of the following rules before transacting business in the account:

- Proper authorization must be given.
- Speculative transactions are generally not permitted.

- Margin accounts are permitted only if the legal documents establishing the fiduciary account authorize them.
- The prudent man rule requires fiduciaries to make prudent (wise and safe) investments.
- Many states publish a **legal list** of securities approved for fiduciary accounts.
- No authority may be delegated.
- The fiduciary may not share in the profits of the account, but may charge a reasonable fee for services.

Power of Attorney

To give another person access to (or control of) an investment account, the client must file a power of attorney.

Full Power of Attorney

A full power of attorney allows someone who is not the beneficial owner of an account to:

- deposit or withdraw cash and/or securities; and
- make investment decisions for the owner of the account.

Limited Power of Attorney

Limited powers of attorney must be filed by clients who want to give their brokers discretionary power over their accounts.

Discretionary Account   *not deposit/ withdraw*

"Discretion" is defined as the *authority to decide*:

- the security
- the number of shares (or units)
- whether to buy or sell

Discretion does not apply to decisions regarding only the timing of the investment or the price at which it is acquired.

Authorization for discretionary accounts. A customer can give a registered rep discretionary power over his account(s) only by filing a limited power of attorney with the registered rep's broker-dealer. The power of attorney remains in force for no more than three years (and must be kept on file for at least three years), at which point it can be renewed at the discretion of the customer.

Regulation of discretionary accounts. Discretionary account business must not be solicited; the customer must request this type of account. Authorization must be in writing from the customer, and the text of the authorization must name the person who will hold discretionary power over the account. The authorization must carry the signature of a partner, officer, or other registered principal of the brokerage house.

Discretionary account business is subject to the following ongoing supervision rules and precautions: *marked as discretionary*

- Each discretionary order must be identified as such at the time it is entered for execution.
- Each order must be approved promptly and in writing by an officer or partner of the brokerage house.
- A record must be kept of all transactions.
- There must not be excessive trading in the account, relative to the size of the account and the customer's investment objectives.
- A designated supervisor or manager (registered principal) must review all trading activity frequently and systematically.

Approval and review. Discretionary accounts must have prior approval in writing from the broker-dealer or a registered principal representing the broker-dealer. Discretionary accounts be must be reviewed frequently by an officer of the member firm. A principal of the firm must approve all trades promptly and in writing. A record must be kept of all transactions, and order tickets must be marked "discretionary."

Third-party Account

Accounts cannot be opened for a third party.

Death of an Account Holder

Single Account

If the owner of a single account dies, all pending transactions and outstanding orders must be *immediately canceled*. At the death of the owner of a single account, the cash and securities in the account are distributed according to the account owner's will, or if the account owner dies without a will, the cash and securities in the account will be distributed according to the laws of the state in which the deceased resided.

Joint Account

Joint tenants with right of survivorship. On the death of any or all of the owners of a JTWROS account, account ownership passes to the survivor(s)—there is a "right of succession."

Joint tenants in common. At the death of one of the owners of a JTIC account, that person's proportionate share of the cash and securities in the account is distributed according to the instructions in the decedent's will to his heirs.

Custodial Account

If the beneficial owner of a custodial account dies, any securities or cash in the account go to the owner's estate. All pending transactions and outstanding orders must be immediately canceled.

If the custodian dies, a new custodian must be named to manage the account.

Partnership Account

If one of the partners in a partnership account dies, all pending transactions and outstanding orders must be immediately canceled and the account closed. The executor of the partner's estate will then instruct the rep as to how the account should be handled or distributed.

Powers of attorney. All trading authorizations cease upon the death of the partner.

Questions

1. An account is owned by three partners, one of whom dies. The registered rep

   A. may continue to trade the account once a letter stating that the partner has died is received
   B. must freeze the account's assets
   C. must close out the account and all outstanding orders because the death of a partner dissolves the partnership
   D. may continue to trade the account only after receiving a certified copy of the partner's death certificate

2. A brokerage firm carrying an account managed by an investment adviser requires all of the following EXCEPT

   A. a written statement of the investment adviser's authority to manage the account
   B. a written statement from the client as to where the confirmations of transactions are to be sent
   C. the name, address and other essential information concerning the client
   D. a list, including addresses and phone numbers, of all of the investment adviser's clients

3. All of the following can grant third-party trading authorizations EXCEPT a(n)

   A. corporation
   B. partnership
   C. individual
   D. custodian

4. Which of the following are considered fiduciaries?

   I. Executor of an estate
   II. Administrator of a trust
   III. Custodian of an UGMA account
   IV. Registered rep granted the authority to choose the security, quantity and action in a client's account

   A. I and II only
   B. I, II and III only
   C. II, III and IV only
   D. I, II, III and IV

5. A customer of an NYSE firm asks her registered rep to exercise discretion over her account. To do so, the rep must

   I. obtain written authorization from the customer for the discretionary account
   II. obtain evidence of written acceptance of the account by a registered principal of the firm
   III. have a principal promptly initial each order
   IV. effect no transaction beyond the customer's financial capability

   A. I only
   B. I and III only
   C. II and IV only
   D. I, II, III and IV

6. The NASD Rules of Fair Practice state that

   I. the member or designated person must approve in writing each discretionary order entered and must frequently review all discretionary accounts to detect excessive trading
   II. a registered representative must have the client's prior written authorization before exercising any discretionary power
   III. transactions in discretionary accounts cannot be excessive in size

   A. I and II only
   B. I and III only
   C. II and III only
   D. I, II and III

7. Which of the following would be considered discretionary?

A. Order that specifies the size of the security but leaves the choice of price and time up to the registered rep

B. Account in which the broker has the power to decide when and what to trade, without specific customer authorization for those trades

C. Account in which the customer has power of attorney over another individual's account

D. Account in which an investment adviser has power of attorney over another individual's account

Answers

1. **B.** The partnership assets will be frozen until receipt of appropriate documentation. The partnership is dissolved, and the other partners cannot trade without a reformation of the partnership.

2. **D.** The adviser does not have to disclose his client list to the broker-dealer. What is required when opening a separate client account is a new account card, a trading authorization and a statement from the client as to who will receive the confirmations.

3. **D.** A custodian is a fiduciary and may not assign a power of attorney or trading authorization to another. The custodian may only resign the position of custodian.

4. **D.** Each of these has a fiduciary relationship to the client or entity involved.

5. **D.** The requirements for a discretionary account include a written authorization from the customer, a written acceptance by the firm, and close supervision of each transaction to ensure suitable transactions in light of the customer's objectives and financial situation.

6. **D.** According to the Rules of Fair Practice, no member or registered representative can exercise discretionary authority over a client's account without prior written authorization. The account must be approved by the member. Discretionary orders must be promptly approved in writing by the member, and the account must be reviewed frequently to prevent over-trading (churning).

7. **B.** An order is *discretionary* when it is placed by the member firm or its representative for a customer's account without the customer's express authorization for that order. Also, for the order to be considered discretionary, the firm must choose more than just the price or time of execution; that is, the size of the trade, whether to buy or sell, and/or the security must be chosen by the firm.

Uniform Gifts to Minors Act Accounts

UGMA accounts require an adult (or bank trust department) to act as custodian for a minor (the beneficial owner). Any kind of security may be given, and there is no limitation on the dollar amount of the gift.

Donating Securities

A gift under UGMA is a complete, irrevocable donation of the donor's interest to another person. Once the gift is donated, the donor gives up all rights to the property.

A gift to a minor through an UGMA gives the minor **indefeasible title**. The minor is considered the beneficial owner of the account and its contents.

Bearer securities are generally not permitted but, if they are, gifts of bearer securities must be accompanied by a **deed of gift**. *Bond.*

Custodian

The custodian has full control over the minor's account and can:

- buy or sell securities
- exercise rights or warrants
- liquidate, trade or hold securities

The custodian may also use the property in the account in any way that person deems proper for the support, education, maintenance, general use or benefit of the minor.

There are some restrictions on UGMAs:

- There may be only one custodian and one minor or beneficial owner for each account.
- A minor can be the beneficiary of more than one account and a person may serve as custodian for more than one UGMA as long as each account benefits only one minor.
- Parents, unless acting as custodians for a minor's account, have no legal control over, or recourse to, the account or any of the securities in it.

Opening an UGMA Account

The rep must ensure that the account application contains the guardian's name, the minor's name and Social Security number, and the state in which the UGMA is registered.

Registration of UGMA Securities

Any securities in an UGMA account are registered in the name of the custodian for the benefit of the minor; they cannot be registered *in street name*. The gift of the securities is considered to have been made when this registration has been completed.

Fiduciary Responsibility

Proper handling of the investments in an UGMA include the following:

- UGMAs may only be opened and managed as cash accounts.
- Securities in the account may not be purchased on margin or pledged by the custodian as collateral for a loan.
- All cash proceeds, dividends and interest must be reinvested by the custodian within a reasonable period of time.
- Investment decisions must take into account the age of the minor and the custodial relationship. Options may not be placed or purchased in a custodial account.
- Stock subscription rights or warrants may be either exercised or sold.
- A custodian for an UGMA may not grant trading authority to a third party.

The custodian may be reimbursed for any reasonable expenses incurred in the management of the account.

Taxation

The minor's Social Security number appears on the account, and the minor must file an annual income tax return and pay taxes on any income produced by the UGMA at *the parent's top marginal tax rate*, regardless of the source of the gift, until the minor reaches the age of 14.

Death of the Minor, Custodian or Donor

If the minor beneficiary of an UGMA dies, the securities in the account pass to the minor's estate, not to the parents' or custodian's estates.

Questions

1. Securities owned by a donor and given to a minor under the Uniform Gifts to Minors Act become the property of the minor

   A. when the securities are paid for by the minor
   B. on the settlement date
   C. when the securities are registered in the custodian's name for the benefit of the minor
   D. when the donor decides to give the securities to the minor

Answers

1.   **C.**   Transfer of securities into the custodial account completes the gift. At that time the minor becomes the owner of the securities.

9 ◆ Brokerage Office Procedures

Brokerage Support Services

Processing an Order

The following departments are involved in processing orders:

- **Order department (wire room, order room).** The order department transmits the order to the proper market for execution.
- **Purchases and sales department.** The P&S department handles all billing—typically a computerized process.
- **Margin or credit department.** This department handles activities involving credit for cash as well as margin accounts.
- **Cashiering department.** This department is responsible for receiving and delivering securities and money.

A clearing corporation totals all trades done on a daily basis for each of its participating firms and balances the books of one firm against those of another.

Other departments are involved in client transactions, including:

- reorganization department
- dividend department
- proxy department
- stock record department
- controller's department

Transactions and Trade Settlement

Receipt and Delivery of Securities

The representative must inquire of and be assured that the customer agrees to receive the securities and will pay for them at the agreed upon price. When a rep accepts a sell order from a customer, the rep must be assured that the customer has the security (in a long position) and can deliver it within five business days of the trade.

Order Memorandum

The following information is required on the order ticket:

- client's identification number;
- registered rep's identification number;
- description of the security (symbol);
- number of shares or bonds to be traded;
- where the security is traded;
- action (buy, sell long, sell short);
- options (buy, write, covered, uncovered, opening, closing);
- price qualifications (at market, GTC, day order, stop order, price limit);
- type of account (cash, margin);
- settlement instructions (if not established when account was opened);
- security instructions;
- payment instructions; and
- location of certificates sold.

error in reporting still does not affect the final trade result.

Report of Execution

A registered rep should never try to correct an error by making additional trades without approval from a principal of the firm.

Incorrectly reported trades. In the event that the details of a trade are reported to a customer incorrectly, the actual trade is binding on the customer.

Route of a Typical Order

When a client places an order, typically the order takes the following route:

1. Client places order with registered rep.
2. Registered rep writes the order ticket.
3. Order department receives ticket and transmits order to proper market for execution.
4. Market or exchange receives order. If the order is executed, it is reported back to the firm's order department.
5. P&S department computes and records all transactions and handles billing and confirmations.
6. Margin department computes the amount clients are required to deposit and transmits this information to them.
7. Cashiering department receives and delivers securities and money. It issues payments as instructed by the margin department.

Trade Confirmations

For each transaction, a client must be sent or given a written confirmation of the trade at or *before the completion of the transaction* (the **settlement date**). An exception to this rule is made for wire order purchases of mutual funds for which confirmation may be sent by the selling agent as late as the day after the settlement date.

Components of the trade confirmation include the following:

- trade date
- account no.
- AE no.
- BOT or SLD
- no. (quantity)

- description
  -- yield to call
  -- CUSIP number
- price
  -- odd-lot differential
- amount
- commission
- inter. or tax
- reg. fee
- net amount

Disclosure of broker-dealer capacity. The confirmation must also show the capacity in which the broker-dealer is acting, and the markup or markdown in cases where the broker-dealer is acting as a principal in a riskless or simultaneous transaction.

Timely mailing of confirmations. Customer confirmations must be sent no later than at or before the *completion of the transaction.*

Customer Account Statements   *at least Quarterly*

The customer statement shows:

- all activity in the account since the previous statement;
- securities positions (long or short); and
- account balances (debit or credit).

Disclosure of Financial Condition

A member firm must be prepared to deliver a copy of its most recently prepared balance sheet to the following:

- any customer with securities or cash held by the member; and
- any other member that has cash or securities on deposit or is transacting business with the member.

Charges for Services Performed

A member broker-dealer's fees and charges must be reasonable, must relate to the work performed, transaction entered or advisory services given, and must not be unfairly discriminatory between customers.

Member firms are prohibited from charging customers for handling or forwarding proxy materials. Proxy-related handling charges are paid by the issuer.

Transaction Settlement Dates and Terms

Settlement date is the date on which ownership changes between buyer and seller.

Regular Way Settlement

Except for transactions in U.S. government securities and money-market instruments, regular way settlement is usually the *fifth business day* following the date of trade. For U.S. government notes and bonds, regular way settlement is always the *next business day*. For money-market securities settlement is the *same day*.

Prepayment. Under NYSE rules, prepayment to the seller usually is not permitted.

Extensions

If for good reason a buyer is unable to pay for a trade within seven business days (Reg T settlement date) from the trade date, the broker-dealer may request an extension from an SRO on the seventh day. The broker-dealer has the option of ignoring amounts of less than $500 without violating Reg T requirements.

Cash Settlement

Cash settlement requires delivery of securities from sellers and payment from buyers on the *same day* the trade is executed (same day settlement).

Frozen accounts. If a customer buys securities in a cash account and sells them before paying for the buy side in full, the account is *immediately frozen*—any additional transactions must be on a cash-and-carry basis. Frozen account status continues for a period of *90 calendar days*.

當日沖銷 ⇒ frozen for 90 days

Seller's Option Contracts

In a seller's option contract, the seller can settle the trade up to *60 calendar days* from the trade date, but no earlier than the *sixth business day*, provided the buyer is given a one-day notice.

A buyer's option contract works the same way, except the option rests with the buyer as to when settlement will take place.

When-, As- and If-issued Contracts

Each time a when issued transaction occurs, a confirmation must be sent by the next business day that includes:

- an adequate description of the security, with the contract price;
- designation of the NASD or another SRO whose rules will govern settlement of the contract; and
- provision for marking the contract to the market.

Unless otherwise agreed, the contract must include:

- accrued interest computed up to the settlement date for bonds and other interest-bearing obligations; and
- mark-to-the-market provisions.

Dividend Department

Dividend Disbursing Agent

The stockholder does not have to do anything in order to receive cash, property or stock dividends, or new shares after a split or a reverse split. The broker-dealer's dividend department will make certain that the distribution of dividends, additional shares and replacement stock to the accounts of the beneficial owners of the stock takes place.

Dividend Disbursing Process

Declaration date. A company's board of directors approves the payment of a dividend, announcing the amount, payment date and date on which it will be determined who is and who is not a registered stockholder (known as the *dividend record date*).

Ex-dividend date. The ex-date is *four business days* before the announced record date. On the ex-date, the opening price of the stock is automatically marked down to compensate for the fact that customers who buy the stock that day or later will not qualify for the dividend. Trades executed regular way on or after the ex-date will not settle until after the record date.

Cash trades. Cash trades settle the same day, so cash trades go ex-dividend on the day after the record date.

Dividend record date. The record date selected by the corporation and is used to determine who is and who is not a stockholder of record for dividend payment or rights distribution purposes.

Payable date. On the payable date the transfer agent cuts dividend checks and mails them to all stockholders whose names appear on the books as of the record date.

Stock Dividends and Splits

The ex-date on stock dividends in excess of 25% and stock splits of 5 for 4 or better is the *first business day* following the payable date.

In adjusting the opening price of a stock on the ex-date, the value of the dividend deducted must conform to the minimum price variation of 1/8th point. If the amount of the cash dividend falls between two standard price variations, the higher price variation will be used as the opening price markdown.

Bonds Traded Flat

Bonds that are traded "flat" will have an ex-date and record date if the issuer declares an interest payment.

Proxy Department

Limited power of attorney. A proxy is a *limited power of attorney* given by a stockholder to another person with which the stockholder gives that person the right to vote on behalf of the stockholder. Proxies are valid only for the specified meeting and are intended to be used to cast votes only on matters addressed at that meeting. The voting authorization given through a proxy is revocable by the stockholder.

Forwarding Proxies and Other Materials

Member firms must vote street name stock in accordance with the wishes of the beneficial owners. If the client does not return the proxy within ten business days, the member firm can vote those shares if the question is of minor importance. If the question is very important and involves a proxy contest, the member firm cannot vote the client's shares.

Don't Know Procedures

If one broker-dealer confirms a transaction but the contra broker-dealer does not confirm, the confirming party can demand that the contra party either confirm or don't know (DK) the trade in question.

Questions

1. Which department in a brokerage firm would handle all credit transactions for a client?

   A. Margin
   B. Cashiering
   C. Purchases and sales
   D. Reorganization

2. Once received, orders flow through a brokerage firm in which sequence?

   I. Wire room
   II. Purchases and sales department
   III. Margin department
   IV. Cashiering department

   A. I, II, III, IV
   B. I, IV, II, III
   C. II, I, IV, III
   D. III, IV, II, I

In questions 3 through 5, write T (True) or F (False) next to each statement.

3. ___ A client must be sent or given a written confirmation at or before the completion of every transaction (the settlement date).

4. ___ The cashiering department handles all credit activities.

5. ___ If there are any errors in the execution of a transaction, you should try to correct them yourself only if it happens in one of *your* client's accounts.

6. Mr. Jones buys 200 shares of RCA at 34 1/2. Later the same day his broker tells him that the report he received was in error and, in fact, the shares were bought for 34 3/4. Mr. Jones

   A. must pay 34 1/2 per share
   B. must pay 34 3/4 per share
   C. may cancel the order
   D. may require that his broker pay the difference

7. According to the 1934 act, an individual or a firm becomes a *participant* in a proxy contest if the individual or firm

   A. gives unsolicited advice to one or more stockholders
   B. gives advice (either solicited or not) to six or more stockholders
   C. gives advice (either solicited or not) to twelve or more stockholders
   D. votes 1,000 or more stocks against the management

8. A customer has an inactive account at a broker-dealer firm. The account does have a few dollars remaining in it as a free credit balance. The firm must report to the customer

   A. monthly
   B. quarterly
   C. semiannually
   D. annually

9. If a registered rep volunteers advice to her clients about how to vote in a proxy contest, she

   A. has acted illegally
   B. may do so only on listed securities
   C. may do so only if her firm specializes in that stock
   D. may have to file under SEC proxy contest rules as a participant

10. When a "contest" condition exists, a member firm can vote stock held *in street name*

   A. if the beneficial owner requests it
   B. only in favor of management
   C. only to oppose management
   D. only if the member firm owns less than 10% of the voting stock of the corporation

11. A sell-out is when

   A. the buyer of a security fails to complete the contract to buy according to its terms and the broker-dealer closes the contract by selling the security for the account of the buyer
   B. the seller of a security fails to complete the contract to sell according to its terms and the buyer closes the contract by buying the security in the best available market and charging the seller
   C. the party who requests the transfer of securities fails to pay the transfer agent's service charges and the transfer agent sells off the securities to cover the deficit
   D. a season ticketholder gives a single game's ticket to a client

12. NASD rules make it clear that any service charges (other than commissions) have to be

   A. limited to less than 1% a year
   B. based on the size and the amount of activity in a client's account
   C. standardized across the board at 5% a year
   D. reasonable and not unfairly discriminatory between clients

13. In a cash transaction on the record date, when is the ex-dividend date?

   A. Record date
   B. Business day following the record date
   C. Four days following the record date
   D. Fourth business day preceding the record date

14. According to NYSE rules, the delivery date for regular way transactions is

   A. the day of the contract
   B. the fifth business day following the day of the contract
   C. within the time specified, but not less than six business days or more than 60 calendar days
   D. the business day following the day of the contract

Answers

1. **A.** The margin department deals with credit transactions.

2. **A.** Once received, the order flows from the order department (wire room), to the purchases and sales department, to the margin department, to the cashiering department.

3. True. A client must be sent or given (not necessarily receive) a written confirmation at or before the completion of every transaction.

4. False. The margin department handles credit transactions.

5. False. You should never try to correct an error through later executions without approval from a principal.

6. **B.** If an error has been made in the notice of execution and reported to a customer, the customer must pay for the shares at the correct price.

7. **A.** Giving any unsolicited advice to a stockholder makes one a *participant* in a proxy contest. Answering customers' questions, however, is allowed and does not mean one is a participant.

8. **B.** A broker-dealer firm must send reports to customers about their accounts at least quarterly.

9. **D.** If the client asks for advice, the registered representative may give it without registering as a participant. But if the registered representative volunteers the information without being asked, she must register as a participant.

10. **A.** It would be preferable if the beneficial owner—the customer—would vote the stock he owns. But if the customer requests it, the member firm may vote the stock.

11. **A.** If a buyer fails to accept delivery of securities as stipulated in the contract and does not provide a properly completed reclamation or rejection form, the broker-dealer can sell out in the best available market and hold the buyer liable for the price of the securities and the resulting transaction costs.

12. **D.** According to the NASD Rules of Fair Practice, charges for services performed, such as the collection of dividends, safekeeping of securities held in street name, etc., must be reasonable and not unfairly discriminating between clients.

13. **B.** In a cash transaction on the record date, the purchaser's trade date and settlement occur on the record date. Therefore, the first date on which the purchaser would not receive the dividend is the business day after the record date.

14. **B.** Settlement (regular way) is the fifth business day after the trade date.

Accrued Interest Calculations

Accrued interest affects bond transactions if a bond trades between coupon dates. The buyer pays the accrued interest to the seller and receives the full interest payment on the next coupon date. Interest begins accruing on the last interest payment date and is computed up to, but not including, the settlement date.

Accrued interest and the dated date. The date from which interest accrual begins is called the *dated date*.

Corporate and Municipal Bonds

Unless the settlement date on a bond transaction coincides with the bond's most current interest payment date, the cost of the bond to the buyer will include accrued interest. The bond proceeds to the seller will include accrued interest. Accrued interest is calculated from the last interest payment date up to, *but not including, the settlement date.*

Transactions in income bonds do not carry accrued interest. These bonds pay interest to bondholders only if such interest is actually earned by the issuing corporation.

Accrued Interest Calculation: 360-day Year

Accrued interest on corporate and municipal bonds is calculated for a 360-day year of 30-day months. For example, if an F&A corporate or municipal bond is traded regular way on Monday, March 5th, the number of days of accrued interest would be:

February	30 days
March 5th trade	11 days (settles March 12th)
	41 days

Therefore, interest would accrue up to, but not including, the settlement date of March 12th (or 5 + 6).

always use this

U.S. Government Bonds

Accrued Interest Calculation: 365-day Year

Calculating time. For calculating time elapsed since the most recent interest payment on a government bond, an actual-days-elapsed method is used instead of the 30-day-month, 360-day-year method used for corporate and municipal bonds. For example, if an F&A government bond is traded regular way on Monday, March 5th, the number of days of accrued interest would be:

February	28 days
March	5 days
	33 days (up to, but not including, the March 6th [next day] settlement date)

Feb 1st Aug 1st paying div.

Questions

1. Sara Long purchased a 7% J&J 15 municipal bond on March 18th in a regular way trade. How much accrued interest will she pay?

   A. $13.04
   B. $13.61
   C. $15.36
   D. $16.52

   next day

2. A customer purchased a T bond in a regular way transaction on Monday, April 4th. Settlement will be on

   A. Monday, April 4th
   B. Tuesday, April 5th
   C. Friday, April 8th
   D. Monday, April 11th

3. A customer purchased a T bond in a regular way transaction on Monday, April 4th. The bond is a J&J bond. How many days of accrued interest will the seller receive?

   A. 79
   B. 80
   C. 94
   D. 95

4. A J&J Treasury bond with a 10 1/4% coupon due July 1, 1999, is purchased in a cash transaction with a settlement date of February 24th. What are the number of days of accrued interest?

   A. 53
   B. 54
   C. 55
   D. 63

5. A bond is dated June 1, 1995. The first interest payment is on January 1, 1996. How many months will the first and second interest payments cover?

   A. 1 month for the first, 5 months for the second
   B. 1 month for the first, 6 months for the second
   C. 7 months for the first, 5 months for the second
   D. 7 months for the first, 6 months for the second

Answers

1.   **B.**   Interest was paid up to but not including January 15th when the last payment was made. This leaves 16 days of interest accrual in January (30 – 14). Settlement on the trade is March 25th (18 + 7 [five business days plus the weekend]). Interest accrues for the seller, then, through March 24th. Interest accrues, therefore, for 70 days (Jan 16 + Feb 30 + Mar 24). The amount of accrued interest is calculated as follows: $70 (annual interest) times 70 divided by 360 (the portion of the year accrued) equals $13.61.

2.   **B.**   Regular way settlement on government securities is the next business day.

3.   **C.**

January	31 days
February	28 days
March	31 days
April	4 days
Total	94 days

Remember that government obligations accrue interest for the actual number of days (up to but not including settlement).

4.   **B.**   A coupon bond starts accruing interest on the payment date of the previous coupon (January 1st) and accrues up to but not including the settlement date (February 24th) because it was a cash settlement. Because accrued interest on government bonds is computed actual days, actual year, 31 for Jan plus 23 for Feb equals 54 days.

5.   **D.**   Because the bond is dated June 1st with the first interest payment the following January 1st, the initial payment covers seven months of interest. Thereafter, the bond will pay interest semi-annually, as bonds normally do.

Rules of Good Delivery

Round lots: stocks. A round lot for common stock is 100 shares or any multiple thereof.

Round lots: bonds. A round lot for bonds is $1,000 face amount or multiples thereof. Good delivery of fully registered bonds is limited to $100,000 face value.

Registered vs. bearer form. Normal delivery, dealer to dealer, is $1,000 or $5,000 bearer bonds.

Overdelivery and underdelivery. If the customer overdelivers or underdelivers, the transaction is not good delivery.

Good delivery clearing rule (100-share uniform units). Odd lot certificates can be used to clear round lot trades provided the odd lot certificates add up to round lots.

Missing coupons. The cash value of missing coupons is deducted from the sale proceeds to the customer.

Partially called bonds. If a particular bond issue (or preferred stock) has been partially called by the issuer, no bonds in that issue are good delivery between brokers. If the entire bond issue has been called, normal good delivery rules apply.

Certificate Negotiability

The final authority on certificate negotiability is the transfer agent. All securities transfers must be accompanied by a **uniform transfer instruction form**.

Assignment. All stock and bond certificates must be *assigned* by the owner(s) whose name is registered on the face of the certificate. Certificates registered in joint name require the signatures of all owners. Endorsement by the customer may be made on the back of the certificate on the assignment line or by signing a detached assignment.

If there has been an alteration or correction to the assignment, a full explanation of the change signed by the person or firm who executed the correction must be attached.

Risk of lost certificate. If there is a risk that the certificate may be lost, the customer should either fill in the line granting power of attorney to another party or use a stock power.

Certificate unavailable. No assignment is necessary if the stock is in street name.

Signature guarantee. All customer signatures must be guaranteed by a member of an exchange, by a national bank or by another party acceptable to the transfer agent.

Signature requirements. The customer's signature must match exactly the name registered on the face of the security, without abbreviation or enlargement. An exception is made for certificates registered in corporate name, in which case the following interchangeable endorsements are acceptable: "Company" or "Co." and "and" or "&."

Legal transfer items. Any form of registration other than individual or joint ownership may require supporting guarantees or documentation to render a certificate negotiable.

Invalid signatures. The executor or administrator of the estate must either endorse the certificate or furnish stock power and must transfer the securities to the name of the estate before they can be sold.

Minors' signatures are invalid for securities registration purposes.

Good condition of security. If a certificate is mutilated or appears to be counterfeit, appropriate authentication by the transfer agent, registrar or issuer must be obtained before the transfer agent can accept the security for replacement. If there is doubt about the authenticity of the certificate, the transfer agent will require a surety bond.

NASD CUSIP Regulations

The CUSIP number is required information on the uniform transfer instruction form, the uniform delivery ticket and the uniform comparison or confirmation.

MSRB Regulations: Legal Opinion

In municipal bond trading, unless the bond is traded and stamped "ex-legal," the legal opinion must be printed on or attached to the bond as evidence of the validity of the bond offering. Securities traded ex-legal are in good delivery condition without the legal opinion.

Questions

1. To be considered in good delivery form, certificates must be

   A. accompanied by a preliminary prospectus

   B. called for redemption by the issuing body

   C. accompanied by an assignment or a stock power

   D. in the name of the deceased person, if he died after the trade date

2. Your client has a certificate registered in his own name. To be a good delivery, the certificate must be accompanied by

   A. a properly executed assignment to the brokerage firm, on the reverse side of the certificate

   B. the promise that it has not been called for redemption

   C. a buyer's option

   D. the legal opinion, unless the client is selling municipal bonds

3. Which of the following would be considered good delivery for a sale of 600 shares of ABC?

   A. 3 certificates for 100 shares each and 8 certificates for 25 shares each

   B. 2 certificates for 100 shares each and 4 certificates for 50 shares each

   C. 6 certificates for 75 shares each and 6 certificates for 25 shares each

   D. 8 certificates for 75 shares each

Answers

1. **C.** To be considered in good delivery form, certificates must be accompanied by an assignment or a stock power.

2. **A.** If the certificate is registered in your client's name, a stock power and a properly executed assignment to the brokerage firm must appear on the reverse side of the certificate.

3. **C.** Each certificate for 25 shares can be matched to a certificate for 75 shares to make a round lot; with six round lots, these certificates would be considered good delivery. Answer A is only 500 shares; Answer B includes only 400 shares; and Answer D cannot be bunched into round lots.

Ethics in the Securities Industry

Prohibited Practices

Manipulative and Fraudulent Devices

NASD member firms are strictly prohibited from using manipulative, deceptive or other fraudulent tactics or methods to effect a transaction or in an attempt to induce the sale or purchase of a security. A customer may bring suit for damages under the act of 1934 within three years of the alleged manipulation and within one year of discovering it. There is no dollar limit placed on damages in lawsuits based on allegations of manipulation.

Outside Business Activity

Associated persons of member firms are prohibited from engaging in **private securities transactions** without the express knowledge and consent of their employing broker-dealers. Violations of the private securities transaction regulations are often referred to as **selling away**.

Suitability of Recommendations to Customers

Investment recommendations must be suitable and in keeping with customer needs and objectives.

Fair Dealing

The NASD's Rules of Fair Practice and the laws of most states require broker-dealers, registered reps and investment advisers to inquire into a customer's financial situation before making any recommendation to purchase, sell or exchange securities. The following activities are considered violations of the rules regarding fair dealing:

- recommending speculative securities without finding out the customer's financial situation and being assured that the customer can bear the risk;
- trading that is excessive in either size or frequency in a customer's account;
- short-term trading of mutual funds;
- setting up fictitious accounts to transact business that otherwise would be prohibited;
- making unauthorized transactions or use of funds;
- recommending purchases that are inconsistent with the customer's ability to pay; and
- committing fraudulent acts.

Excessive Trading: Churning

Engaging aggressively or excessively in trading a customer's account primarily to generate commissions is an abuse of fiduciary responsibility known as *churning* and is strictly prohibited.

Influencing or Rewarding Employees of Other Firms

Member broker-dealers are not permitted to distribute business-related compensation to the employees of other member firms.

Employment contracts. This rule does not apply to legitimate employment contracts in which an employee of one firm supplies or performs services for another firm.

Selling Dividends

A registered representative is forbidden to encourage an investor to purchase fund shares prior to a distribution because of the tax liability, and doing so is known as *selling dividends*.

Breakpoint Sales

Encouraging a customer to purchase investment company shares in an amount just under a dollar bracket amount that would qualify the investment for a reduction in sales charges, or remaining silent when a customer unknowingly requests such a transaction, is highly unethical and a violation of the Rules of Fair Practice.

Borrowing and Lending

Borrowing money or securities from a client. Registered reps and investment advisers are prohibited from borrowing money or securities from a client *unless* the client is a bank, broker-dealer or other financial institution that is in the business of lending money.

Loaning money or securities to a client. Registered reps and investment advisers are prohibited from lending money or securities to clients. This prohibition against lending money does not include broker-dealers making margin loans or investment advisers lending money as part of their normal business practices.

Misrepresentations

Registered reps and investment advisers are prohibited from misrepresenting themselves or their services to clients or potential clients. Included misrepresentations covering:

- qualifications, experience and education
- nature of services offered
- fees to be charged

Prohibitions Against Guarantees and Sharing in Customer Accounts

Broker-dealers, investment advisers and registered reps must not guarantee any customer against a loss or guarantee that a gain will be achieved in his account. Except in limited circumstances, members, advisers and representatives are also prohibited from sharing in any profits or losses in a customer's account. An exception will be made if a joint account has received *prior* written approval, and the registered representative shares in the profits and losses only to the extent of his *proportionate contribution* to the account.

Misuse of Nonpublic Information

The Investment Advisers Act of 1940 established strict regulations concerning the use and misuse of nonpublic (inside) information.

Information Obtained as a Fiduciary

Confidentiality of customer information. Employees of broker-dealers and investment advisers may not divulge personal information about customers without the express permission of the customer.

Numbered accounts. Accounts designated by a number or a letter rather than a name are permitted if the member has on file a signed statement from the customer claiming ownership of that account.

Other Unethical Trading Practices

Artificial Transactions

Artificial transactions of all types are strictly prohibited.

Transactions Involving No Change (Wash Sale) in Beneficial Ownership

Broker-dealers are prohibited from entering orders for the purchase or sale of securities with the knowledge that contra orders for the same stock, in the same amount, at approximately the same price have been or will be placed for the same customer or for different parties working in concert.

Spreading False and Misleading Information

Broker-dealers are prohibited from using their positions as centers of influence and opinion makers to sway customers by promoting and disseminating false or misleading information contrived for the purpose of inducing people to buy or sell a particular stock.

Front-running

When holding a customer's order to sell, a broker-dealer is prohibited from selling stock for a firm trading account at or above the price at which the customer's order is subsequently filled.

Capping

Any attempt to place selling pressure on a stock in order to keep a price low or move it lower is known as *capping* and is prohibited by the NASD's Rules of Fair Practice.

Criminal Penalties

If a person is convicted of willfully violating federal securities regulations, or of knowingly making false or misleading statements in a registration document, that person can be fined up to $1,000,000, sentenced to prison for not more than ten years, or both; the maximum fine is $2,500,000 for other than a natural person.

Questions

1. According to the Securities Exchange Act of 1934, which of the following statements is(are) true?

   A. Matching is prohibited.
   B. Pegging or fixing is not allowed.
   C. Using any means to create the appearance of active trading in a security is prohibited.
   D. All of the above statements are true.

2. Under the Securities Exchange Act of 1934, it is unlawful to

   I. enact a series of trades in a security to make it appear as if it is actively traded
   II. induce the sale of a security through misleading statements
   III. give out information about the actions of a person or a group that might affect the price of a security

   A. I only
   B. I and III only
   C. II only
   D. I, II and III

Answers

1. **D.** *Matching* is entering identical orders to buy and sell a security. It would be done to create the illusion of high activity in a particular stock. It is prohibited activity. *Pegging* is entering bids for a security that is above the offering price. Broker-dealers are prohibited from pegging. Anything that creates an appearance of activity in a stock when it is not really there is considered to be market manipulation and is prohibited by the act of 1934.

2. **D.** All of the activities listed are manipulative or deceptive devices. They are prohibited by the act of 1934.

10 Margin Accounts

Extension of Credit in the Securities Industry

Regulation T

Under **Regulation T (Reg T)**, the FRB sets the minimum amount a customer must deposit when purchasing securities from a broker-dealer or when selling securities short. Currently, the required minimum deposit is 50% of the market value of the securities at the time of purchase. Certain securities are exempt from the Reg T initial margin requirement, including U.S. government securities and municipal bonds.

Customers making purchases in cash accounts must make payment in full not later than the seventh business day after the trade date. Margin account customers must meet initial margin calls on new commitments not later than the seventh business day after the trade date.

7th B. Day

Marginable Securities

Eligible Securities

Marginable securities include:

- stocks and bonds listed on an exchange;
- stocks listed as eligible for trading in the NASDAQ/NMS;

- certain OTC securities designated by the FRB; and
- warrants (for listed and designated securities only).

Noneligible Securities

The following investment instruments cannot be used as collateral for loans, must be purchased in a cash account and must be paid for in full:

- put and call options;
- common and preferred OTC stocks not designated by the FRB;
- rights;
- insurance contracts; and
- new issues for the first 30 calendar days.

Exempt Securities

Securities exempt from Reg T are:

- U.S. Treasury bills, notes and bonds;
- government agency securities;
- municipal securities; and
- corporate straight debt (nonconvertible) securities.

These securities can be bought or sold in a margin account, subject to whatever initial payment the broker-dealer feels is reasonable. However, the NYSE and NASD require member firms to abide by minimum margin maintenance requirements when dealing in exempt securities.

NASD and NYSE Requirements

Minimum Maintenance Requirements

NASD/NYSE margin maintenance requirements come into effect if and when the market moves adversely. A margin maintenance call is a demand that the client make additional payment on his loan at once to the lending broker-dealer. If payment is not made, the broker-dealer will liquidate his securities.

The minimum maintenence requirement for long common stock is 25% of the CMV. In general the minimum maintenance requirements for exempt securities are the same as the initial requirements.

$2,000 Minimum Equity Deposit

The NYSE and NASD require that each new margin account opened be subject to a minimum deposit of $2,000. An investor must meet the larger of either the 50% Reg T requirement or the NASD/NYSE requirement of $2,000. If the initial transaction in a margin account is for less than $2,000, the investor is not required to deposit more than the total cost of the transaction.

Broker-Dealer (House) Requirements

Broker-dealers are free to establish and apply higher minimum requirements for the accounts they hold.

Current Requirements

Initial requirement. A customer buying securities in a margin account is required to deposit initially a certain percentage of the purchase cost of the securities.

Reg T applies to all *nonexempt* margin securities. Margin requirements as set by the FRB are currently 50%. Therefore at 50% margin, for every $100 worth of securities purchased, the customer must deposit $50 and the broker-dealer advances the other $50 as a loan against the securities. The current initial margin requirement of 50% of the trading commitment also means that the *initial loan*

value is 50%. The loan value of a security is the complement of the margin requirement.

Maintenance requirement. A **maintenance call** is sent to a client whose account falls below the required **equity** (**EQ**) level. If a change in market value causes equity to fall below $2,000, no maintenance call will be issued. The NYSE/NASD requirement prevents a brokerage firm from lending money to a client or permitting withdrawals of cash or securities by a client whose account equity is $2,000 or less. A broker may waive the **margin call** if the balance due is less than $500 or if the total purchase is less than $1,000.

Buying power. To calculate the buying power in an account, first take the amount of money in the account and divide it by the current margin requirement (as an example, if there is $2,700 cash in the account, dividing $2,700 by 50% gives you $5,400 in buying power). To this amount, add the additional money that would be available if the marginable securities in the account were fully margined (as an example, if the account holds $12,600 of fully paid, marginable securities, the customer could purchase an additional $12,600 of securities at a 50% Reg T requirement without putting up additional cash). The total of these two numbers ($18,000) is the account's buying power.

When Issued Securities

Purchases of when issued securities are subject to the same Reg T and NASD/NYSE requirements as other securities purchases. If the when issued security is part of a *new issue*, 100% of the purchase price must be deposited. If the when issued security is not part of a new issue (or is not in some other way exempt from Reg T), Reg T margin requirements apply. If Reg T is 50%, a customer must deposit 50% when purchasing nonexempt when issued securities on margin.

Purchasing Bonds in a Margin Account

Initial requirement. Nonconvertible bonds are subject to the NASD/NYSE $2,000 initial margin requirement. Convertible corporate bonds are subject to the same Reg T requirements as marginable (nonexempt) stocks (50%).

Margin Accounting

Initial Requirements

A customer with a margin account has current market value (in this case, of securities), debt (the loan from the firm) on which he pays interest and equity (the difference between the market value and the loan balance).

If the customer makes a purchase of 200 shares of XYZ stock at $34 per share, for example, there will appear a $6,800 debit in the account. The customer must deposit $3,400 in cash to meet the 50% Reg T requirement, which leaves a debit balance of $3,400, the amount the firm has loaned for the purchase.

The customer's margin account now has 200 shares of XYZ with a market value of $6,800, no cash, a debit balance of $3,400, equity of $3,400 and $0 in excess equity. The equity in an account does not represent a cash balance; it represents that portion of the securities fully owned by the customer. In this example, the account balance would appear as follows:

```
$ 6,800   CMV
- 3,400   DR
$ 3,400   EQ
```

Initial Transaction and Reg T Initial Margin

A customer opens a margin account and purchases 500 shares of ALFA at $16 per share, a total of $8,000 worth of ALFA common stock. The first step the firm takes is to issue a Reg T initial margin call for $4,000 (50% of the cost of the stocks). When the customer makes the required deposit, the account is at exactly 50% margin. The equation for a long position in a margin account is CMV minus DR equals customer EQ.

Maintenance Requirements

SRO Maintenance Requirements

NASD/NYSE margin maintenance requirements come into effect if and when the market moves adversely. Maintenance requirements on short sale positions are higher than on long positions because of the greater risks of this trading technique. If a client shorts a low-priced stock, trading—for example—at $1 per share, the $2.50-per-share maintenance requirement would be in effect.

If a client's equity in a margin account falls below the *maintenance* minimum however, a maintenance call will be issued to restore the equity to the proper amount.

$2,000 minimum. If a customer asks to withdraw cash or securities from a margin account, the withdrawal would not be allowed if it would take the account equity below the $2,000 minimum equity threshold. If the customer's equity level declines as the result of lower market prices, a maintenance call will be issued if the decline puts the account under the $2,000 minimum.

House Maintenance Requirements   30% in genal

On long positions, the typical **house maintenance is 30%** rather than 25%. Broker-dealers can set house requirements higher than either Reg T initial or NYSE/NASD initial and minimum maintenance requirements, *but never lower*.

How Changes in Market Value Affect Maintenance Requirements

Increase in Market Value

As the market value of a stock goes up, equity in the account increases; and as the market value falls, equity decreases. The debit balance stays the same until cash is either deposited to or withdrawn from the account.

As an example, look at the account of a customer who purchases 400 shares of DWQ at 38 and deposits $7,600. If DWQ appreciates from $38 to $42 per share, the CMV of the account rises $1,600 (400 shares times $4), from $15,200 to $16,800. The debit remains $7,600. The result is an increase in equity of $1,600, to $9,200. The increase affects the equity dollar for dollar. The Reg T requirement for this account is 50% of the CMV (which is now $16,800), or $8,400.

Excess Equity

Buying power. To determine the buying power of a cash deposit when Reg T is 50%, multiply the amount of cash by two. Reg T excess equity can be withdrawn in cash or used to make new margin commitments.

Using excess equity to purchase stock. The customer from the previous example now has excess equity of $800, which can be used to purchase $1,600 of stock:

$$EE + Reg\ T\ (50\%) = Buying\ power$$

Withdrawing excess equity. A customer can withdraw cash equal to the excess equity. By doing so, the customer will increase his debit by borrowing the money against the increased loan value of the securities.

Cash withdrawals. When a customer withdraws money from a margin account, he is increasing the amount of the loan outstanding on the securities in the account.

Decrease in Market Value

If the stock decreases in value, the equity in the account will fall dollar for dollar with the market value of the stock. The debit balance does not change; it is a record of money borrowed and cash coming into and going out of the account. CMV is a measure of the securities' value in the account. Equity is the CMV minus the debit; it is the customer's share of the market value.

Decline in market value and restricted accounts. Declines in market value impact a customer's equity dollar for dollar (for example, a $12,000 loss in market value results in a $12,000 loss in customer equity). The debit balance remains

unchanged because declines in market value do not change the money amount owed to the broker-dealer.

Nonrequired Cash Deposits

Any deposit of cash that is not needed to meet a margin call is used to pay off part of the debit balance. Anything that reduces the debit balance increases equity. Any nonrequired cash deposit is always available for the customer to withdraw.

New debits that are not related to purchases of additional securities increase the debit balance in the account and decrease equity.

Reg T excess equity. Any margin account in which the customer's equity is more than 50% of the current market value of the securities in the account is said to have Reg T *excess equity*. The customer may withdraw this excess equity, leave it in the account to be applied against the debit balance or use it to purchase additional securities.

Maintenance Calls

If an account drops below the required minimum maintenance level, the firm may *mark to the market* and the client will receive a maintenance call. To calculate the SRO-required minimum maintenance equity, multiply the current market value by 25%.

Calculating Market Value at Minimum Maintenance

(drop ⅓ of original purchase price)

The following formula can be used to calculate how low the value of securities can go in the market before a client is sent a maintenance call.

$$DR + 75\% = CMV\ at\ min.\ maintenance$$

When equity reaches the allowable minimum of 25% of current market value, the debit balance represents the remaining 75%. If the debit exceeds 75% of CMV, equity will be below maintenance and the customer will receive a maintenance call.

Using Fully Paid Securities to Meet Margin Requirements

Fully paid securities may be used to purchase stock in a margin account. When meeting margin requirements, a customer may deposit securities with a loan value equal to the debit in the account. The Reg T loan value of stock is currently 50% of its CMV. The formula for calculating the dollar amount of stock necessary to meet a Reg T call is:

$$\frac{\text{Margin call in \$}}{100\% - \text{Reg T}\%} = \text{Reg T call}$$

Restricted Accounts

[handwritten: eq is < 50% initial > 25% cmv]

A restricted account is a margin account in which the equity is less than the Reg T initial requirement. When equity falls between the 50% Reg T initial margin requirement and the 25% minimum maintenance, the account becomes restricted. When equity falls below 50% of market value and an account becomes restricted, the Reg T *retention requirement* mandates that the customer may not withdraw securities without depositing an amount equal to 50% of whatever is withdrawn. Even in a restricted margin account, Reg T permits 50% of the proceeds of any sale to be made available to the customer.

Activity in a Restricted Account

Purchasing additional shares. If an investor wants to purchase additional shares in a restricted margin account, he must deposit either cash or securities equal to 50% of the purchase price.

Selling shares. Under the retention requirement, 50% of the proceeds of any sale must be made available to the investor. However, because any sale proceeds will have been applied towards reducing the investor's debit balance, any amount subsequently withdrawn from the account will be added to his debit balance.

Cash available for withdrawal. In order to determine how much of the proceeds from a sale is

available to a client who wishes to make a cash withdrawal from a restricted account, two separate calculations must be made. For the first calculation, multiply the proceeds by 50%:

$$50\% \times \text{Proceeds of sale} = \text{Amount available}$$

Then take into account the excess equity that might also be available for withdrawal:

$$\text{EQ} - \text{Margin required} = \text{EE available}$$

Cash withdrawals. A customer with a restricted margin account is entitled to withdraw cash dividends and interest. A dividend or an interest payment received by the account reduces the debit. If the customer withdraws that amount, the debit increases and the account is back where it was before the dividend was received, as if nothing happened.

For any other cash withdrawal, a customer with a restricted account must either deposit additional marginable securities with a loan value equal to the amount of the cash withdrawal or have SMA.

Stock withdrawals. If the customer wants to withdraw stock from his account, he must deposit cash or fully paid stock equal to the retention requirement.

Same-day substitution of stock. A client with a margin account can sell one stock and buy an equivalent amount of stock without incurring a Reg T call, resulting in a same-day substitution.

Deadlines for Meeting Margin Calls

Reg T requires all margin account customers to meet initial margin calls on new commitments not later than the *seventh business day* after the trade date.

Credit extensions for margin customers. A broker-dealer may apply to an SRO for permission to extend credit beyond the seventh business day to margin account customers late in meeting a margin call.

Forced sell-outs. If a margin customer does not meet a Reg T initial margin call by the seventh business day and no extension has been applied for, the broker-dealer must liquidate enough securities in the account to satisfy the call in full. In addition, the firm must *freeze the account for 90 days*. For amounts less than $500, the broker-dealer can choose to take no action.

Short Sales and Margin Requirements

Reg T Margin Requirements on Short Sales

The Reg T initial margin requirement on short sales is 50% of the sale proceeds. Reg T uses the phrase "150% of the current market value of the security" to indicate that the full amount (100%) of the sale proceeds *plus* an additional 50% initial margin on the position must be deposited in the account at the time of the transaction.

NYSE $2,000 minimum. When establishing a short margin position, a client must always deposit a minimum of $2,000.

Margin Maintenance Calls on Short Sales

NASD/NYSE margin maintenance requirements on short positions (30%) are higher than on long positions (25%), and house maintenance requirements on short positions might be higher still.

The equation for determining a client's equity in a short position is:

$$CR - SMV = Client\ EQ$$

To illustrate, assume that a customer sells short 100 shares of DWQ at 35 for proceeds of $3,500 and deposits the 50% Reg T initial margin requirement of $1,750 ($5,250 total). Over the two weeks following the short sale, the market price of the stock advances.

To determine the maximum market value to which a short sale position can advance before a margin maintenance call will be issued, the following formula is used:

about 15.5% increase

Total CR ÷ 130% = Maximum market value

Applying this formula to the previous illustration, the maximum market value to which the short

position could advance would be $4,038.50 ($5,250 ÷ 130%), or 40 3/8 per share.

Short Against the Box

Margin requirement. For margin purposes, the short against the box position is treated as a net-zero position. Because of this, there is no Reg T initial requirement when an investor establishes the short against the box position. In effect, the investor deposits the certificate for the long stock instead of depositing Reg T.

Maintenance requirement. There is, however, a maintenance requirement. The investor must leave on deposit 5% of the market value of the long side. The fact that being short against the box is treated as a net-zero position affects the long side in two more ways: (1) if the investor sells the long stock before replacing the borrowed stock, that sale is considered a short sale (the ticket is marked "short," and the sale is not exempt from the plus tick rule) and (2) the investor may not deliver the long stock if there is a tender offer for it.

Closing a short against the box. A short against the box transaction is closed out when the customer instructs the broker-dealer to release the box stock and pair off the offsetting long and short positions. If the customer switches strategies and elects to sell the box stock, the sale is not a long sale. It must be executed as a short sale subject to the plus tick rule, and the order ticket must be marked "short."

Short Accounts

Credit balance. Clients do not borrow money for short positions; they sell securities, and they make margin deposits to cover their risk. The resulting credit balance represents cash, which is available when a client wants to purchase the securities to close the short position.

Equity. In a short account, equity equals the amount by which the credit balance exceeds the current market value of the securities short in the account.

Buying power. A decline in the market value of a security below the original short sale price may produce excess equity in a client's margin account.

This buying power can be preserved as SMA if not used.

Restricted accounts. In a short account, restriction can take place when a stock appreciates above the selling price.

Effect on SMA. When a short position is closed by purchasing securities to cover the short, however, there is no sale and no automatic 50% release. The SMA will change only if excess equity generated by covering the short position exceeds the existing SMA balance.

Combined Accounts

In combined accounts, long and short positions are netted out and viewed as a single number to determine initial margin requirements and SMA balances.

Determining Customer Equity in a Combined Account

Computing equity. To compute the equity in a combined account, both the long and short formulas are used:

	Long market value
plus	Credit balance
minus	Short market value
minus	Debit balance
equals	Equity

Determining Margin Requirements in a Combined Account

Reg T margin requirement. To calculate the Reg T requirement for a combined account, calculate the Reg T requirement for the long and short accounts separately and then combine them.

Maintenance. To calculate the SRO maintenance requirement for combined accounts, calculate the long and short positions separately. For a long position, the NYSE requirement is 25% of the CMV. For a short position, the NYSE requirement is 30% of the CMV.

Questions

1. A customer's margin account contains the following registered nonexempt securities:

   100 shares of EWH, CMV $40 per share
   100 shares of XYZ, CMV $50 per share
   100 shares of ABC, CMV $80 per share

   The account has a debit balance of $10,800, and the initial margin requirement is 50%. How much equity is in the account?

   A. $4,030
   B. $6,200
   C. $11,050
   D. $17,000

2. In the account described in the preceding question, the excess equity is

   A. $0
   B. $2,300
   C. $6,200
   D. $8,500

Use the following information to answer questions 3 through 6.

With the initial margin requirement at 50%, a customer purchased 100 shares of Xerox (XRX) at $100 per share and deposited $5,000. XRX then increases in value to $150 per share.

3. With XRX at $150 per share, the customer's equity in the account is

   A. $5,000
   B. $7,500
   C. $10,000
   D. $15,000

4. What is the excess equity in the account?

   A. $2,500
   B. $5,000
   C. $7,500
   D. $10,000

5. How much more XRX can the customer purchase without depositing additional cash?

   A. $2,500
   B. $5,000
   C. $7,500
   D. $10,000

6. How much cash can the customer withdraw from the account without selling any XRX?

   A. $2,500
   B. $5,000
   C. $7,500
   D. $10,000

7. When stock held in a margin account appreciates, which of the following increase(s)?

   I.   Current market value
   II. Debit balance
   III. equity

   A. I only
   B. I and III only
   C. II only
   D. I, II and III

8. A client chooses to leave a dividend payment in a margin account; as a result, the

   I.   equity increases
   II. equity decreases
   III. debit balance increases
   IV. debit balance decreases

   A. I and III
   B. I and IV
   C. II and III
   D. II and IV

9. A client has a margin account with $23,000 in securities and a debit of $12,000. Which of the following statements are true? (Reg T is 50%.)

   I.   The account is restricted.
   II. The client will receive a margin call for $500.
   III. The client may withdraw securities if he deposits 50% of the securities' value.
   IV. The account has excess equity of $5,250.

   A. I and II only
   B. I and III only
   C. II, III and IV only
   D. I, II, III and IV

10. A client has a margin account with $23,000 in securities and a debit of $12,000. The stock increases in value to $26,000. How much money may the client withdraw from the account?

    A. $1,000
    B. $2,000
    C. $3,000
    D. $4,000

11. Jan Doe has a margin account with a market value of $8,000 and a debit of $4,200. She would like to withdraw $4,000 of the securities and deposit other securities to satisfy the retention requirement. What dollar value of securities must she deposit?

    A. $2,000
    B. $3,000
    C. $4,000
    D. $4,200

12. A customer sells short against the box 100 shares of ABC at 50. Four months later, when ABC is at 40, the customer delivers the long shares to cover his short position. How much can be withdrawn from the account?

    A. $1,000
    B. $4,000
    C. $5,000
    D. $7,500

13. A customer sells short 100 shares of Xerox at $80 per share and meets the minimum Reg T requirement. Two months later, she covers her short position by buying Xerox at $70 per share. This was her only transaction in the account. What is the maximum amount she can withdraw from the account after closing the short position? (Reg T is 50%.)

   A. $1,000
   B. $4,000
   C. $5,000
   D. $12,000

14. A customer has a short account with $25,000 short market value, $37,000 credit balance and SMA of $500. What is the maximum short market value for this account before the customer will incur an NYSE maintenance call?

   A. $28,462
   B. $33,020
   C. $33,500
   D. $48,100

Answers

1. **B.** The total market value in the account is $17,000. CMV − DR = EQ; $17,000 CMV − $10,800 DR = $6,200.

2. **A.** The required equity is $8,500 (50% × $17,000 CMV). The account has no excess equity. It is, in fact, restricted—that is, it is below the Reg T amount.

3. **C.** The account now looks like this:

$15,000	CMV
− 5,000	DR
$10,000	EQ

4. **A.** The account now looks like this:

$10,000	EQ
− 7,500	Reg T
$ 2,500	EE

5. **B.** The purchasing power is $5,000 ($2,500 EE ÷ 50% Reg T).

6. **A.** The customer could withdraw cash equal to the excess equity.

7. **B.** The debit balance changes only when money is borrowed or deposited. A withdrawal of cash is borrowing against the loan value of the securities in the account and increases the debit balance. A deposit of cash into the account reduces the debit balance.

8. **B.** Any cash deposit lowers the debit balance. A lower debit balance with no change in market value results in higher equity.

9. **B.** The account is restricted by $500. The client will not, however, receive a margin call for the $500 because Reg T applies only to the initial purchase. Because the account is restricted, any withdrawal of securities requires a cash deposit of 50% or a deposit of securities with a loan value of 50% of the value of the securities withdrawn. The

account is $5,250 above the required minimum, but this amount is not considered excess equity.

10. **A.** The account now has equity of $14,000. The Reg T requirement is $13,000. This leaves $1,000 in excess equity that may be withdrawn.

$ 26,000	CMV
− 12,000	DR
$ 14,000	EQ
− 13,000	Reg T
$ 1,000	EE

11. **C.** A withdrawal of $4,000 of securities from a restricted account would require a cash deposit of $2,000 ($4,000 × 50%). If securities are deposited, they must have a loan value of $2,000. Loan value is currently 50%, so Jan must deposit $4,000 in securities ($2,000 ÷ 50%, or $2,000 × 2).

12. **C.** Although the question tells us that the stock was at $40 when the customer delivered the long shares, we do not know what the customer actually paid for the stock. We do know how much the stock was sold for. As soon as the customer delivers the long shares against the short position, he is free to withdraw the sale proceeds. This is virtually the same as if he had bought the stock and then sold it, except that he does not deliver the shares until some time after the sale date.

13. **C.** The customer sold the stock at $80 per share and deposited $4,000 per the Reg T requirement ($8,000 × 50%). She now has an SMV of $8,000 and a credit balance of $12,000 ($8,000 sale proceeds + $4,000 deposit). The market value of the stock is now down to $7,000 and the customer uses $7,000 of her credit balance to purchase the shares and close the short position. The remaining credit balance is all excess equity because she no longer has any short position and the entire amount may be withdrawn. A second way to look at the account is to see that after the short position is closed, the customer may withdraw the Reg T deposit and the $1,000 profit ($8,000 sale proceeds − $7,000 purchase price).

14. **A.** When the account is at minimum maintenance level, the equity will be 30% of market value. Because the formula to compute equity for a short account is CR minus SMV, the credit balance will be 130% of market value when the account is at minimum maintenance. The credit balance will be the only number that is constant as the market increases, so we must use the credit balance to calculate the maximum value the securities can be before a call is issued:

$$\frac{CR}{130\%} = \frac{\$37,000}{1.30} = \$28,461.54$$

Special Memorandum Account

Excess equity in a margin account can be credited to the special memorandum account. SMA is a line of credit, a limit on the amount of money a client can borrow now or in the future. Clients of brokerage firms may withdraw funds from SMAs. When a client withdraws or uses SMA, she is actually borrowing more money from the broker-dealer, thereby increasing the debit balance in her account. The client will owe interest on any amount withdrawn or borrowed.

Clients may always use the balance in their SMAs unless the use will cause the account equity to drop below the minimum maintenance requirement.

The most important characteristics of SMA are:

- SMA *increases* as the excess equity in a margin account increases.
- SMA *does not decrease* as the result of market value decreases.
- SMA may be more than excess equity or may exist even if there is no excess equity in the account.

Generating SMA

An SMA balance can be generated when excess equity is credited to SMA or by any of the following means:

- nonrequired cash deposits
- dividends and interest earned
- loan value

Excess Equity

Excess equity can be borrowed, used to purchase additional securities or left in the account to be credited to SMA. Once SMA is credited to a client's account, only the client's use of it can deplete it. Market or broker actions cannot take away the SMA line of credit.

Selling securities. Reg T retention requirements allow an investor to withdraw or use for additional purchases 50% of the proceeds of any sale in a margin account. If the amount is not used immediately, it is credited to SMA.

New excess equity (resulting from sale proceeds) is not added to the SMA. Excess equity and SMA are always compared, and the greater of the two becomes the new SMA.

Depleting SMA

An SMA balance is depleted by all of the following:

- withdrawing cash from a margin account
- new margin purchases
- withdrawing securities

Using SMA to buy stock. SMA is a line of credit and an investor can use it to meet the margin requirements on stock purchases. SMA can be used to meet a Reg T call, but because it does not represent an actual cash deposit, it does not lower the debit when used.

Withdrawing cash. Clients may use SMA to withdraw money from their margin accounts. To determine how much SMA can be used without going below the 25% minimum requirement, calculate the difference between the existing and the minimum equity; that is the amount that may be withdrawn. The client cannot withdraw the full SMA balance if this action would reduce the equity in the account to an amount less than the required maintenance level. SMA may not be used to meet a maintenance call.

SMA and Restricted Accounts

Withdrawing securities. When withdrawing securities from a restricted account, a client must meet the 50% Reg T retention requirement. This can be done with SMA unless doing so violates maintenance requirements.

Purchasing securities. SMA can be used to purchase new securities only to the extent that its use does not violate the minimum equity requirements of either the NYSE or the firm.

Questions

1. A customer's margin account contains securities with a market value of $50,000, a debit balance of $30,000 and no SMA balance. After the value of the securities increases to $70,000, the customer sells $20,000 worth of securities. What is SMA after the sale? (Reg T is 50%.)

   A. $0
   B. $5,000
   C. $10,000
   D. $15,000

2. A customer has a margin account with $50,000 in securities and a debit of $26,000. SMA is $4,000. How much cash can the customer withdraw from the account?

   A. $0
   B. $2,000
   C. $4,000
   D. $24,000

3. Which of the following can change the balance in SMA?

   I. Sale of securities in the account
   II. Market appreciation of securities in the account
   III. Interest and cash dividends deposited in the account
   IV. Decrease in value of securities in the account

   A. I only
   B. I and II only
   C. I, II and III only
   D. I, II, III and IV

Answers

1. **D.** After the value of the securities in the account increased to $70,000, the customer had equity of $40,000. Because Reg T requires equity of $35,000, the customer had $5,000 in excess equity after the increase in market value. The new excess equity was credited to SMA. When the customer sold $20,000 worth of securities, half of the sale proceeds were automatically released to SMA, as prescribed by retention requirements. The $10,000 in sale proceeds released to SMA increased SMA to $15,000.

2. **C.** The customer may withdraw SMA from the account. SMA may always be withdrawn in cash unless doing so will bring the account below the minimum margin requirements. The minimum market value in this case is $12,500 ($50,000 × 25%). Withdrawal of $4,000 will increase the debit to $30,000, leaving an equity of $20,000—well above the minimum requirements.

3. **C.** The sale of securities in the account (choice I) results in an automatic release of funds to SMA. Nonrequired cash deposits, such as interest and dividends (choice III), will also be automatically credited to SMA. An increase in the value of the securities (choice II) will increase SMA if the excess equity becomes greater than existing SMA. A decrease in the market value of the securities (choice IV) will not increase or decrease SMA.

Hypothecation of Customer Securities

Holding Customer Securities—Hypothecation

When a customer purchases securities in a margin account using money borrowed from the broker-dealer, the securities are pledged to the broker-dealer as collateral for the loan in a process called *hypothecation* of the securities. When a broker-dealer borrows money from a bank using customer securities to finance customer debit balances, the process is called *rehypothecation*.

Rehypothecation of Customer Securities

Customer hypothecation agreement (margin agreement). SEC rules prohibit a broker-dealer from rehypothecating customer securities to a bank as collateral for cash loans unless the customer authorizes this activity.

Commingling of Customer Securities

SEC Rule 15c2-1 prohibits a broker-dealer from commingling one customer's securities with another customer's securities, bundling them together as joint collateral for a bank loan, unless the customers specifically authorize it.

Broker-dealers are prohibited from commingling customer securities with firm securities, pledging them jointly as collateral for a consolidated loan from a bank.

Maximum Hypothecation of Customer Margin Securities

140%

The firm may pledge customer securities only to a maximum of 140% of the customer's net debit balance. For example, if a customer has a net debit balance of $7,000 in a margin account and $13,000 CMV of securities, the firm may rehypothecate up to $9,800 worth of the customer's margined securities ($9,800 is 140% of $7,000).

Customers' fully paid and excess margin securities held by a broker-dealer must be segregated from the firm's own accounts and cannot be commingled with the firm's inventory.

Margin Securities and Excess Margin Securities

Those securities in a margin account that have a market value of up to 140% of the account's debit balance are known as *margin securities*. All of the securities in a margin account more than 140% of the account's debit balance are known as *excess margin securities*. Margin securities are available to broker-dealers and can be used for debit balance financing purposes. Excess margin securities must be segregated, earmarked as the property of the customer.

hypothecation = customer → B-D
rehypothecation = B-D → Bank

Questions

1. All of the following are true statements according to NYSE regulations EXCEPT that

   A. proxies must be forwarded to beneficial owners of the securities held *in street name*

   B. with NYSE approval, member firms may lend client securities without specific client authorization

   C. a corporate margin account can be opened only after it is established that such accounts are not contrary to the firm's charter and bylaws

   D. in order to open an account for an allied member of another member firm, written permission from the person's employer (a general partner, principal executive or supervisory person) must be given

Answers

1. **B.** Clients' securities may never be lent unless they have signed the consent to loan agreement. Fully paid securities must be segregated from the broker-dealer's securities.

Economics and Analysis

Economics

Business Cycles

Long-term business cycles go through four stages:

1. expansion
2. peak
3. contraction
4. trough

Mild, short-term contractions that last two to six consecutive quarters (6 to 18 months) are known as **recessions**. More severe contractions of longer duration may be deemed **depressions**.

Some of the signs of expansion that an economist will look for include:

- increases in industrial production;
- bullish (rising) stock markets;
- rising property values;
- increased consumer demand for goods and services; and
- increasing GNP.

Downturns in the business cycle tend to be associated with:

- rising numbers of bankruptcies and bond defaults;
- higher consumer debt;
- bearish (falling) stock markets;
- rising inventories (a sign of slackening consumer demand in hard times); and
- decreasing GNP.

Gross National Product

The annual economic output of a nation is known as its *gross national product*. During periods of expansion, the GNP increases.

C	Consumption
+ G	Government spending
+ I	Gross investment
GNP	Gross national product

Economists adjust the GNP figures to **constant dollars**.

Price Levels

Inflation. Inflation is a persistent and measurable rise in the general level of prices. Increases in the inflation rate tend to drive up the rate of interest on new fixed income securities; this, in turn, drives down the prices of existing debt securities. Decreases in the inflation rate have the opposite effect: as the inflation rate drops, new debt is issued at lower rates and the prices of existing debt rise.

Deflation. Deflation is a persistent and measurable fall in the general level of prices.

Stagflation. Stagflation is used to describe those periods of high unemployment (stagnation) coupled with rising prices (inflation). *Worst*

Consumer Price Index. The CPI measures the rate of increase or decrease in consumer prices for such things as food, housing, transportation, medical care, clothing, electricity, entertainment and services.

Economic Indicators

Leading indicators. The leading indicators that economists use most often include:

- average work week in manufacturing;
- average weekly initial claims for state unemployment compensation;
- new orders for durable goods;
- slowdowns in deliveries by vendors;
- contracts and orders for plant and equipment;
- building permits (housing starts);
- changes in inventories;
- changes in sensitive materials prices;
- stock prices;
- money supply (M2, which includes M1); and
- changes in business and consumer borrowing.

Positive changes lead economists to believe that there will be more spending, production and employment in days to come. Negative changes give rise to a more pessimistic outlook among economists and politicians, as possible downturns and recessions loom.

Coincident indicators. Coincident indicators used by economists and widely quoted in the national news include:

- nonagricultural employment
- personal income
- industrial production
- manufacturing and trade sales

Lagging indicators. Lagging indicators include: _Loan, profits._

- average duration of unemployment (in months between periods of employment);
- ratio of deflated inventories to sales, manufacturing and trade;
- labor cost per unit of output (manufacturing);
- commercial and industrial loans outstanding;
- corporate profits; and
- ratio of consumer installment credit to personal income.

Economic Theories and the Business Cycle

1. Classical Economic Theory   _1776: Wealth of Nations Adam Smith_

Classical economists reason that in a free enterprise economy there are periods of unemployment and full employment, but that full employment always will prevail if the economy is left to its own devices. This philosophy of governmental nonintervention is known as **laissez-faire economics**.

2. Keynesian Theory → _demand side_

Keynes held that active government intervention was vital to the health, well-being and stability of a nation's economy. Keynes believed that *demand* was the factor that controlled employment and prices. If there were insufficient demand for goods, unemployment would be the end result. If there were an excess of demand, inflation could be expected.

According to Keynesian economists, **consumption** is any spending done by household units to purchase newly produced consumer goods and services. A household's **marginal propensity to consume** is the marginal change in current consumption per dollar change in current income. **Savings** is any personal income not spent on taxes or goods. **Investment** refers to planned or intended investment and not to actual or realized investment.

Economic phases. Keynesian economics established three economic phases:

- equilibrium
- falling production
- rising production

Keynesian Economics and Interest Rates

Liquidity preference is a measure of the supply and demand for money itself and is a strong influence on interest rates. If the demand for money exceeds supply, people will borrow and liquidity preference will cause interest rates to rise. If the supply of money is greater than the demand for it, people will attempt to get rid of the excess and this will force interest rates down. The equilibrium rate of interest occurs at the point where the amount of money people hold is the same as the amount of money they want to hold.

The Government's Role in Keynesian Economics

According to Keynes, the government is expected to intervene in economic interplay and be a major force in moving the economy to prosperity by engaging in activities that affect aggregate demand.

A government can exert forces to reduce consumer and business demand and spending by:

- raising taxes
- reducing the money supply
- reducing government spending

Each of these activities serves to remove money from the country's economic system (a condition known as *tight money*), which discourages demand and spending. A government can exert forces to increase consumer and business demand and spending by:

- reducing taxes
- increasing the money supply
- increasing government spending

These activities inject money into the economy (a condition known as *easy money*) and, as a result, encourage consumer demand and spending.

3 Supply-side Economic Theory   *Arthur Laffer*

The theory on which supply-side economics is based is that drastic reductions in taxes, particularly those paid by businesses and wealthy individuals, would result in an increased level of spending and investment that would benefit society as a whole. Supply-side economists advocate federal income tax reductions and claim that deficits can be avoided by a commensurate reduction in federal spending.

4 Monetarist Economic Theory

Monetarist economic theory states that the *money supply* is the major determinant of price levels, particularly over the long run. Monetarists believe that a well-controlled, slowly increasing money supply will have the most positive impact on the health of the economy—far more than changes in the levels of federal spending could.

Milton Friedman

Questions

1. An improvement in economic conditions is indicated by an increase in all of the following EXCEPT

   A. industrial production
   B. inventories
   C. Standard & Poor's 500
   D. consumer orders

2. Gross national product is the sum of all the

   A. goods and services produced by a country
   B. goods produced by a country
   C. household goods of a country
   D. manufactured and nonmanufactured goods of a country

3. A six-month decline in business activity, employment and stock prices is

   A. a depression
   B. a recession
   C. inflation
   D. stagflation

4. The Consumer Price Index is based on which of the following?

   A. Prices of all items in the GNP
   B. Selected goods in selected cities
   C. Average price of goods and services per person for three months
   D. Cost of food and utilities

5. Which of the following is NOT one of the normal economic phases?

   A. Expansion
   B. Stagflation
   C. Inflation
   D. Recession

6. Which of the following economists is(was) a supporter of supply-side economics?

   A. Adam Smith
   B. John Maynard Keynes
   C. Arthur Laffer
   D. Milton Friedman

7. Which of the following economists is(was) a supporter of demand-side economics?

   A. Adam Smith
   B. John Maynard Keynes
   C. Arthur Laffer
   D. Milton Friedman

8. Which of the following economists is(was) a supporter of classical economics?

   A. Adam Smith
   B. John Maynard Keynes
   C. Arthur Laffer
   D. Milton Friedman

9. Which of the following economists is(was) a supporter of monetarist economics?

   A. Adam Smith
   B. John Maynard Keynes
   C. Arthur Laffer
   D. Milton Friedman

10. According to monetarist economic theory, an economy's health can be ensured if the government

    A. cuts taxes for businesses and the wealthy
    B. increases aggregate demand
    C. increases the money supply
    D. leaves the economy alone

11. According to Keynesian economic theory, an economy's health can be ensured if the government

    A. cuts taxes for businesses and the wealthy
    B. increases aggregate demand
    C. increases the money supply
    D. leaves the economy alone

12. According to supply-side economic theory, an economy's health can be ensured if the government

    A. reduces taxes for businesses and the wealthy
    B. increases aggregate demand
    C. increases the money supply
    D. leaves the economy alone

13. According to classical economic theory, an economy's health can be ensured if the government

    A. reduces taxes for businesses and the wealthy
    B. increases aggregate demand
    C. increases the money supply
    D. leaves the economy alone

14. What kind of economist would encourage a government to spend money to move the economy into an expansionary phase?

    A. Classical
    B. Keynesian
    C. Supply side
    D. Monetarist

15. What kind of economist would encourage a government to cut business taxes to move the economy into an expansionary phase?

    A. Classical
    B. Keynesian
    C. Supply side
    D. Monetarist

16. What kind of economist would encourage a government to increase the money supply to move the economy into an expansionary phase?

    A. Classical
    B. Keynesian
    C. Supply side
    D. Monetarist

17. What kind of economist would encourage a government to not intervene in the workings of the economy?

    A. Classical
    B. Keynesian
    C. Supply side
    D. Monetarist

18. What term do economists use to describe a downturn in the economy that lasts more than two consecutive quarters?

    A. Inflation
    B. Stagflation
    C. Depression
    D. Recession

19. What term do economists use to describe a downturn in the economy that lasts several years and is accompanied by extremely high unemployment?

    A. Inflation
    B. Stagflation
    C. Depression
    D. Recession

20. What term do economists use to describe a downturn in the economy characterized by increasing price levels?

    A. Inflation
    B. Stagflation
    C. Depression
    D. Recession

21. What term do economists use to describe a downturn in the economy that is characterized by both unemployment and rising prices?

    A. Inflation
    B. Stagflation
    C. Depression
    D. Recession

22. New orders for durable goods is what kind of economic indicator?

    A. Leading
    B. Coincident
    C. Coterminous
    D. Lagging

23. Slowdowns in deliveries is what kind of economic indicator?

    A. Leading
    B. Coincident
    C. Coterminous
    D. Lagging

24. Industrial production is what kind of economic indicator?

    A. Leading
    B. Coincident
    C. Coterminous
    D. Lagging

25. Manufacturing sales is what kind of economic indicator?

    A. Leading
    B. Coincident
    C. Coterminous
    D. Lagging

26. Commercial loans outstanding is what kind of economic indicator?

    A. Leading
    B. Coincident
    C. Coterminous
    D. Lagging

27. Changes in the money supply is what kind of economic indicator?

    A. Leading
    B. Coincident
    C. Coterminous
    D. Lagging

28. Nonagricultural employment is what kind of economic indicator?

    A. Leading
    B. Coincident
    C. Coterminous
    D. Lagging

29. Initial state unemployment claims is what kind of economic indicator?

    A. Leading
    B. Coincident
    C. Coterminous
    D. Lagging

30. Changes in which industry would be considered a *leading indicator* for economic growth trends?

    A. Home appliances
    B. Natural gas
    C. Retailing
    D. New housing

Answers

1. **B.** Increasing inventories means that consumer demand is slackening. Thus, disposable income is dropping and economic conditions are deteriorating.

2. **A.** The GNP is the sum of all goods and services produced in the United States.

3. **B.** Two or more consecutive quarters of decline are termed a *recession*.

4. **B.** The CPI is a composite of selected items (housing, food, clothing, transportation) in selected cities. Answer C is incorrect because the CPI is an index of average prices paid during a one-month period, not a three-month period.

5. **B.** Economists consider expansion (recovery) as the beginning of the business cycle, followed by the peak (prosperity), the contraction (recession or deflation) and the trough. Stagflation is an unusual situation combining characteristics of expansion (inflation) with contraction (unemployment).

6. **C.** Professor Arthur Laffer was a proponent of supply-side economics in the 1970s and believed that tax cuts for businesses and the wealthy would help the economy as a whole.

7. **B.** John Maynard Keynes was the first demand-side economist and believed that by increasing the income available for spending and saving, a government could increase demand and improve the country's economic well-being.

8. **A.** Adam Smith is often referred to as the father of economics. His theory that the economy does best when left to its own devices is known as *classical economics*.

9. **D.** Milton Friedman is probably the best known monetarist; he supports the theory that the determining factor of an economy's health is the size and rate of growth of its money supply.

10. **C.** Monetarists theorize that a controlled, gradually increasing money supply will result in the healthiest economy.

11. **B.** Keynesians theorize that government efforts to increase aggregate demand by increasing its own purchases of goods and services will result in the healthiest economy.

12. **A.** Supply-siders believe that cutting taxes for businesses and the wealthy will result in the healthiest economy.

13. **D.** Classicists believe in what is known as *laissez-faire* economics, a French phrase that translates as *allow to do*, or *leave it alone*.

14. **B.** Keynesians advocate government intervention in the workings of the economy through increased government spending, which in turn increases aggregate demand.

15. **C.** Supply-siders advocate government intervention in the workings of the economy through tax cuts for businesses and the wealthy, which in turn provides increased supplies of goods.

16. **D.** Monetarists believe that a healthy economy is based on a controlled, slowly increasing money supply.

17. **A.** Classical economists believe that the government should not intervene in the workings of the economy and that the efforts of individuals to improve their own lot will result in the best economic situation for all.

18. **D.** An economic downturn that lasts for more than two consecutive quarters (six months) is known as a *recession*.

19. **C.** A long-term economic downturn with unemployment reaching 15% or more is known as a *depression*.

20. **A.** Inflation is the overall increase of price levels that occurs when spending is increasing faster than the supply of goods on the market.

21.   **B.**   "Stagflation" is the term used to describe the unusual combination of inflation and unemployment (stagnation).

22.   **A.**   New orders for durable goods is a leading economic indicator.

23.   **A.**   Slowdowns in deliveries is a leading economic indicator.

24.   **B.**   Industrial production is a coincident economic indicator.

25.   **B.**   Manufacturing sales is a coincident economic indicator.

26.   **D.**   Commercial loans outstanding is a lagging economic indicator.

27.   **A.**   Changes in the money supply is a leading economic indicator.

28.   **B.**   Nonagricultural employment is a coincident economic indicator.

29.   **A.**   Initial state unemployment claims is a leading economic indicator.

30.   **D.**   A leading indicator is one that predicts future growth trends. The usual indicators involve increases in basic productive processes such as steel shipments and housing starts. Durable goods (autos, home appliances) tend to be lagging indicators. Natural gas usage and retail sales are generally noncyclical.

Government Economic Policy

The president's and the federal government's policies on taxation and spending make up the country's **fiscal policy**. The FRB's policies on the size, movement and growth of the money supply compose its **monetary policy**.

Monetary Policy

Money and Banking

A demand deposit is money left with a bank that the depositing customer has the right to withdraw on demand. A time deposit is a deposit of money that the depositing customer has agreed not to withdraw for a specified period of time or without sufficient advance notice to the depository bank.

Creating Money

By granting loans to establish demand deposits, banks actually can create money.

Definition of Money

To an economist, money includes loans, credit and an assortment of other liquid instruments. Economists divide money into four categories, depending on the type of account in which it is kept:

1. **M1.** M1 consists of currency and demand [*checking*] deposits that can be converted to currency immediately.
2. **M2.** M2 includes M1 and some time deposits that are fairly easy to convert into demand deposits. [*+ saving + one day repo*]
3. **M3.** In addition to M1 and M2, M3 includes time deposits of more than $100,000 and repurchase agreements with terms longer than one day. [*+ CD*]
4. **L.** L includes M1, M2 and M3 plus other long-term liquid assets.

M1 is the largest component of the money supply.

The Federal Reserve Board

The Fed performs the following functions:

- acts as an agent of the U.S. Treasury;
- regulates the U.S. money supply;
- sets reserve requirements for members;
- supervises the printing of currency;
- clears fund transfers throughout the system; and
- examines members to ensure their compliance with federal regulations.

The FRB affects the money supply through its use of three monetary tools:

1. changes in reserve requirements
2. changes in the discount rate
3. open-market operations

Federal Funds

Commercial banks are required by the Federal Reserve Board (FRB) to keep on deposit an amount of cash equal to a certain percentage of their depositors' money (called the **reserve requirement**). The term "federal funds" commonly is used to describe all money deposited by commercial banks at a Federal Reserve Bank, including any money in excess of the reserve requirement.

When a bank falls short of its reserve requirement, it may borrow the federal funds of another member bank. The effective rate of interest is the daily average rate of interest costs as negotiated between the banks through the Federal Reserve System and is called the **federal funds rate**. The federal funds rate fluctuates daily and is one of this country's most volatile rates.

Reserve Requirements   [*7% – 22%*]

The FRB requires member banks to have reserves equal to a certain percentage of their deposits, a percentage that can vary from 7% to 22%. After depositing the specified percentage of any demand deposit it takes in, the bank may make the remaining amount available for loan. Changing reserve requirements is one way the FRB tries to control inflation.

The amount of money available to businesses and consumers multiplies rapidly when banks lend because banks can lend more money than they take in. This expansion of the money supply is called the **multiplier effect**.

Discount Rate

The Fed's second most important tool for affecting the money supply is raising and lowering the discount rate—the interest rate the Fed charges its members for certain very short-term loans. If a member has a reserve deficiency, it can borrow funds from its Federal Reserve district bank. Lowering the discount rate tends to counteract a recessionary trend. Raising the discount rate tends to counteract inflation.

Open-market Operations

The Federal Reserve's most important and flexible tool is *open-market operations*. The Fed buys and sells government securities in the secondary market in order to expand and contract the money supply.

When the Fed buys, bank excess reserves go up; when the Fed sells, bank excess reserves go down. When the Fed buys securities, it *expands* the money supply; when the Fed sells securities, it *contracts* the money supply. Because most of these transactions involve next-day payment, the effects on the money supply are immediate—making open-market operations the Fed's most efficient tool.

Other Methods

By changing margin requirements, the Fed can limit the extent to which brokers, dealers, banks and others can extend loans to purchase securities. The effect of changing margin requirements is more limited than that of changing reserve requirements because it affects a smaller segment of the economic community.

The Fed can use **moral suasion** by suggesting to member banks that its unofficial policies and banking directives be followed. It does this through warnings and speeches by Board members. If moral suasion is not effective, the Fed may have to make official policies it can enforce.

Fiscal Policy

Fiscal policy includes increases or decreases in:

- federal spending
- money raised through taxation
- federal budget deficits or surpluses

Fiscal policy is based on the assumption that by using the tools and policies at its disposal, the government can:

- reduce the rate of inflation by reducing aggregate demand for goods and services if price levels are excessive; or
- increase the rate of inflation by increasing aggregate demand if low inflation is causing unemployment and economic stagnation.

Disintermediation

Disintermediation is the flow of money from low-yielding accounts in savings institutions to higher yielding investments in the marketplace.

International Monetary Factors

Balance of Payments

The largest component of the balance of payments is the **balance of trade**—the export and import of merchandise (not services). On the U.S. credit side are sales of U.S. products to foreign countries. On the debit side are U.S. purchases of foreign goods that cause U.S. dollars to flow out of the country.

Questions

1. The short-term effect of the Federal Reserve's buying and selling securities in the marketplace is to
   A. check inflation
   B. stop a recession
   C. make credit more or less available
   D. do all of the above

2. Of the following, the item the Federal Reserve Board changes most often is the
   A. federal funds rate
   B. prime rate
   C. discount rate
   D. reserve rate

3. Which of the following actions by the Federal Reserve would result in a decrease in the money supply?
   A. Selling securities in the open market
   B. Changing the federal income tax rates
   C. Decreasing the discount rate
   D. Decreasing the reserve requirement

Answers

1. **C.** The short-term effect is to make credit more or less available. The long-term effect is to check inflation or to create a situation where the economy can recover from a recession.

2. **C.** Of the items listed, the FRB changes the discount rate most frequently. It seldom changes the reserve rate. It does not change the federal funds rate or the prime rate. These rates are both market rates and are changed by market forces and by banks.

3. **A.** When securities are sold by the Fed, money is being taken out of circulation by purchasers who buy the securities. Tax changes are not used to control the money supply. Increasing discount rates and reserve requirements, not decreasing them, contracts the money supply.

Technical Analysis

Market Averages and Indexes

Technical analysts place a great deal of value on the averages and indexes that show price changes in the securities markets. Moving averages are computed over time. Other factors that technical analysts take into account include trading volume and advances/declines.

Dow Jones averages. The Dow Jones averages are based on the prices of a limited number of stocks from four categories:

1. Industrial Average (30 stocks)
2. Transportation Average (20 stocks)
3. Utilities Average (15 stocks)
4. Composite Average (the 65 stocks from the three other averages)

The Dow Jones averages are not weighted by the relative size of an issue or a corporation.

Standard & Poor's 500. Standard & Poor's 500 stock index (S&P 500) is based on the prices of 400 industrials, 20 transportation stocks, 40 financial stocks and 40 public utility stocks. Each stock is weighted according to the aggregate value of shares outstanding.

NYSE index. The NYSE Composite Index is based on the prices of all common stocks listed on the Exchange. Like the S&P 500, it is weighted by the total value of shares outstanding for each stock.

NASDAQ-OTC price indexes. In addition to compiling the NASDAQ composite index, the NASD provides group indexes for industrials, banks, insurance stock, other finance stocks, transportation issues and utilities.

Value Line. The *Value Line* Composite Index consists of 1,700 NYSE, AMEX and OTC stocks.

Wilshire 5,000 Equity Index. The Wilshire 5,000 is a value-weighted index composed of 5,000 NYSE, AMEX and OTC common stocks.

Charting Stocks

Trendlines

A trendline connects the reaction lows in an uptrend and the rally highs in a downtrend. Three common patterns in stock price trendlines are consolidation, reversals and support and resistance levels.

Consolidation. If a market is staying within a narrow price range, it is said to be *consolidating*.

Reversals. A reversal indicates that an upward or a downward trendline has halted and the stock's price is moving the other way. One reversal patterns is called a saucer (reversal of a downtrend) or an inverted saucer (reversal of an uptrend). Another reversal pattern is the head-and-shoulders pattern.

A head and shoulders top pattern indicates a bearish trend—the upward trend of the stock has been reversed. A head and shoulders bottom indicates a bullish reversal.

Support and resistance levels. When prices hover in a narrow range for an extended period, the bottom of this trading range is known as the support level; the top of the trading range is called the resistance level.

If the price on a particular stock penetrates either the support or the resistance level, such a penetration is known as a **breakout**. Breakouts usually signal the beginning of a new upward or downward trend.

Technical Market Theories

Dow theory. The Dow theory is used to confirm the end of a major market trend. According to the theory, there are three types of changes in stock prices: primary trends (one year or more), secondary trends (three to twelve weeks) and short-term fluctuations (hours or days).

According to the Dow theory, the primary trend in a bull market is a series of higher highs and higher lows. In a bear market, the primary trend is a series of lower highs and lower lows. Daily fluctuations are considered irrelevant.

Odd-lot theory. When odd-lot traders are buying, odd-lot theorists are bearish. When odd-lot traders are selling, odd-lot theorists are bullish.

Short-interest theory. Some analysts believe high short interest is a bullish indicator, and low short interest is a bearish indicator.

Confidence theory. *Barron's Confidence Index* is based on comparisons of the yields of a group of high-grade bonds with the yields of lower ranked bonds.

Modern portfolio theory. Investment managers who subscribe to MPT focus on the relationships among all the investments in a portfolio. Adherents to MPT say that securities markets are efficient markets.

Random walk theory. This theory states that the direction in which a stock's or market's prices will go is no more predictable than the direction of a drunkard's walk.

Questions

1. Which of the following is the narrowest measure of the market?

    A. NYSE Composite Index
    B. *Value Line* Index
    C. Dow Jones Industrial Average
    D. Standard & Poor's 100

2. The NYSE Composite Index consists of

    A. common stocks
    B. preferred stocks
    C. certain listed bonds
    D. all of the above

3. The stock index that contains the securities of 400 industrial corporations is the

    A. Dow Jones Composite Index
    B. NASDAQ Index
    C. NYSE Index
    D. Standard & Poor's 500

4. The value of the Dow Jones averages would be most affected by a change in the value of which of the following stocks?

    A. Utility
    B. Industrial
    C. Transportation
    D. Growth

5. What is the largest component of the NYSE Composite Index?

    A. Transportation
    B. Industrial
    C. Utilities
    D. Finance

6. A fundamental analyst would be interested in all of the following EXCEPT

    A. statistics of the U.S. Department of Commerce on disposable income
    B. daily trading volumes on the NYSE
    C. corporate annual reports
    D. innovations within the automotive industry

Answers

1.   **C.**   Of those listed, the *Value Line* Composite, consisting of approximately 1,700 NYSE, AMEX and OTC stocks, is the broadest index. The second broadest is the NYSE Composite, containing all of the common stocks on the NYSE (about 1,500). The third broadest is the Standard & Poor's 100, made up of 100, mostly NYSE-traded, industrial stocks, for which options are available on the CBOE. The Dow Jones Industrial Average, containing 30 actively traded blue chip stocks, is the narrowest measure of the market.

2.   **A.**   The NYSE Composite Index is composed of only common stocks.

3.   **D.**   The Standard & Poor's 500 contains 400 industrials. The other 100 stocks are divided among financials, utilities and transportation stocks.

4.   **B.**   The Dow Jones Composite Index consists of 65 stocks: 30 industrial, 20 transportation and 15 utilities issues. Because industrials are the largest component, changes in their prices have the greatest effect on the averages.

5.   **B.**   Industrial stocks are the largest component of the NYSE Composite Index, the Standard & Poor's 500 and the Dow Jones Composite Index.

6.   **B.**   Trading volume interests the technical analyst, who looks at fluctuations in the market, not at fundamental economic values.

Fundamental Analysis

Industry Analysis

Fundamental analysts look at particular industries to see which are likely to fare best as the economy proceeds along its upward or downward course. Four types of industries and investments are: defensive, cyclical, growth and special situation.

Defensive industries. Defensive industries are those industries that are least affected by normal business cycles. Investment in defensive industries tends to involve less risk and, consequently, less opportunity for a high return on investment.

Cyclical industries. Cyclical industries are highly affected by business cycles and price changes. Investments in cyclical industries tend to involve greater risks and greater opportunities for a high return on investment.

Growth industries. An industry is considered in its growth phase if the industry is growing faster than the economy as a whole because of technological changes, new products or changing consumer tastes.

Special situation stocks. Special situation stocks are stocks of a company with unusual profit potential due to nonrecurring circumstances.

Corporate Analysis

Fundamental analysts are concerned with the growth and stability of a company. They look at the quality of the firm's management and historical earnings trends. They plot how its projected growth compares with that of its competitors and whether its growth is stable or erratic. Fundamental analysts also examine a corporation's capitalization and use of working capital.

Financial Statements

The balance sheet and income statement, however, are critical tools for analyzing a company's financial situation and for evaluating the viability of the company's securities investments.

Balance Sheet

The balance sheet shows what the company owns (its assets), what it owes (its liabilities) and the excess of the book value of assets over the book value of liabilities (its equity). A balance sheet reports on a company's financial position in dollars and cents.

Assets

In general, assets are listed on the balance sheet in order of liquidity. Balance sheets commonly include three types of assets: current assets, fixed assets and other assets.

Current assets. Current assets include all cash and other items expected to be converted into cash within the next accounting cycle, including:

- cash and equivalents
- accounts receivable
- inventory
- prepaid expenses

Fixed assets. Fixed assets cannot be easily liquidated. Fixed assets can be **depreciated** and their cost deducted from taxable income in annual installments to compensate for loss in value.

Other assets. Other assets may include relatively permanent investments. Intangible assets are nonphysical properties.

Liabilities

Total liabilities on a balance sheet represent all financial claims by creditors against the assets of a corporation. Balance sheets usually include two main types of liabilities: current liabilities and long-term liabilities.

Current liabilities. Current liabilities are corporate debt obligations due for payment within the next twelve months, including:

- accounts payable
- accrued wages payable
- current long-term debt

A balance sheet might also include as current liabilities:

- notes payable
- accrued taxes

Long-term liabilities. Long-term debts are financial obligations due for payment after twelve months. Funded debt is any long-term debt that is payable in five years or more.

Shareholders' Equity

Shareholders' equity represents the stockholders' residual claims against the assets. Shareholders' equity is equal to total assets less total liabilities. Shareholders' equity is represented by three items:

1. capital stock at par.
2. capital in excess of par
3. retained earnings

Liquidity

The formula for working capital is:

$$\text{Current assets} - \text{Current liabilities} = \text{Working capital}$$

Capitalization = long term debt + stock + capital in excess of par

A company's capital structure is the sum of a company's long-term debt, stock accounts and capital in excess of par.

Changes that Affect the Balance Sheet

Every change in the financial structure of the business will require entering two changes on the balance sheet.

Depreciating Assets

Depreciation deduction. Depreciation is an operating expense and is calculated as a percentage of the cost of an asset. The actual amount of the deduction would be determined from tables published by the IRS.

When depreciation is calculated by the straight-line method, the same amount is deducted each year over the useful life of the asset. Accelerated depreciation methods speed up the recovery of an asset's cost by allocating higher deductions in earlier years.

Depreciation and the balance sheet. Depreciation affects the balance sheet in two ways: accumulated depreciation reduces the value of fixed assets, and depreciation deduction reduces tax liability.

Valuing Inventories

FIFO. FIFO is based on the assumption that items acquired first are sold first. During times of inflation, using the FIFO method has two consequences:

1. FIFO assigns the highest possible value to inventory because it assumes that the latest received (and most expensive) items remain unsold.
2. FIFO assigns the lowest possible value for COGS because it assumes the first (and cheapest) items are sold first.

LIFO. LIFO is based on the assumption that goods acquired last are sold first. In times of inflation when prices are rising, LIFO produces a higher figure for COGS and, therefore, the lowest profits for a given amount of sales. When prices are falling, however, using LIFO results in higher profits and taxes than using FIFO does.

Capital Structure

A corporation builds its capital structure with four elements:

1. long-term debt
2. capital stock
3. capital in excess of par
4. earned surplus

Issuing securities. If a corporation issues additional shares, the balance sheet will change in two ways: net worth (shareholders' equity) will increase by the additional capital raised and, as the stock is sold, the amount of cash assets on the opposite side of the balance sheet will also increase.

Convertible securities. When a stockholder converts convertible debentures into shares of common stock, the amount of liabilities decreases, while equity increases.

Bond redemption. The redemption of bonds reduces liabilities on the balance sheet. The offsetting change would be a decrease in cash assets on the opposite side of the balance sheet.

Dividends. When a cash dividend is declared, retained earnings are lowered, as is the cash balance. When a stock dividend is declared, retained earnings are lowered, while the total amount of capital stock and capital in excess of par increases.

Stock splits. A stock split does not affect shareholders' equity. On the balance sheet, only the par value and number of shares outstanding change.

Financial Leverage

A company with a high ratio of long-term debt to common stock is said to have *high leverage*. Stockholders benefit from leverage if the return on borrowed money exceeds the debt service costs.

Income Statement

The income statement summarizes a corporation's revenues and expenses for a fiscal period.

The income statement is a history of the company's operations for the period.

The income statement is used by fundamental analysts to judge the efficiency of a company's operation. From the income statement, analysts generate ratios.

Net sales. Net sales are gross sales minus returns.

Costs of goods sold. Cost of goods sold are subtracted from net sales, along with operating expenses, to calculate operating income.

Operating expenses. Operating expenses are subtracted from net sales to arrive at operating income.

Operating income. Operating income is a company's profit from the year's business operations.

Nonoperating income. Other sources of revenue are listed separately on the income statement.

Interest expense. Interest payments on outstanding debt are not considered part of operating expenses nor part of the corporation's taxable income. The corporation reduces operating income by the amount of interest charges.

Net income after taxes. Dividends are paid to stockholders out of net income.

Earnings per share. Earnings per share is calculated after payment of interest on debt securities, taxes and the payment of preferred dividends. Earnings per share are computed by dividing the earnings available to common by the number of shares of common stock outstanding.

Earned surplus. Earnings not paid out in interest, dividends to preferred and common stockholders, or taxes are called earned surplus. = retained earnings

Extraordinary items. Extraordinary items are listed separately on the income statement.

Questions

1. As a result of corporate transactions, a company's assets remain the same and its equity decreases. Which of the following statements is true?

   A. Prepaid expenses decrease.
   B. Total liabilities increase.
   C. Accrued expenses decrease.
   D. Net worth increases.

2. A company has been experiencing increased earnings but has kept its dividend payments constant. Due solely to this, the company's balance sheet would reflect

   A. decreased net working capital
   B. decreased net worth
   C. decreased retained earnings
   D. increased shareholders' equity

3. The difference between current assets and current liabilities is called

   A. net worth
   B. working capital
   C. cash flow
   D. quick assets

4. Earned surplus is

   A. net profits
   B. operating income
   C. cumulative earnings after dividends have been paid from net income
   D. cumulative earnings paid in dividends

5. All of the following can be said of accumulated depreciation EXCEPT that it

   A. provides funds for the actual cost of replacement
   B. is accumulated against liabilities
   C. is used to reduce the carrying value of fixed assets
   D. is a balance sheet item

6. During an inflationary period, FIFO will

   A. decrease profits
   B. decrease tax liabilities
   C. increase costs of goods sold
   D. increase profits and value of inventory on hand

7. Which of the following is NOT affected by the issuance of a bond?

   A. Assets
   B. Total liabilities
   C. Working capital
   D. Shareholders' equity

8. If a company redeems an outstanding debenture, working capital

   A. increases
   B. is not affected because debentures are long-term debts
   C. is not affected because cash and liabilities decrease equally
   D. decreases

9. Under what circumstances will a dilution of equity occur?

   A. Stock dividend
   B. Stock split
   C. Conversion of convertible bonds into common stocks
   D. Issue of mortgage bonds to replace debentures

10. A company that is highly leveraged has as the smallest portion of its capitalization

    A. preferred stock
    B. common stock
    C. debentures
    D. convertible debentures

11. A corporation that is highly leveraged is generally MORE attractive to

    A. secured bondholders
    B. general creditors
    C. preferred stockholders
    D. common stockholders

12. Which of the following statements is(are) true?

    I. The higher the bond rating, the lower the yield.
    II. Deep discount bonds have a high degree of safety.
    III. Interest rates can affect the discount on bonds.

    A. I
    B. I and III
    C. II
    D. II and III

13. Quantitative measures for corporate bonds include all of the following EXCEPT

    A. yields
    B. debt ratios
    C. net fixed assets per bond
    D. industry stability

14. When analyzing the investment quality of a mortgage bond, which of the following would be LEAST useful?

    A. Rating assigned the obligation by a nationally recognized rating service
    B. Information pertaining to the collateral that backs the obligation
    C. Name of the trustee that holds title to the collateral
    D. General trends in the economic cycle

Answers

1. **B.**   The formula for the balance sheet is: assets = liabilities + shareholders' equity. If assets stay the same and equity (net worth) decreases, liabilities must increase. Answer A is incorrect because prepaid expenses are assets; answer C is incorrect because accrued expenses are liabilities.

2. **D.**   If earnings increase, retained earnings also increase. If the increased retained earnings are not paid out as dividends, shareholders' equity increases.

3. **B.**   Working capital (or net working capital) is, by definition, the difference between current assets and current liabilities.

4. **C.**   Earned surplus (also called *retained earnings)* is created by earnings of the company that have not been paid out in the form of dividends.

5. **B.**   Accumulated depreciation offsets the value of fixed assets (not liabilities) on the balance sheet. The depreciation deduction reduces tax liability, keeping the balance sheet in balance. Depreciation expense is a deduction representing the decline in value of a fixed asset as it wears out. The deduction is based on a percentage of the asset's actual cost—not its current market value. The deduction reduces taxable income each year, which reduces taxes. Because of this income reduction, depreciation deductions are said to provide funds for the asset's replacement when it wears out.

6. **D.**   When FIFO is used during periods of inflation, inventory purchased some time ago at a lower price is continually being charged against current sales. This practice results in higher profits on the income statement. The remaining inventory is valued at the latest price paid. In an inflationary economy, this inventory will be priced higher than the inventory charged against sales. Thus, the cost of inventory carried on the balance sheet has been increased.

7. **D.**   On the issuance of a bond, cash is received (thus increasing current assets) and long-term debt increases (increasing total liabilities). Because there is no corresponding increase in current liabilities, working capital will increase. It would have no effect on shareholders' equity.

8. **D.**   The debenture, representing long-term debt, is part of the capitalization of a company. Cash is paid out to redeem the long-term debt. Therefore, cash, a current asset, has been reduced without a corresponding reduction of current liabilities. Consequently, working capital (current assets minus current liabilities) will decrease.

9. **C.**   Dilution of equity occurs when each existing stockholder is affected by a change in capital structure that reduces his percentage interest in the company. A stock dividend or stock split does not change a stockholder's percentage of ownership. Refunding debts (answer D) has no effect on stockholders. However, if bonds are converted, more common shares are issued and the shareholder's equity is diluted.

10. **B.**   The question defines a highly leveraged company. With a substantial amount of debt outstanding, highly leveraged companies have relatively little common stock. Remember: total capitalization = long-term debt + equity. So, if a company increases its long-term debt, a smaller percentage of its total capital will represent shareholders' equity.

11. **D.**   High leverage tends to benefit common stockholders by magnifying the effect of increasing sales and earnings upon returns on common equity. Creditors, bondholders and preferred stockholders receive a fixed return. Any earnings above the amount necessary to pay that fixed return will apply to common stockholders' accounts.

12. **B.**   Deep discount bonds may have a degree of uncertainty surrounding the safety of the investment and the ability of the issuer to continue interest payments.

13. **D.**   Industry stability is a qualitative factor.

14.   **C.** Rating services evaluate risk. The value of pledged collateral affects the safety of a bond investment. Economic trends affect the ability of an issuer to pay debt service and interest rates that, in part, determine the resale value of a bond. The trustee named in the bond indenture, however, assumes no liability for repaying the bond issuer's debt and does not guarantee repayment.

Financial Ratios

Capitalization Ratios

Risk of bankruptcy. Analysts assess the risk that a company will go bankrupt by studying its capitalization and its degree of leverage.

Ratios. When assessing a company's capitalization, analysts use ratios that express the percentage of capitalization composed of long-term debt, common stock and preferred stock. Bond analysts use the following three capitalization ratios to assess the degree of safety of a corporation's bonds.

$$\frac{\text{Long-term debt}}{\text{Total capitalization}} = \text{Bond ratio}$$

$$\frac{\text{Common} + \text{Capital in} + \text{Retained}}{\text{stock} \quad \text{excess of par} \quad \text{earnings}}{\text{Total capitalization}}$$

$$= \text{Common stock ratio}$$

$$\frac{\text{Preferred stock}}{\text{Total capitalization}} = \text{Preferred stock ratio}$$

The **bond ratio** measures the percentage of total capitalization that is provided by long-term debt financing. It is sometimes called the **debt ratio**. The **common stock ratio** measures the percentage of total capitalization contributed by common stockholders. The **preferred stock ratio** measures the percentage of total capitalization that is in preferred stock.

Leverage. The **debt-to-equity ratio** provides a common measure of leverage:

$$\frac{\text{Total long-term debt}}{\text{Total shareholders' equity}} = \text{Debt-to-equity ratio}$$

Liquidity Ratios

Liquidity ratios measure the firm's ability to meet its current obligations. Working capital is the amount of liquid assets available to meet new short-term obligations.

$$\begin{matrix}\text{Current} \\ \text{assets}\end{matrix} - \begin{matrix}\text{Current} \\ \text{liabilities}\end{matrix} = \begin{matrix}\text{Working} \\ \text{capital}\end{matrix}$$

The **current ratio** measures the amount of current assets in relation to current liabilities.

$$\frac{\text{Current assets}}{\text{Current liabilities}} = \text{Current ratio}$$

Quick assets takes into account the size of the company's unsold inventory. Analysts use quick assets instead of current assets in the **acid-test ratio**. Most accountants believe that the acid-test ratio is a better measure of a company's liquidity than is the current ratio.

$$\text{Current assets} - \text{Inventory} = \text{Quick assets}$$

$$\frac{\text{Quick assets}}{\text{Current liabilities}} = \text{Acid-test ratio}$$

(liquidity)

The final liquidity ratio, the **cash assets ratio**, measures only the cash assets (including marketable securities) in relation to current liabilities.

Efficiency Ratios

The **inventory turnover ratio** expresses the number of times a corporation's average inventory investment is turned into income dollars.

$$\frac{\text{COGS}}{\text{Year-end inventory}} = \text{Inventory turnover ratio}$$

Profitability Ratios

Ratios that demonstrate how high a company's profits are in relation to its sales include the **margin of profit ratio** and the **net profit ratio**.

$$\frac{\text{Operating profit}}{\text{Net sales}} = \text{Margin of profit ratio}$$

$$\frac{\text{Net income}}{\text{Net sales}} = \text{Net profit ratio}$$

Profitability is also reflected in a firm's return on assets, which analysts measure with the following ratios:

$$\frac{\text{Net income (after taxes)}}{\text{Shareholders' equity}} = \text{Return on equity}$$

$$\frac{\text{Net income (after taxes)}}{\text{Total tangible assets}} = \text{Return on equity (assets)}$$

Asset Coverage and Safety of Income

Net asset value per bond. The ratio of net asset value (NAV) to the number of bonds outstanding gives bondholders some information about the assets available to back up the company's obligations to short- and long-term creditors.

$$\frac{\text{Net tangible assets} - \text{Current liabilities}}{\text{Number of bonds outstanding}} = \text{NAV per bond}$$

Bond interest coverage. The likelihood that a company will have sufficient earnings to cover its interest payments can be measured by the number of times earnings before interest and taxes (EBIT) exceeds annual interest on the company's outstanding bonds.

$$\frac{\text{EBIT}}{\text{Annual interest payable to bonds}} = \text{Bond interest coverage}$$

The bond interest coverage ratio is also called the *interest coverage ratio, times interest earned ratio, fixed charge coverage ratio* and *times fixed charges earned ratio.*

Debt service ratio. An issuer's ability to meet principal and interest payments on bonds can be calculated by including principal payments in the denominator of the bond interest coverage ratio. This modified version of the ratio is called the *debt service ratio.*

$$\frac{\text{EBIT}}{\text{Annual interest} + \text{Principal payments}} = \text{Debt service ratio}$$

Book value per share. The book value of a company's assets is determined by deducting all liabilities and the value of any preferred stock from the company's tangible assets. Dividing this by the number of outstanding shares of common stock shows how far a company's assets might go toward reimbursing stockholders for their losses in bankruptcy.

$$\frac{\text{Shareholders' equity} - \text{Par value of pref. stock} - \text{Intangible assets}}{\text{No. of shares of common stock outstanding}}$$

$$= \text{Book value per share}$$

Collection ratio. A company's relative efficiency in collecting debts can be measured by the collection ratio.

$$\frac{\text{Receivables} \times 360}{\text{Net sales}} = \text{Collection ratio}$$

Valuation Ratios

Earnings per share. Earnings per share (EPS), measures the value of one share against the earnings of the company.

$$\frac{\text{Earnings available to common}}{\text{Number of common shares outstanding}} = \text{EPS}$$

The concept of EPS applies only to common stock. Preferred stockholders have no claims to earnings beyond the stipulated preferred stock dividends.

Earnings per share after dilution. If a corporation has rights, stock options, warrants, convertible preferred stock or convertible bonds, the EPS after dilution is used. EPS after dilution assumes that all convertible securities have been converted.

Dividends per share. The dividends per share is simply the dollar amount of cash dividends paid on each common share during the year.

$$\frac{\text{Annual dividends}}{\text{No. of common shares outstanding}} = \frac{\text{Dividends}}{\text{per share}}$$

Price-earnings ratio. The price-earnings (PE) ratio formula is:

$$\frac{\text{Current market price of com. stock}}{\text{EPS}} = \text{PE ratio}$$

Current yield. The current yield of a common stock expresses the annual return on the investment as a percentage of the market value.

$$\frac{\text{Ann. dividends/common share}}{\text{Market value/common share}} = \text{Current yield}$$

Dividend payout ratio. The dividend payout ratio is used to measure the proportion of common earnings actually paid to common stockholders as dividends.

$$\frac{\text{Ann. dividends/common share}}{\text{EPS}} = \frac{\text{Dividend}}{\text{payout ratio}}$$

Competitiveness (Comparative Performance)

Return on common equity. The numerator of the return on common equity formula is the same as that for calculating EPS. The denominator is the amount of equity attributable to common stockholders.

$$\frac{\text{Earnings available to common}}{\frac{\text{Common}}{\text{par value}} + \frac{\text{Capital in}}{\text{excess of par}} + \frac{\text{Retained}}{\text{earnings}}}$$

$$= \text{Return on common equity}$$

Analyzing Corporate Debt

Bond interest coverage ratio. This ratio (described previously) is perhaps the most important single tool for analyzing the security of a bond.

$$\frac{\text{Income before interest and taxes}}{\text{Annual interest charges}}$$

$$= \text{Bond interest ratio}$$

Net fixed assets per bond. The ratio of net fixed assets per bond is the most cautious method of evaluating net fixed assets and excludes intangible assets, working capital and accumulated depreciation.

$$\frac{\text{Net fixed assets}}{\text{No. of bonds in funded debt}} = \frac{\text{Net fixed}}{\text{assets per bond}}$$

Bond ratio. The bond ratio is the percentage of capital structure composed of bonds:

$$\frac{\text{Value of bonds}}{\text{Total long-term capitalization}} = \text{Bond ratio}$$

Credit risk. To measure the credit risk of a company, use the ratio of total debt to net tangible assets.

Questions

1. The bond interest coverage ratio is

   A. sales ÷ inventory
   B. receivables ÷ sales
   C. total debt ÷ net worth
   D. net income before taxes and interest ÷ interest expense

2. A corporation has annual sales of $15,000,000, operating expenses of $9,000,000, interest expense of $2,000,000 and principal payments on bonds totaling $1,000,000. What is the company's debt service ratio?

   A. 2 to 1
   B. 3 to 1
   C. 4 to 1
   D. 5 to 1

3. XYZ Corporation has total current assets of $40,000,000, $20,000,000 in inventory, total assets of $110,000,000, current liabilities of $10,000,000 and long-term debts totalling $50,000,000. What is the current ratio for XYZ corporation?

   A. 1 to 2
   B. 2 to 1
   C. 4 to 1
   D. 8 to 1

4. Which of the following is the most stringent test of liquidity?

   A. Assets ÷ Current liabilities
   B. Current assets ÷ Current liabilities
   C. (Current assets – Inventory) ÷ Current liabilities
   D. (Cash + Marketable securities) ÷ Current liabilities

5. A corporation has $12,000,000 net income after taxes, 5,000,000 common shares outstanding and $10,000,000 of 6% preferred stock ($100 par). What is the corporation's earnings per share?

   A. $1.20
   B. $2.15
   C. $2.28
   D. $2.40

6. Which of the following would increase earnings per share?

   I. Tax loss carryover
   II. Cash dividends paid
   III. Bond interest received
   IV. Retirement of debt

   A. I, III and IV only
   B. I and IV only
   C. III and IV only
   D. I, II, III and IV

Answers

1. **D.** The bond interest coverage (or times interest earned ratio) is operating income divided by interest expense. Operating income can also be described as *net income before taxes and before interest*.

2. **A.** The corporation has operating income before taxes and interest of $6,000,000 ($15,000,000 in sales less $9,000,000 operating expenses). The debt service ratio is: operating income of $6,000,000 divided by interest plus principal of $3,000,000, which equals a debt service ratio of 2 to 1.

3. **C.** The current ratio is: current assets of $40,000,000 divided by current liabilities of $10,000,000, which equals a current ratio of 4 to 1.

4. **D.** Of the answers given, answer D, the cash assets ratio, is the most stringent because it excludes inventories and accounts receivable.

5. **C.** Begin by calculating how much of the net income is available for common stockholders: net income after taxes minus preferred dividends equals earnings for common. The preferred stockholders receive $600,000 in dividends ($10,000,000 × 6% preferred stock = $600,000). To compute earnings per share: net income after taxes of $12,000,000 minus preferred dividend of $600,000, divided by the number of shares of common outstanding (5,000,000) equals $2.28 EPS.

6. **A.** When net income after taxes increases (for example, if there is a tax loss carried forward or bond interest is received), EPS will increase. Retirement of debt ends interest payments, thereby increasing net income and EPS. Payment of cash dividends has no effect on earnings, so choice II is incorrect.

12 ◆ Investment Recommendations and Taxation

Know Your Customer

Financial Profile

Customer's Balance Sheet

Before you enter the first trade for a new customer, it is important to find out as much about that person's financial status as you can. You can determine the status of your customer's personal balance sheet by asking questions about:

- assets;
- liabilities;
- investments and securities;
- investment accounts; and
- IRAs, Keoghs, corporate pension or profit-sharing plans, annuities, life insurance.

Customer's Income Statement

In order to make appropriate investment recommendations, you need to determine what your customer's income statement looks like. You can do this by asking questions about:

- total gross income and total family income, including anticipated changes;
- monthly expenses, including anticipated changes; and
- net spendable income after expenses.

Other Financial Elements

You will also want to learn about the investor's:

- home ownership
- insurance
- tax bracket
- credit problems

Nonfinancial Investment Considerations

Nonfinancial considerations often carry more weight than the financial information. Some of the items you will want to ask your customer about include:

- age
- marital status
- number and ages of dependents
- employment
- employment of family members
- current and future family educational needs
- current and future family health care needs

To understand better a customer's aptitude for investment, ask questions similar to the following:

- What kind of risks can you afford to take?
- How liquid must your investments be?
- How important are tax considerations?
- Are you seeking long-term or short-term investments?
- What is your investment experience?

- What types of investments do you currently hold?
- How would you react to a loss of 5% of your principal? 10%? 50%?
- ✓ What level of return do you consider good? Poor? Excellent?
- What combination of risks and returns would you feel comfortable with?
- What is your investment temperament?
- Do you get bored with stable investments?
- Can you tolerate market fluctuations?

Customer Investment Outlook

safety ⇒ **Preservation of capital**. When clients speak of *safety*, they usually mean preservation of capital from losses due to credit, or financial, risk. Financial risk is the danger of losing all or part of the principal amount a person has invested.

Current income. Corporate bonds, municipal bonds, government and agency securities, income-oriented mutual funds, some stocks, money-market funds, annuities and some DPPs are among the investments that can contribute current income through dividend or interest payments.

Capital growth. Growth refers to an increase in the value of an investment over time. This growth can come from increases in the value of the security, the reinvestment of dividends and income, or both.

Tax advantages. Some products allow interest to accumulate tax deferred. Other products offer tax-free interest income.

Portfolio diversification. When concentrations of investments in one or a few industries or securities expose customers to much higher risks, portfolio diversification becomes an important objective.

Liquidity. A product is liquid if the customer can sell it quickly at face amount or at a fair market price without losing significant principal.

Speculation. Speculation is a legitimate investment objective, and most customers would be well advised to place at least some of their investable assets in speculative, high-potential-return investments and securities.

Questions

1. Which of the following considerations must you take into account when recommending suitable investments for clients?

   A. Client's age and marital status
   B. Current investment portfolio
   C. Investment objectives
   D. All of the above

2. "Growth" refers to

   A. the value of the investment increasing over time
   B. increasing principal and accumulating interest and dividends over time
   C. investments that appreciate tax-deferred
   D. all of the above

3. Credit risk involves

   A. safety of principal
   B. fluctuations in overall interest rates
   C. the danger of not being able to sell the investment at a fair market price
   D. inflationary risks

4. Bonds with long maturities offer

   I. stability of income
   II. stability of market value
   III. fluctuation of income
   IV. fluctuation of market value

   A. I and II
   B. I and IV
   C. II and III
   D. III and IV

5. Which of the following investments is LEAST appropriate for a client who is concerned primarily with liquidity?

   A. Preferred stock
   B. Municipal bond mutual funds
   C. Bank savings accounts
   D. Direct participation programs

6. Which of the following securities generates the greatest current return with moderate risk?

A. Common stock of a new company
B. Security convertible into the common stock of a company
C. Fixed-income security
D. Income bond

Answers

1. **D.** A thorough investigation of a customer's situation, needs and objectives would take all of these factors into account before making an investment recommendation.

2. **A.** The term "growth" refers to an increase in the value of a product, not to an accumulation of undistributed interest or dividends.

3. **A.** This is the danger of losing all or part of one's invested principal. Answer B is market risk; answer C is marketability risk; and answer D is purchasing power risk.

4. **B.** If you buy one $1,000 bond with an 8% nominal (or coupon) yield, you will receive stable income: $80 every year. However, your principal (the current market value of the bond) will fluctuate, depending on the prevailing interest rates.

5. **D.** Clients who are concerned about liquidity risk should not invest in products like DPPs that do not have an active secondary market and, therefore, are not considered liquid investments.

6. **C.** Of the answers offered, in order to generate the greatest return a fixed-income security (a bond) is most suitable. Common stock is definitely not suitable; convertibles (either bonds or preferred) generally pay out a lower income rate than nonconvertibles because the investors receive benefit from the conversion feature; income bonds pay interest only if the corporation meets targeted earnings levels.

Analyzing Financial Risks and Rewards

Investment Risks   *10 kinds*

Inflationary Risk

Also known as **purchasing power risk**, inflationary risk measures the effects of continually rising prices on investments.

Capital Risk

Capital risk is the potential for an investor to lose all of her money or capital under circumstances unrelated to the financial strength of the issuer.

Selection Risk

When all other factors have been accounted for and an investor chooses an investment, there is always the possibility that the choice will be a poor one. This is known as *selection risk*.

Timing Risk

The risk to an investor of buying or selling at the wrong time and incurring losses or lower gains is known as *timing risk*.

Interest Rate Risk

Bond investors risk not being able to reinvest their interest income or principal at the same rate. This is known as *interest rate risk* or **reinvestment risk**.

Market Risk

Market risk is the risk that investors may lose some of their principal due to price volatility in the market.

Credit Risk   *↙ capital risk*

Credit risk (also called **financial risk** or **default risk**) involves the danger of losing all or part of one's invested principal through failure of the issuer.

Liquidity Risk

The risk that a client might not be able to liquidate her investment at a time when she needs cash is known as *liquidity risk* or **marketability risk**.

Legislative Risk

Congress has the power to change existing laws affecting securities. The risk that such a change in law might affect an investment adversely is known as *legislative risk*.

Call Risk

Related to reinvestment risk, call risk is the risk that a bond might be called before maturity and investors will be unable to reinvest their principal at the same (or a higher) rate of return.

Analyzing Investment Returns

Holding period return. Determining the holding period rate of return involves calculating the total return from capital gains and dividend income without taking into consideration how long the investment was held.

$$P * R^y = F$$

Present value. Present value calculates today's value of a future payment or stream of payments, discounted at a given compound interest rate.

Internal rate of return. The internal rate of return (IRR) is the discount rate at which the present value of future cash flows of an investment equals the cost of that investment.

Questions

1. Geographical diversification of municipal investments can protect against all of the following EXCEPT

   A. adverse legislation in one area
   B. economic decline in one region
   C. increasing interest rates
   D. default by a particular issuer

2. Which of the following securities carries the highest degree of purchasing power risk?

   A. Short-term note
   B. Blue chip stock
   C. Long-term, high-grade bond
   D. Convertible cumulative preferred stock

3. Bondholders risk the value of their bonds falling as interest rates rise. This is known as what type of risk?

   A. Credit
   B. Reinvestment
   C. Marketability
   D. Market

Answers

1. **C.** Geographical diversification cannot protect an investor against a loss in the value of an investment due to rising interest rates.

2. **C.** The longer you hold a fixed-income investment, the more vulnerable you are to purchasing power risk from inflation. Although preferred stock is also a fixed-income investment, convertible preferred will increase in value with the underlying common stock.

3. **D.** Among the different forms of market risk is the risk that fixed-income securities prices will drop as interest rates rise.

Portfolio Analysis

Portfolio Management Strategies

A **portfolio** is an individual's or business's combined holdings of stocks, bonds, cash equivalents, packaged investment products and other investment securities. A portfolio of securities offers the investor **diversification**.

Aggressive Investment Strategies

Aggressive investors pursue aggressive policies to buy and sell securities, including:

- selecting stocks with high betas) *more volitile*
- buying securities on margin
- using put and call option strategies
- employing arbitrage techniques

Defensive Investment Strategies

Defensive investors are willing to accept potentially lower total returns in order to minimize investment risk and preserve their capital. Investors who apply defensive strategies to their portfolios place a high percentage of their investable capital in bonds, cash equivalents and stocks that are likely to fare well in recessionary times, including stocks in defensive industries.

Balanced Investment Strategies

A **balanced** (or **mixed**) **portfolio** will have securities of many types in it, including bonds, stocks, packaged products and cash equivalents.

Modern Portfolio Theory

Modern portfolio differs from traditional securities analysis in that it shifts the emphasis away from analyzing the specific securities in the portfolio to determining the relationship between risk and reward in the total portfolio.

Systematic and Nonsystematic Risk

Beta

Systematic risk. The tendency for security prices to move together is known as *systematic risk.*

α

Nonsystematic risk. Nonsystematic risk is associated with the underlying investment itself. The larger and more diversified an investor's portfolio, the less subject it is to nonsystematic risk.

Risk Management Techniques

Diversification. A portfolio can be diversified in many ways, including:

- type of instrument
- industry
- companies within an industry
- length of maturity
- investment rating
- geography

Dollar cost averaging. Dollar cost averaging consists of making periodic purchases of a fixed dollar amount in one or more common stocks or mutual funds. In a fluctuating market, the average *cost* of the stock purchased in this manner is always less than the average market *price*.

Constant ratio plan. The strategy behind a constant ratio plan is that securities should be bought and sold in such a manner as to keep the portfolio balanced between equity and debt securities.

Constant dollar plan. The constant dollar plan's primary goal is to buy and sell securities so that a set dollar amount remains invested at all times. By employing this technique, the client is selling as prices rise and buying as prices fall.

Measuring Stock Price Volatility

Alpha coefficient. The alpha coefficient of a stock is a measure of the projected rate of change of a stock's price independent of market-related factors.

Beta coefficient. Beta coefficients quantify the degree to which a stock's price changes in comparison to changes in the market. Stocks with a beta of 1 move with the market. Stocks with a beta greater than 1 (such as 1.5) move more than the market. Stocks with a beta less than 1 (such as .75) move less than the market. In general, the greater the beta coefficient, the more risk associated with the security.

$$\beta x + \alpha = y \qquad \text{(market)}$$

Questions

1. Which of the following constitutes a constant dollar plan?

    A. 60% equities, 40% fixed income
    B. 40% equities, 60% fixed income investments
    C. Fixed amount in the portfolio regardless of market price
    D. Fixed amount in fixed-income investments regardless of market price

2. An investor who makes transactions once a month using dollar cost averaging would

    A. buy the same dollar amount of a stock
    B. buy the same number of shares of a stock
    C. put 70% of the money in a bond fund and buy stocks with the rest
    D. buy equal amounts of speculative and blue chip securities

3. Mr. Smith is pursuing an aggressive stock buying strategy. Which of the following is most suitable for him?

    A. ABC stock with a beta coefficient of 1.0
    B. DEF stock with a beta coefficient of .93
    C. GHI stock with a beta coefficient of 1.04
    D. Convertible bonds of a blue chip company

Answers

1. **C.** In a constant dollar plan, a fixed dollar amount is invested in the portfolio. If the market value rises, the excess is sold. If the market value falls, the securities are purchased to restore the "constant" dollar position.

2. **A.** Because the dollar amount remains constant, the investor will automatically buy more shares when the price is low, thus reducing the average cost.

3. **C.** Beta coefficients over 1 signify that the stock will fluctuate more than the market as a whole. In general, the higher the beta, the greater the risk. Such risk-taking is appropriate for investors who seek aggressive stock-buying strategies and have both the financial ability and the temperament to withstand downturns in the market.

Federal and State Taxation

Income Taxes

Federal income taxes are imposed on three types of income: earned, passive and portfolio.

Earned income. Earned income includes salary, bonuses and income derived from active participation in a trade or business.

Passive income. Passive income and losses come from rental property, limited partnerships and enterprises (regardless of business structure) in which the individual is not actively involved.

Portfolio income. Portfolio income includes dividends, interest and net capital gains derived from the sale of securities. *Shedule B/E*

No matter what the source of the income, it is taxed in the year in which it is received.

Income Tax Brackets

TRA 1986 defines two tax brackets: a 15% rate and a 28% rate.

Taxation and Investment Portfolios

Interest Income

Based on the **doctrine of mutual reciprocity**, there is a reciprocal agreement between governments. The federal government does not tax state and municipal issues. In turn, state and local governments usually do not tax federal securities.

Corporate bonds. Interest income on corporate bonds is taxable by federal, state and some local governments.

U.S. government securities. Interest income on direct federal debt is exempt from state and local taxes, but is federally taxable.

Agency obligations. The interest income on most federal agency debt, like that on Treasury securities, is taxable by the federal government but is exempt from state and local taxes. Agency issues that are fully taxable at all levels include:

- GNMAs
- FNMAs
- securities of the IADB

Accrued interest. Interest income includes accrued interest received when bonds are sold between interest payment dates. The accrued interest is taxable income to the seller.

Tax-exempt Interest Income

Municipal securities. Interest on municipal bonds issued before August 7, 1986, and on municipal bonds with a public purpose issued after that date is exempt from federal taxes. *may pay state tax*

Interest on a municipal bond or note may or may not be taxable for residents of the state in which the bond or note is issued.

Dividend Income

Dividend income received from stocks and mutual funds is taxed in the same manner as interest income received from debt securities.

Dividend income from mutual funds. The tax consequences of dividend checks received from mutual funds depends on what types of securities are in the underlying portfolio.

- Municipal bond mutual funds or unit investment trusts distribute federally tax-free dividends to shareholders.
- Dividend distributions from taxable mutual funds are taxable in the year they are received by the investor. Reinvested dividends are considered constructively received and also are taxable in the year they are distributed.

Taxable on Receipt

Interest and dividends are taxable only in the year they are *received*.

Capital Gains (and Losses)

Adjusting Cost Basis

The cost basis of an investment is used to determine whether there is a taxable gain or tax-deductible loss when the asset is sold.

Capital gains. A capital gain occurs when capital assets are sold at prices that exceed the adjusted cost basis.

Capital losses. A capital loss occurs when capital assets are sold at prices that are less than the adjusted cost basis.

Net capital gains and losses. To calculate tax liability, taxpayers must first add all capital gains for the year. Then, they separately add all capital losses. Finally, they offset the totals to determine the net capital gain or loss for the year. Net capital losses are deductible against earned income to a maximum of $3,000 per year. Any capital losses not deducted in a taxable year may be carried forward indefinitely to lower taxable income in future years.

Wash sales. Capital losses may not be used to offset gains or income if the investor sells a security at a loss and purchases the same (or a substantially identical) security within 30 days before or after the trade date establishing the loss.

Bonds Purchased at a Discount

Original issue discount (OID). If an OID bond is sold before it matures, the cost basis of the bond is adjusted by **accreting** the amount of the discount annually as determined by the issuer.

Secondary market discount. The cost basis of a bond bought at a discount in the secondary market is not adjusted.

Margin Expenses

Interest paid for securities margin loans is a tax-deductible expense. _up to investment income_

Alternative Minimum Tax

AMT for individuals. The AMT is a flat rate of 26%. To determine whether an individual is subject to the AMT:

1. Add all preference items to the taxpayer's AGI.
2. From this amount, subtract $40,000 (married, filing jointly), $30,000 (single) or $20,000 (married, filing separately).
3. Multiply this amount by a flat 26%. The result is the minimum tax liability. If the taxpayer's standard tax is less than this figure, the individual must pay the AMT.

Tax preference items. Certain preference items receive favorable tax treatment. These items must be added back into taxable income for the AMT. They include:

- accelerated depreciation on property placed in service after 1986;
- certain costs associated with DPPs, such as research and development costs and intangible drilling costs;
- local tax and interest on investments that do not generate income;
- tax-exempt interest on private purpose municipal bonds issued after August 7, 1986;
- untaxed appreciation on charitable contributions of appreciated property; and
- incentive stock options in excess of their fair market value.

Corporate Income Taxes

The following rules apply:

- Corporations are subject to a maximum tax rate of 34%.
- Dividends paid from one corporation to another are 70% exempt from taxation.
- Corporations do not pay federal taxes on income received from municipal obligations.

Questions

1. A couple who file a joint tax return has $275 in corporate preferred dividends. According to the tax law, this couple can exclude how much of this dividend income?

   A. $0
   B. $100 on a joint return
   C. $200 on a joint return
   D. All of it

2. Which of the following bonds is totally tax exempt?

   A. Hawaii GO bond
   B. U.S. government bond
   C. Puerto Rico GO bond
   D. U.S. Steel bond

3. Dr. Nichols invests $5,000 in the following new issue:

   > Ohio General Telephone Company
   >
   > $20,000 9% debentures
   >
   > Price 97
   >
   > To yield 9.2%

   The bonds listed above are

   A. federal and state tax exempt
   B. state tax exempt
   C. federal and state tax exempt if purchased by an Ohio resident
   D. fully taxable

4. A customer owns five 6% U.S. government bonds. The customer is in the 28% federal tax bracket and the 14% state tax bracket. What is her income tax liability on the interest?

   A. $0
   B. $42
   C. $84
   D. $126

5. The income from all of the following securities is fully taxable at the federal, state and local levels EXCEPT

   A. Ginnie Maes
   B. Treasury bonds
   C. reinvested mutual fund dividends
   D. IADB securities

6. Assuming that each of the bonds under consideration has the same maturity, place the following bonds in order of their pretax yields, from highest to lowest.

   I. U.S. government bonds
   II. AAA municipal bonds
   III. AA corporate bonds

   A. I, II, III
   B. II, I, III
   C. III, I, II
   D. III, II, I

7. A corporation announces a redemption call on March 15th for its $9 cumulative convertible preferred stock. The redemption is to be made at 100 plus a $.80 accrued dividend. The preferred stock, which is trading at 98, is convertible into 1.4 shares of common trading at 73 1/2. If the customer buys 100 shares of the preferred stock, converts the stock into common and sells the common at the market, what would be the resulting gain or loss?

   A. $490 profit
   B. $2,500 loss
   C. $7,790 loss
   D. $10,290 profit

8. Which of the following statements are true concerning the 1991 tax treatment of mutual funds?

    I. Dividend payments and capital gains distributions will not be subject to taxation as long as they are reinvested in the fund.
    II. Dividend payments and capital gains are both taxed at the same rate.
    III. The IRS treats exchanging shares within the same family of funds as a sale and repurchase of securities.

    A. I and II only
    B. I and III only
    C. II and III only
    D. I, II and III

9. Losses from direct participation programs can be used to offset

    A. earned income from salary or commissions
    B. portfolio income
    C. income from limited partnerships
    D. none of the above

10. Interest expense incurred to purchase which of the following types of securities is NOT federally tax deductible?

    A. Corporate bonds
    B. Treasury securities
    C. Municipal bonds
    D. Common stocks

Answers

1. **A.** Individual taxpayers must pay taxes on the full amount of their dividend income.

2. **C.** Bonds issued by territories and political subdivisions of the United States (Puerto Rico, Guam and the U.S. Virgin Islands) are exempt from federal, state and local taxes.

3. **D.** These bonds are issued by General Telephone, a publicly held corporation located in the state of Ohio. Like all corporate bonds, the interest income is fully taxable.

4. **C.** U.S. government bonds are exempt from state and local taxes, but the interest is taxed by the federal government. The customer earned $300 annual interest ($5,000 × 6%). The federal tax liability is $84 ($300 × 28%).

5. **B.** Dividends (whether reinvested or not), Ginnie Maes, Fannie Maes and IADB securities are all fully taxable. U.S. government securities are exempt from state and local taxes.

6. **C.** Normally, the greater the risk, the higher the yield that must be offered to potential investors. Therefore, government securities yield less than corporate securities. In this problem, you must also take into account the difference in taxable bonds (corporate and governments) versus tax-free bonds (municipals). This difference in taxation causes the pretax yield of municipals to be lower than that of corporate and government bonds.

7. **A.** One hundred preferred shares cost $9,800 (100 × $98). These 100 shares convert into 140 shares of common (100 × 1.4). The 140 shares of common stock are worth $10,290 (140 × $73.50). The profit is the sale proceeds on the common stock less the cost of the preferred, or $490 ($10,290 − $9,800).

8. **C.** Both dividend payments and capital gains distributions are taxed at ordinary income tax rates (choice II). Investors must report and pay taxes on all such distributions even if they are

automatically reinvested in the fund (so choice I is false). The exchange of mutual fund shares within a family of funds is treated as a sale and repurchase of securities, so taxable capital gains or losses are incurred when shares are exchanged.

9. **C.** Passive losses can be used only to offset passive gains.

10. **C.** Interest expense incurred to purchase a security that offers federally tax exempt income cannot be deducted.

13

U.S. Government and State Rules and Regulations

Insider Trading Act of 1988 { 1mil or 300% profit ↑ 10 ye

Policies and Procedures

Insiders may be held liable for more than just transactions in their own accounts. Investors who have suffered monetary damage because of insider trading now have legal recourse against the insider and against any other party who had control over the misuse of nonpublic information. The SEC can levy a penalty of up to three times the amount of profit made (or loss avoided) if inside information is used. To determine whether information is nonpublic, the SEC considers the method by which the information is released to the public and the timing of trades relative to when other people also have the information.

Written supervisory procedures. All broker-dealers must establish written supervisory procedures specifically prohibiting the use of material nonpublic information.

SEC investigations. The SEC has the right to investigate any person who has violated or is suspected of violating any of the provisions of the Insider Trading Act.

Civil Penalties

Under the act, the person controlling the incident may be liable for civil penalties of up to the greater of $1 million or 300% of profits made (or losses avoided). Any person who knowingly violates these rules can be imprisoned for up to ten years.

Control. The simple fact that a person would normally have control over another does not imply guilt. The Commission would establish the full extent of that person's control and involvement before it exacted any penalties.

Short-swing profits. Insiders may not retain short-swing profits in securities, and any short-swing profit can actually be reclaimed by the stockholders of the company. Insiders are prohibited from establishing short-against-the-box positions and entering short sales.

Insider Trading Rules

The key elements of tipper and tippee liability under the insider trading rules are as follows:

- Does the *tipper* owe a *fiduciary duty* (to a company, its stockholders, etc.), and has he breached it?
- Does the *tipper* meet the *personal benefits test* (even something as simple as enhancing a friendship or reputation)?
- Does the *tippee know or should the tippee have known* that the information was inside or confidential?
- Is the *information material and nonpublic*?

Given these elements, a "slip of the tongue" by a corporate insider could leave that person liable under the rules, and anyone who trades on information that she knows or should know is not public is also liable.

Chinese Wall Doctrine

Those departments or branches of a broker-dealer that have access to material nonpublic information may not disseminate this information to anyone who could conceivably trade on it.

Questions

1. Which of the following statements about insider transactions are true?

    I.   After filing an initial statement of holding, an insider must see that every change in securities holdings thereafter is recorded by the SEC.
    II. Selling short and selling short against the box are prohibited.
    III. An insider may not earn long-term capital gains on her own company's securities.
    IV. Insiders may not make securities transactions based on nonpublic information.

    A. I, II and IV only
    B. I and III only
    C. II, III and IV only
    D. I, II, III and IV

Answers

1. **A.** All statements are true except choice III. An insider may take long-term gains. It is short-term gains that may not be made by an insider. If an insider does make a short-term capital gain on securities of that company, the gain must be given to the company.

Securities Investor Protection Corporation

All broker-dealers registered with the SEC must be SIPC members. Exempt from membership are:

- broker-dealers handling exclusively open-end investment company shares or unit trusts;
- broker-dealers handling exclusively variable annuities or insurance; and
- investment advisers.

The SIPC Fund

SIPC collects from its members an annual assessment based on a percentage of a member's gross revenues from the securities business.

SIPC has been given SEC authority to borrow from the U.S. Treasury to meet claims.

Protection of Customers

If the SEC or any SRO finds indications that a broker-dealer is in financial difficulty, SIPC will be notified immediately. If SIPC determines that the member has failed or is in imminent danger of failing, it may petition a federal court to take action by appointing a trustee to liquidate the firm and protect its customers. Once a trustee has been appointed, the member firm is prohibited from engaging in business as a broker-dealer.

Liquidation Proceedings

The trustee is required to *promptly*:

- deliver securities that are registered in a customer's name back to the customer;
- assign ownership and distribute street name securities to customers;
- sell or transfer branches or other offices of the failed broker-dealer to raise capital; and
- liquidate the business of the broker-dealer.

Notification. The appointed trustee must notify by mail all customers of the firm during the preceding twelve months about the liquidation proceedings and publish a notice of the liquidation in one or more general-circulation newspapers. Customer claims are based on the customers' net equity as of the valuation date of their accounts.

Payment of customers. The trustee will distribute the securities held by the broker-dealer according to the following guidelines:

- Securities registered in customer name are returned to the owners without dollar limit.
- Securities held in street name and cash are distributed to customers on a pro rata basis.
- After the distribution of street name securities and cash, SIPC funds are available to meet remaining claims of each customer up to a *maximum of $500,000*, with *cash claims* not to exceed *$100,000* of the $500,000 total.
- For claims in excess of $500,000, the customers become general creditors of the broker-dealer and share pro rata with all other general creditors.

Customer Account Coverage

Individuals. Under SIPC rules, each *separate customer account* is entitled to coverage up to SIPC limits. "Separate customer accounts" are defined as those accounts with *unique beneficial owners*.

Coverage limits. Customer accounts are covered to a *maximum of $500,000*, with *cash claims* not to exceed *$100,000*. Only claims for securities and cash are covered; claims resulting from open positions in commodity futures contracts do not fall under SIPC coverage.

Advertising SIPC Membership

SIPC bylaws allow members to put up a sign indicating a firm's coverage under SIPC as long as the term "SIPC" does not appear larger than the firm's own name and as long as the sign does not imply that the member can offer SIPC benefits not afforded by other members.

Questions

1. Which of the following is NOT true of SIPC?

   A. It is a nonprofit corporation designed to protect the public in the event a broker-dealer fails.
   B. It is a government agency designed to protect the public.
   C. It is funded by broker-dealers.
   D. It is subject to an SEC overview.

2. Under SIPC, each customer's account is insured for

   A. $100,000 in cash
   B. $500,000 in bonds
   C. $500,000, with cash not to exceed $100,000
   D. $600,000 in bonds and cash

3. Claims for more than the maximum allowable coverage are settled under SIPC in which of the following manners?

   A. Rejected in whole
   B. Paid to the maximum coverage, with the excess rejected
   C. Paid to the maximum coverage, with the excess becoming the claim of a general creditor
   D. Paid to the maximum coverage, with the excess becoming a subordinated claim paid after the general creditors are paid

4. If a SIPC member corporation were to go bankrupt, the trustee appointed would be responsible for all of the following EXCEPT

   A. informing the firm's clients about the liquidation
   B. distributing identifiable customer-owned securities held by the firm
   C. supervising the distributions for commodity accounts
   D. supervising the liquidation of the firm and seeing that it is done methodically

Answers

1. **B.** Answer B is untrue. The other answers are true. SIPC is a private organization that was set up as a nonprofit corporation. It was designed by Congress to protect the public even if the broker-dealer fails. SIPC is funded by broker-dealers and is subject to SEC overview.

2. **C.** SIPC insures accounts for a total of $500,000 with maximum coverage of $100,000 in cash.

3. **C.** Any claim exceeding the maximum coverage becomes a claim as a general creditor. The amount that is covered by SIPC insurance will be paid in full by SIPC.

4. **C.** SIPC does not cover commodity accounts.

Other Federal and State Legislation

Federal Regulations

Maloney Act

The Maloney Act provided for the creation of the NASD and its registration with the SEC.

Trust Indenture Act of 1939

The Trust Indenture Act of 1939 specifies that any corporate bond issue of more than $5 million and a maturity date more than nine months in the future must be issued with a trust indenture.

Investment Company Act of 1940

The purpose of the Investment Company Act of 1940 is to regulate investment companies in order to ensure that they adhere to specific rules and regulations and to keep investors fully informed about investment company operations.

Investment Advisers Act of 1940

This act requires that if an individual is in the business of giving investment advice (gives such advice and charges a fee for the advice), she must register as an investment adviser.

Securities Acts Amendments of 1975

MSRB

The Securities Acts Amendments of 1975 established the **Municipal Securities Rulemaking Board (MSRB)**. This board makes rules pertaining to the issuance and trading of municipal securities.

State Regulations

State securities laws are known as **blue-sky laws**. The **Uniform Securities Act (USA)** serves as model legislation that each state may follow or adapt to its own needs.

Most states require broker-dealers that do business in a particular state to register with that state's securities commission. Salespeople associated with a broker-dealer must also be registered in the state(s) where they do business.

In most states, securities must be registered before they can be sold to the public. There are three ways to register a security in a state:

1. **Coordination**. At the same time the issuer files with the SEC, it files with the state.
2. **Notification**. If an issuer meets certain criteria, it can notify the state that it is about to sell a security.
3. **Qualification**. The issuer files with the state a registration statement that meets the state's requirements.

The securities and transactions exempt from state securities registration include:

- securities listed on SEC-registered stock exchanges;
- nonprofit organizations;
- insurance companies;
- banks;
- building and loan associations;
- public utilities and railroads;
- cooperative associations; and
- private placements.

Under blue-sky laws, most states require that all advertising be submitted for approval to the state securities administration.

Questions

1. Which of the following is(are) objectives of the Investment Company Act of 1940?

   A. To ensure that the individual investor is fully informed about the affairs of the investment company and is treated fairly by its management

   B. To require minimum financial and accounting standards of all broker-dealers engaged in interstate commerce

   C. To control the size of individual investment companies and their impact on securities markets

   D. All of the above

2. All of the following statements are true of blue-sky laws EXCEPT that

   A. they attempt to protect the public from the fraudulent sale of securities within a particular state

   B. the Securities Act of 1933 sets forth certain standard provisions that must appear in all blue-sky laws

   C. an issuer that intends to offer securities for sale in several states must comply with the provisions of the Securities Act of 1933 and all securities laws of the appropriate states

   D. a state securities division has the power to revoke the license of any securities salesperson for violation of its laws

3. A state requires registration for which of the following?

   I. In-state salesperson
   II. In-state broker-dealer
   III. Out-of-state salesperson doing business in that state
   IV. Out-of-state broker-dealer doing business in that state

   A. I and II only
   B. II and IV only
   C. III and IV only
   D. I, II, III and IV

4. In which of the following circumstances can a registered representative purchase a security for a client who lives in a certain state when the security is not registered in the state?

   I. The security is NYSE listed.
   II. The security is exempt from registration.
   III. The security is listed on the Canadian Stock Exchange.
   IV. The security has been publicly traded for at least twelve months.

   A. I and II only
   B. I, II and IV only
   C. II only
   D. I, II, III and IV

5. In some states, registration of securities with the state securities division may be accomplished through

   I. notification
   II. substitution
   III. qualification
   IV. coordination

   A. I and II
   B. I, II and IV
   C. I, III and IV
   D. II and III

6. Which of the following legislative acts exclusively regulates debt securities?

   A. Securities Act of 1933
   B. Securities Exchange Act of 1934
   C. Trust Indenture Act of 1939
   D. Investment Advisers Act of 1940

Answers

1. **A.** A "rules and regulations" question tempts one to pick "all of the above." But, in this case, answers B and C do not apply to the Investment Company Act of 1940.

2. **B.** The Securities Act of 1933 is a federal statute—the federal government does not dictate state law. Blue-sky laws protect the public from securities fraud in each state and must be complied with by issuers and by broker-dealers.

3. **D.** A broker-dealer or salesperson doing business in the state must be registered in that state.

4. **A.** To sell a security in a given state, the security must be registered in the state. This is required unless the security is exempt. Most states exempt listed securities from state registration (a *blue chip* exemption). In addition, exempt securities under the act of 1933 are also exempt from state registration.

5. **C.** "Substitution" is not a method of registering securities with a state securities administrator. The other answers are ways in which a security can be registered.

6. **C.** The Trust Indenture Act of 1939 protects investors in corporate bonds in the case of the default of the issuing company.

14 Other SEC and SRO Rules and Regulations

Registration and Regulation

Securities Exchange Act of 1934

Broker-dealers that transact securities business with customers or with other broker-dealers must apply and be approved for registration with the SEC.

SEC Sanctions against Broker-Dealers

The SEC is entitled to:

- censure
- limit activities, functions or operations
- suspend
- revoke registration
- fine
- seek civil monetary penalties

Associated person. An associated person also can be suspended, censured, restricted in his activities, fined or barred from association with a broker-dealer. If the SEC has barred an associated person, no broker-dealer may allow that person to associate with it without the express permission of the Commission.

Fingerprinting

Registered broker-dealers are required to have fingerprint records made for all of their employees, directors, officers and partners, and are required to submit those fingerprint cards to the U.S. attorney general for identification and processing. Certain employees (typically clerical and ministerial) are exempt from the fingerprinting requirement if they:

- are not involved in securities sales;
- do not handle or have access to cash or securities or to the books and records of original entry relating to money and securities; and
- do not supervise other employees engaged in these activities.

Questions

1. Under the Securities Exchange Act of 1934, the SEC does which of the following?

   I. Regulates securities exchanges.
   II. Requires the registration of brokers and dealers.
   III. Prohibits inequitable and unfair trade practices.
   IV. Regulates over-the-counter markets.

   A. I and II only
   B. I and IV only
   C. II, III and IV only
   D. I, II, III and IV

2. The Securities and Exchange Commission was established under the

   A. Securities Act of 1933
   B. Securities Exchange Act of 1934
   C. Investor Protection Act of 1970
   D. Federal Reserve Board

Answers

1. **D.** Although the SEC has delegated some of the responsibility of overseeing the OTC markets to the NASD, it is still ultimately responsible for their regulation.

2. **B.** Although a primary responsibility of the Securities and Exchange Commission is to review registration statements for new issues of nonexempt securities (which must register under the act of 1933), the SEC was not formed until 1934 under the Securities Exchange Act. Before the formation of the SEC, issues were registered with the Federal Trade Commission.

NASD Bylaws

Self-regulatory Organizations

The largest of the SROs, and their jurisdictions, are the following:

- **National Association of Securities Dealers (NASD).** Regulates all matters related to investment banking (securities underwriting) and trading in the OTC market and the conduct of NASD member firms and associated persons.
- **New York Stock Exchange (NYSE).** Regulates all matters related to trading in NYSE-listed securities and the conduct of NYSE member firms and associated persons.
- **Municipal Securities Rulemaking Board (MSRB).** Regulates all matters related to the underwriting and trading of state and municipal securities (the MSRB regulates but does not have enforcement powers—it depends on other SROs for the enforcement of its rules).
- **Chicago Board Options Exchange (CBOE).** Regulates all matters related to writing and trading standardized options and related contracts listed on that exchange.

Administration of the NASD

Membership Corporation

The NASD is a membership corporation incorporated under the laws of the State of Delaware. The purposes and objectives of the NASD are to:

- promote the investment banking and securities business, to standardize principles and practices, to promote high standards of commercial honor and to encourage the observance of federal and state securities laws;
- provide a medium for communication among its members, and between its members, the government and other agencies;

- adopt, administer and enforce the NASD's Rules of Fair Practice and rules designed to prevent fraudulent and manipulative practices, as well as to promote just and equitable principles of trade; and
- promote self-discipline among members and investigate and adjust grievances between the public and members and between members.

Districts. The NASD has divided the United States into 13 districts in order to facilitate operation. Every year, each district committee appoints a **District Business Conduct Committee (DBCC)**, which handles the trade practice complaints that arise in the district.

NASD Dues, Assessments and Other Charges

The annual fee charged to members includes the following:

- basic membership fee;
- assessment based on gross income;
- fee for each principal and registered representative; and
- charge for each branch office.

Use of the Corporate Name

Members of the NASD are prohibited from using the name of the Association in any manner that would suggest that the member's registration with the NASD means that the Association has passed upon or approved its financial standing, business or conduct.

NASD Manual

The *NASD Manual* describes the following four sets of basic rules and codes by which the OTC market is regulated:

1. Rules of Fair Practice
2. Uniform Practice Code
3. Code of Procedure
4. Code of Arbitration Procedure

NASD Membership and Registration

Broker-Dealer Registration

Any broker-dealer that is registered as such with the SEC is eligible and may apply for membership in the NASD. Application for membership in the NASD specifically carries the applying firm's agreement to:

- comply with the rules and regulations of the Association;
- comply with federal securities laws; and
- pay dues, assessments and other charges in the manner and amounts fixed by the Association.

Branch Offices

Registration. Each branch office must be registered with the NASD.

Executive representation. At a national level, each member firm is entitled to appoint an executive representative to act in the firm's interest on business and political issues brought before the NASD in Washington, D.C.

Associated Person Registration

Any person who is or becomes associated with an NASD member firm and who intends to engage in the investment banking or securities business must be registered with the NASD as an associated person.

Registration Rules and Regulations

Qualifications investigated. Prior to submitting an application to enroll any person with the NASD as a registered representative, the member firm is obligated to investigate and ascertain the person's business reputation over the previous ten years, good character, educational institutions attended, qualifications and experience.

Registered persons changing firms. NASD registration is *nontransferable*. If a registered person leaves one member firm to join another firm, he must terminate registration at the first firm and reapply for registration with the new employing member firm. If a person has terminated his registration with one firm, he must register with another firm within two years or he will be required to requalify for his license.

Exemptions from Registration

Foreign associates. Non-U.S. citizens employed by NASD member firms are not subject to registration and licensing with the Association.

Clerical and ministerial personnel and corporate officers. A member firm's employee whose function is purely clerical or ministerial does not have to register with the Association.

Qualifications Examinations

Registered Representatives

All associated persons engaged in the investment banking and securities business are considered registered representatives, including any:

- assistant officer who does not function as a principal;
- individual who supervises, solicits or conducts business in securities; and
- individual who trains others to supervise, solicit or conduct business in securities.

Following are the primary registrations available at this time.

Series 7. The Series 7 General Securities Representative license allows a registered rep to sell all types of securities products, including corporate stocks and bonds, government and municipal securities, options, direct participation programs (DPPs), investment company products and most other types of securities.

Series 6. The Series 6 Investment Company/Variable Contract Products Limited Representative license entitles a representative to sell mutual funds and variable annuities and is used by many firms that are engaged primarily in the sale of insurance-related products.

Series 11. The Series 11 Assistant Representative—Order Processing license allows a registered sales assistant to take unsolicited orders, enter order tickets, update client information, fill out client new account forms and provide customers with quotes and other pro forma information relating to securities.

Ineligibility and Disqualifications

NASD membership will be denied and status as an associated person will be refused to any firm or individual candidate who fails to meet the Association's eligibility standards.

Disqualifications. A broker-dealer or an individual must be treated as a nonmember if the firm or person:

- has been and is expelled or suspended from membership or participation in any other SRO;
- is under an SEC order denying, suspending or revoking the broker-dealer's SEC registration or barring the individual from association with a broker-dealer; or
- has been found to be the cause of another broker-dealer or associated person being expelled or suspended by another SRO or the SEC.

Any of the following also will disqualify an applicant:

- misstatements willfully made in an application for membership or registration as an associated person;
- a felony conviction within the previous ten years or a misdemeanor charge involving securities or money; or
- court injunctions prohibiting the firm or individual from acting as an investment adviser, an underwriter or a broker-dealer.

Questions

1. A person who has just passed the Series 7 examination (NASD/NYSE exams) is now
   A. registered to sell securities to residents of all states
   B. registered to sell securities to residents of her state
   C. allowed to sell securities to residents of her state after she has registered with the securities department of that state
   D. allowed to sell securities in her NASD district

2. You are a registered representative and you are resigning from a member firm. In order to join another firm as a registered rep, you should
   A. transfer your registration
   B. take the Series 7 exam again immediately and reapply for membership when you pass
   C. resign in writing, notify the NYSE and file a new application form with the firm you are joining
   D. notify the NASD and serve a 90-day apprenticeship with your new firm

3. The NASD Uniform Practice Code was established to
   A. require that practices in the investment banking and securities industry be just, reasonable and nondiscriminatory between investors
   B. eliminate advertising and sales literature the SEC considers to be in violation of standards
   C. provide a procedure for handling trade complaints from investors
   D. maintain similarity of business practices among member organizations in the securities industry

Answers

1.   **C.**   A person who passes the Series 62 or 7 examination must register with the securities commission in each state in which she wants to do business. Most states require that a person passes the Series 63 (blue-sky) examination.

2.   **C.**   You cannot transfer your registration. You must terminate employment with your present employer by filling out a U-5 Form, and then you must reapply for registration with the new employer.

3.   **D.**   The Uniform Practice Code is designed to make uniform the customs, practices and trading techniques employed in the investment banking and securities business.

NASD Codes of Procedure and Arbitration

Code of Procedure

complaint → member & Assoc. person

The NASD's Code of Procedure was developed as a guide to settling complaints that arise between and among members and associated persons.

Sources of complaints. When a customer, another member firm or one of the NASD's own committees lodges a complaint, an NASD examiner investigates the accused member's premises and inspects the books in an effort to substantiate or discredit the complaint.

Complaint resolution process. The DBCC notifies the accused member in writing, advising it as to the specifics of the complaint, identifying who has filed the complaint and requesting a response from the accused member within 20 calendar days of the date of receipt.

Request for hearing. When the regular complaint proceeding is chosen, the member firm or associated person will either deny the charge of rule violation or make an offer of settlement.

Decision of the committee. The DBCC will issue a written decision and announce the sanctions being imposed on the member firm or associated person as disciplinary action.

Summary complaint. In a summary complaint, the complainant usually has sufficient evidence on hand to support the complaint that a violation has occurred. If amenable to the settlement terms stated in a summary complaint, the member firm or associated person named in the complaint signs and returns a *letter of acceptance, waiver and consent.*

Penalties. If the DBCC finds that a rule violation has occurred, one or more of the following sanctions may be imposed:

- censure
- fine
- suspension
- expulsion
- barring

Appeal and review. A respondent in receipt of the DBCC's findings in favor of the complainant has 15 calendar days from the date of receipt to appeal the decision to the NASD Board of Governors.

Appeal to SEC. If either the complainant or the respondent feels aggrieved by the decision of the NASD Board of Governors, application can be made to the SEC for a review.

Code of Arbitration Procedure

The arbitration process is geared towards resolving problems and financial losses that usually can be traced to misunderstandings and faulty communications or to the failure of one person to live up to another person's expectations (Uniform Practice Code violations). Arbitration offers participants a relatively easy method of settling disputes at a cost that is usually significantly lower than the cost of settling a dispute through the courts.

Matters eligible for submission. Any dispute, claim or controversy may be submitted to the NASD's National Arbitration Committee for resolution and settlement.

Required submissions. Internal disputes between member firms and between associated persons must be submitted for resolution and settlement via arbitration.

Arbitration involving customers. Customers are under no obligation to submit any matter of dispute or claim to the NASD's Board of Arbitration.

No redress through the courts. Findings under the Code of Arbitration are binding on all parties involved in the dispute.

Simplified industry arbitration. Disputes not involving customers can be submitted for resolution under simplified industry arbitration procedures provided the dollar amount of the claim does not exceed $10,000.

Simplified customer arbitration. As with simplified industry arbitration, the dollar amount in dispute must not exceed $10,000.

Questions

1. An NASD member can take a final appeal of disciplinary action to the

    A. Board of Governors
    B. SEC
    C. civil district court
    D. Supreme Court

2. If a case has gone to the Board of Arbitration of the NASD or NYSE, the decisions made are

    A. not binding on a client but are binding on the member
    B. binding only if the two parties agree on the decision
    C. not binding if the two parties decide not to accept the decision
    D. always binding on all parties to the arbitration

Answers

1.   **D.**   The District Business Conduct Committee and the Board of Governors are the two bodies that are empowered to hear and pass upon all complaints concerning the Rules of Fair Practice. The District Business Conduct Committee has first jurisdiction over these complaints, and the Board of Governors acts as an appellate body. A decision by the Board of Governors can be appealed to the SEC, and an SEC decision can be appealed through the federal court system to the Supreme Court.

2.   **D.**   The decisions of the board of arbitration are final and are binding on the parties involved. There is no appeal of these decisions.

— much stringent rules than NASD

NYSE Constitution and Rules

*{ 10 Exchange member
10 Public Rep
1 Chairperson*

Organization

The NYSE is a corporation operated by a board of directors consisting of ten Exchange members, ten public representatives and one chairperson. The board is responsible for setting policy, supervising Exchange and member activities, listing securities, overseeing the transfer of members' seats on the Exchange and judging whether an applicant is qualified to be a specialist.

Membership   *at 1,366 fix*

The number of memberships, or **seats**, on the NYSE is fixed at 1,366.

Only individuals can own seats on the Exchange.

Member Firms

A member firm must obtain prior approval from the Exchange in order to open a branch office. Every branch must be supervised by a principal who has passed the appropriate principal's examination.

The principal's supervisory duties include:

- approving new accounts;
- reviewing all correspondence, trade blotters and registered representatives' client statements;
- reviewing all transactions with clients and representatives' accounts of clients; and
- initialing all of the above items.

Registration of Employees

All employees of NYSE member firms must be registered through their firms with the NYSE. Registered reps who work for a member firm must exhibit high standards of business conduct and integrity, must pass an examination and must have reached the age of majority.

A registered rep cannot be employed in name only. Registered reps must, in most cases, work full time for the firm. Transfer of registration is not permitted; a rep must resign from one employer and reapply for registration with the new firm.

Registered reps must sign statements agreeing to abide by certain regulations. A person who wishes to become a registered representative must agree to read the NYSE constitution and regulations and abide by them.

Employment other than with the employing broker-dealer. Under NYSE rules, a registered rep must have her firm's written permission before taking a second job.

Compensation. The representative can receive compensation for securities transactions only from her employer. Permission from the Exchange is needed in order to be paid by any other firm for securities trades.   *$50 is OK*

Arbitration

The NYSE Board of Arbitration hears and settles disagreements between members, allied members, member organizations and their employees. Nonmembers may voluntarily submit to arbitration in a dispute with members or employees. Decisions of the arbitrators are final.

Discipline

Disciplinary hearing. A grievance or complaint against an employee of a member organization must be made in writing.

Penalties and review. The hearing panel may impose on a member found guilty of a violation any of the following penalties:

- censure
- fine
- suspension
- expulsion
- barring

Questions

1. The objectives of the NYSE include which of the following?

    I. To maintain high standards of commercial honor
    II. To promote just principles of trade
    III. To provide a place for the transaction of a member's business

    A. I only
    B. I and III only
    C. II and III only
    D. I, II and III

2. An NYSE registered representative

    A. can, at his discretion, give evidence to an investigating body at the request of the Exchange
    B. must give evidence on any subject under investigation but is not required to produce relevant documents or records
    C. must produce relevant documents or records but is not required to give oral testimony
    D. must not fail to give evidence on any subject under investigation and must produce, on request of the Exchange, all relevant records or documents

3. All of the following statements are true EXCEPT that

    A. unless Exchange permission is granted, registered representatives cannot devote less than full time to the duties of their member employers
    B. the term *registered representative* applies to someone who solicits orders for the purchase or sale of securities for her employer's clients
    C. testimonials are representative of the experience of one or a few clients and are not necessarily indicative of future market performance
    D. compensations by members to an employee of another member firm are acceptable as long as they don't exceed the limit of $75

4. The NYSE requires a general partner or an officer of the member organization to

    A. supervise diligently all accounts handled by registered representatives of the organization
    B. use due diligence to learn the essential facts relative to every client
    C. specifically approve the opening of any account prior to or promptly after the completion of any transaction for the account of a client
    D. do all of the above

5. As a means of protecting the investing public from possible member organization financial failure, the NYSE

    A. charges a large price for membership
    B. requires an annual audit of the books of member firms by outside certified auditors
    C. insists that margin accounts be maintained at 50% of market value
    D. requires all of the above

6. How does one become an NYSE-registered representative?

A. Fill out an application and pay a fee to the New York Stock Exchange.
B. Pass an exam.
C. Be sponsored by a member broker-dealer firm, exhibit high standards of integrity and pass an exam.
D. Serve a 90-day apprenticeship.

7. NYSE registered representative agreements include which of the following provisions?

A. Not to guarantee clients against loss
B. Not to accept any kind of compensation from a source other than her employer without prior written consent of the Exchange
C. Not to offer part of her commission to anyone as an inducement to obtain securities business
D. All of the above

Answers

1. **D.** The NYSE maintains high standards of honor, promotes fair trade and provides the location for the trading of securities.

2. **D.** When a person becomes a registered representative, he agrees to appear before Exchange committees and to produce documents as requested by the Exchange.

3. **D.** Gifts by member firms to employees of another member firm are limited to $50 in any year.

4. **D.** All of the answers seem to be protective of the client. So, if you were in doubt about any of them, you could be quite sure that statements that protect the client are probably true.

5. **B.** SIPC protects investors from actual financial failure of member firms, but an annual audit might avert a failure before it happens.

6. **C.** Answers A and B are incorrect because there are more requirements than passing the exam and paying fees. The rep, moreover, is not a member of the Exchange; the rep is associated with the member firm.

7. **D.** Answers A, B and C are all true.

Communications with the Public

Advertising and Sales Literature

Advertising materials. Advertising includes copy and support graphics and/or other support materials intended for:

- publication in newspapers, magazines or other periodicals;
- radio or TV broadcast;
- prerecorded telephone marketing messages and tape recordings;
- videotape displays;
- signs or billboards;
- motion pictures and filmstrips;
- telephone directories; and
- *any other use of the public media.*

Sales literature. Sales literature is *any written communication distributed to customers* or available to people upon request, and includes materials such as:

- circulars;
- research reports;
- market letters;
- form letters;
- options worksheets;
- performance reports and summaries;
- text prepared and used for educational seminars;
- prepared scripts for public interest radio and TV interview programs; and
- reprints and excerpts from any advertisement, sales literature or published news item or article.

Sales literature can be distributed in either written or oral form. Standardized sales pitches, telephone scripts and seminar tapes are all classed as sales literature, and are therefore subject to the same rules and regulations that apply to printed literature.

Form letters. A letter becomes a form letter if it is sent to more than 25 persons within any 90 consecutive days.

Generic advertising (Rule 135a). Institutional advertising uses general terms and phrases and often includes information about:

- the securities offered by investment companies;
- the nature of investment companies;
- services offered in connection with the described securities;
- explanations of the various types of investment companies;
- descriptions of exchange and reinvestment privileges; and
- where the public can write or call for further information.

All generic advertisements must contain the name and address of the registered sponsor of the advertisement.

Tombstones (Rule 134 advertisements). Rule 145 makes it unlawful to solicit stockholders unless a prospectus accompanies the solicitation. Under Rule 134, advertising copy and other sales materials will not be deemed a prospectus if the body copy is limited to the following:

- the name of the issuer of the securities being offered;
- a brief description of the business of the person making the offer;
- the date, time and place of the meeting at which stockholders are to vote on or consent to the proposed transaction;
- a brief description of the planned transaction (material facts and financial information); or
- any legend or disclaimer statement required by state or federal law.

Advertisements that meet these restrictions are more commonly known as **tombstones** or **Rule 134 advertisements**. Any advertising copy in a tombstone must also contain the following disclaimers:

- that the registration statement has been filed by the issuer but is not yet effective;
- that the communication does *not* represent an offer to sell the securities described—securities are sold **by prospectus only;**

- the name and address of the person (or firm) to contact for a prospectus; and
- that a response to this advertisement does not obligate the prospect to a buying commitment of any kind (i.e., that it represents only an **indication of interest**).

Hiring New Registered Representatives

Recruitment advertisements must be truthful, informative and fair in representing the opportunities in the industry and must not contain exaggerated or unwarranted claims. Broker-dealers are permitted, in this one instance, to run blind advertisements.

Approval and Filing Requirements

Seminars and Public Lectures

Under NYSE rules, a member firm must keep a log of all seminars. For each seminar, the log must include the topic and the names of the speaker(s) and sponsor.

Exceptions to Filing Requirements

The following types of advertisements or sales literature are excluded from filing and spot check procedures:

- those relating solely to changes in a member's name, personnel, location, ownership, business structure, officers or partners, telephone, facsimile or teletype numbers, or to mergers involving and/or acquisitions by another member;
- those identifying only a member's NASDAQ symbol or the NASDAQ symbol and security in which the member makes a market;
- those identifying only the member and/or offering a security at a stated price; and
- those for internal distribution only and not distributed to the public.

Also excluded from the filing requirements are prospectuses, preliminary prospectuses, offering circulars and similar documents used in connection with the offering of securities that have been filed with the SEC or any state.

Customer Recommendations

Disclosure requirements. Proposals and written presentations that include specific recommendations must have reasonable bases to support the recommendations, and the member firm must provide these in the proposal or other written document, or offer to furnish them upon request. In any event, the member should have reasonable grounds for believing that a security is a suitable investment for a customer before recommending its purchase.

In addition to meeting these requirements, the firm making the recommendation must not:

- imply that there are any guarantees accompanying the recommendation;
- compare the recommended security to dissimilar products;
- make fraudulent or misleading statements about the recommended security; or
- make any predictions about the future performance or potential of the recommended security.

Other Communication Prohibitions

Claims and opinions couched as facts and conclusions. It is unprofessional and a violation of these regulations to pass off opinions, projections and forecasts as guarantees of performance or as scientific evidence.

Testimonials. Testimonials and endorsements by celebrities and public opinion influencers related to specific recommendations or investment results must not be misleading or suggest that past performance is an indication of future performance.

Other rules. The following is a list of rules regarding unprofessional practices:

- A communication must not state or imply that research facilities are more extensive than they actually are.

- Hedge clauses, caveats and disclaimers must not be used if they are misleading or inconsistent with the content of the material.
- If periodic investment plans are being promoted, the material must caution that such plans do not ensure a profit.
- Ambiguous references to the NASD or other SROs must not be made with the aim of leading people to believe that a broker-dealer is acting with the endorsement and approval of the Association (or one of the other SROs).
- If advertisements or sales literature includes price performance information in the form of charts, graphs or statistical tables prepared by or obtained from outside sources, the source of the data must be disclosed.

Legal Recourse of Customers

The Securities Exchange Act of 1934, and the acts of 1933 and 1940, all contain sections prohibiting the use of any fraudulent or manipulative device in the selling of securities to the public.

The rules make it unlawful for any person to use the mails or any facilities of interstate commerce to "… employ, in connection with the purchase or sale of any security … any manipulative or deceptive device … in contravention of such rules and regulations as the Commission may prescribe as necessary."

Any client may sue for damages if he believes that the broker-dealer employed any form of manipulative or deceptive practices in the sale of securities. The client must bring the lawsuit within three years of when the manipulative act occurs and within one year of his discovery of the manipulation or deception.

15 Municipal Securities

Municipal Bond Characteristics

Municipal securities are considered second only to U.S. government and U.S. government agency securities. Each new municipal issue is accompanied by documentation that:

- sets forth the terms of the loan and the schedule of repayment;
- attests to the issuing municipality's authority to issue the debt obligation;
- lists the specific features of the issue;
- describes the intended use of the borrowed funds; and
- provides financial information about the economic health of the municipality and the community.

Tax Benefits

The interest paid by most municipal securities is exempt from federal income taxation. The **doctrine of reciprocal immunity** was established by the Supreme Court in a decision handed down in 1895.

Municipalities are able to offer tax-exempt bonds at lower interest rates than offered by similar taxable bonds.

Issuers

The three primary entities legally entitled to issue municipal debt securities are territorial possessions of the United States, state governments and legally constituted taxing authorities.

Municipal Security Registration Documents

Bond contract. This is the contract a municipal issuer enters into with the underwriters of and investors in its securities.

Bond resolution. The municipality authorizes the issuance and sale of its securities through the bond resolution.

Trust indenture. This serves as a contract between the bond's issuer and an appointed trustee on behalf of the bond's investors.

Official statement (OS). This is the municipal securities industry's equivalent to the corporate prospectus. It serves as a disclosure document and contains any material information an investor might need about an issue.

Preliminary official statement. This discloses most of the same material information as the official statement, with the exception of the interest rate(s) and offering price(s) of the issue.

Legal opinion. This states that the issue conforms with applicable laws, the state constitution and established procedures. It is issued as either a **qualified opinion** or an **unqualified opinion**.

General Obligation Bonds

GO bondholders have a legal claim to the revenues received by a municipal government for payment of the principal and interest due them. Their financial support is ad valorem taxes for city, county and district bonds and sales and income taxes for state bonds. GOs are also known as *full faith and credit bonds*.

Sources of Funds

GOs are backed by taxes.

Legal Limitations

Statutory or constitutional limits on municipal debt. The amount of debt municipal governments are allowed to incur may be subject to local and state statutory debt limitations.

Voter approval. GOs must be approved by vote of the taxpayers in a referendum.

Tax limits. Property taxes are limited by some states to a certain percentage of the assessed property value or to a certain percentage increase in any single year.

Overlapping debt. Municipal entities that have overlapping boundaries are often described as **coterminous**, and their debt as coterminous debt.

Revenue Bonds (like Corp. Income Bond)

Revenue bonds can be used to finance any municipal function that generates income. The typical sources of revenue that finance the principal and interest payments to revenue bondholders include user charges for public utility facilities; tolls, concessions and fees from the operation of turnpikes, bridges, airports and other facilities; and rental payments under lease-rental arrangements between the issuing authority and a state or political subdivision.

Revenue bonds are payable only from the earnings of specific revenue-producing enterprises.

Revenue bonds are subject to no statutory debt limits and require no voter approval.

Sources of Revenue

The interest and principal payments of revenue bonds are payable to bondholders only from the specific earnings of revenue-producing facilities. They are not payable from general or real estate taxes and are not backed by the full faith and credit of the issuer.

Protective Covenants

The face of a revenue bond certificate usually refers to a trust indenture. This is a statement of the terms of agreement between the issuing municipality and the trustee appointed to act on behalf of the bondholders.

The trust indenture usually includes provisions for the following protective covenants:

- rate covenant
- maintenance covenant
- insurance covenant
- issuance of additional bonds
- sinking fund
- catastrophe clause
- flow of funds
- call features

Special Revenue Bonds

Industrial development revenue bonds. Industrial revenue bonds (IDRs or IDBs) and pollution control bonds are issued by a municipal authority to construct facilities or purchase equipment, which is then leased to a corporation. The ultimate responsibility for the payment of principal and interest rests with the corporate lessee.

Special tax and special assessment bonds. Special tax bonds are issued for specific projects and are payable only from the proceeds of a special tax.

New Housing Authority bonds. New Housing Authority bonds are backed by the full faith and credit of the U.S. government.

Double-barreled bonds. Interest and principal are paid from the earnings of the facility. The bonds are also backed by the taxing power of the state or municipality.

Moral obligation bonds. If revenues backing the bond are not sufficient to meet debt service requirements, the state has the authority to authorize payment on the debt through legislative appropriation.

Municipal Notes

Municipal notes fall into several categories:

- Tax anticipation notes (TANs)
- Revenue anticipation notes (RANs)
- Tax and revenue anticipation notes (TRANs)
- Bond anticipation notes (BANs)
- Construction loan notes (CLNs)
- Grant anticipation notes (GANs)
- Variable-rate demand notes

Questions

1. Municipal bonds are issued for all of the following EXCEPT

   A. sewers
   B. GNMAs
   C. hospitals
   D. capital improvements

2. Municipal bonds pay interest

   A. monthly
   B. quarterly
   C. semiannually
   D. annually

3. In safety of principal, municipal bonds are considered second only to

   A. preferred stock
   B. common stock
   C. U.S. government agency bonds
   D. FNMA securities

4. Which of the following is(are) a type of municipal bond?

   I. Collateral trust
   II. Revenue
   III. General obligation
   IV. Income

   A. I, II and III
   B. I, II and IV
   C. II and III
   D. III

5. A general obligation bond is backed by

   A. tolls
   B. special taxes
   C. public housing
   D. the full faith and credit of the issuing municipality

6. A bond issue backed by both net revenue rentals and the full faith and credit of the U.S. government is a

   A. Fannie Mae
   B. Ginnie Mae
   C. T bill
   D. New Housing Authority bond

7. A legal opinion on a municipal bond is prepared by

   A. the underwriter
   B. the trustee
   C. the municipality
   D. an independent bond attorney

8. All of the following would be found in the legal opinion of a municipal revenue bond EXCEPT

   A. the statutory, constitutional and other legal authority required to issue the bonds
   B. any call provisions
   C. a guarantee that revenue generated will be sufficient to pay the interest when due and the principal at maturity
   D. a description of the bonds

9. All of the following are examples of short-term, tax-exempt municipal issues EXCEPT

   A. BANs
   B. PNs
   C. AONs
   D. TANs

10. Short-term municipal notes normally have all of the following characteristics EXCEPT that they

   A. mature in less than one year
   B. are issued in anticipation of a bond sale
   C. pay interest every six months
   D. pay interest that is exempt from federal taxation

11. Revenue bonds are backed by all of the following EXCEPT

   A. tolls
   B. rental fees
   C. federal revenue sharing
   D. tuitions

12. Which of the following are characteristics of revenue bonds?

   I. They are usually free from debt limitations.
   II. They usually contain a rate covenant.
   III. They can be issued by interstate port authorities.

   A. I only
   B. I and II only
   C. II and III only
   D. I, II and III

13. To fund debt service on a general obligation bond, a municipality may use

   I. direct taxes
   II. special assessments
   III. fines
   IV. collection of delinquent funds

   A. I and II only
   B. I, III and IV only
   C. III and IV only
   D. I, II, III and IV

14. Special assessment bonds are backed by

   A. property taxes
   B. unlimited property claims
   C. charges against benefitted property
   D. gasoline, liquor and similar taxes

15. The taxing power of an issuer of a limited-tax bond is limited to a specified

   A. minimum rate
   B. maximum rate
   C. tax source
   D. method of taxation

16. All of the following statements are true of industrial revenue bonds EXCEPT that

   A. they are issued by municipalities to provide local industries with funds for pollution control equipment
   B. they are issued by municipalities to provide local industries with funds to purchase plants and equipment
   C. interest is paid from rental payments received from corporations that lease the property or equipment from the municipality
   D. the credit rating of the bonds is dependent on the credit rating of the municipality

17. A municipal bond is issued with a covenant that the state legislature has the authority to appropriate funds necessary to meet payments if revenue collections are not sufficient to do so. This bond is a

   A. contingent liability bond
   B. moral obligation bond
   C. general obligation bond
   D. double-barreled bond

18. A double-barreled municipal bond is backed by municipal

   A. revenues
   B. taxes
   C. taxes and revenues
   D. taxes and U.S. government taxes

19. A municipal bond issued to finance the construction of a new office complex will most likely be serviced and retired from

   A. a special tax
   B. a moral obligation
   C. lease payments from pooled rentals
   D. refunding

Answers

1. **B.** GNMAs are federal obligations.

2. **C.** Most municipal bonds, like most debt instruments, pay interest semiannually.

3. **C.** Municipal bonds are second only to U.S. government bonds in safety.

4. **C.** Municipal bonds include revenue and general obligation bonds. Corporate bonds include the income or adjustment bond and the collateral trust bond. The question requires only that you distinguish between the types of bonds issued by municipalities and those issued by corporations.

5. **D.** General obligation bonds are, as the name indicates, general obligations of the municipality. They are not tied to specific revenue sources, such as tolls, special taxes or properties.

6. **D.** New Housing Authority bonds (NHAs) are backed by the U.S. government, as well as by the issuing municipality's rental revenue from the facility. Federal backing makes them especially safe from default risk.

7. **D.** The legal counsel must be independent of the issuer.

8. **C.** The legal counsel cannot guarantee that the project will go as planned or that the city will remain solvent. The legal opinion examines only the legal aspects of the bond issue. The official statement, which is similar to a prospectus, contains among other things information about the issuer's financial status.

9. **C.** An all or none (AON) is a type of order; the term has nothing to do with short-term tax-exempt notes.

10. **C.** Short-term notes normally pay interest at maturity. The other answers are true of short-term municipal notes.

11. **C.** Revenue bonds are backed by revenues from the facility (such as tolls, rentals or tuition), not by federal revenue sharing.

12. **D.** All of the characteristics listed are true of revenue bonds. They are not subject to debt limits; they are free from debt limitations; they contain a rate covenant requiring that revenues be high enough to provide operation, maintenance and debt service; and they are issued by interstate port authorities (such as the Milwaukee Port Authority).

13. **B.** General obligation bonds may be funded by tax revenues, fines or collections of delinquent obligations. Special assessments are used to pay off special assessment bonds—a type of revenue bond.

14. **C.** Municipalities finance the installation of streets, curbs and gutters, sidewalks and similar amenities by issuing special assessment bonds. Property holders are assessed for the increased value of their property and the money from assessments is used to repay bondholders.

15. **B.** A limited-tax municipal bond is issued under statutory or constitutional limitations on the maximum tax that a government entity can charge.

16. **D.** Industrial revenue bonds are a primary obligation of the corporation—the municipality acts as a conduit in issuing the bonds. The bond's credit rating, therefore, is dependent on the corporation's rating.

17. **B.** The legislature has the authority and a moral obligation (but not a legal obligation) to appropriate any additional funds necessary to pay off the issue if revenues are insufficient. A double-barreled bond would be a GO; that is, the municipality is obligated to back the bond.

18. **C.** A double-barreled bond is a bond backed by two different sources—income from a revenue-producing facility plus the full faith and credit of a municipal issuer with taxing power.

19. **C.** Office buildings are often financed with lease rental bond issues. This is a revenue bond backed by lease payments to the issuing authority.

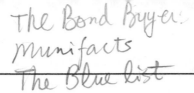
The Bond Buyer
Munifacts
The Blue List

Issuing Municipal Securities

Negotiation vs. Competitive Bidding

Negotiated Underwriting

Most revenue bonds are issued through a negotiated underwriting, and the issue can be distributed as either a public offering or a private placement.

Competitive Bidding

GOs are awarded to an underwriter through competitive bidding. Investment bankers form **syndicates** to prepare bids for the securities. Syndicates can obtain *bid worksheets* from *The Bond Buyer*.

The syndicate submits a bid outlining proposed interest rates and other conditions for conducting the underwriting. The municipality awards the bond issue to the bidder offering to sell the bonds at the lowest net cost to the issuer. The price at which the bonds are then sold to the public is known as the **reoffering price**.

Official notice of sale. The notice of bond sale includes the following information:

- date, time and place of sale;
- name and description of issuer;
- type of bond;
- interest payment dates;
- dated date, interest accrual date and first coupon payment date;
- maturity structure;
- call provisions (if any);
- name of the firm providing the legal opinion; and
- criteria for awarding the issue.

The bond's rating and the name of the underwriter are not included in a notice of sale because they have not yet been determined.

Functions of a Municipal Bond Attorney

The legal opinion. In addition to the statement about tax exemption, the legal opinion contains a description of the bonds, statements concerning the statutory basis for bond issuance, any tax limitation of the issuer and any call provision of the issue.

The underwriter's counsel. The underwriter's counsel is not responsible for the legal opinion and is employed to represent the interests of the underwriter, not those of the investors.

Municipal Securities Publications

Market and Index Information

The Blue List Total is a measure of the total par value of all municipal securities offered for sale in *The Blue List*.

The Bond Buyer publishes a number of indexes, including:

- 11 Bond GO Index
- 20 Bond GO Index
- 25 Bond Revenue Index (Revdex)

The Bond Buyer Municipal Bond Index is published daily and is a composite of the prices of 40 issues as determined by a group of five municipal brokers' brokers.

Sources of Information on Proposed Issues

Information can be obtained from the following publications:

- *The Bond Buyer* publishes the **30-day visible supply** and the **placement ratio**. *The Bond Buyer* also publishes **new issue worksheets** for the municipal industry.
- *Munifacts* is a wire service source of prices, information about proposed new issues and general news relevant to the municipal bond market.
- *The Blue List* lists the par value, issuer, interest rate, maturity date, price or yield and offering dealer for current municipal bond

secondary offerings of banks and brokers across the nation, and a limited amount of information about new issues.

The tombstone. Tombstones contain only limited information about the issue, including the type of bond, dated date, maturity date, interest rate, minimum denomination and syndicate manager(s).

Formation of the Underwriting Syndicate

Once an issuer's notice of sale has circulated, those investment bankers interested in placing a competitive bid for an issue form syndicates. Participants formalize their relationship by signing a syndicate letter (in a competitive bid) or a syndicate contract or agreement among underwriters (in a negotiated underwriting).

Types of Accounts

Western account. The Western account is a **divided account**. Each underwriter is responsible for its own underwriting allocation. An underwriter's financial liability ends once it has distributed its allocated bonds.

Eastern account. An Eastern account is an **undivided account**. Each underwriter is responsible for its own allocation *plus* a percentage of any unsold bonds. The responsibility for any unsold bonds continues until the entire issue has been sold.

Due Diligence

A due diligence investigation is conducted through a **feasibility study**, which focuses on information such as the projected revenues and costs associated with the project and on an analysis of competing facilities.

Establishing the Syndicate Bid

The process of establishing the yield for each maturity is called **writing a scale**. A scale is the list of the different maturities of the bond issue. If the coupon rate has already been determined, each maturity listed is assigned a yield. The underwriters also determine the premium, or discount, at which the bonds are to be offered.

Firm commitment. Competitive bids are submitted as firm commitments.

Awarding the Issue

The issuer meets in private with its attorneys and accountants to analyze each bid and then awards the municipal bond issue to the syndicate that offers to underwrite the bonds at the lowest **net interest cost (NIC)**, or **true interest cost (TIC)**, to the issuer.

Breakdown of the Spread

The spread is the difference between the price the syndicate pays to the issuer and the price at which the syndicate offers the bonds to the public.

Management fee. The managing underwriter receives from the spread a per-bond fee for its work in bringing the new issue to market.

Underwriting fee. Each syndicate member receives a share of the underwriting fee (or syndicate fee) according to its designated bracket or percentage of commitment. The managing underwriter would be entitled to its percentage of the syndicate fee *in addition to* the management fee it receives.

Takedown. The percentage of the spread that remains after subtracting the manager's and syndicate fees is called the *takedown*.

A member that has purchased bonds at the takedown can then either sell its bonds to customers at the POP or sell them to a dealer in the selling group at something less than full price.

Concession and reallowance. The discount a selling group dealer receives from a syndicate member is called the *concession*. Dealers are said to buy bonds from syndicate members *at the concession*.

When the member does not sell the bonds directly to the public, it *concedes* a portion of the takedown to the seller. The remainder is kept by the member and is called the **additional takedown**.

Allocation Priorities

The normal priority is as follows:

1. presale order
2. group net order
3. designated order
4. member-at-the-takedown order

Payment and Delivery

Confirmations of sales to customers. Final confirmations are mailed to investors who purchased the bonds from the underwriters. The investors' confirmations disclose the purchase price and settlement date (if known) for the transaction. The investor must pay any interest that has accrued between the dated date and the settlement date. The underwriters then deliver the bonds, accompanied by the legal opinion, to the investors.

Bonds are usually sold on a **when issued (WI)** basis. After the settlement date has been determined, sales between dealers or to investors are reconfirmed as regular way trades.

Official Statement

Any broker-dealer involved in the sale of a new issue must furnish a final official statement to every customer who has purchased part of that new issue, including other broker-dealers. A typical official statement will include all of the following information:

- offering terms;
- summary statement;
- purpose of issue;
- authorization of bonds;
- security of bonds;
- description of bonds;

- description of issuer;
- construction program;
- project feasibility;
- regulatory matters;
- specific provisions of the indenture or resolution;
- legal proceedings; and
- tax status.

Analyzing the Official Statement

Analysts study the various documents included in the official statement to determine the financial condition of the issuer at the present and in the foreseeable future.

Future financial needs. The official statement should be scrutinized for indications of future debt requirements.

The debt statement. The estimated full valuation of taxable property, the estimated assessed value of property and the assessment percentage, and the estimated population are all included in the debt statement.

Questions

1. If a municipality appoints an underwriter to offer a new issue, the underwriting is

   A. negotiated
   B. a competitive bid
   C. proportionate
   D. an Eastern agreement

2. Which of the following new bond issues would most probably be purchased through competitive bidding?

   A. Corporate bonds
   B. General obligation bonds
   C. Income bonds
   D. Debentures

3. An official notice of sale would include all of the following EXCEPT the

   A. authority for sale
   B. date and time of sale
   C. amount of issue
   D. bond rating

4. A municipal dealer considering placing a bid in a competitive general obligation bond offering would obtain information from

   A. *The Yellow Sheets*
   B. *The Bond Buyer*
   C. *The Blue List*
   D. Standard & Poor's *Bond Guide*

5. Interested parties wishing to submit bids on competitive municipal underwritings can obtain bid worksheets through a service provided by

   A. *The Bond Buyer*
   B. *The Blue List*
   C. *Munifacts*
   D. Moody's

6. When evaluating the validity of a new municipal issue, the bond counsel examines

   I. municipal statutes
   II. the state constitution and amendments
   III. judicial edicts
   IV. the legislative authority of the issuer

   A. I and II only
   B. I, II and III only
   C. III and IV only
   D. I, II, III and IV

7. The manager of a municipal syndicate is a dealer that will

   A. act for the underwriting group
   B. take the largest position
   C. act for the issuing authority
   D. provide the legal opinion

8. What is a "scale" on a municipal bond offering?

   A. List of bonds that have been redeemed
   B. List of bonds showing their yield to maturity and maturity date
   C. Description of how the municipality pays its debts
   D. Rating system for municipal bonds

9. In a competitive bid municipal underwriting, the completed bid form includes all of the following EXCEPT the

   A. reoffering scale
   B. bond interest rates
   C. premiums or discounts
   D. identity of the bidder

10. Which of the following statements is true of the good faith deposit of a competitively bid municipal offering?

    A. The deposit is returned by the issuer to the winning syndicate.
    B. The deposit is used to reduce the payment upon delivery of the bonds.
    C. The deposit is returned by the issuer to the underwriters if the underwriters suffer a loss as a result of syndicate operations.
    D. The deposit is treated as a portion of the settlement with the bond purchasers.

11. In a competitive bidding for a municipal bond to be issued at par, the underwriter will be selected on the basis of the

    A. refunding capabilities
    B. lowest interest rate offered
    C. highest dollar bid
    D. sinking fund provisions

12. A municipal syndicate account letter includes all of the following EXCEPT the

    A. final reoffering scale
    B. duration of the account
    C. participation of each member
    D. designation of the manager as the agent for the new issue underwriting

13. In a municipal securities underwriting, which of the following signs the agreement among underwriters?

    A. Members of the syndicate
    B. Issuer
    C. Bond counsel
    D. Trustee

14. The takedown in a municipal bond offering is the discount given to

    A. members of the syndicate
    B. nonmembers of the syndicate
    C. large institutional accounts
    D. members of the selling group

15. The date on which the interest on a new municipal issue will begin accruing is the

    A. filing date
    B. delivery date
    C. closing date
    D. dated date

16. All of the following are used to determine the bid for a municipal bond offering EXCEPT

    A. a good faith check
    B. yield
    C. maturity
    D. the type of bond

17. In an Eastern account, the broker-dealer is underwriting 200 bonds. If the firm sells its 200 bonds but other bonds remain unsold, it is liable for

    A. all of the unsold bonds
    B. none of the unsold bonds
    C. a maximum of 200 additional bonds
    D. a percentage of the unsold bonds equal to its percentage participation in the original allotment

18. A broker-dealer commits to $500,000 in bonds out of a total offering of $5 million in a Western syndicate. The broker-dealer sells $300,000 of the bonds. Of the total offering, $1 million of the bonds remain unsold. What is the syndicate member's remaining liability?

    A. $100,000
    B. $200,000
    C. $300,000
    D. $1,000,000

19. The issuer appoints the underwriter if the underwriting is

    A. negotiated
    B. competitive
    C. Eastern
    D. Western

20. The trust indenture of a revenue bond will show all of the following EXCEPT

    A. reoffering yields
    B. application of flow of funds
    C. discrimination covenant
    D. rate covenant

21. In a gross revenue pledge, which of the following is paid first?

    A. Debt service
    B. Operation and maintenance
    C. Surplus
    D. Debt service reserve

22. When an authority sets aside money for additions and improvements, this is what type of fund?

    A. Renewal and replacement
    B. Sinking
    C. Operations and maintenance
    D. Surplus

23. When a municipality is allocating funds from a revenue-producing facility under a net revenue pledge, the first priority is to

    A. pay operations and maintenance
    B. pay debt service, including principal and interest
    C. establish a reserve for retirement of bonds
    D. accumulate a surplus for expansion of the facility

Answers

1. **A.**   In a negotiated underwriting, the issuer selects an underwriter and negotiates the terms of the offering with that firm. In a competitive bid underwriting, the issuer selects the firm that offers the most attractive terms.

2. **B.**   Municipalities are usually required to sell general obligation bonds on a competitive bid basis.

3. **D.**   The official notice of sale is provided by the issuer. The bond rating is determined by rating companies.

4. **B.**   *The Bond Buyer* contains public notices of invitations to bid, the 30-day visible supply, the placement ratio, etc.

5. **A.**   *The Bond Buyer* provides bid worksheets.

6. **D.**   The legal opinion examines all aspects of the validity of the bond, including its tax-exempt status, relevant statutes and the issuer's authority to issue the bond.

7. **A.**   The manager of a municipal syndicate is the broker-dealer that acts with the issuer on behalf of the syndicate. The managing underwriter manages the entire underwriting process for the syndicate.

8. **B.**   A "scale" is a list of all bonds in an offering with their prices or their yields to maturity, ranging from early to later maturities.

9. **A.**   The completed bid form contains the yields and prices on the bonds according to the rates that the issuer will pay. It does not contain the reoffering scale—the prices at which the bonds will be sold to the public.

10. **B.**   The good faith deposit is used to reduce the total price due to the issuer. Good faith deposits are returned to the syndicates that do not

win the bid. Any loss incurred in the sale of the bonds is a loss to the underwriters; the deposit will not be returned by the issuer in such a case. The bond purchasers know nothing of the good faith deposit.

11.   **B.**   The issuer awards a competitive underwriting based on the lowest total cost to the issuer. The interest cost on the bonds is the cost to the issuer, and so bids are awarded to the syndicate that proposes the lowest coupons or yields.

12.   **A.**   The syndicate account letter identifies the syndicate manager and details terms of the syndicate agreement: duration of the account, participation and retention of each member, and priority of order allocation. The syndicate letter does not include the reoffering scale.

13.   **A.**   The issuer, the bond counsel and the trustee are not concerned with the agreement among underwriters. The agreement among underwriters is a document signed by members of the syndicate.

14.   **A.**   Takedown is the discount given to a syndicate member that buys bonds from the syndicate. The concession is a discount given to a nonmember that buys from a member.

15.   **D.**   The dated date is the date on which interest begins to accrue.

16.   **A.**   The bid on a municipal bond issue is determined by the type of bond, maturity dates and yields on the scale. The good faith check is for an amount stipulated by the issuer—usually a percentage of the offering.

17.   **D.**   An Eastern account is undivided. Each broker-dealer is responsible for the same percentage of unsold bonds as its percentage of participation in the offering.

18.   **B.**   A Western account is divided. The broker-dealer is responsible only for the bonds it is committed to sell. The broker-dealer committed to sell $500,000 in bonds but sold only $300,000; it is responsible for the remaining $200,000 in bonds.

19.   **A.**   In a negotiated offering, the underwriter and the issuer negotiate an agreement.

20.   **A.**   The trust indenture is the contract under which the revenue bond is issued. It lists the responsibilities of the issuing authority, including the application of funds, the covenant (or promise) not to discriminate and the rate covenant, which is a promise to charge rates sufficient to pay debt service.

21.   **A.**   Under a gross revenue pledge, debt service is the first item paid. The more common net revenue pledge applies gross revenues first to operations and maintenance and then pays debt service out of the remaining net revenues.

22.   **D.**   The word "authority" tells you that this is a revenue bond. An authority that issues a revenue bond establishes an operations and maintenance fund to meet expenses of operating and maintaining the facility, a sinking fund for debt service payment, a debt service reserve fund to ensure availability of money to pay debt service for a given period (typically one year), a renewal and replacement fund to cover major repairs or replacement of equipment, a reserve maintenance fund to cover extraordinary repair or maintenance expenses and a surplus fund to meet expenses not covered by other funds.

23.   **A.**   Under a net revenue pledge, the first obligation is to pay operations and maintenance. The remaining funds (the net revenues) are applied to bond interest, the sinking fund, the debt service reserve fund, the renewal and replacement fund, the reserve maintenance fund and the surplus fund—in that order. Under a gross revenue pledge, the first priority is to pay debt service.

Municipal Trading and Taxation

Quotations

The term "quotation" means any bid for or offer of (or broker-dealer request for a bid for or offer of) municipal securities. Any indication of interest or solicitation by a municipal broker-dealer (such as "bid wanted" or "offer wanted") would be considered a quotation request.

Bona fide. If a broker-dealer gives, distributes or publishes a quotation for a security, that quote must be bona fide, and the dealer must be prepared to trade the security at the price specified in the quote. All quotations have at least a *reasonable* relationship to fair market value.

Types of quotations. The bid price at which a dealer states its willingness to purchase securities from another dealer is called a **workable indication**. A dealer that offers a **nominal** (or **subject**) **quotation** intends only to indicate an approximate market value for a security.

Holding a quote. If a municipal dealer wants to guarantee that it will fill a market order at the current bid or offer for a certain period of time, he can do this by giving an **out firm** quotation.

Broker-Dealer Regulation

Customer Communications

Recommendations. Municipal securities brokers and dealers are required to make reasonable and suitable recommendations to customers. **Churning**—increasing commissions through excessive trading—is prohibited.

Protecting customer accounts. Broker-dealers are not permitted to *guarantee* customers against loss or to *share in the profits or losses* of a customer's account.

Confirmations

Customers must receive a written confirmation of each municipal securities transaction they have entered. The confirmation must describe the security accurately; list the trade date, settlement date and amount of accrued interest; and indicate whether the firm acted as agent or principal in the trade.

Dollar bonds. Some municipal revenue bonds are traded on a dollar basis (percentage of par) rather than on a YTM basis. These municipal bonds are commonly called *dollar bonds*. Dollar bonds usually are term bonds.

Disclosing yield. MSRB Rule G-15 requires that a confirmation for a trade effected on the basis of dollar price include that price and indicate the lowest potential yield (yield to premium call, to par option or to maturity) the customer might receive.

Required information on confirmations. Confirmations must include the following information:

- in agency transactions, the name of the party on the other side of the transaction and the source and amount of any commission;
- the dated date if it affects the interest calculation;
- the first interest payment date if payments are not semiannual;
- whether the securities are fully registered, registered as to principal only or available in book-entry form;
- whether the securities are called or prerefunded, as well as the date of maturity fixed by the call notice and the amount of the call price; and
- any special qualification or factor that might affect payment of principal or interest.

Taxation of Municipal Issues

Adjusting the Cost Basis of Debt Securities

Bonds bought at a premium or discount will usually produce capital gains or losses at the time of their sale, and the ultimate tax treatment will depend on the type of bond purchased.

Municipal bonds bought at a premium. The investor who buys a municipal bond at a premium must amortize the amount of the premium over the life of the bond. If the bond is sold before it matures, its cost basis must be adjusted by the amount of the amortized premium.

Original issue discount (OID). If an OID bond is sold before it matures, the cost basis of the bond is adjusted by **accreting** the amount of the discount on a straight-line basis.

Secondary market discount. The cost basis of a municipal bond bought at a discount in the secondary market is not adjusted.

Tax Benefits

To determine a bond's tax-equivalent yield, divide the tax-free yield (yield to maturity) by 100% *less* the investor's tax rate, as follows:

$$\frac{\text{Tax-free yield}}{100\% - \text{Tax rate}} = \text{Tax-equivalent yield}$$

$$\frac{5\%}{72\%} = 6.9\%$$

Bond Swaps

Bond swapping is a technique used by investors in bonds to generate current tax losses, improve yields or quality, or extend the maturity of their portfolios. The investor swaps by selling bonds that she already holds and replacing them with other bonds that better meet her investment objectives.

To avoid having a legitimate bond swap classified as a wash sale by the IRS, the replacement bonds purchased must differ in some significant respect from those sold. The IRS will not consider a bond swap a wash sale if the new bonds represent a change in issuer, maturity date, rating or coupon.

Questions

1. Which of the following best describe *municipal dollar bonds*?

   I. Term
   II. Serial
   III. Series
   IV. Callable

   A. I and II
   B. I and IV
   C. II and IV
   D. III and IV

2. All of the following describe term bonds EXCEPT that they

   A. mature entirely on a single date
   B. are called *dollar bonds*
   C. are not callable
   D. are quoted at a percentage of par

3. On what basis are municipal serial bonds quoted?

   A. Yield to maturity
   B. Discount yield
   C. Current yield
   D. Dollar price basis

4. What term describes the excess of the purchase price over the par value of a municipal bond?

   A. Spread
   B. Discount
   C. Premium
   D. Reallowance

5. A common feature shared by almost all revenue bonds is that they are

   A. issued at an original discount
   B. callable
   C. double-barreled
   D. term bonds rather than serial bonds

6. If interest rates rise, municipal bond prices should

   A. rise
   B. decline
   C. fluctuate
   D. stay the same

7. A customer purchases a public purpose municipal bond at $900 in the primary market. The bond matures in ten years. All of the following statements regarding the purchase are true EXCEPT that the

   A. interest is exempt from federal income tax
   B. customer will have no gain or loss if the bond is held to maturity
   C. customer will realize a capital gain of $100
   D. customer will not have to pay tax on the accrued discount each year

8. Which agency has the ultimate authority for determining the amount of the discount on original issue discount municipal bonds?

   A. IRS
   B. FRB
   C. SEC
   D. MSRB

9. A customer buys $100,000 of newly issued municipal bonds at a price of 105. The bonds mature in five years at par. Two years later, the customer sells the bonds at 95. What is the customer's loss for tax purposes?

   A. $3,000
   B. $5,000
   C. $8,000
   D. $10,000

10. A public purpose municipal bond is purchased at a discount in the secondary market at 90. The face amount is $10,000 and the bond has ten years to maturity. The bond is sold for 97 after five years. What is the taxable gain?

    A. $0
    B. $200
    C. $700
    D. Capital gains on municipal bonds are not taxable.

11. A customer buys a new issue municipal bond at $1,060 with an eight-year maturity. After four years, he sells the bond. What is the unamortized premium?

    A. $20
    B. $24
    C. $30
    D. $36

12. An investor purchases a 20-year municipal bond at $10 over par and sells the bond ten years later at 103. The investor has a

    A. loss of $20
    B. loss of $7
    C. loss of $2
    D. gain of $25

13. Interest expense incurred to purchase which of the following types of securities is NOT federally tax deductible?

    A. Corporate bonds
    B. Treasury securities
    C. Municipal bonds
    D. Common stocks

14. A financial institution buys $90,000 of 8%, 20-year revenue bonds. For book purposes, the institution uses straight-line accretion, but for tax purposes the institution uses cost. The bonds are sold after three years for $99,000. What will be the taxable gain?

    A. $3,000
    B. $5,000
    C. $7,500
    D. $9,000

15. A taxpayer in the 28% bracket would net the highest aftertax income from a

    A. 5% municipal bond ∿6.94
    B. 5 1/2% T bill
    C. 6% income bond
    D. 6 1/2% corporate bond

16. The current yield of a municipal bond

    A. is the annual interest divided by the market price
    B. reflects the time until maturity
    C. reflects the interest paid since issuance
    D. includes capital gains as well as interest payments

17. A municipal securities dealer buys $500,000 of 6% bonds at par and immediately reoffers the bonds. Under MSRB rules, which two of the following would most likely be considered bona fide quotes?

    I.   4.10 net
    II. 5.8 less 1/2
    III. 101
    IV. 108

    A. I and III
    B. I and IV
    C. II and III
    D. II and IV

18. According to the terms of the trust indenture, funds for the retirement of municipal revenue bonds would be deposited in what type of fund?

    A. Construction
    B. Maintenance
    C. Sinking
    D. Reserve

19. On January 1, 1996, a municipality publishes a notice that it has deposited sufficient U.S. government securities with the trustee to pay interest and principal on outstanding bonds maturing in the year 2000. This is termed

    A. refinancing
    B. refunding
    C. prerefunding
    D. replacement

Answers

1. **B.** Municipal dollar bonds are term bonds quoted at a percentage of par. These quotes, unlike quotes made on a yield basis, are easily converted into dollars. Most term bonds are callable prior to maturity. Serial bonds are quoted on a yield basis and can also be callable.

2. **C.** All bonds in a term bond issue mature on the same date. They are known as *dollar bonds* because, unlike other municipal issues, they are quoted at a percentage of par rather than at yield. Issuers of term bonds create sinking funds to allow them to call bonds and repay the principal before maturity.

3. **A.** Municipal serial bonds are quoted on a yield-to-maturity basis.

4. **C.** When a bond is trading at a price greater than $1,000 par value, it is trading at a premium. "Spread" is the difference between the bid and ask prices. "Discount" describes a bond trading at less than par. "Reallowance" refers to the compensation of nonsyndicate members for their role in the sale of a new municipal bond issue.

5. **B.** Almost all revenue bonds are callable. If revenue exceeds projections, the excess funds can be used to pay off some of the bonds. To ensure that the bonds are available for purchase, they are issued with a call provision.

6. **B.** An inverse relationship exists between interest rates and bond prices. As current market interest rates rise, bond prices fall. As current market interest rates fall, bond prices rise.

7. **C.** The discount on OID bonds must be accreted annually. For municipals, this amount is nontaxable because the interest income on municipals is federally tax-exempt. If the bond is held to maturity, the entire discount is accreted, and the bond is valued at par; therefore, there is no gain or loss.

8. **A.** The IRS would ultimately decide the discount on an OID bond because the discount must be accreted annually and is treated as interest income. As the discount is accreted, the adjusted cost basis of the bond is increased, which changes the capital gain or loss that would be realized each year if the bond were sold.

9. **C.** The premium on a municipal bond must be amortized. The five-point premium on a five-year bond will reduce the cost basis by one point per year. After two years, the bonds purchased at $105,000 will be written down to $103,000. If the bonds are sold at $95,000, the tax loss is $8,000 ($103,000 – $95,000).

10. **C.** Because the municipal bond was bought at a discount in the secondary market, there is no requirement to accrete the discount. The bond is valued at cost ($9,000) for tax purposes. If the bond is sold for $9,700, the taxable gain is $700.

11. **C.** New issue municipal bonds purchased at a premium must amortize the premium on a straight-line basis. Thus, this bond has a $60 premium and an eight-year maturity so that $7.50 of the premium must be deducted from the bond's cost basis each year ($60 ÷ 8 = $7.50). After four years, $30 of the $60 premium will have been amortized ($7.50 × 4 = $30), leaving only $30 unamortized.

12. **D.** The bond is purchased $10 over par at 101. The premium must be amortized on a straight-line basis over the remaining life of the bond. Ten years later, the adjusted basis of the bond will be $1,005. One-half of the $10 premium will have been amortized. The sale price of $1,030 less the adjusted basis of $1,005 will result in a gain of $25.

13. **C.** Because the income generated by the bond is tax-free, the IRS does not allow taxpayers to deduct for interest expense incurred in the purchase of municipal bonds.

14. **D.** Because the institution only accretes the bond for its books, while it values the bond at cost for tax purposes, the tax cost is $90,000. If the bonds are sold for $99,000, the taxable gain is $9,000. Remember, you do not accrete secondary

market discount municipal bonds for tax purposes. Only new issue discount municipal bonds must be adjusted.

15.   **A.**   Municipal bonds are exempt from federal taxation and in most cases from taxation by the state in which they are issued. Income bonds, corporate bonds and T bills are fully taxed. This particular investor would be taxed at the 28% level. The equivalent yield on a corporate bond would be 6.94% (5% ÷ 72%).

16.   **A.**   Current yield on a bond is the annual interest received divided by the bond's market price. It does not include capital gains or the number of years remaining until maturity, which are considered in the yield to maturity compensation.

17.   **C.**   Under MSRB rules, markups that dealers charge on bonds must be fair and reasonable, with the dealer considering the security's availability, its judgment of the current market and the fact that it is entitled to a reasonable profit on the trade. Of the quotes given, two represent small markups and two represent very large markups. Because the bonds were bought at par, a quote of 101 is a more reasonable markup than a quote of 108. Because the bonds have a 6% coupon, a quote of 5.8% less 1/2 a point is a more reasonable quote than a quote of 4.10 net.

18.   **C.**   The question defines a sinking fund— a fund set aside for the accumulation of money needed to retire a bond issue at maturity.

19.   **C.**   The question defines prerefunded or advance-refunded bonds, which are sometimes called *escrowed* bonds.

Analysis of Municipal Securities

General Obligation Bonds

General wealth of the community. GOs can be analyzed for safety by evaluating the general wealth of the community through examining a community's:

- property values
- retail sales per capita
- local bank deposits and bank clearings
- diversity of industry in its tax base

Characteristics of the issuer. An analysis of population, property values and per capita income would constitute a **quantitative analysis** of the municipality. An analysis of other factors—including benefits available to industries located in the area, trends in the growth or decline of the population, property value trends and plans and projects being undertaken in the area—would constitute a **qualitative analysis** of the municipality.

Debt limits. Statutory limits may be placed on the amount of debt a municipality can assume. The state constitution and a municipality's articles of incorporation will usually place a **constitutional debt limit** on the dollar amount of GOs that a city may issue and have outstanding.

Overlapping debt. A municipality's share of any debt issued by its political subdivisions is part of overlapping (**coterminous**) debt.

Income of the municipality. The largest source of city income is normally the tax on real property.

Ad valorem taxes. Property taxes are based on a property's assessed valuation, which is a percentage of the estimated market value. GOs, backed by the power to tax and seize property, are considered safer than revenue bonds of the same issuer and, therefore, can be issued with a lower interest rate.

Revenue Bonds

Revenue bonds are rated according to the potential of a facility to generate money to service the bond debt. Revenue bonds are not repaid from taxes, and are not subject to statutory debt limits the way GOs are. When assessing the quality of revenue bonds, an investor should consider the following factors:

- economic justification
- competing facilities
- sources of revenue
- call provisions
- flow of funds

Applications of Revenues

The issuer pledges to pay the various expenses involved in a particular order, called the **flow of funds**. In most cases, a **net revenue pledge** is used, and the first payments cover operating and maintenance expenses. The remaining funds, or *net revenues,* are used to pay debt service and other expenses.

If the issuer does not need to commit any revenues to operating and maintenance expenses first, the first disbursements go directly to debt service. When debt service is paid first, the flow of funds is called a **gross revenue pledge**.

Flow of Funds in a Net Revenue Pledge

In a net revenue pledge, the gross revenues are disbursed in the following order:

1. operations and maintenance
2. debt service account
3. debt service reserve fund
4. reserve maintenance fund
5. renewal and replacement fund
6. surplus fund

Municipal Debt Ratios

Some of the more commonly used ratios include the following:

- net debt to assessed valuation
- net debt to estimated valuation
- debt per capita
- debt service to annual revenues
- debt trend
- collection ratio
- coverage ratio
- taxes per person or per capita

Other Sources of Information for Municipal Bond Analysis

Interest Rate Comparisons

A **bond appraisal** is an approximate valuation of a bond that is based on the current market prices of similar bonds.

Municipal Bond Insurance

Municipal bond insurance is available from the investor-owned Municipal Bond Investors Assurance Corp. (MBIA) or AMBAC Indemnity Corporation (AMBAC). Standard & Poor's has agreed to rate all AMBAC- and MBIA-insured bonds AAA. Moody's does not take into consideration purchased insurance when it rates municipal bonds.

Questions

1. A qualitative analysis of a general obligation bond that is to be issued would take into consideration all of the following factors EXCEPT the

   A. tax base of the community
   B. economic character of the community
   C. dollar denominations of the bonds to be issued
   D. makeup of the community's population

2. Which of the following is NOT considered when evaluating municipal revenue bond credit risk?

   A. Competing facilities
   B. Quality of management
   C. Coverage ratios
   D. Interest rate movements

3. A bond analyst checking a general obligation municipal bond will examine the

   I. past performance of the payment of interest
   II. per capita income of the citizens
   III. population growth of the area
   IV. industrial development of the area

   A. I, II and III only
   B. I, II and IV only
   C. II, III and IV only
   D. I, II, III and IV

4. A municipal bond issue would be nonrated when the

   A. municipality's credit is not good
   B. municipality's debt is too small to be rated
   C. amount of the issue is too small to be rated
   D. municipality has an outstanding bond in default

5. The number of times by which the annual net revenues of a facility exceed the annual interest charges and principal payments is called the

   A. working capital ratio
   B. dividend payout ratio
   C. debt service coverage ratio
   D. collection ratio

6. All of the following would be considered when analyzing an airport revenue bond issue EXCEPT

   A. energy costs
   B. per capita debt
   C. passenger traffic trends
   D. tourism in the area

7. Which of the following would a customer examine to evaluate the credit quality of a new municipal security?

   A. Official statement
   B. Legal opinion
   C. Prospectus
   D. Trust indenture

8. In analyzing the general obligation debt of a municipality, which of the following is LEAST important?

   A. Direct debt
   B. Authorized debt
   C. Matured debt
   D. Overlapping debt

9. The city of Bondville (population 10,000) has just issued $1 million in general obligation bonds and already has an outstanding debt of $2 million. The city is located in a municipal county with $1,500,000 in debt outstanding, most of which is funded from ad valorem taxes. Bondville makes up 70% of the county. What is the net direct debt per capita of Bondville?

   A. $150
   B. $300
   C. $405
   D. $450

10. All of the following would indicate deteriorating credit conditions EXCEPT an increase in

    A. bankruptcies
    B. consumer debt
    C. bond defaults
    D. assessed valuations

11. A corporation owns a building with an estimated market value of $400,000. How much tax will be due if the county assesses the building at $200,000 and applies a 10 mill tax rate?

    A. $200
    B. $400
    C. $2,000
    D. $4,000

12. The debt of other districts for which the residents of a municipal district may also be responsible is what kind of debt?

    A. Funded
    B. Floating
    C. Overlapping
    D. Unsecured

13. If a municipal issuer is in financial difficulty, which of the following could insure payment of principal and interest on the municipality's outstanding debt?

    I. MBIA
    II. AMBAC
    III. SIPC
    IV. FDIC

    A. I and II only
    B. I, II and III only
    C. III and IV only
    D. I, II, III and IV

Answers

1. **C.** The dollar denomination of bonds to be issued has no bearing on a GO bond analysis. The tax base, economic character and population makeup would all be considered.

2. **D.** Interest rate movements have no bearing on determining the quality of revenue bond issues.

3. **D.** The past payment record indicates the reliability of earnings. Per capita income, population growth and industrial development all indicate how large a source of tax revenue backs the bond.

4. **B.** The size of the municipality does not count, but the size of the debt outstanding for a municipality does. A municipality with a small amount of debt will not have enough activity in those debt instruments to warrant a rating by a rating agency.

5. **C.** The debt service coverage ratio shows the number of times that interest and principal can be paid with net revenues.

$$\frac{\text{Annual earnings for debt service}}{\text{Annual interest charges} + \text{Principal payment}}$$

= Debt service coverage

6. **B.** Airport revenue bonds are paid off by revenues from the facility; therefore, an analyst would consider passenger traffic trends, tourism and energy costs. Per capita debt is a measure used in analyzing GO issues.

7. **A.** The official statement is an offering document that discloses material information on a new issue of municipal securities. Because it commonly includes information concerning the purpose of the issue, how the securities will be repaid and the financial, economic and social characteristics of the issuer, it is an appropriate place to review the creditworthiness of an issue. The legal opinion reviews the legality of the issue (including certain legal exemptions). A prospectus is the document that provides material information about a nonexempt security being publicly distributed. The trust indenture is the basic bond contract between the issuer and the trustee that represents the bondholders.

8. **C.** Debt that has already matured is meaningless in evaluating a municipality's debt load.

9. **B.** The direct debt of Bondville is $3 million divided by 10,000 residents, which equals $300 direct debt per capita.

10. **D.** When credit conditions deteriorate, bankruptcies rise, bond defaults increase and consumer debt increases (answers A, B and C). An increase in assessed valuation (property value) would indicate a strengthening economy.

11. **C.**

$200,000.00	Assessed value
× .01	.001 × 10 mill tax rate
$ 2,000.00	

12. **C.** Districts, counties and cities may have overlapping debt; a state does not.

13. **A.** MBIA and AMBAC insure municipal bonds.

Municipal Securities Rules and Regulations

The Securities Acts of 1933 and 1934

The 1933 and 1934 acts protect investors considering the purchase of new-issue securities by requiring issuers to meet certain registration requirements and by requiring broker-dealers to comply with very strict antifraud provisions. Among the provisions of the 1933 act are the:

- requirement that all new issues to be distributed interstate be registered;
- requirement that the issuer provide full and fair disclosure about itself and the offering;
- requirement that the issuer make available all material information necessary for an investor to judge the merit of the issue;
- regulations concerning the underwriting and distribution of primary and secondary issues; and
- provisions for criminal penalties for fraud in the issuance of new securities.

Municipal and government securities are exempt from the registration requirements of the Securities Act of 1933. Municipal issuers, underwriters, brokers and dealers are, however, always subject to the 1934 act's antifraud provisions.

Municipal Securities Rulemaking Board

The MSRB is an independent self-regulatory organization (SRO) established by the Securities Acts Amendments of 1975. The act of 1975 requires underwriters and dealers of securities to protect the interests of investors (as well as themselves), be ethical in offering advice and be responsive to complaints and disputes.

The MSRB is the organization that makes rules pertaining to the issuance and trading of municipal securities.

Rule enforcement. The MSRB does not have the authority to enforce the rules it makes. The rules that pertain to broker-dealers are enforced on its behalf by the NASD and SEC, and the comptroller of the currency enforces MSRB rules that pertain to national banks. Neither the MSRB nor the SEC has any authority over municipal issuers.

General Regulations

Rule G-1. Separately identifiable department or division of a bank.

Rule G-2. Standards of professional qualification.

Rule G-3. Classification of principals and representatives.

Rule G-4. Statutory disqualifications.

Rule G-5. Disciplinary actions by appropriate regulatory agencies.

Rule G-6. Fidelity bonding requirements.

Rule G-7. Information concerning associated persons.

Rule G-8. Books and records to be made.

Rule G-9. Preservation of records.

Rule G-10. Delivery of investor brochure.

Rule G-11. Sales of new issue municipal securities during the underwriting period.

Rule G-12. Uniform practice.

Rule G-13. Quotations relating to municipal securities.

Rule G-14. Reports of sales or purchases.

Rule G-15. Confirmation, clearance and settlement of customer transactions.

Rule G-16. Periodic compliance examination.

Rule G-17. Conduct of municipal securities business.

Rule G-18. Execution of transactions.

Rule G-19. Suitability of recommendations and transactions, discretionary accounts.

Rule G-20. Gifts and gratuities.

Rule G-21. Advertising.

Rule G-22. Control relationships.

Rule G-23. Activities of financial advisers.

Rule G-24. Use of ownership information obtained in a fiduciary capacity.

Rule G-25. Improper use of assets.

Rule G-26. Customer account transfers.

Rule G-27. Supervision.

Rule G-28. Transactions with employees and partners of other municipal securities professionals.

Rule G-29. Availability of MSRB rules.

Rule G-30. Prices and commissions.

Rule G-31. Reciprocal dealings with municipal securities investment companies.

Rule G-32. Disclosures in connection with new issues.

Rule G-33. Calculations of accrued interest.

Rule G-34. CUSIP numbers

Rule G-35. Arbitration.

Questions

1. Which of the following are NOT directly regulated by the MSRB?

   A. Bank dealers
   B. Issuers of municipal bonds
   C. Broker-dealers that deal in municipal bonds
   D. Federal Reserve Board

2. Which of the following statements are true?

   I. The MSRB was formed as a result of the Securities Exchange Act of 1934.
   II. The MSRB is a self-regulating organization.
   III. The MSRB does not enforce its own rules.
   IV. The MSRB controls the over-the-counter market.

   A. I and II
   B. I and III
   C. II and III
   D. II and IV

3. The MSRB is responsible to

   A. the NASD
   B. the SEC
   C. the NYSE
   D. no one, because it is a self-regulatory organization

4. Municipal securities issuers and dealers are subject to which of the following?

   I. Antifraud provisions under Rule 10b-5 of the Securities Exchange Act of 1934
   II. Issuer reporting requirements to the Securities and Exchange Commission under the Securities Exchange Act of 1934
   III. Prospectus delivery requirements to purchasers of new issues under the Securities Act of 1933

   A. I only
   B. I and II only
   C. II and III only
   D. I, II and III

5. Which of the following enforce(s) the rules of the MSRB?

   I. Comptroller of the Currency
   II. FDIC
   III. Federal Reserve Board

   A. I only
   B. II only
   C. II and III only
   D. I, II and III

6. A municipal securities principal at a bank is in charge of supervising all of the following EXCEPT

   A. writing legal opinions
   B. processing trades in municipal securities
   C. maintaining municipal securities records
   D. bank employees involved in municipal transactions

7. Which of the following statements about MSRB rules is true?

   A. The FDIC enforces MSRB rules governing brokerage firms.
   B. A broker expelled by the NYSE would not be disqualified by the MSRB.
   C. MSRB rules do not allow representatives to receive part of a client's profits instead of a commission.
   D. The MSRB has adopted the 5% markup policy.

8. An MSRB dealer opens an account for a customer. The dealer should ask about the customer's

   I. tax status
   II. investment objectives
   III. financial background
   IV. education

   A. I and II only
   B. I, II and III only
   C. II only
   D. I, II, III and IV

9. The municipal principal must approve all orders in writing taken for the account of

   I. individuals
   II. trust departments
   III. insurance companies
   IV. commercial banks

   A. I only
   B. I, II and III only
   C. III and IV only
   D. I, II, III and IV

10. According to the MSRB, if a customer wishes to purchase municipal bonds when the registered representative feels that the trade would be unsuitable, the trade

    A. may be executed if approved by the MSRB
    B. may be executed if the customer specifically directs that it be done
    C. may be executed only if the customer has previous trading experience
    D. cannot be executed

11. Advertising related to municipal securities must be approved by which of the following?

    A. MSRB
    B. SEC
    C. Municipal securities principal
    D. General securities principal

12. A municipal dealer that receives an advisory fee from a client must, according to MSRB rules, notify the client in writing of

    A. the credit rating of any security recommended
    B. any financial interest the dealer may have in an underwriting of a security recommended for purchase
    C. the yearly trading range of any security recommended for purchase
    D. all of the above

13. According to MSRB rules, under which of the following conditions may a municipal dealer share in the profits of a customer's account?

   A. If the dealer effected the transaction for the customer
   B. If the dealer receives compensation on an offsetting transaction
   C. If a written guarantee is signed by the customer
   D. Under no circumstances

14. According to MSRB rules, one municipal dealer must notify another municipal dealer if relatives of employees of the second municipal dealer wish to open an account. Which of the following would trigger the notification requirement?

   A. Twenty-five-year-old daughter of an employee
   B. Spouse of an employee
   C. Aunt of an employee
   D. Son-in-law of an employee

15. Under MSRB rules, all of the following would be considered advertisements EXCEPT

   A. offering circulars
   B. market letters
   C. official statements
   D. summaries of official statements

16. According to the MSRB, a control relationship would exist between a municipal broker-dealer and an issuer when

   A. senior officers of the municipal dealer live in the municipality
   B. the firm recently completed a negotiated underwriting for the municipality
   C. an officer of the underwriter is in a position of authority over the issuer of the municipal bonds
   D. the dealer has an inventory of the issuer's bonds that are trading at a premium

17. MSRB rules would treat as "material"

   A. a gift of less than $50
   B. World Series tickets valued at $75
   C. reminder advertising valued at $25
   D. vintage wine valued at $125

18. A municipal bond is issued with five years of call protection. The bonds are callable after that date with a scale of declining premiums. The bond has been prerefunded and the proceeds of the refunding issue deposited in an escrow account and invested in direct federal debt issues. The bonds are sold at a dollar price, so the confirmation must show the

   A. lowest yield to maturity or yield to call
   B. yield to the maturity date established by the refunding
   C. yield to the longer call with the lower resulting yield
   D. yield to the longer call with the higher resulting yield

19. MSRB rules prohibit municipal securities firms from engaging in which of the following activities with investment companies?

   A. Accepting a presale order for a new municipal issue
   B. Hiring investment company officers
   C. Soliciting municipal transactions from the investment company as compensation for shares sold of the investment company
   D. Any transactions in municipal securities by investment companies

20. According to MSRB rules, all of the following is required customer account information EXCEPT the

    A. tax ID or Social Security number
    B. age and birth date
    C. name and address of employer
    D. signature of the municipal securities representative or general securities representative introducing the account and of a municipal securities principal or general securities principal indicating acceptance of the account

21. A registered representative qualified to sell only municipal securities may solicit orders for which of the following?

    I. Sewer and water revenue bonds
    II. General obligation bonds
    III. Municipal unit investment trusts
    IV. Open-ended municipal bond funds

    A. I and II only
    B. I and III only
    C. II and IV only
    D. I, II, III and IV

22. The first action to be taken by a municipal securities dealer upon receipt of a customer complaint is to

    A. notify the examining regulatory authority
    B. submit to arbitration
    C. refund any money to the customer making the complaint
    D. accept the complaint and record the action taken

23. Municipal bonds are MOST suitable for

    A. individual retirement accounts
    B. corporations in the maximum tax bracket
    C. pension plans
    D. individuals in the 15% tax bracket

24. Which of the following is the LEAST important factor contributing to the diversification of a municipal bond portfolio?

    A. Maturity
    B. Issuer location
    C. Denomination
    D. Quality

Answers

1. **B.** Because municipal bond issues are exempt from registration with the SEC, neither the SEC nor the MSRB has any direct authority over the issuers of municipal securities.

2. **C.** The MSRB was formed as a result of the Securities Acts Amendments of 1975. It is a self-regulatory organization but does not enforce its own regulations. Regulations are enforced by another SRO (such as the NASD), which has authority over the municipal dealer. Although municipal bonds are sold in the over-the-counter market, the MSRB does not control that market; the NASD does.

3. **B.** It is true that the MSRB is a self-regulatory organization but it still is responsible to the SEC. The MSRB was formed to carry out the wishes of the SEC.

4. **A.** Municipal securities are exempt under the acts of 1933 and 1934. However, the 1934 act specifically states that its provisions for fraud pertain to municipal dealers and issuers. The issuer-reporting requirements of the SEC (such as annual and quarterly reports) apply to corporate issuers, not to municipal issuers. Prospectus delivery rules apply only to corporate issuers, not to municipal issuers.

5. **D.** The Comptroller of the Currency enforces MSRB rules in national banks. The Federal Reserve Board enforces the rules in nonnational banks that are members of the Federal Reserve System. The FDIC enforces MSRB rules for nonnational banks that are not members of the Federal Reserve System. The NASD and NYSE supervise member firms' compliance with MSRB rules.

6. **A.** An independent bond counsel writes legal opinions for the issuer of a municipal security. The municipal securities principal at a bank would have no authority over this aspect of municipal bond underwriting.

7. **C.** Registered representatives cannot share in the profits of a client's account. The rep can receive compensation only from the firm.

8. **B.** In opening an account for a customer, municipal rules limit the dealer to asking about tax status, investment objectives and financial background.

9. **D.** The municipal principal is required to approve all orders on a timely basis.

10. **B.** If a customer wishes to purchase a security that the registered representative feels is unsuitable, the trade may be entered if the customer specifically directs that it be done. The trade ticket should be marked "unsolicited." (Most firms require the customer to sign a nonsolicitation letter for this type of trade, meaning that the customer was not solicited by the firm to make this trade.)

11. **C.** Municipal advertising must be approved by a municipal principal prior to first use.

12. **B.** Because a municipal bond dealer must always act in the best interests of the client, it must disclose to the client any personal interest it may have in a recommended security.

13. **D.** A representative may only share in the profits of an account owned jointly with another person. Even then, the rep may share in profits only to the extent of his interest in the account.

14. **B.** The rules governing opening accounts for other securities professionals apply to the immediate family members of those professionals. The immediate family member in this instance speaks of a financial unit. The spouse of the employee would be automatically in that family unit. A twenty-five-year-old offspring is not likely to be supported by the municipal employee, nor is the son-in-law. If they were, they also would be subject to the reporting requirements.

15. **C.** MSRB rules consider all forms of mass public communication to be advertising, except listings of dealer inventories, official statements and preliminary official statements.

16.   **C.**   The officer of the broker-dealer has control over both the broker-dealer and the issuer. This could open doors for possible manipulation, which is why the control relationship is forbidden.

17.   **D.**   The word "material" indicates that an *excessive* gift cannot be given by a municipal firm to employees of another municipal firm. The dollar value the MSRB considers "material" is $100. The vintage wine valued at $125 exceeds this limit.

18.   **B.**   The bond has been refunded. The money is in the escrow account. The outstanding bonds will be called as soon as possible. With these conditions, the date and the price at which the bonds will be called are known. The maturity date is established by the refunding. The yield that is to be shown on the confirmation is the yield to call established by that refunding.

19.   **C.**   The idea behind the municipal antireciprocal rule is that investment companies should not attempt to induce municipal broker-dealers to sell shares of the fund. This could be done if the investment company ran its portfolio trades only through those broker-dealers that sold the most fund shares. This practice is prohibited under MSRB rules. Of course, presale orders for new municipal issues may be accepted and transactions between investment companies and municipal broker-dealers are allowed. (Otherwise, how could the fund's portfolio be traded?)

20.   **B.**   The age or birth date is not required customer information.

21.   **A.**   Persons licensed to sell only municipal securities must limit their activities to securities issued by municipal issuers, the federal government and government agencies; sewer and water revenue bonds and general obligation bonds are securities of municipal issuers. Municipal bond mutual funds or investment trusts are investment company securities; sale of these securities requires either a general securities or an investment company/variable contracts representative license.

22.   **D.**   Upon receipt of a customer complaint, accept the complaint, record the action taken, put it in a complaint file and respond; record the response.

23.   **B.**   The tax-exempt status of municipal bonds makes them especially appealing to two types of investors: individuals in high tax brackets and corporations in the maximum (34%) tax bracket. Because pension and profit-sharing plans are exempt from current federal income tax, they usually do not invest in municipals. For the same reason, municipal bonds are not suitable for IRAs. Tax-deferred plans prefer the higher rates associated with corporate and government bonds.

24.   **C.**   Bond denominations have no bearing on the diversification of a portfolio. Obviously, maturity, issuer location and quality are all important factors to consider when diversifying a portfolio.

16 ⬦ Option Contracts and Option Markets

Introduction to Options

Calls and Puts

An option is a **contract** between two people.

The purchaser of the contract has paid money for the *right* to buy or the *right* to sell securities. The seller of the option contract, on the other hand, has accepted money for taking on an *obligation*.

The option seller *must* buy or *must* sell the specified security if asked to do so by the option's buyer. A stock option contract represents an agreement between two people to buy or sell a round lot of stock.

There are two types of options: calls and puts.

- A **call option** is the *right to call* a security away from someone else.
- A **put option** is the *right to put* a security to someone else.

A *call* is the right to *buy* a set amount of a specific investment instrument at a set price for a set period of time. A *put* is the right to *sell* a set amount of a specific investment instrument at a set price for a set period of time.

Disposing of an Option

The holder of an option contract can:

- **exercise** the option
- let the option **expire**
- **sell** the option

Underlying Instruments

Options are available on the following underlying instruments:

- corporate stock;
- broad- and narrow-based indexes;
- Treasury bonds, Treasury notes and Treasury bills; and
- major foreign currencies.

Questions

1. Angus Bullwether is long 10 ABC Jul 50 calls. Identify the three choices he can make regarding his option position.

   _____

   _____

   _____

Questions 2 through 6 are about Karen Kodiak's option position: Karen is long 10 ABC Jul calls at 4 1/2.

2. How many options does Karen own?

   _____

3. What is the name of the underlying instrument?

   _____

4. Does the contract give Karen the right to buy or sell stock?

   _____

5. What is the total premium Karen paid for her position?

   _____

6. How many shares of stock will change hands if Karen exercises her option?

   _____

7. Which of the following investors will purchase stock if the option is exercised?

   I. Owner of a call
   II. Owner of a put
   III. Writer of a call
   IV. Writer of a put

   A. I and II
   B. I and IV
   C. II and III
   D. III and IV

8. Which of the following investors will sell stock if the option is exercised?

   I. Owner of a call
   II. Owner of a put
   III. Writer of a call
   IV. Writer of a put

   A. I and II
   B. I and IV
   C. II and III
   D. III and IV

Answers

1. Exercise the option.
   Let the option expire.
   Trade the option in a closing sale.

2. 10.

3. ABC common stock.

4. Buy.   A call is the right to buy stock.

5. $4,500.   4 1/2 × 100 shares per contract × 10 contracts = $4,500.

6. 1,000.   100 shares per contract × 10 contracts.

7. **B.**   A call owner has the right to purchase stock from a call writer. A put writer has the obligation to purchase stock if a put buyer chooses to exercise the option.

8. **C.**   A put owner acquires the right to sell stock by exercising the option. A call writer undertakes the obligation to sell stock if a call owner exercises the option.

Equity Options

The Option Contract

Exercise prices. An option's exercise price is the price at which the owner of the contract will be entitled to buy the underlying security and the price at which the seller has an obligation to deliver that security. If the advance or decline of the price of the underlying stock warrants it, the Options Clearing Corporation (OCC) will create new options with different strike prices.

Strike prices are usually created in multiples of $2.50 and $5, but may be adjusted later for stock splits and dividends. Options are not adjusted for ordinary cash dividends.

Expiration dates. The OCC standardizes the expiration dates of listed options. Each class of listed options has a set of four expiration months (known as a **cycle**). Each option contract must expire on the preset option expiration day in one of those months.

At any point in time, four option contracts are available for trading by investors: the **spot** (current) month, the **nearby** month and the next two options in the expiration cycle (JAJO, FMAN or MJSD).

e.g. JAN → JAN, FEB, {Apr July or may Aug or mar, Jun

Type, Class and Series

- **Type**. There are two types of options: calls and puts.

- **Class**. All options of the same type on the same underlying security are considered as being of the same class.

- **Series**. All options of the same class, exercise price and expiration month are in the same series.

The Four Basic Options Transactions

Long options. The owner of an option is said to have a **long position**.

- The investor with a **long call** has the right to *purchase* the underlying security at a speci-

fied price at any time through the expiration date.
- The investor with a **long put** has the right to *sell* the underlying security at the specified strike price until the expiration date.

Short options. The seller of an option is said to have a **short position**.

- The investor who is **short a call** is obligated to *sell* the underlying security at the specified strike price to the person who is long the call if the option is exercised by the expiration date.
- The investor who is **short a put** is obligated to *buy* the underlying security at the strike price at any time through the expiration date if the put owner exercises the option. For agreeing to the terms of the contract, the put writer receives the premium.

How the Options Market Functions

Exchange-traded. Listed options have standardized strike prices and expiration dates.

Listing requirements. In order to qualify for trading on a listed options exchange, the security underlying the option contract must meet the following requirements:

- minimum of 7,000,000 shares outstanding;
- minimum of 2,000 holders of the stock;
- volume in all markets of at least 2,400,000 shares in the preceding twelve months; (2 month)
- market price of at least $7.50 for the last three months; and
- issuer must be in compliance with the Securities Exchange Act of 1934.

Delisting. If a listed option's underlying stock no longer meets the exchange's listing requirements, no new contracts will be issued. A market will delist an option if:

- there are fewer than 6,300,000 shares outstanding;
- there are fewer than 1,600 holders of the stock;

- trading volume in all markets for the last twelve months falls below 1,800,000 shares; or
- the market price closes below $5 for the last six months.

The CBOE. Each OBO on the CBOE maintains in his order book a record of all limit orders on a particular class of options. The OBO displays the high bids and low offers for the option and executes any open order within the action of the trading crowd.

Options Clearing Corporation

The OCC's three-part mission is to standardize options contracts, issue options to buyers and sellers and guarantee performance of the contracts. Options are issued by the OCC *without a certificate*.

The investor long an option closes the position by entering a closing sale of an identical contract. The investor who is short an option closes the position by making a closing purchase of an identical contract.

OCC Options Disclosure Document. The OCC publishes an options disclosure document, called "The Characteristics and Risks of Standardized Options," that outlines the risks and rewards associated with investing in options. An investor must receive this document from the broker-dealer prior to or at the same time as the investor receives approval for options trading. The disclosure document must also accompany any options sales literature a client is sent.

Options agreement. A broker-dealer must obtain from any customer who intends to invest in options a signed options agreement within 15 days of approving the account for trading.

Option Contract Adjustments

Cash dividends. The OCC does not adjust the strike price of standardized options for ordinary cash dividends.

Stock splits. Options are adjusted for stock splits, reverse stock splits, stock dividends and rights offerings. When a stock splits, so does the option. The aggregate exercise price remains the same. If a stock split does not work out to even round lots, the OCC adjusts the number of shares in the contract.

Stock dividends. If a company declares a stock dividend, the OCC can adjust the strike price, the number of shares in the contract or both as it deems necessary.

Rounding. Adjustments to exercise prices are rounded to the nearest 1/8th, and adjustments in the number of underlying shares are rounded down to the next whole share.

Position Limits

In general, the exchanges limit investors to the following number of equity option contracts on the same side of the market:

- 8,000 contracts—options on heavily traded stocks
- 5,500 contracts—options on less heavily traded stocks
- 3,000 contracts—options on the least heavily traded stocks

Under the OCC's three-tier system of exercise limits, investors may not exercise more than the allowed number of contracts within *five consecutive business days*. The position limit on index options is 25,000 contracts on the same side of the market, with no more than 15,000 in the nearest term month. The exercise limit is 15,000 contracts in five days. For foreign currency options (FCOs), the position and exercise limits are the same, 100,000 contracts on the same side of the market.

Expiration, Trading and Exercise

The key option expiration times and dates are as follows:

- 4:00 pm EST (3:00 pm CST) on the third Friday of the month of expiration—listed equity options cease trading.
- 5:30 pm EST on the Friday of the month of expiration—options can no longer be exercised by their holders.
- 11:59 pm EST on the Saturday following the third Friday of the expiration month—options expire.

Automatic exercise. In the absence of instructions to the contrary, the OCC will automatically exercise any contracts owned by public customers that are 3/4ths of a point in the money and any contracts owned by member firms that are 1/4th of a point in the money.

Assignment of exercise. When an option owner notifies the OCC that he wants to exercise his option, the OCC randomly selects a firm to which it assigns the exercise. The assignment of the exercise notice to one of its customers by the broker-dealer may be done randomly or on a FIFO basis.

Questions

Use the options table in Figure 1 to answer questions 1 through 5.

1. What is the closing price of All Swel stock?

    _____

2. The number 30 appears to the right of "ALFA Inc." What does the number signify?

    _____

3. What is the closing premium of the ALF Jan 35 calls?

    _____

4. What does the small letter *r* mean?

    _____

5. How much would an investor pay for an option granting the right to buy 100 shares of Bulln Bar stock at $25 per share before the expiration date in March?

    _____

Figure 1

CHICAGO BOARD							
Option & NY Close	Strike Price	Calls-Last			Puts-Last		
		Jan	Feb	Mar	Jan	Feb	Mar
Adm Fam	40	1 3/8	3 5/8	r	3/16	7/8	1 1/4
41 1/8	45	1/2	1 1/2	2 1/8	3 7/8	r	5 1/4
41 1/8	50	r	3/8	5/8	s	s	12
ALFA Inc	30	7 7/8	9 1/8	11	r	r	1/8
37 7/8	35	3 1/8	4 1/2	6 3/4	r	1/4	1/8
37 7/8	40	3/4	1 5/8	3	3/4	7/8	r
All Swel	25	1/4	1 3/8	2	1/8	1	1 5/8
25 1/4	30	r	1/8	7/8	3 3/4	4 5/8	7
Bulln Bar	20	r	r	r	r	r	7/8
24	22 1/2	1	r	r	r	r	r
24	25	5/16	1	2 1/4	r	r	2 5/8

Total call vol 1,240,086   Call open int 3,038,532
Total put vol   105,755   Put open int   941,395
r - Not Traded. s - No Option.

6. Who or what issues a listed option?

    A. Member firm of the option writer
    B. Exchange on which the option is purchased
    C. Investor who writes the option
    D. Options Clearing Corporation

7. An investor buys 1 LMN Apr 70 call at 5, giving him the right to buy 100 shares of LMN at $70 per share. Which aspect of the transaction is not set or standardized by the OCC?

    A. Contract size of 100 shares
    B. Premium of 5
    C. Exercise price of 70
    D. Expiration date in April

8. All of the following are characteristics of nonstandardized options EXCEPT

    A. negotiated exercise prices
    B. active secondary trading
    C. premiums determined by the market
    D. negotiated expiration dates

Choose from the following list of options to answer questions 9 through 11.

    A. XYZ Jul 60 put at 3
    B. MNO Jul 45 put at 2
    C. MNO Aug 50 put at 4
    D. MNO Aug 50 call at 5

9. ___ Which of the options, if any, are of the same type?

10. ___ Which of the options, if any, are of the same class?

11. ___ Which of the options, if any, are of the same series?

12. It would be fair and equitable for a brokerage firm to assign an option exercise notice to which of the following customers?

    A. Customer with the largest open position in that option
    B. Customer who first wrote that option
    C. Either A or B
    D. Neither A nor B

The OCC sets standard expiration dates and exercise times for all listed options. Use the July calendar below to answer questions 13 through 15 concerning an ABC Jul 40 call option: in each case, write the time of day, day of the week and date.

July						
S	M	T	W	T	F	S
						1
2	3	4	5	6	7	8
9	10	11	12	13	14	15
16	17	18	19	20	21	22
23	24	25	26	27	28	29
30	31					

13. What is the deadline for selling the call in the open market?

    _____

14. What is the deadline for exercising the call?

    _____

15. When does the option expire?

    _____

16. A customer first discusses options trading with a registered representative on July 3rd. On July 7th the customer is approved for trading listed options and on July 12th he enters the first trade. Using the July calendar below, on which of the following dates must the customer receive an options disclosure document?

A. July 3rd
B. July 7th
C. July 12th
D. July 13th

July						
S	M	T	W	T	F	S
						1
2	3	4	5	6	7	8
9	10	11	12	13	14	15
16	17	18	19	20	21	22
23	24	25	26	27	28	29
30	31					

Answers

1. 25 1/4. The closing price of the underlying stock is listed under the stock's name.

2. 30. This is the strike price of the option.

3. 3 1/8 ($312.50).

4. The option did not trade.

5. $225. 2 1/4 per share × 100 shares.

6. **D.** The Options Clearing Corporation (OCC) issues all listed options.

7. **B.** The OCC sets standard exercise prices and expiration dates for all listed options, but the premiums that buyers pay for options are determined by the market.

8. **B.** Unlike listed options, unlisted options do not trade continuously in an organized secondary market. Trades are negotiated between individuals.

9. **A, B, C.** All are puts.

10. **B, C.** Both are MNO puts.

11. None. Options of the same series are of the same class, with the same expiration date and strike price.

12. **B.** Firms can choose one of two methods to assign an exercise: random; and first in, first out. Answer B describes the first in, first out method.

13. 4:00 pm Eastern time on Friday, July 21st. Note that July has five Saturdays and only four Fridays. This is why the rule reads "the business day immediately preceding the Saturday that follows the third Friday of the expiration month."

14. 5:30 pm Eastern time on Friday, July 21st.

15.   11:59 pm Eastern time on Saturday, July 22nd.

16.   **B.**   The options disclosure document must precede or accompany approval for trading listed options.

Option Trading and Strategies

Value of an Option

in, at, out the money.

A call is **in-the-money** whenever the stock's market price exceeds the option's strike price. A put is in-the-money whenever the stock price is less than the strike price.

A call is **out-of-the-money** if the stock price is below the exercise price. A put is out-of-the-money if the stock price is above the exercise price.

When the underlying stock is trading exactly at the exercise price of the option, the option is said to be **at-the-money**.

Intrinsic value. Intrinsic value is the positive difference between the option's strike price and the underlying stock's price. A call option has intrinsic value when the price of the underlying stock is above the option's exercise price. A put option has intrinsic value when the price of the underlying stock is below the option's exercise price. An out-of-the-money option has no intrinsic value.

Time value. The amount an investor is willing to pay above an option's intrinsic value in order to buy and hold that option for the time remaining until the option expires is the time value. As the option's expiration date approaches, the time value tends to diminish. On the last trading day before expiration, the time value is gone and the premium usually equals the intrinsic value. To find the time value of an option, calculate the intrinsic value and subtract it from the premium.

Buying and Selling Options

Buying Calls

An equity call option is the right to buy 100 shares of a specific stock at a specific price for a specific period of time. When an investor buys a call, he does so in anticipation that the price of the underlying stock will go up between the purchase date and the expiration date. If he is right and the call is trading higher than the strike price near the expiration, he can purchase shares for the strike price by exercising his call. If he is wrong and the price of the stock drops below the strike price, he will either let the option expire or try to sell it to someone else to recoup at least some of the premium he paid.

Options are wasting assets; the passage of time depletes their value. If an option is allowed to expire unexercised, the buyer loses 100% of the premium he paid at the opening transaction.

Objectives of Call Buyers

Call buyers are generally bullish on the underlying stock.

Speculative profit. The most common reason for buying calls is to make a speculative profit with as little cash outlay as possible. Using options provides the investor with greater leverage.

Deferring a decision. Investors can defer a decision to buy (or not to buy) a stock until near the expiration date of the option.

Diversifying holdings. Buying inexpensive calls can allow the investor to profit from any rise in the stock price through the option premiums without having to own the stock.

Writing Calls

An option seller is willing to take on the obligations of the contract in return for being paid the premiums. An investor writes a call in the belief that the stock will stay the same or drop in price.

Objectives of Call Writers

Call writers are generally bearish on the underlying stock. If the call is still unexercised at expiration, the call writer gets to keep the premium without having to deliver the stock to the buyer.

Increasing yield. Investors in many stocks use covered call writing to increase the yield of their securities.

Locking in a sale price. If an investor has already made a profit in a stock she holds and is interested in selling it if she can get a good price for it, she can write a call at a strike price that will lock in that profit.

Buying Puts

Investors in puts expect that the underlying security will drop in price during the life of the option. If this bearish view is correct, the investor can exercise the put option and sell the stock at a strike price that is higher than the market price of the stock.

Objectives of Put Buyers

Put buyers are generally bearish on the underlying stock. Investors typically purchase puts because they expect the underlying security to decline in value.

Speculating on a decline in a stock. A put buyer may wish to profit from a decline in the price of a stock that he does not own. If the stock becomes worthless, the investor will make his maximum gain, which is the exercise price less the premium paid. The investor's maximum loss is the premium he paid for the option.

Deferring a decision. Buying puts allows an investor to defer a decision to sell stock she owns until near the expiration date of the option.

Writing Puts

In return for assuming the obligation to buy stock at the put owner's discretion, put writers receive cash premiums.

Objectives of Put Writers

Put writers are generally bullish on the underlying stock.

Generating a large return. The premium a put buyer is willing to pay for the put option is the return the put writer wants.

Buying stock below its current price. Some put writers want the option exercised against them and consider short puts a good way to buy stock cheap because the premium received, in effect, reduces the cost of the stock when the stock is put to them in an exercise.

Maximum Gains, Losses and Breakeven Points

Long Calls

Maximum gain. Theoretically, there is no limit on the potential gains available to call owners because there is no limit on a rise in stock price.

Maximum loss. On a long call, investors risk losing 100% of the premium paid.

Breakeven point. A call buyer breaks even when the price of the underlying stock rises to the point where the investor could sell the option and make back the original premium she paid.

Short Calls

Maximum gain. The writer's gain is limited to the amount of the premium originally received.

Maximum loss. Theoretically, there is no limit on a call writer's potential loss.

Breakeven point. Call writers receive the premium, so they will break even when the value of their option rises an equal amount.

Long Puts

Maximum gain. The buyer of a long put is bearish, and his maximum gain is the strike price of the option less the premium he paid.

Maximum loss. A put buyer's maximum potential loss is the premium she paid.

Breakeven point. The breakeven point on a put option will be reached when the market price of the stock is below the strike price by the dollar amount of the premium.

Short Puts

Maximum gain. The writer of a put's greatest potential gain is the premium received.

Maximum loss. A put seller's maximum potential loss occurs if the stock price drops to zero—she is out the exercise price minus the premium received in the opening transaction.

Breakeven point. The put seller will lose money with the market price below the strike price by the amount of the premium received.

Questions

Use the following information and chart to answer questions 1 through 3.

$45 calls on XYZ have an intrinsic value and are in-the-money by $3. The market value of the XYZ stock ($48) is greater than the strike or exercise price of the call option by $3. The 45 calls have a $3 intrinsic value, regardless of the expiration date. The 45 calls with the December expiration have $1 of time value. Time value is the premium on the option less the option's intrinsic value.

Option & NY Close	Strike Price	Calls—Last		
		Dec	Jan	Feb
XYZ	45	4	6	7
48	50	1 1/2	3 1/2	4 1/2

1. What is the time value of the XYZ Jan 45 calls?

   _____

2. What is the time value of the XYZ Feb 45 calls?

   _____

3. With the market value of XYZ at 48, the $50 calls are out-of-the-money and have no intrinsic value. The market value is less than the exercise price. What is the time value of the XYZ 50 calls that expire in each of the following months?

   a. December _____

   b. January _____

   c. February _____

4. A call is in-the-money when the market price of the underlying stock is

A. equal to the strike price
B. more than the strike price
C. less than the strike price
D. more than it was at the previous day's close

5. PQR stock is trading at 25 3/4. PQR Jul 25 calls are trading at a premium of 2. What is the intrinsic value of these calls?

A. $0
B. $75
C. $125
D. $200

6. PQR stock is trading at 25 3/4. PQR Jul 25 calls are trading at a premium of 2. What is the time value of the Jul 25 calls?

A. $0
B. $75
C. $125
D. $200

7. Angus buys 1 ABC Jul 70 call at 2 1/2 when the market is at 71. As time passes, the market price of ABC remains stable at 71. The premium, therefore, will probably

A. stay the same
B. go up
C. go down
D. exhibit extreme volatility

8. Adam buys 1 XYZ 50 call at 4. What is the risk on this position?

A. Loss of $400
B. Loss of $500
C. Loss of $5,000
D. An unlimited amount

Figure 1

CHICAGO BOARD

Option & NY Close	Strike Price	Calls-Last Jan	Feb	Mar	Puts-Last Jan	Feb	Mar
Adm Fam	40	1 3/8	3 5/8	r	3/16	7/8	1 1/4
41 1/8	45	1/2	1 1/2	2 1/8	3 7/8	r	5 1/4
41 1/8	50	r	3/8	5/8	s	s	12
ALFA Inc	30	7 7/8	9 1/8	11	r	r	1/8
37 7/8	35	3 1/8	4 1/2	6 3/4	r	1/4	1/8
37 7/8	40	3/4	1 5/8	3	3/4	7/8	r
All Swel	25	1/4	1 3/8	2	1/8	1	1 5/8
25 1/4	30	r	1/8	7/8	3 3/4	4 5/8	7
Bulln Bar	20	r	r	r	r	r	7/8
24	22 1/2	1	r	r	r	r	r
24	25	5/16	1	2 1/4	r	r	2 5/8

Total call vol 1,240,086   Call open int 3,038,532
Total put vol 105,755   Put open int 941,395
r - Not Traded. s - No Option.

Use the options table in Figure 1 to answer questions 9 through 14.

9. What is the time value of the ALFA 35 calls that expire in

a. January? _____
b. February? _____
c. March? _____

10. What is the maximum gain a writer can earn and the maximum loss a writer can suffer by writing an option on each of the following ALFA 35 calls?

	Max. Gain	Max. Loss
a. Jan		
b. Feb		
c. Mar		

11. What is the maximum gain a writer of the Mar 45 Adm Fam calls can earn?

_____

12. What is the intrinsic value of the Feb 25 All Swel calls?

_____

13. What is the time value of the Feb 25 All Swel calls?

_____

14. What is the most a writer of the Jan 30 ALFA calls can lose?

_____

In questions 15 through 21, identify each situation by using the following terms:

   A. Buying calls
   B. Buying puts
   C. Writing calls
   D. Writing puts

15. ____ Angus sells 1 ABC Nov 45 put at 2 1/2.

16. ____ Belle receives a $400 premium for 1 Oct XYZ put.

17. ____ Angus has the obligation to buy 100 shares of ABC at 50 if the option is exercised.

18. ____ Adam has the right to sell 100 shares of MNO at 60 any time between July and October.

19. ____ Karen is long 1 ZYX Apr 30 put.

20. ____ Belle pays $225 for the option to buy 100 shares of ZYX at 25.

21. ____ Karen must sell 100 shares of PQR at 25 on demand; she owns 500 shares of PQR.

22. Which of the following investors are bearish?

   I. Buyer of a call
   II. Writer of a call
   III. Buyer of a put
   IV. Writer of a put

   A. I and II
   B. I and IV
   C. II and III
   D. III and IV

In questions 23 through 29, indicate whether you think the position would be taken by an investor who is a bull or an investor who is a bear.

23. ____ Long 1 XYZ Jul 60 put

24. ____ Short 1 XYZ Oct 60 put

25. ____ Buy 10 MNO Jul 35 puts

26. ____ Sell 10 ABC Jan calls

27. ____ Write 1 ABC call

28. ____ Buy 1 JKL call

29. ____ Write 10 KLM puts

Option Trading and Strategies

30. Belle tells her broker that she thinks the price of ABC is going to go up, but currently she does not have the money to buy 100 shares. By which methods could she use options to profit from a rise in the stock's price?

    I. Buy calls on ABC
    II. Write calls on ABC
    III. Buy puts on ABC
    IV. Write puts on ABC

    A. I and II
    B. I and IV
    C. II and III
    D. II and IV

In questions 31 through 36, refer back to Figure 1 and indicate whether the option is in-, at- or out-of-the-money.

31. ___ Adm Fam Mar 45 puts

32. ___ Adm Fam Feb 50 calls

33. ___ ALFA Jan 40 calls

34. ___ Bulln Bar Mar 20 puts

35. ___ All Swel Feb 25 puts

36. ___ All Swel Jan 25 calls

37. All of the following are objectives of call buyers EXCEPT

    A. speculating for profit on the rise in price of stock
    B. delaying a decision to buy stock
    C. hedging a long stock position against falling prices
    D. diversifying holdings

Answers

1. $3. $6 premium minus $3 intrinsic value

2. $4. $7 premium minus $3 intrinsic value

3.   a. $1 1/2.
    b. $3 1/2.
    c. $4 1/2. The option has no intrinsic value; its premium, in each case, is all time value—the more time, the more value. Investors believe the market value has more chance of being greater than the strike price in January or February than in December.

4. **B.** Options are in-the-money when they are worth exercising. Calls are worth exercising when the strike price is less than the market price of the underlying stock.

5. **B.** The intrinsic value of an option is the amount that the option is in-the-money. When PQR is trading at 25 3/4, the calls with a strike price of 25 are in-the-money by 3/4, which is $.75 a share, or $75 for all 100 shares of the underlying stock.

6. **C.** The time value is the premium minus the intrinsic value. The premium is 2 (or $200) and the intrinsic value is $75; $200 − $75 = $125.

7. **C.** Remember that options are wasting assets. As the expiration date approaches, the option's time value diminishes. Time, therefore, is against the option owner. In this case, the intrinsic value stays the same because the stock price remains stable at 71. (Intrinsic value for a call is the difference between the strike price and the market price—if the strike price is lower.)

8. **A.** The call buyer's risk is the amount of the premium paid for the option. If the call expires, the owner receives no return on investment.

9.   a. $25 (or 1/4). The premium is 3 1/8. The intrinsic value is the market value of the underlying stock (37 7/8) minus the strike price (35), or 2 7/8. The time value is the premium minus the

intrinsic value, or 3 1/8 minus 2 7/8, which equals 1/4.

     b. $162.50 (or 1 5/8). Premium (4 1/2) minus intrinsic value (2 7/8) equals time value (1 5/8).

     c. $387.50 (or 3 7/8). Premium (6 3/4) minus intrinsic value (2 7/8) equals time value (3 7/8).

10.   a. $312.50; unlimited. The maximum gain a writer can earn is the premium received—in this case, 3 1/8 (or $312.50). The maximum loss a call writer can suffer is unlimited.
     b. $450; unlimited
     c. $675; unlimited

11.   2 1/8.   The premium received is the maximum gain. The premium is 2 1/8 per share or $212.50 per contract.

12. $25.   The intrinsic value is the market value of the underlying security minus the exercise price of the option: or 25 1/4 minus 25, which is 1/4.

13.   1 1/8.   The Feb 25s are trading at 1 3/8, or $137.50 per contract. The intrinsic value as calculated in the preceding question is 1/4 (or $25). Time value is equal to the premium minus the intrinsic value—in this case, 1 3/8 minus 1/4, which is 1 1/8, or $1.125 per share.

14.   A call writer has a potentially unlimited loss.

15.   **D.**   *Writing* is the same as *selling*.

16.   **D.**   The writer (or seller) receives the premium.

17.   **D.**   Writers undertake obligations; buyers acquire rights. A put writer is obligated to buy stock from a put owner, who exercises the option.

18.   **B.**   The put buyer has the right to sell stock to a put writer, who is obligated to buy that stock.

19.   **B.**   *Buying, owning* and *being long* are synonymous.

20.   **A.**   Call buyers have the right, or option, to buy stock from call writers.

21.   **C.**   Call writers must sell stock to call buyers, who exercise their options.

22.   **C.**   Remember that diagonal positions (those positions that are total opposites—Buys vs. Sells and Puts vs. Calls) are on the same side of the market.

23.   Bear.   Put owners have the right to sell stock by exercising their options. The lower the market price of the underlying stock, the more you profit from the right to sell stock at a price fixed by the option.

24.   Bull.   When the market price goes up, put owners will sell stock in the market rather than exercise their options. Put writers, therefore, will not have to take delivery of stock. The options will expire, and the writers will keep the premium received.

25.   Bear.

26.   Bear.   The seller of a call receives a premium and is obligated to sell the underlying stock if a call buyer exercises the option. When the market price of the stock falls, call owners will be more likely to buy at the market price than to exercise their options to purchase stock at the strike price.

27.   Bear.   *Writing* means the same as *selling*.

28.   Bull.   Call buyers have the right to buy stock from call writers. The more the market price of the stock rises, the more attractive is the fixed strike price of the option.

29.   Bull.   *Writing* a put is the same as *shorting* a put.

30.   **B.**   The bullish strategies are buying calls and writing puts.

31.   In-the-money.

32.   Out-of-the-money.

33.   Out-of-the-money.

34.   Out-of-the-money.

35.   Out-of-the-money.

36.   In-the-money.

37.   **C.**   The right to purchase more shares of stock does not provide a hedge against falling prices.

Multiple Option Strategies

Spreads, Straddles and Combinations

Spreads

A spread is the purchase of one option and sale of another option of the same class. Investors can establish both **call spreads** and **put spreads**. A call spread is a long call and short call. A put spread is a long put and short put. The two options in a spread are of the same class, but are of different series.

Types of spreads. When the two options in a spread differ only in strike price, the investor has established a **price spread**. When the two options differ only in expiration date, the investor has established a **time spread**. When the options differ in both price and time, the investor has established a **diagonal spread**.

Straddles and Combinations

Straddles. The two options in a straddle are on the same stock, have the same strike price and have the same expiration date. A **long straddle** is the purchase of a call and put. A **short straddle** is the sale of a call and put.

Combinations. In a combination the investor purchases or sells options that differ in strike price, expiration date or both.

Risks and Rewards of Multiple Option Strategies

Maximum Gains, Losses and Breakeven Points

The rules for determining whether a multiple option strategy is bullish or bearish are the same as they are for single option investments. Bulls buy calls and call spreads. Bears buy puts and put

spreads. Bulls sell puts and put spreads. Bears sell calls and call spreads.

An investor who establishes a spread does so for either a **net credit** or a **net debit**.

Debit Call Spreads

Investor objectives. A bullish investor buys a call or call spread because she expects that its net market value will increase along with the underlying stock's price. If it does, she can exercise the long option of the spread and buy stock below the market price. And even if the short option is exercised against her, she will be able to deliver the stock she just bought and keep the difference between the strike prices.

Maximum gain. The investor will realize her maximum gain any time the stock's market price is at or above the strike price of the higher option.

Maximum loss. If the stock's price falls to or below the strike price of the lower option, both calls will expire worthless. As a general rule, the maximum loss on any debit spread is the initial debit.

Breakeven. The breakeven point on a debit call spread is the lower strike price plus the initial debit.

Debit Put Spreads

Investor objectives. A bearish investor buys a put or put spread because he expects that the spread's net market value will increase as the underlying stock's price decreases. If it does, he can exercise the long put of the spread and sell stock above the current market price. If the short put is exercised against him, he will have to buy the stock, but by exercising the option he owns, he can then sell at the higher strike price and keep the difference.

Maximum gain. The investor will realize his maximum gain any time the stock's market price is at or below the strike price of the lower option.

Maximum loss. If the stock's price rises to or above the strike price of the higher option, both puts will expire worthless. The maximum loss on any debit spread is the initial debit.

Breakeven. The breakeven point on a debit put spread is the higher strike price minus the initial debit.

Credit Call Spreads

Investor objectives. Bearish investors sell calls and call spreads because they expect the underlying stock's price to go down.

Maximum gain. The maximum gain on a credit call spread, as with any position established for a credit, is the initial credit.

Maximum loss. The maximum loss on a credit call spread is the difference between strike prices less the initial credit.

Breakeven. The breakeven point will be the lower strike price plus the initial credit.

Credit Put Spreads

Investor objectives. Bullish investors sell puts and put spreads because they expect the stock's price to go up.

Maximum gain. The maximum gain on a credit put spread is the initial credit.

Maximum loss. The maximum loss on a credit put spread is the difference between strike prices minus the initial credit.

Breakeven. The breakeven point on a credit put spread is the higher strike price minus the net premium.

Spread Between Premiums

Investors in credit spreads keep the credit received initially if the options become worthless and the spread between the premiums of two options *narrows*.

Investors with debit spreads make their maximum gain when both options are in-the-money and the spread between premiums *widens*.

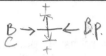

Long Straddles

Investor objectives. Straddles are used by investors who think a stock's price is going to be volatile, but are not sure which direction the price will take.

Maximum gain. The maximum gain for a long straddle is the maximum gain for the call.

Maximum loss. A long straddle investor loses the entire premium if the options expire at-the-money because she paid for both and neither is worth exercising or selling.

Breakeven. A long straddle breaks even when the stock price is equal to the strike price plus or minus the debit.

Short Straddles

Investor objectives. The straddle writer believes the stock price will not change much and will *not move* outside the breakeven points.

Maximum gain. The maximum potential gain for a short straddle is the initial premiums received.

Maximum loss. The maximum loss for a short straddle is the maximum loss for the short call.

Breakeven. A short straddle breaks even when the stock price is equal to the strike price plus or minus the credit.

Hedging with Options

Long Stock and Short Calls (Covered Call Writing)

Covered call writers reduce the downside risk of long stock positions by the dollars they receive in premiums from selling the call, and the long stock position gives the call writer something to deliver if the call is exercised against him.

Long Stock and Long Puts

Hedging against price declines. If an investor owns stock, she can hedge her downside risk by purchasing puts at the purchase price. Her long stock position is hedged against a drop in price by the put options as long as they remain in effect.

Short Stock and Long Calls

Insurance to hedge a short stock position. Purchasing a call limits an investor's risk to the difference between the strike price of the call and the price he received for the borrowed stock. The purchase of the call reduces the overall profit potential on the short position by the amount of the premium.

Short Stock and Short Puts

A customer with a short put position may partially hedge the short position by selling short the stock at the same price. If the stock rises in value, the investor is partially protected by the amount of money received in premiums.

Questions

In questions 1 through 6, identify the positions described by indicating one of the following terms.

A. Price spread
B. Long straddle
C. Time spread
D. Short straddle
E. Diagonal spread
F. Combination

1. ___ Buy 1 XYZ May 40 call; sell 1 XYZ May 50 call.

2. ___ Buy 1 XYZ May 40 call; buy 1 XYZ May 40 put.

3. ___ Buy 1 XYZ Aug 40 call; sell 1 XYZ Dec 40 call.

4. ___ Buy 1 ABC May 30 call; buy 1 ABC Jul 40 put.

5. ___ Write 1 ABC Jan 30 call; write 1 ABC Jan 40 put.

6. ___ Buy 1 ABC Mar 35 call; write 1 ABC Jun 45 call.

7. Which two of the following are spreads?

   I. Long 1 ABC May 40 call; short 1 ABC May 50 call

  II. Long 1 ABC May 40 call; long 1 ABC May 50 call

 III. Long 1 ABC Aug 40 call; short 1 ABC May 40 call

 IV. Long 1 ABC Aug 40 call; short 1 ABC Aug 50 put

A. I and II
B. I and III
C. II and III
D. II and IV

8. Angus Bullwether sells an XYZ Mar 35 call. To establish a straddle, he would

   A. sell an XYZ Mar 35 call
   B. buy an XYZ Mar 35 put
   C. sell an XYZ Mar 35 put
   D. buy an XYZ Mar 40 call

9. Angus buys 1 ABC Nov 70 put and sells 1 ABC Nov 60 put when ABC is selling for 65. This position is a

   A. bull spread
   B. bear spread
   C. combination
   D. straddle

10. ADM issues a news release that your customer believes will strongly affect the market price of ADM stock. Your customer is not, however, sure whether the effect will be positive or negative. In this situation, which of the following strategies would be best?

   A. Buy a call
   B. Write a call
   C. Write a straddle
   D. Buy a straddle

11. All of the following are credit spreads EXCEPT to

   A. write 1 Nov 35 put and buy 1 Nov 30 put
   B. buy 1 Apr 40 call and write 1 Apr 30 call
   C. buy 1 Jul 50 call and write 1 Jul 60 call
   D. buy 1 Jan 50 put and write 1 Jan 60 put

In questions 12 through 19, identify which are bull spreads and which are bear spreads.

12. Write 1 Nov 35 put; buy 1 Nov 30 put.

   _____

13. Buy 1 Jan 70 call; write 1 Jan 75 call.

   _____

14. Write 1 Apr 30 call; buy 1 Apr 40 call.

   _____

15. Write 1 Dec 45 put; buy 1 Dec 60 put.

   _____

16. Buy 1 Jul 50 call; write 1 Jul 60 call.

   _____

17. Buy 1 Dec 45 put; write 1 Dec 40 put.

   _____

18. Write 1 Jan 60 put; buy 1 Jan 50 put.

   _____

19. Buy 1 May 25 put; write 1 May 20 put.

   _____

20. In which of the following cases would the investor want the spread to widen?

   I. Buy 1 May 30 put; write 1 May 25 put.
   II. Write 1 Apr 45 put; buy 1 Apr 55 put.
   III. Buy 1 Nov 65 put; write 1 Nov 75 put.
   IV. Buy 1 Jan 40 call; write 1 Jan 30 call.

   A. I and II
   B. I and IV
   C. II and III
   D. III and IV

21. Belle Charolais purchases 2 XYZ Jul 30 calls at 2 and 2 XYZ Jul 30 puts at 2 1/2. She will break even when the price of the underlying stock is

   I.   25 1/2
  II.   27 1/2
 III. 32
 IV. 34 1/2

  A. I and IV
  B. II and III
  C. III
  D. IV

In questions 22 through 25, calculate the break-even points on each position.

22. Buy 1 MNO Jan 40 call at 2 3/8; write 1 MNO Jan 45 call at 7/8.

_____

23. Buy 1 XYZ Apr 30 put at 3 3/8; write 1 XYZ Apr 35 put at 5 7/8.

_____

24. Write 1 ABC Dec 50 call at 5 1/4; buy 1 ABC Dec 55 call at 2.

_____

25. Write 2 XYZ Apr 30 calls at 2 1/4; write 2 XYZ Apr 30 puts at 2 1/8.

_____

Use the following information to answer questions 26 through 28.

Karen Kodiak writes 1 XYZ Apr 50 call at 4 and buys 1 XYZ Apr 40 call at 8 when XYZ is trading at 47.

26. If both calls expire unexercised, what will be Karen's gain or loss?

  A. $400 loss
  B. $600 gain
  C. $700 loss
  D. $1,100 gain

27. Excluding commissions, the breakeven point on Karen's position is

  A. 40
  B. 44
  C. 46
  D. 50

28. What will Karen's profit be if the underlying stock is trading at $52 at expiration?

  A. $200
  B. $400
  C. $600
  D. $800

In questions 29 through 32, indicate the maximum possible gain and the maximum possible loss for each spread.

29. Write 1 MNO Oct 30 call at 3 3/16; buy 1 MNO Oct 40 call at 1/16.

Max. gain: _____

Max. loss: _____

30. Buy 1 MNO Jan 40 put at 6 1/2; write 1 MNO Jan 30 put at 2 1/8.

Max. gain: _____

Max. loss: _____

31. Buy 1 ABC Oct 80 call at 8; write 1 ABC Oct 90 call at 2 3/4.

    Max. gain: _____

    Max. loss:_____

32. Write 1 XYZ Jan 130 call at 26 3/4; buy 1 XYZ Jan 140 call at 19 1/2.

    Max. gain: _____

    Max. loss:_____

Use the following information to answer questions 33 and 34.

Adam writes an Apr 60 call on PNY stock at 7 and covers the option by purchasing 100 shares of the underlying stock at $55 per share.

33. What is the initial cost of this covered call?

    _____

34. What is the breakeven point on Adam's position?

    _____

35. What is the breakeven point if you buy 100 ABC at 53 and sell 1 50 call for 7 1/2?

    _____

36. What is the breakeven point if you buy 100 Big Tractor at 58 1/4 and sell 1 60 call at 6 1/2?

    _____

Use the following information to answer questions 37 through 41.

An investor buys 100 Big Tractor at 58 1/4 and sells 1 Big Tractor 55 call for 7.

37. What is the price received when selling the stock at the exercise price?

    _____

38. What are the dollar proceeds from the call?

    _____

39. What would be the sale proceeds from the sale of the stock if the option is exercised?

    _____

40. What was the cost of the stock?

    _____

41. What is the maximum profit potential?

    _____

42. Adam is short 100 shares of MNO and wants a hedge against a rise in the market price of the stock. What should be his strategy?

    _____

43. Angus buys 500 shares of XYZ. What strategy would provide insurance against a drop in the stock's market value?

    _____

In questions 44 through 47, identify the option strategy that might help the investor achieve the specified goal.

    A. Sell covered calls.
    B. Sell naked calls.
    C. Sell puts.

44. ___ Karen thinks ABC is going to drop sharply in price. What could she do if she wants to make a speculative profit on that drop, and is willing to take considerable risk?

45. ___ Angus owns 100 shares of HIJ stock. He is worried that the price may drop but does not want to sell his stock. How could he partially ensure against falling market prices?

46. ___ Belle owns a large block of XYZ. How could she generate extra income from her stock?

47. ___ How could Karen buy MNO common stock at a price below the market?

Use the following information to answer questions 48 through 50.

Max Leveridge is long 100 shares of This Can't Be Sushi (TCB) at 51. He establishes a short straddle on TCB with a strike price of 50. The premium on the call is 3 1/4 and the premium on the put is 2 1/4.

48. What is Max's maximum gain on the position?

    A. 2 1/4
    B. 3 1/4
    C. 5 1/2 $(5\frac{1}{2} - 1)$
    D. 4 1/2

49. What is Max's maximum loss on the position?

    A. 45 1/2   at 0   51+50-5½
    B. 47 3/4   = 95½
    C. 51
    D. 95 1/2

50. What is Max's breakeven point on the position?

    A. 47 3/4
    B. 50 1/4
    C. 55 1/2
    D. 56 1/2

51. Which of the following is the riskiest options position?

    A. Covered call writing
    B. Uncovered call writing
    C. Writing puts
    D. Buying puts

52. All of the following are suitable objectives for a covered call writer EXCEPT

    A. hedging a long stock position
    B. increasing return on a long stock position
    C. speculating that a stock will not rise in price
    D. buying stock below the market

Answers

1. **A.** The most common spread, and the one you're most likely to see on the Series 7 exam, is the price spread, in which the two options have the same expiration date but different exercise prices.

2. **B.** The investor is long a call and long a put with the same strike price and expiration date; this is a long straddle.

3. **C.** Also called a *horizontal* or *calendar* spread, a time spread involves two options with different expiration dates.

4. **F.** A combination is similar to a straddle in that the investor buys or sells a call and a put. With a combination, however, the strike prices, expiration dates or both are different.

5. **F.** The investor is selling a call and a put with different strike prices.

6. **E.** Both the expiration date and the price are different.

7. **B.** Choices I and III fit the definition of a call spread because each includes one long and one short option of the same type with either different strike prices (choice I) or different expiration dates (choice III). Choice II involves options of the same type but both are long. Choice IV involves options of different types.

8. **C.** Straddles involve options of different types, but either both options must be long or both must be short. They must have the same expiration date and strike price.

9. **B.** This put spread is established at a debit, because the investor pays more for the 70 put than he receives for the 60 put. Bears buy puts and put spreads.

10. **D.** If the stock goes either up or down sharply, your customer will profit from owning a straddle.

11. **C.** The lower the strike price, the more expensive the call option. The higher the strike price, the more expensive the put option. Because the investor has purchased the more expensive option with the lower strike price, this is a debit spread.

12. **Bull spread.** This is a put credit spread. The investor receives more for the Nov 35 put than she pays for the Nov 30 put. Bulls sell put spreads. The put with the higher strike price is more likely to be in-the-money as the market falls.

13. **Bull spread.** This is a call debit spread. Bulls buy calls. A lower strike price call is more likely to be in-the-money as the market rises.

14. **Bear spread.** This is a call credit spread. Bears sell calls.

15. **Bear spread.** This is a put debit spread. Bears buy puts. The 60 put is worth more because it has a higher strike price.

16. **Bull spread.** This is a call debit spread. Bulls buy calls.

17. **Bear spread.** This is a put debit spread. Bears buy puts.

18. **Bull spread.** This is a put credit spread. Bulls sell puts.

19. **Bear spread.** This is a put debit spread. Bears buy puts.

20. **A.** Choices I and II are debit spreads. An investor wants a debit spread to widen. As the distance between the premiums increases, the investor's potential profit also increases. This is because the investor intends to sell the option with the higher premium and buy back the option with the lower premium and, therefore, wants the selling

price of one to be as much above the buying price of the other as possible.

21. **A.** Belle buys calls and puts with the same strike price and expiration date, so the position is a straddle. Straddles have two breakeven points—the strike price plus and minus the sum of the two premiums.

22. 41 1/2. Because this is a call spread, you find the breakeven point by adding the initial debit of 1 1/2 to the lower strike price: 40 + 1 1/2 = 41 1/2.

23. 32 1/2. This is a put spread established at a credit of 2 1/2. To find the breakeven point on a put spread, subtract the initial credit or debit from the higher strike price. (PSH: Puts Subtract from Higher). In this case, subtract the credit of 2 1/2 from the higher strike price of 35.

24. 53 1/4. To find the breakeven point on this call credit spread, add the initial credit of 3 1/4 to the lower strike price of 50.

25. 25 5/8, 34 3/8. A straddle, whether long or short, has two breakeven points: the strike price plus and minus the sum of the premiums paid or received. In this case, the sum of the premiums received for the two short options is 4 3/8, and the strike price is 30. At any stock price greater than 34 3/8 or less than 25 5/8, the investor who wrote this straddle will lose money.

26. **A.** If both options expire unexercised, Karen will lose her original investment in the position—a $400 debit derived from buying a call for $800 and selling one for $400.

27. **B.** Remember CAL: add the original debit of 4 to the lower strike price of 40 to find the breakeven point of 44.

28. **C.** At any stock price equal to or greater than the higher strike price of 50, Karen realizes her maximum gain—the difference between the strike prices minus the initial debit: 10 − 4 = 6, or $600 on the 100 shares in the contract.

29. Max. gain: $312.50. The maximum potential gain on a credit spread is the initial credit.
    Max. loss: $687.50. The maximum potential loss on a credit spread is the difference between the strike prices minus the initial credit: 10 − 3 1/8 = 6 7/8; 6 7/8 × 100 shares = $687.50.

30. Max. gain: $562.50. The maximum gain on a debit spread is the difference between the strike prices minus the initial debit: 10 − 4 3/8 = 5 5/8; 5 5/8 × 100 shares = $562.50.
    Max. loss: $437.50. The maximum loss on a debit spread is the initial debit.

31. Max. gain: $475. The maximum gain on a debit spread is the difference between the strike prices minus the initial debit: 10 − 5 1/4 = 4 3/4; 4 3/4 × 100 shares = $475.
    Max. loss: $525. The maximum loss on a debit spread is the initial debit.

32. Max. gain: $725. The maximum gain on a credit spread is the initial credit received.
    Max. loss: $275. The maximum loss on a credit spread is the difference between the strike prices minus the initial credit: 10 − 7 1/4 = 2 3/4; 2 3/4 × 100 shares = $275.

33. $4,800. The total debit for the position is $4,800. Adam pays $55 a share for 100 shares ($5,500) and receives $700 for writing the call: $5,500 − $700 = $4,800.

34. Adam pays $4,800 for his position—equivalent to $48 per share for the stock. Therefore, when the stock is trading for $48, he can sell it for $4,800 and break even. At that price, the call expires worthless. If the stock price rises to more than 60, the call will be in-the-money. Even if Adam's call is exercised, however, he will receive $60 per share ($6,000 for 100 shares) and make money on his position.

35. 45 1/2. 53 − 7 1/2 = 45 1/2. He paid 53 for the stock and offset the cost by selling a call for 7 1/2.

36. 51 3/4. 58 1/4 − 6 1/2 = 51 3/4.

37. $5,500.   Remember, the call is exercisable at 55.

38. $700.   The premium of $7 per share on a 100-share contract yields $700 to the writer.

39. $6,200.   The strike price of 55 plus the premium of 7, times 100 shares.

40. $5,825.   This is $58.25 per share.

41. $375.   The stock was purchased at 58 1/4. If the market goes up, the call will be exercised. The stock will be delivered at the exercise price of $55 plus the premium received on the call, for sale proceeds of $62 per share. The net profit, therefore, will be 3 3/4 per share (62 − 58 1/4).

42.   Buy calls.   Short sellers are bearish. They have borrowed and sold stock; they must replace the borrowed shares. If they need to buy those shares in the market, they want the market price to fall, not rise. A call option provides insurance against a rising market price because it gives the owner the right to buy stock at the predetermined exercise price.

43.   Buy puts or sell calls.   Puts lock in a selling price for the underlying stock. Angus knows, therefore, that he can always sell his stock at the exercise price of the put, no matter how far the market may drop. The bearish put position is a hedge against losses on the bullish stock position. Selling calls would provide only a partial hedge against falling prices, to the amount of the premium received for writing the call.

44.   B.   Sell naked calls.   Because Karen is willing to take a risk, she can write naked calls. If the stock price drops, she will keep the premium. If it does not drop, she risks having to buy stock at a high market price to deliver at the exercise price.

45.   A.   Sell covered calls.   The covered call writer buys stock and, at the same time, writes a call on it. If the stock price drops, the investor will keep the option premium; that amount of money will compensate, to a degree, for loss on the long stock position.

46.   A.   Sell covered calls.   The premiums received for writing the calls increase the yield from the position.

47.   C.   Sell puts.   If a writer sells a put with an exercise price near the current market price and if the stock is put to writer, the effective cost of the stock is the strike price minus the premium. That effective cost may be less than the market price at the time the put is sold.

48.   D.   When trying to determine the maximum gain, maximum loss or breakeven, it is the underlying stock position (the long-term investment) that counts. In order to determine Max's profit, loss or breakeven, you have to make the assumption that he will close out his position at that point. This is the easiest way to calculate the net value of all account debits and credits.

In this problem, we are dealing initially with 100 shares of stock purchased at 51, a 50 call sold at 3 1/4 and a 50 put sold at 2 1/4. Our starting position, then, is a net debit of 51 and a net credit of 5 1/2. Now we must determine what will happen as the stock price moves up or down.

At any stock price exceeding 50, the put will expire worthless and the call will be exercised. If the call is exercised at 50, Max will lose $100 on the stock (cost basis of 51 minus the selling price of 50) but will still realize a net gain of $450 (net credit of 5 1/2 minus the 1-point loss). No matter how high the stock's price rises, the maximum gain on this position is $450.

49.   D.   If the stock falls to less than 50, the call will expire worthless but the put will be exercised and Max will have to buy another 100 shares. To determine his loss if this happens, assume that Max will sell the 100 shares put to him at the market, and then net that loss first against the credit he received for selling the straddle and then against his cost basis in the original 100-share investment.

As an example, assume that TCB goes to 45. The call will expire, and the put will be exercised against Max at 50. Max will have to buy the 100 shares at 50 and then sell those shares at 45, taking a 5-point loss on the stock. The net credit he received for the straddle (5 1/2) will offset the loss on the stock put to him, leaving him with a 1/2-point credit. This 1/2-point credit is then applied against the 6-point loss he faces on his original 100 shares (cost basis of 51 minus the 45 market value). At a market price of 45, Max realizes a 5 1/2-point loss.

If TCB goes to 0, Max will be put the 100 shares at 50 and be unable to sell them at 0, taking a 50-point loss on the stock. The net credit he received for the straddle (5 1/2) will only slightly offset the loss on the stock put to him, leaving him with a 44 1/2-point loss. This 44 1/2-point loss is then added to the 51-point loss he faces on his original 100 shares (cost basis of 51 minus the 0 market value). At a market price of 0, Max's maximum loss is 95 1/2 points.

50.   **A.**   In this breakeven problem, Max must be concerned not only with the possible loss on his long TCB position, but also on a second 100 shares of stock that will be put to him if the price of the stock drops to less than 50. To determine Max's breakeven, the first step is to calculate the average cost basis of these two positions. To do this we take the cost basis of his long stock (he purchased it at 51), add the cost basis of the stock that will be put to him (at a strike price of 50) and then divide that number by two to get his average cost basis. 51 + 50 = 101; 101 ÷ 2 = 50 1/2.

The next step is to apply the net premium against the two stock positions in the same way. Max's net premium for writing this straddle is 5 1/2 (3 1/4 for the call and 2 1/4 for the put). Because we are dealing with two stock positions, this premium must cover potential losses on both. To calculate the amount of protection this net premium offers, divide the premium by 2. 5 1/2 ÷ 2 = 2 3/4. Each position has downside protection of 2 3/4 points.

Finally, we can establish the breakeven for the entire strategy by subtracting the average downside protection (2 3/4 points) from the average cost basis for the stock (50 1/2). 50 1/2 − 2 3/4 = 47 3/4. Max's breakeven will occur at a stock price of 47 3/4.

To prove this, assume the stock drops to 47 3/4. Max would have a loss of 3 1/4 points on his long stock position (51 − 47 3/4). In addition, he is now obligated to buy another 100 shares at $50 per share and sell it at 47 3/4, a loss of 2 1/4. His total loss is 5 1/2 points (3 1/4 + 2 1/4). This loss is exactly covered by the 5 1/2 points in premiums he received for writing the straddle.

Here is a summary of the steps we took to find Max's breakeven point:

1. Find the average cost basis: (51 + 50) ÷ 2 = 50 1/2.
2. Find the average premium protection: 5 1/2 ÷ 2 = 2 3/4.
3. Subtract the average protection from the average cost basis: 50 1/2 − 2 3/4 = 47 3/4.

51.   **B.**   Uncovered call writing is very risky and can produce potentially unlimited losses.

52.   **D.**   A covered call writer has taken on the obligation to sell stock if the call is exercised, not to buy stock.

Introduction to Nonequity Options

Index Options

Broad-based indexes. Options are available on the S&P 100 Index (OEX), the S&P 500 Index (SPX), the AMEX Major Market Index (XMI) and the *Value Line* Index, among others.

Narrow-based indexes. Narrow-based indexes include the Technology Index and the Gold/Silver Index. *group*

Options on indexes. Index options make it possible for investors to profit from the swings in the market or to hedge against losses that market movement can cause in individual stock positions.

Multiplier. For the OEX, the multiplier is 100. An OEX Jun 380 call at 12 is actually worth $38,000 (380 × 100) and would cost an investor a premium of $1,200.

Call options. A call on an index gives its owner the right to receive, in cash, the option's intrinsic value at an assigned time on the day of exercise.

Put options. A put on the index gives its owner the right to put the index to the put writer and to receive the option's intrinsic value at the close on the day of exercise.

Exercise settlement. Index option writers deliver cash. Cash settlement creates a special risk because it means that all short calls on index options are naked.

Dates and times. Trading of index options occurs between 9:30 am and 4:15 pm EST. The daily exercise cut-off occurs at 4:15 pm EST. Settlement occurs one business day after exercise.

Position and exercise limits. The position limit for index options is 25,000 contracts on the same side of the market, and the exercise limit is 15,000 contracts in five days on the same side of the market.

25,000/15000
↓
5 day

Interest Rate Options

Investor objectives. Investors in interest rate options hope to profit from changes in the prices of debt securities or to hedge existing portfolios of debt securities against price declines caused by increased interest rates.

Treasury bills. The underlying instrument for calls and puts on T bills is the most current 13-week (91-day) Treasury bill. One T bill option represents $1 million worth of some future issue of 13-week bills rather than a specific security.

To turn a T bill premium quote into a dollar figure, multiply it by $2,500. The premium is an annualized percentage of the face value, $1 million. Although 1% of $1 million is $10,000, the T bill's life span is 13 weeks, just one-fourth of a 52-week year. Annualized, therefore, each point equals $2,500 (one-fourth of $10,000).

Treasury notes and bonds. An option on either a note or a bond represents a specific underlying security with a face value of $100,000. Upon exercise, the owner of a put or the writer of a call must deliver a note or bond from that particular issue. Strike prices for notes and bonds are quoted at a percentage of face value.

Expiration and exercise. Expiration of interest rate options is the Saturday following the third Friday of the month. Two business days after the exercise of the option, the call writer must deliver (or the put writer receive) the underlying note or bond. The investor who receives the security must pay the exercise price plus the interest that has accrued since the last payment.

Hedging with long call positions. An investor who fears that long-term bond interest rates will head down and thus wants to lock in high current rates can purchase calls.

Hedging with short put positions. An investor who anticipates a near-term decline in interest rates and who hold a long-term position in Treasury bonds can write puts.

Hedging with long put positions. As a hedge against rising interest rates (and falling note prices), investors sometimes buy at-the-money puts on T notes.

Increasing yields with call writing. A fund manager can write call to generate increased investment income on a portfolio of Treasury securities.

Hedge strategies. The need to hedge currency exchange is a major reason for the existence of options on currencies.

Foreign Currency Options

Investors trade foreign currency options to profit from fluctuating exchange rates and to hedge against the risks arising from fluctuating exchange rates.

Characteristics of FCOs. Underlying each FCO is an arbitrary amount of foreign money as set by the PHLX. The strike price of the option is set at a certain amount of U.S. money. Each option contract represents the right to buy or sell the foreign currency for the specified amount of U.S. currency.

Price of the underlying currency. Exchange rates are quoted in U.S. cents per unit of the underlying currency, with two exceptions: French francs trade in 1/10ths of a cent per franc; Japanese yen trade in 1/100ths of a cent per yen.

Expiration cycles. The PHLX trades FCOs on a three-six-nine-month schedule and has the option of adding a twelve-month contract.

Expiration date and last trading day. All FCOs expire on the Saturday preceding the third Wednesday of the month. Trading ceases at 1:30 pm EST the last business day before the expiration date.

Position and exercise limits. On the PHLX, position and exercise limits are 100,000 contracts on the same side of the market.

Exercise settlement. The PHLX uses the American exercise system, which allows owners to exercise their options at any time up to and including the last business day before expiration. When an FCO is exercised, the owner of the put or writer of the call must deliver the currency of the country of origin.

Strategies. Investors trade FCOs for two reasons: to profit from fluctuating exchange rates or to hedge against the risks arising from fluctuating exchange rates.

Questions

1. The OEX and Major Market Indexes are examples of which of the following?

   A. Broad-based indexes
   B. Narrow-based indexes

Use the following information to answer questions 2 and 3.

On November 4th, Angus Bullwether writes an OEX Jun 220 put at 6.

2. The maximum potential gain on Angus's position is

   _____

3. Angus will achieve the maximum gain on his position if, on the expiration date, the OEX closes at what price?

   _____

4. Karen Kodiak writes an XMI 450 call at 13. The market closes that day at 462.34. Karen will break even on her short call if, on the expiration date, the index closes at which of the following prices?

   A. 437
   B. 450
   C. 462.34
   D. 463

Use the following information to answer questions 5 through 7.

Adam establishes a spread by purchasing an OEX Jul 285 call and writing a Jul 280 call.

5. Is his position a credit spread or a debit spread?

   _____

6. Does Adam want his spread to widen or narrow?

   _____

7. The index closes at 280 on expiration date. Does Adam realize his maximum gain or maximum loss?

   _____

8. Refer to the Major Market Index options table (similar to what might appear in *The Wall Street Journal*) shown in Figure 1. If the multiplier for Major Market Index options is 100, what is the dollar amount of the premium for Jan 405 calls?

   _____

Figure 1

American Exchange
Major Market Index

Strike Price	Calls--Last Jan	Feb	Mar	Puts--Last Jan	Feb	Mar
375	14 1/4	....	....	2 7/8	13 1/8	....
380	10 1/8	18	16 3/4	4 3/8	16 3/4	....
385	6 3/8	18 1/4	....	5 3/8	20 1/2	....
390	4 1/2	14 1/2	18	8 3/8	21 1/2	....
395	2 3/8	12 1/4	....	11 1/2		....
400	1 1/4	9 3/4	....	14 1/4	25	34
405	3/4	8 1/8	....	19 1/2	....	....
410	1/8	7 3/4	....	30	33	....
415	3/16	6	10	30	....	....

Total call volume 24,480   Total call open interest 37,170
Total put volume 26,652   Total put open interest 24,062
The index: High 391.22; Low 378.56; Close 386.65; -4.57

9. Karen is short 1 XMI Mar 380 call. If she is assigned an exercise on March 15th, when the index closes at 386.65, how much will she owe? (Trades involving index options must be settled in cash.)

_____

Use the following information and Figure 1 to answer questions 10 through 12.

Belle Charolais is short 1 XMI Jan 400 put.

10. If Belle decides to close her position, how much will she pay to do so?

_____

11. How much of the amount paid in Belle's closing transaction is due to the premium's intrinsic value?

_____

12. How much of the premium is due to time value?

_____

Calculate the breakeven point for the positions in questions 13 through 15.

13. Karen sells 1 OEX 285 call at 5. She will break even when the index is at

_____

14. Belle is long 10 470 puts on the AMEX Major Market Index. She initially paid an aggregate premium of $6,000. Her breakeven point comes with the index at

_____

15. Adam writes a spread on the PHLX Gold/Silver Index. He is long 1 Dec 105 put at 1 3/4 and short 1 Dec 110 put at 4 3/8. The breakeven point on this credit spread is an index value of

_____

16. An investor is long 10,000 OEX calls. How many OEX puts can the investor purchase?

A. 5,000
B. 15,000
C. 25,000
D. Any number

17. Armand A. Legge owns a large, diversified portfolio of stocks. While he is confident that his securities are well selected for the long term, he is concerned that he may be subject to market risk in the short run. What positions could he take in index options to hedge against a downturn in the market?

_____

18. Belle Charolais is bullish on the market. If she buys 1 Jul 490 call on the XMI, which of the following options might she write to create a debit spread?

I.   Jan 485 call
II. Jan 490 call
III. Jan 500 call
IV. Jan 505 call

A. I
B. I and II
C. II, III and IV
D. III and IV

Use the following information to answer questions 19 and 20.

In November, June Polar writes 1 Mar 102 call at 1.20 on a 9 5/8%, five-year Treasury note when the note is trading at 101 22/32.

19. How much does June receive for writing the option?

   A. $1,031
   B. $1,200
   C. $1,625
   D. $2,000

20. As a call writer, June is bearish on the price of T notes. She will break even on her investment when the price of the underlying note is which of the following?

   A. 98 12/32
   B. 101 11/32
   C. 102
   D. 103 20/32

21. Tex Longhorn purchases 1 Nov 106 put on five-year 10 3/4% Treasury notes and sells 1 Nov 108 put on the same notes. Which of the following statements are true?

   I. He believes interest rates are going to decline.
   II. He is bearish on the price of Treasury securities.
   III. He has created a debit spread.
   IV. If he closes his position with the notes selling at 108, he will realize his maximum gain.

   A. I and II
   B. I and IV
   C. II, III and IV
   D. II and IV

Figure 2

Chicago Board Options Exchange U.S. TREASURY BOND--$100,000 PRINCIPAL VALUE							
		Calls--Last			Puts-Last		
Underlying Issue	Strike Price	Dec	Mar		Dec	Mar	
10 5/8%	98	...	...	...	0:07	0:12	...
due 8/2015	100	3:20	...	...	0:16	1:22	...
	102	2:05	2:12	...	...	2:20	...
	104	0:26	1:18	...	2:10	3:17	...
				...			

Use Figure 2 and the following information to answer questions 22 and 23.

June Polar buys 1 Mar 98 put on the 10 5/8% bond (due 8/2015).

22. What is June's maximum potential loss?

_____

23. What is June's breakeven point?

_____

24. Using Figure 2, if Klaus Bruin establishes a bear put spread with Mar 102 and Mar 104 options on the 10 5/8% Treasury bond, which option will he buy and which will he sell?

_____

_____

25. Using Figure 2, what is Klaus' maximum potential loss on the bear put spread with Mar 102 and Mar 104 options on the 10 5/8% Treasury bond?

   A. $906.25
   B. $970
   C. $1,060
   D. $2,000

Figure 3

Foreign Currency Options
Philadelphia

Friday, January 18th, 1994

Option & Underlying	Strike Price	Calls--Last Feb	Mar	Jun	Puts--Last Feb	Mar	Jun
50,000 Australian Dollars-cents per unit.							
ADollr	77	r	r	r	0.35	r	r
79.56	78	r	r	r	r	r	0.67
31,250 British Pounds-cents per unit.							
BPound	165	r	14.10	r	r	r	r
179.44	170	r	9.40	r	r	r	r
179.44	175	5.10	r	r	r	1.70	3.80
179.44	177 1/2	3.15	3.90	r	r	2.40	r
6,250,000 Japanese Yen-100ths of a cent per unit.							
JYen	73	1.92	2.45	2	0.48	0.79	r
74.58	74	1.40	1.95	3.0	0.75	1.15	r
74.58	75	0.95	1.48	r	1.34	r	2.20

---

26. As investment manager for an insurance company, Greta Guernsey is in charge of a portfolio that includes a large holding in U.S. Treasury bonds. She is anticipating Congressional action that will, in the long run, bring down the federal budget deficit while keeping interest rates down and bond prices up. In the near term, though, she expects an increase in business activity to bring interest rates up. Using interest rate options, devise a strategy to meet her long- and short-term goals.

_____

_____

_____

27. A portfolio manager would like to increase the yield on Treasury notes in the portfolio. She believes that interest rates are about to rise. Which of the following strategies will provide a relatively safe, low-risk way to increase yield?

    A. Write covered calls on Treasury notes.
    B. Write puts on Treasury notes.
    C. Write calls on T bills.
    D. Buy puts on Treasury notes.

28. In reading the foreign currency option quotes in Figure 3, you find that the exchange rate for British pounds is listed as 179.44. What does this mean?

    A. One U.S. dollar is equivalent to 17.944 pounds.
    B. One U.S. dollar is equivalent to 1.7944 pounds.
    C. One pound is equivalent to 1.7944 U.S. dollars.
    D. One pound is equivalent to 179.44 U.S. cents.

29. Your client owns a portfolio of blue chip stocks. She informs you that she believes that the securities will provide good, long-term appreciation but she is fearful that the market will decline over the short term. Which index options strategy should you recommend that will protect against the expected decline and still allow for long-term capital appreciation?

    A. Buy puts
    B. Buy calls
    C. Sell covered puts
    D. Sell covered calls

30. An investor exercises 1 PHLX Jan 40 call on the deutsche mark. The aggregate exercise price for this option is which of the following? (Each contract is for 62,500 DM.)

    A. $5,000
    B. $25,000
    C. $40,000
    D. $50,000

Calculate the aggregate exercise price of a Mar 90 call on T bills using the step-by-step procedure below.

31. The annualized discount on 1 Mar 90 call is:

_____

32. The percent discount for 91 days is:

_____

33. The dollar amount of the discount is:

_____

34. The aggregate exercise price is:

_____

Answers

1. **A.** Broad-based indexes attempt to reflect the status of the market as a whole, not the status of particular market segments.

2. $600. The potential gain on a short option is the premium received on the opening transaction.

3. 220. At (or above) the strike price of 220. At this price and above, the put expires worthless, and Angus keeps the premium he received for writing the option.

4. **D.** To break even, Karen must lose an amount equal to her initial gain—13 points. This will occur if her short call is in-the-money by 13 points and she is assigned an exercise.

5. Credit. Adam sold the call with the lower strike price. The lower the strike price of a call, the higher the premium. So he received more for his short call than he paid for his long one. He has a credit spread.

6. Narrow. The investor who opens a credit spread wants the spread between premiums to narrow. At best, both premiums become zero, and there is no spread between them. The writer keeps the net premium received.

7. Gain. As the writer of a bear credit spread, Adam wants the price of the index to drop until the calls expire worthless, and he keeps the initial credit.

8. $75. The Jan 405 calls are trading at a premium of 3/4, which is $75.

9. $665. Karen owes the difference between the strike price and the value of the index: 386.65 − 380 = 6.65.

10. $1,425. Belle pays the premium, which is 14 1/4.

11. $1,335.   With the index at 386.65, the put has 13.35 in intrinsic value (400 − 386.65 = 13.35).

12. $90.   The remaining .90 represents its time value (14 1/4 premium − 13.35 = .90).

13.   290.   Strike price of 285 plus the premium of 5. The writer of a call is bearish and does not want the index to go up. If the index is greater than the strike price, the call may be exercised against the writer.

14.   464.   Strike price of 470 minus the premium of 6 ($6,000 ÷ 10 contracts ÷ 100 shares per contract). Long puts are bearish; the writer wants the index value to go down.

15.   107 3/8.   Remember, PSH: Puts Subtract from Higher. Here you subtract the initial credit of 2 5/8 from the higher strike price of 110, for a breakeven point of 107 3/8.

16.   C.   The position limit of 25,000 contracts applies to options on the same side of the market. Long calls and long puts are on opposite sides of the market.

17.   Armand is bullish in the long term and wants insurance against losses in a bear market. He needs options that will be profitable in a bear market; therefore, he can buy puts or sell calls.

18.   D.   Belle would create a credit spread by selling the 485 call. Because it has a lower strike price, it would be more expensive than the 490 call. If Belle sold a 490 call, she would be both long and short the same option, creating neither a debit nor a credit. (She would be creating a lot of commissions!) If Belle sold either a 500 call or a 505 call, she would have a debit spread because she has purchased the more expensive call—the one with a lower strike price.

19.   C.   In premium quotes for options on Treasury notes and bonds, 1.0 = $1,000; 0.20 = 20/32; 20/32 × $1,000 ($625); or 20 × $31.25.

20.   D.   June receives the premium of 1 20/32. When the bond price moves against her by that amount to the strike price plus 1 20/32, she stands to lose as much as she gained on the opening sale.

21.   B.   Tex has written the spread at a credit. Because bulls write puts and put spreads, you know he is bullish on the price of the notes. If the price of the T notes goes up, interest rates will be going down. Tex hopes to keep the credit received when the puts expire worthless, which will happen at 108 or any higher price.

22. $375.   The premium of 12/32 of 1% times the $100,000 principal.

23.   97.20.   97 20/32, or the strike price of 98 minus the premium of 12/32.

24.   Klaus will buy the Mar 104 put at 3.17 and write the Mar 102 put at 2.20 to create the spread at a debit.

25.   A.   The net debit is the spread between premiums: 3 17/32 − 2 20/32 = 29/32, or .90625, which is $906.25. The net premium on a debit spread is the maximum potential loss.

26.   Over the long run, Greta believes interest rates will stay down, so the bonds she holds will remain attractive. In the short run, though, as rising interest rates drive down the prices of debt securities, she might want to hedge her portfolio against losses by writing covered T bond calls to capture the premiums as bond prices go down. She might also buy puts, reselling them as falling bond prices bring up their value.

27.   A.   The calls will provide premium income and expire unexercised if rates rise. Short puts will cost money to buy back if T note prices fall. The calls on T bills will appreciate if the portfolio manager is right, but T bill calls cannot be covered and are risky. Puts on T notes will also appreciate if rates rise, but the buyer risks the entire premium if she is wrong about the market. Writing calls meets her objective of increasing the portfolio yield better than if she bought puts.

28.   D.   The exchange rate refers to U.S. cents per British pound. 179.44 cents is $1.7944.

29. **A.** Because your client is long the stock, her position would be hurt by a drop in the market. To hedge against that risk, she must take an option position that appreciates in value as the market declines: long puts or short calls. Because your client also wishes to benefit from any appreciation, the long put is the better hedging vehicle. If the market averages increase, the put position would lose only the premium, and your client could still gain on her stocks.

30. **B.** Deutsche marks are quoted in cents per underlying currency unit. A 40 deutsche mark call represents a price of 40 cents per unit, or $.40 times 62,500 deutsche marks for a total exercise price of $25,000.

31. 10%. $100\% - 90\%$

32. 2.52778%. $10\% \times 91 \div 360$

33. $25,277.80. $2.52778\% \times \$1$ million

34. $974,722.20. $\$1$ million $- \$25,277.80$

Margin Rules for Options

Client accounts. A customer can enter into an option transaction in a *cash* account only if he is buying options or selling *fully secured and covered* calls and puts. If the customer is buying an option as part of a spread, both option transactions must be executed in the customer's margin account.

Long option positions. Options cannot be bought on margin. The option buyer must pay 100% of the purchase price of the option. For all option purchases, the option buyer must pay for the purchase in full not later than the next business day after the trade date.

Margin Requirements for Covered Options

Covered Calls

In a margin account, a call is covered and the writer will not be required to meet option margin requirements if he deposits into the account or presents:

- the *stock* underlying the call;
- an *escrow agreement (receipt)* for the underlying stock;
- a security that is *convertible* into the underlying stock;
- a *long call* on the same stock with a later expiration date, a lower exercise price or both; or
- a *warrant* to purchase the underlying security, provided the exercise price of the warrant is the same or less than the exercise price of the short call.

In a cash account, a call is covered and the writer will not be required to meet option margin requirements if she deposits into the account or presents:

- the *stock* underlying the call option;
- an *escrow agreement (receipt)* for the underlying stock; or

- a security that is *convertible* into the underlying stock.

Covered Puts

In a margin account, a put is covered and the writer will not be required to meet option margin requirements if he deposits into the account, presents or enters:

- *cash equal to the exercise price* of the put;
- a *bank guarantee letter* or a *bank agreement*;
- a *short sale of the underlying stock*; or
- a *purchase of a put* on the same stock with the same or a higher strike price, the same or a later expiration date, or both.

In a cash account, a put is covered and the writer will not be required to meet option margin requirements if the writer deposits into the account or presents:

- *cash equal to the exercise price* of the put;
- an *escrow agreement*;
- *money-market securities* with a current market value equal to or greater than the exercise price of the put; or
- an *escrow agreement* for any of the above.

Margin Requirements for Uncovered Options

An investor who writes an uncovered option is required to deposit:

- 100% of the current option premium,
- *plus* 20% of the market value of the underlying security,
- *less* any amount the option is out-of-the-money.

Options accounts are marked to the market daily. The margin requirement is recalculated by the broker-dealer every day, using the new market value of the security and the new premium on the option.

Listed stock options. The formula for listed stock options margin requirements is:

- 100% of the option premium,
- *plus* a percentage of current market value,
- *less* any amount out-of-the-money.

The percentage of market value used changes with different types of options contracts.

Minimum margin requirements. When dealing with an out-of-the-money option, the deposit required is the greater of the initial or minimum margin requirement. For most securities, the minimum requirement is 100% of the current premium plus 10% of the current market value of the underlying security. If the equity option is out-of-the-money, the minimum margin requirement is:

	Current premium
plus	10% of the security's CMV
equals	Minimum margin requirement

Required cash deposit. The cash deposit required when writing an option is:

	Margin requirement
minus	Premium received
equals	Required cash deposit

Margin Requirements for Nonequity Options

The initial requirement for a nonequity option is the current premium plus a percentage of the underlying market value less any out-of-the-money amount. The minimum requirement is the current premium plus a lesser percentage of the underlying market value. The cash deposit required is the margin requirement minus the premium received. Options on Treasury securities are the single exception. For these options, the percentage of the underlying amount is a percentage of face value, not market value.

Margin on Spreads

The maintenance requirement for a limited-risk credit spread is the dollar amount of the actual risk (i.e., the difference between the options' strike prices). The investor's cash deposit will be the maintenance requirement less the net premium received.

The margin requirement for debit spreads is also the dollar amount of the maximum risk (i.e., the maximum risk is the net debit). As with the purchase of any option, Reg T requires that the long option be fully paid for.

Margin Requirements for Straddles and Combinations

An investor who opens a long straddle or combination must deposit 100% of the combined premiums.

The margin required for short straddles and combinations is the greater of the two margin requirements for the individual options plus the current market value of the other option (that is, the other option's premium).

Questions

1. An investor writes 10 uncovered XYZ Oct 50 calls for 3. The market value of XYZ is currently $47 a share. What is the margin requirement for this position? (Hint: calculate for one option and then multiply by the number of contracts.)

   _9400_

   _____

2. An investor writes 10 uncovered XYZ Oct 50 calls for 3. The market value of XYZ is currently $47 a share. What is the cash deposit required?

   _____

3. An investor opens a margin account and writes 1 naked 50 put for 2. The stock is currently trading at $49 per share. What is the margin required?

   _____

4. Joe Kuhl writes 7 uncovered ABC 45 calls for $2. The market value of ABC is $39 per share. What is the required margin?

   _____

5. A call writer can be covered by which of the following?

   I. Long the underlying stock
   II. Long a convertible security
   III. Escrow receipt
   IV. Long a call with a lower strike price

   A. I only
   B. I and II only
   C. I and III only
   D. I, II, III and IV

6. What will an escrow receipt show?

   I. Name of the account
   II. Number of shares
   III. Name of the stock
   IV. Number of contracts, expiration date and exercise price

   A. I only
   B. I and II only
   C. I, II and III only
   D. I, II, III and IV

7. Which of the following cannot be used to cover a short call in an account?

   A. Escrow receipt
   B. Underlying stock
   C. Convertible bond
   D. Guarantee letter from a bank

8. Which of the following covers a customer who has sold 1 Jul 50 put at 4?

   A. Long 1 Jul 50 call
   B. Long 1 Jul 50 put
   C. Short 1 Jul 50 put
   D. Short the underlying stock

9. An investor writes a call and receives a net premium of $375. That same day he purchases the stock for $6,750. Margin requirements are at 50%. What is the net cash deposit required in the investor's margin account?

   A. $2,000.00
   B. $3,000.00
   C. $3,187.50
   D. $3,375.00

Answers

1. $9,400.

$ 300	100% of current premium
+ 940	20% CMV ($4,700 × .20)
− 300	Out-of-the-money amount
$ 940	Margin per call
× 10	Number of contracts
$9,400	Total margin required

2. $6,400.

$ 940	Margin per call
− 300	Premium received
$ 640	Deposit per call
× 10	Number of contracts
$6,400	Total deposit required

Alternatively, $9,400 (margin required) minus $3,000 (premium) equals $6,400 deposit.

3. $2,000.

$ 200	100% of current premium
+ 980	20% CMV ($4,900 × .20)
− 0	Out-of-the-money amount
$1,180	Total margin required

The minimum requirement is $2,000 per account.

4. $4,130.

Margin Req.		Minimum Req.
$ 200	100% premium	$ 200
+ 780	20% CMV *or* 10% CMV	+ 390
− 600	Out-of-the-money	− 0
$ 380	Minimum is greater	$ 590
	Number of contracts	× 7
		$4,130

This minimum amount is also greater than the $2,000 requirement.

5. **D.** All of the choices cover a short call position.

6. **C.** The escrow receipt states what securities the customer has on deposit at the bank. It does not discuss the options contract, which is a concern of the broker-dealer.

7. **D.** A guarantee letter states that the customer has enough money to cover a short put position. If a short put is exercised, the customer will be required to purchase the stock at a specified price. The guarantee letter does not cover a written call because the writer has to purchase the stock at an unknown price in the market to deliver against the call, if exercised.

8. **D.** If another put is used to cover a written put, it must be long and have a later expiration date, a higher strike price or both. None of the three answers fulfills these requirements. A short sale of the stock will cover the short position. The account will contain the sale proceeds from the short sale as well as the required margin deposit from the customer. If the put is exercised, the writer can deliver the shares he is obligated to buy against the short stock position.

9. **B.** The written call is covered by the purchase of the stock, so no margin is required for the call itself. The margin required for the purchase of the stock is $3,375 ($6,750 × 50%). The investor may use the proceeds from the written call to meet the margin requirement, so the required cash deposit is $3,000 ($3,375 margin requirement − $375 premium proceeds).

Tax Rules for Options

Taxable Option Events

Call or put option expires. An option that expires unexercised results in a capital loss for the person who paid the premium to buy it. The writer of the option received the premium and, if the option remains unexercised at expiration, realizes a capital gain from that premium.

Call or put position is closed. The tax effects of a closing purchase or sale are as follows:

- A capital gain will result if the sale price of the option is greater than the purchase price.
- A capital loss will result if the sale price is less than the purchase price of the option.

Call option is exercised. When a call is exercised, the holder of the option buys the stock at the call's strike price. The total cost basis for the stock is the strike price plus the premium on the call.

Put option is exercised. When a put is exercised, the premium of the option is subtracted from the cost basis (or sale proceeds) of the stock.

Establishing gains or losses. If the stock is being sold through exercise, you need to know the original purchase price. If the stock is being purchased through exercise, you need to know the price at which the investor later sells the stock.

Effect of Options on Stock Holding Periods

Long stock and long a put. If an individual owns stock and buys a put option on that stock, he has effectively locked in a sale price for the life of that option. The IRS has ruled that the purchase of a put on stock held six months or less automatically caps that stock's holding period at six months. Any gain on that stock will be treated as short term. If the stock was held more than six months before the purchase of the put, the holding period is unaffected.

Long stock and short a call. The sale of a call that is deep in-the-money automatically caps the holding period on stock held six months or less at six months. Any gain on that stock will be treated as short term.

Writing a call that is only slightly in-the-money also caps the holding period at six months, but in the event a closing purchase of a call is entered, the holding period of the stock resumes.

If the stock was held more than six months before the sale of the call, the holding period is unaffected. If the investor writes an out-of-the-money call, the stock's holding period is similarly unaffected.

Questions

1. In September, an investor sells 2 ABC Jan 60 puts at 3. If the investor buys the 2 puts back at 4 1/2, the result for tax purposes is a

   A. $150 capital gain
   B. $150 capital loss
   C. $300 capital gain
   D. $300 capital loss

2. In September, an investor sells 2 ABC Jan 60 puts at 3. If the 2 ABC Jan 60 puts expire in January, what are the tax consequences for the seller?

   A. $600 gain realized in September
   B. $600 loss realized in September
   C. $600 gain realized in January
   D. $600 loss realized in January

3. On January 1st, an investor buys 1 XYZ Apr 50 call at 4 and 1 XYZ Apr 50 put at 2 1/2. Both options expire unexercised. What are the tax consequences for the investor?

   A. $150 net capital gain
   B. $150 net capital loss
   C. $400 gain on the call, $250 gain on the put
   D. $400 loss on the call, $250 loss on the put

4. Sally Smith buys 1 XYZ Oct 50 call at 3. She exercises the option to buy 100 shares when the market is at 60. What is the cost basis of the 100 shares?

   A. $5,000
   B. $5,300
   C. $6,000
   D. $6,300

5. A customer writes 1 Jul 50 put at 7. The put is exercised when the market price is 40. For tax purposes, what is the effective cost basis of the stock put to the seller?

   A. 40
   B. 43
   C. 50
   D. 57

Answers

1. **D.** The closing cost of $900 minus $600 opening sale proceeds equals a $300 loss.

2. **C.** Expiration of a short option generates a gain at the time the option expires.

3. **D.** In a straddle, the options are treated separately for tax purposes. The investor has a $400 capital loss on the call and a $250 capital loss on the put.

4. **B.** The cost basis of the 100 shares is the total amount Sally spent to acquire them. She paid $300 to purchase the call option. When she exercised the call, she purchased 100 shares of XYZ at $50 per share, for a total price of $5,000. The cost basis therefore is $5,300.

5. **B.** The cost basis is 50 (the price at which the writer must buy) minus 7 (the premium the writer was paid), or $43 per share.

17 Investment Company Products

Investment Company Offerings

The Investment Company Act of 1940

The act of 1940 states:

". . . investment companies are affected with a national public interest in that:

- the securities they issue constitute a significant percentage of all securities publicly offered;
- their process of issuing redeemable securities and their redemption of those securities is continuous; and
- the investing, reinvesting and trading of investment companies constitutes a significant percentage of all transactions in the securities markets of the nation."

Types of Investment Companies

Face-amount Certificate Company

A face-amount certificate is a contract between an investor and an issuer in which the issuer guarantees a payment of a **stated** sum to the investor at some set date in the future.

Unit Investment Trust

The primary characteristics that set UITs apart from other types of investment companies are that UITs:

- do not have a board of directors;
- do not employ an investment adviser; and
- do not actively manage their own portfolios (trade securities).

A UIT sells redeemable shares (units of beneficial interest) in a portfolio of securities.

Management Companies

Management companies actively *manage* a portfolio of securities in accordance with the investment objectives stated in their prospectuses.

Closed-end Investment Companies

When all of the shares that a closed-end investment company has registered to sell have been distributed by the underwriters, the public offering period comes to a close. The fund's capitalization is basically fixed. Closed-end investment companies are more commonly known as **publicly traded funds**.

Open-end Investment Companies

An open-end investment company (or **mutual fund**), unlike the closed-end company, does not specify the exact number of shares it intends to sell; rather, it registers an open offering with the SEC. The open-end investment company can raise an unlimited amount of investment capital by continuously selling new shares in its portfolio of investments. The shares that an open-end investment company sells are known as **redeemable securities.**

Diversified vs. Nondiversified

Diversified. Under the Investment Company Act of 1940, a management company will qualify as a diversified investment company if it meets the following **75-5-10** test:

- *75%* of total assets must be invested in securities issued by companies *other than the investment company itself* or its affiliates.
- No more than *5%* of total assets can be invested *in any one corporation's* securities.
- No more than *10%* of an outside corporation's *voting class securities* can be owned by the management company.

Nondiversified. A nondiversified company is any company that fails to meet one or more of these criteria.

Questions

1. "Mutual fund" is a popular name for

    A. all investment companies
    B. open-end investment companies
    C. closed-end investment companies
    D. a company that invests pooled funds

2. Which of the following are covered under the Investment Company Act of 1940?

    I. Unit investment trusts
    II. Face-amount companies
    III. Open-end management companies
    IV. Closed-end management companies

    A. I and II only
    B. I, III and IV only
    C. III and IV only
    D. I, II, III and IV

3. What kind of investment company has no provision for redemption of outstanding shares?

    A. Open-end company
    B. Closed-end company
    C. Unit investment trust
    D. Mutual fund

4. Diversified management companies must be invested so that

    I. they own no more than 5% of the voting stock of a single company
    II. no more than 5% of their assets are invested in any one company
    III. they own no more than 10% of the voting stock of any one company
    IV. if they own more than 25% of a target company, they do not vote the stock

    A. I and II
    B. I, II and IV
    C. II and III
    D. II, III and IV

5. Which type of mutual fund is sold at net asset value?

A. Open-end
B. Closed-end
C. Front-end load
D. No-load

6. All of the following statements about diversified and nondiversified investment companies are true EXCEPT that

A. a nondiversified company is any management company not classified as a diversified company
B. to be considered diversified, an investment company must invest 75% of its total assets in cash, receivables or securities
C. both diversified and nondiversified companies are examples of management companies
D. to be considered a nondiversified company, an investment company must invest the majority of its total assets in one industry

7. The Investment Company Act of 1940 regulates all of the following EXCEPT

A. face-amount certificates
B. holding companies
C. closed-end funds
D. unit investment trusts

8. Which of the following statements describe open-end investment companies?

I. Shares are redeemable on demand at the net asset value.
II. Shares are always sold by prospectus.
III. Only a limited number of shares are offered.
IV. Shares are sold on securities exchanges.

A. I and II only
B. I and III only
C. III and IV only
D. I, II, III and IV

9. According to the Investment Company Act of 1940, an investment company with a fixed portfolio, redeemable shares and no management fee is classified as a

A. face-amount certificate company
B. management company
C. unit investment trust
D. closed-end investment company

10. All of the following terms describe a fixed unit investment trust EXCEPT

A. liquidity
B. manageability
C. redeemability
D. classification as an investment company

11. Open-end investment companies, but not closed-end investment companies

I. can make continuous offerings of shares provided the original registration statement and prospectus are periodically updated
II. can be listed on registered national exchanges
III. always redeem their shares
IV. can issue only common stock

A. I, II and III
B. I and III
C. I, III and IV
D. II and IV

Answers

1. **B.** The term "mutual fund" is synonymous with "open-end investment company."

2. **D.** All are covered under the act of 1940. Unit investment trusts, face-amount and management investment companies are all mentioned in this act. Remember, both open-end and closed-end management companies are management investment companies.

3. **B.** The closed-end company does not redeem shares that it issues. The closed-end company has a fixed capitalization and, like regular corporations, outstanding shares trade on the open market.

4. **C.** A diversified investment company:

- must have at least 75% of its assets invested in cash, securities or both;
- may own no more than 10% of the voting stock of a company; and
- may have no more than 5% of its total assets invested in one company.

5. **D.** A no-load fund is sold at NAV with no sales charges. A closed-end company may trade at NAV, but market price does not necessarily correlate with the NAV.

6. **D.** A nondiversified investment company does not meet one or more of the requirements of a diversified company. There are many diversified investment companies that invest primarily in a single industry.

7. **B.** Holding companies are subject to the Holding Company Act, a federal act distinct and separate from the Investment Company Act of 1940. Under the act of 1940, investment companies are divided into three major classifications: face-amount certificates, unit investment trusts and management companies (including closed-end companies and open-end investment companies).

8. **A.** Only choices I and II are true. Open-end investment companies must be prepared to redeem shares at net asset value. Open-end investment companies continually issue new shares that are sold by prospectus. Unlike open-end investment companies, closed-end investment companies issue a limited number of shares that may be sold on an exchange.

9. **C.** Unlike unit investment trusts, which issue redeemable securities, face-amount certificate companies issue installment certificates with guaranteed principal and interest. A unit investment trust has a diversified portfolio that, once established, does not change. Therefore, it cannot be called a "management company." A closed-end investment company is a type of management company.

10. **B.** A unit investment trust is one of the three major types of investment companies. Because it is a fixed, redeemable portfolio of securities, it is not managed.

11. **C.** Open-end investment companies, but not closed-end investment companies, can make continuous offerings of shares, can redeem their shares and can issue only common stock.

Characteristics of Mutual Funds

The Mutual Fund Concept

Each investor in the mutual fund's portfolio owns an undivided interest in the portfolio. All investors in the open-end fund are mutual participants; no one investor has a preferred status over any other investor. Mutual funds issue only one class of common share; no preferred class of shares or debt can be issued.

Advantages to Investors

An open-end mutual fund must redeem shares presented to it by investors at the NAV within seven days. A mutual fund offers professional portfolio management. Mutual fund shares offer diversification.

Investment Objectives

An investment company's objective must be clearly stated in the prospectus and can be changed only by a majority vote of the fund's outstanding shares.

Diversified Common Stock Funds

Growth funds. Growth funds invest in equity securities of companies expected to increase in value more rapidly than the overall market.

Income funds. An income fund stresses current yield, or income.

Combination funds. A combination fund combines the objectives of growth and current yield by diversifying its portfolio among companies showing long-term growth potential and companies currently paying high dividends.

Specialized (Sector) Funds

Funds that specialize in particular sectors of the economy or in specific industries are known as *sector funds*.

Balanced Funds   *Growth + Income*

Balanced funds attempt to combine the objectives of growth and income by investing in different vehicles.

Asset Allocation Funds

Asset allocation funds split investments between stocks, bonds and money-market instruments or cash in an attempt to provide a consistent return for the investor.

Bond and Preferred Stock Funds

If income is a primary investment objective, it is often obtained by investing in bonds.

Tax-free (Tax-exempt) Bond Funds

Tax-exempt funds contain instruments such as municipal bonds or notes that produce income exempt from federal income tax.

U.S. Government and Agency Security Funds

U.S. government funds purchase securities backed by the U.S. Treasury or issued by an agency of the U.S. government, such as Sallie Mae or Ginnie Mae.

Dual-purpose Funds

Investors seeking income purchase income shares and receive all the interest and dividends earned by the fund's portfolio. Other investors interested in capital gains purchase the gains shares and receive all gains on portfolio holdings.

Money-market Funds

Money-market funds are usually no-load, open-ended mutual funds. The management invests the fund's capital in money-market instruments that have high interest rates and short maturities, such as Treasury bills, Treasury bonds with a short time to maturity, commercial paper, bankers' acceptances and certificates of deposit (CDs). The net asset value of money-market funds is set at $1.00 per share. The fund is managed so as to maintain it regardless of market changes.

Comparing Mutual Funds

Fund Expenses and Expense Ratio

The expense ratio of a fund relates the expenses of operating the fund, such as costs of administration and fees paid to the custodian, adviser or transfer agent, to the net assets of the fund (that is, the expenses of the fund divided by its average net assets). Typically, the more aggressive a fund, the higher its expense ratio.

Questions

1. An investor looking for current income would be LEAST interested in

   A. bond funds
   B. preferred stock funds
   C. common stock funds
   D. gains shares in a dual-purpose fund

2. Money-market funds usually offer which of the following?

   I. Daily interest calculations
   II. Check-writing privileges
   III. No-load funds
   IV. Long-term growth potential

   A. I and II
   B. I, II and III
   C. I, II and IV
   D. II, III and IV

3. The Investment Company Act of 1940 requires that redemption of mutual fund shares be made within how many days of tender?

   A. 5
   B. 7
   C. 10
   D. 30

4. An investor purchases shares in a sector fund. Which of the following statements describe this investment?

   I. The fund invests in a particular industry.
   II. The fund's objective is current income rather than capital growth.
   III. The fund invests primarily in common stocks.
   IV. The companies in which the fund invests must be within a specific region of the United States.

   A. I and II
   B. I and III
   C. II and III
   D. III and IV

5. Mr. Smith is interested in investing in an open-end investment company. His objective is high current yield, but he is uncomfortable with high risks. His registered representative should recommend what type of fund?

   A. Oil industry
   B. Balanced
   C. Growth
   D. Income

6. The greatest expense of an open-end investment company is

   A. the management fees
   B. salaries
   C. overhead
   D. custodial fees

7. The greatest cost in operating a money-market fund is

   A. custodial fees
   B. brokerage fees
   C. management fees
   D. overhead

Answers

1. **D.** Dual-purpose funds offer a choice between income shares and gains shares. Income shares receive interest and dividends from the fund, while gains shares receive capital gains. Thus, an investor interested in earning current income would not invest in gains shares.

2. **B.** Money-market funds are made up of short-term, high-yield debt instruments, are sold no-load, calculate interest daily and offer check-writing privileges. Because their purpose is to provide income, money-market funds usually offer limited growth.

3. **B.** The Investment Company Act of 1940 requires that payment be made within seven days of receiving a redemption order.

4. **B.** Sector funds concentrate their investments in common stocks in a specific industry. Most industry funds seek capital growth rather than current income. An industry fund is not limited by geographic area.

5. **B.** An income fund provides current income rather than capital growth, with above-average risk. Balanced funds are less risky than the other investments listed and are, therefore, the appropriate choice. Oil industry funds and growth funds are not appropriate for Mr. Smith because of the high degree of risk.

6. **A.** The management fee is a mutual fund's greatest expense.

7. **C.** Management fees are the greatest cost of operating money-market funds.

Investment Company Registration

A company must register as an investment company with the SEC if:

- the company is in the business of investing, reinvesting, owning, holding or trading in securities; or
- 40% or more of the company's assets are invested in securities.

Registration of Investment Companies

An investment company is not allowed to issue securities to the public unless it has:

- private capitalization of at least $100,000
- 100 investors
- clearly defined investment objectives

The company must clearly define an investment objective under which it plans to operate. Once defined, the objective may only be changed with a majority vote of the company's outstanding shares.

Open-end companies. The act of 1940 requires open-end companies to have the following:

- no more than one class of security
- a maximum asset-to-debt ratio of 300%

Open-end management companies may issue only one class of security and they are permitted to borrow from banks. They may borrow money as long as the company's asset-to-debt ratio is not less than 3-to-1.

SEC Registration and Public Offering Requirements

In filing for registration as an investment company with the SEC, a corporation must provide the following information in its registration form:

- the type of investment company it intends to be;
- any plans the company has to raise money by borrowing;
- the company's intention (if any) to concentrate its investments in a single industry;
- any plans for investing in real estate or commodities;
- conditions under which investment policies may be changed by a vote of the shareholders;
- the full names and addresses of each affiliated person; and
- a description of the business experience of each officer and director during the preceding five years.

Continuous Public Offering Securities

Open-end management company shares must be sold by prospectus only. All sales must be accompanied by a prospectus.

Purchasing Mutual Fund Shares on Margin

Mutual fund shares may not be purchased on margin. They may be used as collateral in a margin account, however, if they have been held fully paid for 30 days.

Securities Issued by Investment Companies

Common stock (equity securities). Investment companies allow investors to participate in their portfolios by selling shares (comoon stock) of the fund.

Bonds (debt securities). Closed-end investment companies are permitted to issue debt securities. A closed-end company may issue either bonds or debentures, provided that, after they have been issued, the company maintains an asset-to-debt coverage ratio of at least 300%.

Preferred stock (equity securities). A closed-end investment company can issue preferred stock with the approval of its common shareholders. In order to conduct an offering of preferred stock, the company must be able to maintain a 200% asset-to-preferred-stock coverage ratio.

Restrictions on Operations

The act of 1940 states that an investment company may not:

- make securities purchases on margin;
- sell securities short; or
- participate in joint investment or trading accounts.

Shareholders' Right to Vote

Among the changes that would require a majority vote of the shares outstanding are the following:

- changes in borrowing by open-end companies;
- issuing or underwriting other securities;
- purchasing or underwriting real estate;
- making loans;
- change of subclassification;
- making changes in sales load policies;
- ceasing business as an investment company; and
- changes in investment policy.

In addition to the right to vote on these items, stockholders retain all rights normally accorded to the holders of any corporate stock.

Questions

1. Shareholders of mutual funds have all of the following rights EXCEPT

   I. voting rights
   II. proxies
   III. receiving semiannual reports
   IV. preemptive rights

   A. I and II
   B. I, II and III
   C. II and IV
   D. IV

2. The Investment Company Act of 1940 states that

   A. it is unnecessary for the prospectus to disclose the management fee
   B. open-end companies may issue common stock only
   C. an investment company must have $5 million capital before its securities can be offered to the public
   D. no more than 50% of the board of directors of an investment company may be officers or employees of the company or investment advisers to the company

3. According to the Investment Company Act of 1940, borrowing by an open-end investment company

   A. is prohibited
   B. is permitted, but only by issuing bonds
   C. is limited to 33% of its net assets
   D. must conform to the 20-to-1 rule

4. According to the Investment Company Act of 1940, an investment company

   A. owns investment securities exceeding 50% of its total assets, excluding government securities

   B. is engaged primarily in investing in and trading securities, has a net worth in excess of $100,000 and has 40% or more of the value of its total assets in investment securities

   C. has a net invested worth of $100,000 and its outstanding securities are beneficially owned by more than 100 persons

   D. is engaged primarily in investing or trading in securities, defined as 50% or more of a company's total invested assets

5. The Investment Company Act of 1940 states that if an investment company's investment policy is stated in the company's registration statement and is not in contravention of SEC rules, the company can do which of the following?

   I. Purchase securities on margin
   II. Borrow money
   III. Make loans
   IV. Purchase and sell real estate

   A. I and II only
   B. I, II and IV only
   C. III and IV only
   D. I, II, III and IV

Answers

1. **D.** Shareholders of mutual funds have all of the rights mentioned except a preemptive right—the right for existing shareholders to maintain a proportionate ownership in the company. Other rights include approval of changes in investment objectives and approval of the investment advisory agreement.

2. **B.** The prospectus must state the management fee. An investment company needs only $100,000 and 100 investors in order to offer itself to the public. No more than 60% of the board of directors can be made up of officers or employees of the company. Open-end companies may issue only one class of equity—common stock.

3. **C.** The 1940 act limits borrowing. Any investment company must have 300% asset coverage, which means borrowing is limited to 33% of the net assets.

4. **B.** An investment company, as broadly defined in the 1940 act, is a company engaged primarily in the business of investing, reinvesting or trading in securities. It must have net worth in excess of $100,000 and own investment securities in an amount exceeding 40% of its total assets.

5. **D.** If the policy is stated in the investment company's registration statement and is not in contravention of SEC rules, an investment company can perform each of the listed functions.

Management of Investment Companies

Board of Directors

40% independent

The shareholders of an investment company elect the board of directors to make decisions and oversee operations. At least 40% of the directors must be independent. This means that no more than 60% of the board members may be interested persons, including attorneys on retainer, accountants and any persons employed in similar capacities with the company. No one may serve on a board of directors who has been convicted of either a felony (of any type) or of a misdemeanor involving the securities industry.

Investment Adviser

The board contracts with an outside investment adviser (portfolio manager) to invest the company's assets, implement investment strategy and manage the day-to-day trading of the portfolio. Investment advisers earn management fees for their services, typically a set annual percentage which is paid from the net assets of the fund.

The act of 1940 requires:

- a written contract, which must be approved initially by a vote of the shareholders, and approved annually thereafter by a vote of the shareholders and/or by the board of directors; and
- that the advisory contract has a *maximum life of two years,* during which time the contract must be *approved annually* by the directors and/or by a majority vote of the shares.

Affiliated and Interested Persons

Affiliated Person

An affiliated person is in a *control* position within the company; in general, an affiliated person controls the investment company's operations. Those persons considered affiliated include:

- anyone with 5% or more of the outstanding voting securities of the investment company;
- any corporation in which the investment company holds 5% or more of its outstanding securities;
- any person controlled in whole or in part by the investment company;
- all officers, directors, partners and employees of the investment company;
- the investment adviser; and
- in the absence of a board of directors, the individual who deposits the assets of the UIT into the account at the custodial bank (also known as the *depositor*).

Interested Person

An interested person is in a position to *influence* the operations of an investment company. All of the following are considered interested persons:

- person associated with the investment company, its investment adviser or its principal underwriter, including the immediate families of any affiliated person;
- person employed by the investment company, the investment adviser or the principal underwriter;
- person who, within the last two years, has acted as legal counsel to any affiliated person;
- broker-dealer registered under the Securities Exchange Act of 1934; and
- any other person deemed by the SEC to be interested because of business dealings with the company, its investment adviser or its principal underwriter.

Restrictions

An affiliated or interested person is prohibited from:

- borrowing money from the investment company; or
- selling any security or other property to the investment company or to any company controlled by the investment company.

Custodian Bank

The bank performs a safekeeping role as custodian of the company's securities and cash and receives a fee for its services. The custodian will handle most of the clerical functions the investment company might need.

Once a custodian bank has been designated by an investment company, the bank must:

- keep the investment company's assets physically segregated at all times;
- allow withdrawal only under the rules of the SEC; and
- restrict access to the account to certain officers and employees of the investment company.

Transfer Agent (Customer Services Agent)

The transfer agent issues and redeems fund shares, sends out customer confirmations and sends out fund distributions.

Underwriter

The underwriter markets fund shares, prepares sales literature and, in return, receives a percentage of the sales charge paid by the client.

Financial Reporting and Auditing

The act of 1940 requires that shareholders receive financial reports at least semiannually (every six months). These reports must contain:

- the investment company's balance sheet;
- a valuation of all securities in the investment company's portfolio on the date of the balance sheet;
- the investment company's income statement;
- a complete statement of all compensation paid to the board of directors and to the advisory board; and
- a statement of the total dollar amount of securities purchased and sold during the period.

Questions

1. The custodian of a mutual fund usually does which of the following?

    A. Approves changes in investment policy.
    B. Holds the cash and securities of the fund and performs clerical functions.
    C. Manages the fund.
    D. Does cleaning and related duties on the fund's properties.

2. Investment company financial statements are sent to shareholders

    A. monthly
    B. quarterly
    C. semiannually
    D. annually

3. The role of a mutual fund's underwriter is to

    A. hold the fund's assets and perform clerical responsibilities
    B. administer and supervise the investment portfolio
    C. market shares
    D. provide investment advisory services

4. When a bank is serving as the custodian of a mutual fund, it always

    A. manages the portfolio
    B. signs all margin agreements
    C. holds the cash and securities and performs other clerical functions
    D. serves as the distributor of the fund and manages interactions with other underwriters

5. Typically, the largest single expense of a mutual fund is the

    A. custodian fee
    B. registration fee
    C. management fee
    D. brokerage fee

Answers

1. **B.** The main functions of the custodian, usually a commercial bank, are to hold the fund's cash and assets for safekeeping and to perform related clerical duties. The custodian may also issue and redeem customer shares, send out customer confirmations and hold customer shares.

2. **C.** Investment company financial statements must be sent to shareholders at least semiannually.

3. **C.** The underwriter markets the fund's shares. Answer A is the responsibility of the custodian, answer B is the responsibility of the fund, and answer D is the responsibility of the manager.

4. **C.** The primary function of a mutual fund's custodian bank is to safeguard the physical assets of the fund, hold the cash and securities and perform other purely clerical functions. It does not manage the portfolio or serve in a selling capacity for the fund.

5. **C.** Typically, the largest single expense for a mutual fund is the management fee—the fee paid to the management company for buying and selling securities and managing the portfolio. A typical annual fee is 1/2 of 1% of the portfolio's asset value.

Mutual Fund Marketing, Pricing and Valuation

Methods of Marketing Mutual Fund Shares

Sales at the Public Offering Price

Any sale of fund shares to a *customer* (a member of the general public who is *not* a member of the NASD) must be made at the public offering price. Only an NASD member acting as a dealer or an underwriter may purchase the fund shares at a discount from the issuer.

Determining the Value of Mutual Fund Shares

The act of 1940 requires mutual funds to calculate the value of the fund shares at least once per business day. Shares are purchased (or redeemed) at the NAV next determined after the request to purchase (or redeem) is received by the fund, a process known as **forward pricing**. Purchases are made at the NAV *plus* any sales charge and redemptions are made at the NAV *minus* any redemption fee.

purchase: NAV + Sales
sale: NAV − redemptions

Net Asset Value per Share

A fund's NAV is the price on which sales of new shares to investors is based. The actual price is referred to as the public offering price (POP), which is equal to the NAV plus a sales charge. When a customer sells, the liquidation price is always equal to the current NAV. NAV per share is computed as follows:

$$\frac{\text{Total assets} - \text{Total liabilities}}{\text{Total shares outstanding}} = \text{NAV}$$

POP = NAV + sales charge.

Changes in NAV

The events that may change a fund's NAV per share include but are not limited to:

- an *increase* in the NAV per share *if* portfolio securities increase in value or the portfolio receives income (interest on debt) from the securities held in the portfolio;
- a *decrease* in the NAV per share *if* portfolio securities decrease in value or portfolio income or gain is paid out to shareholders (dividends or gains distributions); and
- *no change* in the NAV per share *if* there is a sale (issuance) or redemption of fund shares or if there is a sale or purchase of portfolio securities.

Sales Charges *< 8.5% on POP*

The underwriter (or sponsor) is the key sales organization hired by the investment company. The underwriter is compensated for distributing the fund's shares by adding a sales charge to the NAV of the shares sold.

The NASD prohibits its members from assessing sales charges *in excess of 8.5%* of the POP on mutual funds purchases by customers. Closed-end (publicly traded) funds do not carry a sales charge. The investor pays a brokerage commission to buy or to sell or a markup or markdown if a principal transaction is being executed.

Front-end Loads

Front-end load sales charges are added to the NAV of the shares at the time the investor purchases the shares.

Back-end Loads

Back-end sales loads (or contingent-deferred loads) are those charged at the redemption of mutual fund shares or variable contracts. The sales load is a *declining percentage charge* that is reduced *annually* and that is applied to the proceeds of any shares sold in that year.

12b-1 Asset-based Fees

Under section 12b-1 of the securities acts, a company may collect a fee for promotion, sale or another activity in connection with the distribution of its shares. There are certain requirements:

- The percentage of net assets charged must be reasonable.
- The fee must reflect the anticipated level of distribution services.

The payments represent charges that would have been paid to a third party (underwriter) had sales charges been negotiated for sales promotion, services and related activities.

Misuse of no-load terminology. To assert that a fund or contract being offered is a no-load fund or contract is a material misrepresentation if the fund indeed has a contingent deferred sales load or has an asset-based 12b-1 fee.

Mutual Fund Pricing

Pricing Management Company Shares

The formula for determining the POP of mutual fund shares is:

NAV + Sales charge = Offering price

The basic formula for determining the sales charge on mutual fund shares is:

Offering price − NAV = Sales charge

To determine the POP when you know only the NAV of a mutual fund share, divide the NAV by the complement of the sales load (100% − SL%). The formula is as follows:

$$\frac{\text{Net asset value}}{100\% - \text{Sales charge}} = \text{Public offering price}$$

The sales charge is always based on the POP, not the NAV.

Computing the Sales Charge Rate

When the NAV and the POP are known, the sales charge percentage included in the POP can be determined this way:

POP − NAV = Sales charge (dollar amount)

$$\frac{\text{Sales charge (dollar amount)}}{\text{POP}} = \text{Sales charge \%}$$

Reductions in the Permitted Maximum Sales Charge

To qualify for the maximum 8 1/2% sales charge, the investment company must offer all of the following:

- automatic reinvestment of income distributions at NAV;
- a scale of reduced sales charges for lump-sum investments; and
- rights of accumulation.

Sales Charges and Quantity Discounts

Breakpoints

The schedule of discounts offered by a mutual fund is called the fund's *breakpoints*. Breakpoints are available to any person. The following is an example of a breakpoint schedule:

Purchases		Sales Cost
$1 to $9,999	=	8 1/2%
$10,000 to $24,999	=	7 1/2%
$25,000 to $49,999	=	7%
$50,000 plus	=	6 1/2%

Statement of Intention (Letter of Intent)

Investors who do not have a large enough amount of money to invest at their initial purchase to qualify for a breakpoint may file a letter of intent (LOI). In the LOI, they indicate their intent to invest the additional funds necessary to reach the breakpoint at some time during the next 13 months.

The LOI is a unilateral contract that is binding only on the fund.

Backdating the LOI

Most investment companies permit the client to sign a letter of intent as late as the 90th day after a purchase. The letter of intent is then backdated to the date of the original purchase. The LOI may be backdated by up to 90 days to include prior purchases, but may not cover more than 13 months in total.

Rights of Accumulation

Rights of accumulation allow the investor to qualify for reduced sales charges. The client may qualify for reduced loads any time the aggregate value of shares previously purchased and shares currently being purchased in the account is over a breakpoint. The investment company will base the quantity of securities owned on:

- the current value of the securities at either NAV or POP;
- total purchases of such securities at the actual offering price; or
- the higher of current NAV or the total of purchases made to date (typically how it is valued).

Combination Privilege

Funds that have the same principal underwriter may grant an investor the privilege of combining separate investments in two or more funds under the same management towards a breakpoint. In this way, the investor would qualify for a reduced sales charge on his total investments.

Breakpoint Sales

The NASD prohibits registered reps from the practice of selling investment company shares in dollar amounts just below the point at which the sales charge is reduced *in order to make the higher commission* (known as a *breakpoint sale*).

Redemption of Fund Shares

Forward Pricing

By law, an open-end investment company must redeem shares tendered to it *within seven days* of receipt of a *written request* for redemption. The redemption price is the NAV next calculated after the investment company receives the redemption request (known as *forward pricing*).

Questions

1. In order for a company to charge the maximum sales charge of 8 1/2%, it must offer all of the following EXCEPT
    A. automatic reinvestment of dividends and capital gains at NAV
    B. breakpoints
    C. automatic reinvestment at POP
    D. rights of accumulation

Use the following breakpoint schedule to answer questions 2 through 4.

Purchases	Sales Cost
$1 to $9,999	8 1/2%
$10,000 to $24,999	7 1/2%
$25,000 to $49,999	7%
$50,000 to $99,999+	6 1/2%

2. Skyhawk Fund has an NAV of $9.15 and a POP of $10. A customer wants to invest $30,000. How many shares of the fund will the customer receive?
    A. 2,951
    B. 3,000
    C. 3,049
    D. 3,279

3. A customer currently has $20,000 to invest but signs a letter of intent for $25,000. The NAV is $12 a share. What is the price the customer will pay per share?
    A. $12.00 plus a commission
    B. $12.90
    C. $12.97
    D. $12.97 for the first $20,000 and $12.90 for the remainder

4. An investor purchases an income fund for himself and deposits $5,000. He also purchases a growth fund for his minor child and deposits $20,000. Which of the following would represent his sales charges if both funds have the same management and breakpoints?
    I. $5,000 at 8 1/2%
    II. $20,000 at 7 1/2%
    III. $25,000 at 7%
    IV. $25,000 at 7 1/2%

    A. I and II
    B. III
    C. IV
    D. None of the above

5. A mutual fund is quoted at $16.56 NAV and $18.00 POP. The sales charge is
    A. 7 1/2%
    B. 7 3/4%
    C. 8%
    D. 8 1/2%

6. Acme Fund has an NAV per share of $9.20 and an 8% sales load. What is the dollar amount of the sales charge?
    A. $.60
    B. $.74
    C. $.80
    D. $10.00

7. A mutual fund has a 7% sales load, a 1 1/2% dealer concession and an NAV of $10.80. To determine the offering price, divide the NAV by
    A. 7%
    B. 8 1/2%
    C. .915
    D. .93

8. Redemption of a no-load fund may be made at the
    A. NAV minus the sales charge
    B. POP minus the sales charge
    C. NAV plus the sales charge
    D. NAV

no sales charge could have redemption fee

9. A client owns 100 shares of a no-load mutual fund. When she redeems those shares, she will receive the net asset value

   A. plus a sales charge
   B. minus a redemption fee
   C. minus a sales charge
   D. minus both a redemption fee and a sales charge

10. Your client owns shares in an open-end investment company. The shares are currently quoted in the newspaper at $10 bid and $10.80 ask. Within the past twelve months, the investment company has distributed capital gains of $1.20 per share and dividends of $.60 per share. What is the current yield on your client's shares?

    A. 1.8%
    B. 5.0%
    C. 5.6%
    D. 6.0%

11. Ms. Johnson purchased mutual fund shares with a net asset value of $7.82 and an 8% sales charge. Ms. Johnson paid a sales charge of

    A. $.68
    B. $.74
    C. $.80
    D. $.87

12. John Smith purchased mutual fund shares with a bid price of $15.50 and an 8% sales charge. At the time of his purchase, what was the price of his shares?

    A. $12.40
    B. $14.26
    C. $16.74
    D. $16.85

13. An open-end investment company receives a redemption request from an investor early in the day on Friday, June 23rd. The basis for the redemption price the investor receives is the

    A. net asset value on Friday, June 23rd
    B. net asset value on Monday, June 26th
    C. ask price on Friday, June 23rd
    D. ask price on Monday, June 26th

14. In reference to open-end investment companies, all of the following terms are synonymous EXCEPT

    A. bid price
    B. net asset value
    C. redemption price
    D. current price

15. Which of the following statements are true regarding a letter of intent and breakpoints?

    I. The letter of intent can be backdated a maximum of 30 days.
    II. The letter of intent is valid for 13 months.
    III. The investor is legally bound to meet the terms of the agreement.
    IV. The fund may hold shares in escrow.

    A. I and II
    B. II and III
    C. II and IV
    D. III and IV

16. Which of the following investors can take advantage of breakpoints?

    I. Individual
    II. Investment club
    III. Trust
    IV. Corporation

    A. I and II
    B. I, III and IV
    C. II, III and IV
    D. III and IV

17. The XYZ Mutual Fund has an 8% sales load, a redemption fee of one-half of 1% and a current offering price of $10.70. If your customer redeemed 1,000 shares of the fund, he would receive

A. $9,572.38
B. $9,794.78
C. $9,844
D. $10,646.50

18. An investor purchasing 1,000 shares of a certain mutual fund that has a maximum sales charge of 8 1/2% and an NAV of $10.30 at the time of purchase will pay a total sales charge of (rounding to the nearest dollar)

A. $88
B. $96
C. $875
D. $957

19. A certain mutual fund has a bid price of $9.15 and a sales charge of 8.5%. What is the price an investor will pay for each share of this fund? (Round to the nearest cent.)

A. $8.37
B. $9.93
C. $10.00
D. $10.76

Answers

1. **C.** The maximum sales load is 8 1/2% *only* if the company offers rights of accumulation, breakpoints and automatic reinvestment at NAV, not at POP.

2. **C.** The offering price with a 7% sales charge is computed as follows: POP = NAV + (100% − SC) = 9.15 + (100% − 7%) = 9.15 ÷ .93 = $9.84. $30,000 ÷ $9.84 = 3,049 shares (rounded). Or, $30,000 − $2,100 (7%) = $27,900; $27,900 ÷ $9.15 (NAV) = 3,049 shares.

3. **B.** When the customer signs the letter of intent, she is entitled to the reduced sales load on the total amount of her investment. She has 13 months to complete the terms of the letter of intent. The offering price will be $12.90 (NAV of $12 + 93%).

4. **B.** Investors are permitted to combine investments to reduce sales loads. This is true for a parent and minor child in two separate accounts as long as the investments are in the same family of funds.

5. **C.** The formula is sales cost divided by public offering price. The sales cost is the difference between NAV and POP, or $1.44 per share. $1.44 ÷ $18 = 8%.

6. **C.** If the fund has an NAV of $9.20 and a sales load of 8%, the offering price is $9.20 ÷ (100% − SC) = 9.20 ÷ .92 = $10.00. The sales charge is the 80-cent difference.

7. **D.** The formula used to determine the offering price is:

$$\frac{NAV}{100\% - \text{Sales charge}} = POP$$

The sales load and sales charge are synonymous and the dealer concession is part of that figure. 100% − 7% = 93%, or .93.

8. **D.** No-load funds are redeemed at net asset value. Mutual funds may also charge a redemption fee, which is subtracted from the NAV.

9. **B.** Mutual fund shares are redeemed at net asset value minus any redemption fee. Sales charges are paid when the shares are purchased, not on redemption.

10. **C.** In open-end investment companies, current yield is calculated as follows: Annual dividends divided by asked price equals yield. Your client would find the yield of his open-end investment company as follows: $.60 ÷ $10.80 = 0.0555 = 5.55% (5.6% rounded).

11. **A.** To find the dollar amount of the sales charge when you know the NAV and the sales charge percentage, calculate the complement of the sales charge by subtracting the sales charge from 100%. (100% − 8% = 92%.) Then divide the NAV by the complement of the sales charge to find the offering price ($7.82 ÷ .92 = $8.50, the offering price). The dollar amount of the sales charge is the offering price minus the NAV. $8.50 − $7.82 = $.68, the sales charge.

12. **D.** The terms "bid price" and "net asset value" are synonymous, and the terms "current price" and "offering price" are synonymous. Divide the bid price by the complement of the sales charge to find the current price: $15.50 ÷ .92 = $16.85.

13. **A.** When an investor redeems shares, the redemption price is based on the next computed NAV following the investment company's receipt of the redemption request. This is the NAV computed at the end of the day on which the company receives the request.

14. **D.** "Current price" is synonymous with "public offering price." Current price is not the same as bid price, net asset value or redemption price.

15. **C.** Only choices II and IV are true. Choice I is false because the letter of intent can be backdated 90 days. Choice III is false because the investor is not required by law to satisfy the letter of intent although, in the case of default, she will pay a higher sales charge.

16. **B.** Breakpoint advantages are available only to "individuals." An investment club is not considered an individual, but trusts and corporations are.

17. **B.** The 1,000 shares have an offering price value of $10,700. The net asset value would be 92% of that amount, or $9,844. Then subtract 1/2 of 1% of $9,844 for the redemption fee, to arrive at a net figure of $9,794.78.

18. **D.** The 1,000 shares have a net asset value of $10,300. Divide that amount by the complement of 8 1/2% (100% ÷ 8.5% = 91.5%, or .915). The result is $11,257, which is the amount of the current offering price. The difference is $957.

19. **C.** To calculate the offering price when you know the bid price (the NAV) and the percentage of sales charge, divide the bid price ($9.15) by the complement of the sales charge (91.5%). This equals $10.00, the offering price.

Mutual Fund Purchase and Withdrawal Plans

Types of Mutual Fund Accounts

Open Account

The client can make additional investments to an open account at any time and without limit as to dollar amount—that is, no such limit is set by law, although each fund may set its own minimums.

Voluntary Accumulation

Under a voluntary accumulation plan, the client opens an account and voluntarily commits to additional periodic investments. Because the plan is voluntary, should the client miss a payment, the fund can in no way penalize the investor. The plan may be discontinued at any time by the client.

Accumulation Plans 9%

Voluntary accumulation plans. Voluntary accumulation plans allow the customer to deposit regular periodic investments on a voluntary basis in preset amounts.

Contractual accumulation plans. A contractual plan differs from a voluntary plan in that the investor signs an agreement to invest an agreed upon dollar amount over a specified period of time. The agreement is binding on the company only; the investor cannot be held to the contract.

The Investment Company Act of 1940 allows a maximum of 9% in sales charges by contractual plans.

Lump-sum accounts. The investor buys shares in the fund by depositing the entire amount he intends to invest all at once.

Periodic Payment Plans (Contractual Plans)

Contractual plans enable the investor who would like to accumulate a sum of dollars over a fixed period of time to invest in a mutual fund on a periodic basis. The investor will sign an agreement stating that she intends to invest a fixed number of dollars over a defined period of time. This agreement is not binding on the investor.

Characteristics of Contractual Plans

Separate products/separate prospectuses. When a contractual plan is sold, two interrelated sales are taking place. First, the customer is agreeing to make periodic payments to a contractual plan company. Evidence of this agreement takes the form of a plan certificate issued by the contractual plan company. Second, as periodic payments are made by the customer, the plan company uses the money to buy shares in the mutual fund.

Contractual plan companies are organized as **UITs.** The customer's units represent an undivided interest in the pool of underlying mutual fund shares.

Plan custodian. The plan company custodian is responsible for:

- safekeeping assets underlying the plan;
- issuing a confirmation form to the customer designating the number of shares owned;
- taking care of any assignments or transfer of fund shares; and
- sending out the letter notifying the customer of the free-look period (45-day letter).

Front-end Load and Spread Load

Front-end load. The Investment Company Act of 1940 allows the plan company to charge up to 50% of the investor's deposits in the first year (known as a *front-end load plan*). The seller is allowed to charge a maximum sales charge equal to 9% of the total payments stipulated in a contractual plan, as follows:

- 50% of the total payments made during the first twelve months (first year) may be deducted and applied against total sales charges due over the life of the plan.

- Over the remaining life of the plan, deductions for sales charges may be calculated in any reasonable manner.

1970 →

Spread load. The Investment Company Act Amendments of 1970, which amends the 1940 act, allows the company to charge up to 20% of the investor's deposit in any one year as long as the average charge over the first four years does not exceed 16% annually. This arrangement is known as a *spread-load plan*.

- Over the *first four years* of the plan, *an average of 16%* of all payments made by the investor may be deducted and applied against the total sales charges called for over the life of the plan.
- In *each* of the *first four years*, the sales charge rate and dollar amount deducted for the year must be *uniformly applied* to each month's payment.
- The rates at which sales charge deductions are made during each of the first four years are subject to the restriction that *the first year's deduction cannot exceed 20%* and the average over the four-year period cannot exceed 16%.

Whether the plan company operates under the act of 1940 or the act of 1970, the maximum sales charge allowable is 9% over the life of the plan.

Investor Right to Terminate a Plan

Right of withdrawal (45-day free look). The customer, if so inclined, may surrender the certificate and terminate the plan *within 45 days* from the mailing date of the custodian's written notice. If the customer surrenders the certificate within that time, he is entitled to:

- a 100% refund of all sales charges paid to date, *plus*
- the current value of the investment.

Right to refund (18-month partial refund period). If a customer requests termination of a front-end load plan within the *first 18 months* from the

issuance date of the periodic payment plan certificate, she is entitled to a refund of:

- all sales charges paid to date *in excess of 15% of the total (gross) payments* made to date, *plus*
- the current value of the investment, which is liquidated at current NAV.

The right to refund policy also applies if the investor abandons the plan prior to the end of the 18-month refund period.

Notice of right to refund. If a contractual plan has reached its *fifteenth-month anniversary* and the investor has missed *three or more* monthly payments, the custodian (or the plan company) must issue a *right to refund notice* to the investor.

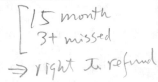

Dollar Cost Averaging

Dollar cost averaging allows the investor to purchase more shares when prices are low and fewer shares when prices are high. In a fluctuating market, the average cost per share over a period of time will be lower for the investor than the average price of the shares for the same period.

Withdrawal Plans

Fixed dollar. A client may request the withdrawal of a fixed amount of money periodically.

Fixed percentage or fixed share. Under a fixed-percentage or fixed-share withdrawal plan, either a fixed number of shares or a fixed percentage of the account will be liquidated each period.

Fixed time. Under a fixed-time withdrawal plan, clients liquidate their holdings over a fixed period of time.

Questions

1. In which of the following circumstances will dollar cost averaging result in an average cost per share that is lower than the average price per share?

   I. The price of the stock fluctuates over a period of time.
   II. A fixed number of shares is purchased regularly.
   III. A fixed dollar amount is invested regularly.
   IV. A constant dollar plan is maintained.

   A. I and II
   B. I and III
   C. I, III and IV
   D. II and III

2. What type of investment company is a contractual plan company?

   A. Unit investment trust
   B. Balanced fund
   C. Management company
   D. Closed-end fund

3. All of the following statements regarding dollar cost averaging are true EXCEPT that

   A. dollar cost averaging results in a lower average cost per share
   B. dollar cost averaging is not available to large investors
   C. more shares are purchased when prices are lower
   D. in sales literature, dollar cost averaging cannot be referred to as *averaging the dollar*

4. A contractual plan is MOST likely to be classified as a(n)

   A. closed-end investment company
   B. open-end investment company
   C. face-amount certificate
   D. unit investment trust

Answers

1. **B.** Dollar cost averaging benefits the investor if the same amount is invested on a regular basis over a substantial period of time, during which the price of the stock fluctuates. A constant dollar plan (choice IV) is one in which the investor maintains a constant dollar value of securities in the investment portfolio.

2. **A.** A contractual plan is usually a unit investment trust; it is not a management company.

3. **B.** Dollar cost averaging is available to both small and large investors.

4. **D.** Contractual plans are usually unit investment trusts. Both closed-end and open-end investment companies are types of management companies, but a contractual plan is not. Face-amount certificates are a different classification of investment company.

Mutual Fund Distributions and Taxation

Distributions from Mutual Funds

Net Investment Income

Dividends are paid from the net investment income of the mutual fund. To calculate net investment income, the fund totals dividends received from common and preferred stock held in the portfolio and adds all interest income received from bonds and other debt instruments. The sum of dividends and interest equals the gross investment income of the fund. From gross investment income, the fund subtracts its expenses for operation. The result is net investment income.

Calculating Fund Yields

The dividend paid from the net investment income is divided by the current offering price to calculate yield. All yield quotations must disclose the:

- general direction of the stock market for the period in question;
- NAV of the fund at the beginning and at the end of the period in question; and
- percentage change in the fund's price during the period in question.

Current yield calculations may be based only on income distributions for the preceding twelve months. Gains distributions may not be included in the yield calculations.

The mutual fund must disclose the source of any dividend payment if it is from other than retained or current income. The ex-dividend date for mutual funds is set by the board of directors.

Distribution from Capital Gains

Once a year

Capital gains distributions are derived from the activities of the investment adviser trading securities held in the fund's portfolio. Capital gains distributions (long term) may not be made more frequently than once per year. Any distribution of gains from an open-end investment company will be long term. Short-term gains are considered income distributions and will be identified and distributed as dividends.

Selling dividends. A registered representative is forbidden to encourage investors to purchase fund shares prior to a distribution because of this tax liability, and doing so is known as *selling dividends*.

Reinvestment of Dividend and Gains Distributions

The shareholder may elect to reinvest the cash distributions to purchase additional shares of the mutual fund. This reinvestment of distributions is called *automatic reinvestment*.

Source of distributions. The fund must disclose the source and character of distributions, either from income or from capital transactions, as each distribution is made.

Realized and Unrealized Appreciation

The tax liability of a shareholder who sells shares will depend on the difference between the original cost for the shares and the appreciated selling price. The gain, whether long or short term, will be taxed at the investor's ordinary income tax bracket.

Taxation of Mutual Funds

Investment Income: IRC Subchapter M

90% income must be distributed

Conduit (pipeline) theory. Subchapter M requires that the investment company distribute at least 90% of its net investment income to shareholders. If the company distributes 89%, the company is liable for tax on 100% of net investment income.

Capital Gains

The investment company designates to the shareholder of record a proportionate share of any undistributed capital gain. This amount is included on the shareholder's 1040 as reportable income. The regulated investment company pays tax on amounts designated to shareholders, but the tax paid is treated as an advance payment by the shareholder. *(withhold)*

Fund Share Liquidations to the Investor

Cost base is that amount of money invested that has already been taxed. Upon liquidation, cost base represents a return of capital and is not subject to a tax liability. The difference between cost base and the current value of the investor's shares represents his taxable gain or loss.

Accounting Methods   *default is FIFO*

The calculation of cost base can be accomplished by electing one of two accounting methods: **first in, first out (FIFO)** or **share identification**. If the investor fails to choose, the IRS assumes the investor is liquidating shares on a FIFO basis.

Share Identification

With share identification, the investor keeps track of the cost of each share purchased. Upon selling the shares, the investor decides which shares to liquidate. He then identifies the cost base of each share liquidated in whichever order provides the necessary tax benefit.

Questions

1. Which of the following decides when a mutual fund goes ex-dividend?

   A. NASD
   B. NYSE
   C. SEC
   D. Board of directors of the fund

2. Mr. Lindquist buys 100 shares of a mutual fund on December 28, 1984, for $4,000. He receives a capital gains distribution of $2.40 per share on March 6, 1985. He sells his 100 shares for $4,300 on June 19, 1985. For tax purposes, these transactions will result in

   A. a $240 capital gain
   B. a $300 capital gain
   C. both A and B
   D. neither A nor B

3. The conduit theory

   A. is described in the Investment Company Act of 1940
   B. refers to a tax treatment available to investment companies
   C. was developed by the NASD
   D. is stated in the SEC statement of policy

Use the following information to answer questions 4 and 5.

Last year, a certain mutual fund paid dividends of $1.50 per share and distributed 80 cents per share in capital gains. The fund has a bid price of $13.50 and an asked price of $14.20. An investor, who purchased shares in this fund nine months before the distributions, received $100 in eligible dividend income and $53 in capital gains.

4. If this is his only investment, the investor will

    I. not be required to pay any federal taxes on the dividend income

    II. be required to pay federal taxes at the ordinary income rate on the dividend income

    III. be required to pay tax on the $53 capital gain at the ordinary income tax rate

    IV. not be required to pay capital gains tax on $53

    A. I and III
    B. I and IV
    C. II and III
    D. III and IV

5. What is the yield of the fund?

    A. 4.92%
    B. 10.00%
    C. 10.56%
    D. 16.20%

Answers

1. **D.** The ex-date for a mutual fund is set by the board of directors.

2. **C.** Mr. Lindquist will realize a $240 capital gain on the distribution and a $300 capital gain on the sale of the stock.

3. **B.** Regulated companies under Subchapter M of the IRS code are allowed to *pass through* income to beneficial owners without a tax at the fund level on the distributed income. This is known as *conduit* or *flow-through* of income and taxation.

4. **C.** This investor will pay taxes on the dividend income, and he will pay capital gains tax on the $53.

5. **C.** Divide the dividend of $1.50 by the asked price of $14.20.

REITs and REMICs

Real Estate Investment Trusts

A real estate investment trust (REIT) is a company that manages a portfolio of real estate investments in order to earn profits for shareholders. REITs allow gains, profits and income to pass through to investors. The REIT investor, however, cannot deduct operating or capital losses. REIT portfolios are composed of professionally managed real estate holdings, typically either in direct ownership of income property or in mortgage loans.

Under the guidelines of Subchapter M of the Internal Revenue Code, a REIT can avoid being taxed as a corporation by receiving 75% or more of its income from real estate and distributing 95% or more of its taxable income to its shareholders.

Real Estate Mortgage Investment Conduits

A real estate mortgage investment conduit (REMIC) passes interest and gains through to investors, and those REMICs that meet certain distribution of income tests qualify for conduit treatment of passed-through income. REMICs do not pass through deductions to investors.

Owners of regular REMIC interests are treated like bondholders and are entitled to the interest generated by the underlying mortgages. Owners of residual REMIC interests are treated like shareholders and are entitled to any resulting capital gains.

REMICs can be organized as corporations (most frequently as subchapter M corporations), trusts or partnerships.

Retirement Planning and Annuities

Retirement Plans

Qualified Retirement Plans

ERISA guidelines for regulation of retirement plans include:

- participation
- funding
- vesting
- communication
- nondiscrimination

Defined benefit or defined contribution. A defined benefit plan specifies the total amount of money to be received upon retirement. A defined contribution plan specifies the amount an employer will contribute to the plan annually.

Taxation of qualified plans. A contribution to a qualified plan is exempt from income tax in the year it is made. With qualified plans, the tax is deferred until the individual receives the money as income.

Nonqualified Retirement Plans

Contributions to nonqualified plans are not exempt from current income tax. With nonqualified plans, the tax is paid on the amount of contribution in the year the contribution is made. Nonqualified plans are not subject to the same stringent ERISA reporting and disclosure requirements as are qualified plans.

Payroll Deduction Plan

In a payroll deduction program, the employee authorizes a deduction from his check on a weekly, monthly or quarterly basis. The money is deducted after taxes are paid and may be invested in any number of investment vehicles at the employee's option. A payroll deduction plan may be either qualified or nonqualified.

Deferred Compensation Plan

A deferred compensation plan represents a *contractual agreement* between a firm and an employee by which the employee agrees to defer receipt of current compensation in favor of a larger payout at retirement.

Deferred comp plans are normally set up as nonqualified retirement plans, do not require IRS approval and do not have to meet ERISA standards regarding participation, funding, vesting or fiduciary responsibility.

Funding. Deferred compensation plans may be either funded or unfunded.

Taxation. The employer does not receive a deduction for contributions until payments are made to the employee. The income tax on the earnings of

343

the program, if funded, is paid by the employer. Upon retirement, the employee will receive the deferred payment as ordinary income.

Nonqualified Variable Annuity Contract

Annuities are products of the insurance industry. An annuity represents a contract between an individual (the **annuitant**) and an insurance company.

Annuities provide a means by which invested capital can be distributed over a lifetime.

Individual Retirement Accounts

Tax Benefits

For individuals whose gross income exceeds $35,000 or couples whose combined gross income exceeds $50,000, there is no allowable deduction.

IRA Contributions

The maximum annual IRA contribution that an employed individual can make is subject to the following limitations:

- for an individual account, 100% of earned income or $2,000, whichever is less; and
- for a spousal account, 100% of earned income or $2,250 (divided between two accounts), whichever is less.

IRA owners are always *100% vested* in their contributions to their accounts.

$2,000 contribution limit. Anyone under age 70 1/2 who has earned income is eligible to open an IRA and make annual contributions.

Excess Contributions

Annual IRA contributions in excess of the maximum are subject to a 6% penalty tax if the excess is not removed by the time the taxpayer files the tax return.

Participation in an IRA

Any taxpayer reporting earned income for a given tax year may participate in an IRA. Earned income is from the performance of personal services and is not passive income. The taxpayer must not have reached the maximum age of 70 1/2 during the tax year.

Participating (covered) employees. If the taxpayer is actively participating in an employer-sponsored pension or profit-sharing plan, the person's total earnings for the year will determine the extent to which self-funded, personal IRA contributions will be tax deductible.

IRA Investments

Permissible investments. IRA investments may include stocks, bonds, UITs, mutual funds, limited partnerships, government securities, U.S. government-issued gold and silver coins, annuities and many others.

Ineligible investments. There are certain investments that are considered ineligible for use in an IRA. Collectibles are not acceptable IRA investments. Life insurance contracts (*cash value*, *term* and *decreasing term* insurance with no cash surrender value) may not be purchased in an IRA. Annuity contracts and endowment policies may be eligible under certain conditions.

IRA Rollovers and Transfers

Rollovers

Rollovers into another account must be completed within 60 days of the original funds' withdrawal from the qualified plan.

Transfers

There is no limit to the number of times per year a person can transfer investments between qualified plans, provided the assets in the accounts do not pass through the hands of the taxpayer.

IRA Withdrawals

Withdrawals may not begin before age 59 1/2 and must begin by the year after the year in which the account owner reaches age 70 1/2.

Taxation on IRA Distributions

IRA Abuses and Tax Penalties

There are three situations in which a taxpayer's IRA activity will lead to penalties being levied by the IRS.

1. Excess contributions over the maximum annual limits will subject the taxpayer to a tax penalty of *6% of the excess amount.*
2. Early withdrawals will be subject to a *tax penalty of 10%*, in addition to the full amount of the early withdrawal being treated as ordinary income.
3. Failure to start distributions by the year after the year in which the taxpayer reaches age 70 1/2 will cause the IRS to impose a special penalty on the taxpayer. 50%

Questions

1. The maximum allowable contribution to an IRA is

   A. $2,250 per individual account
   B. $2,000 per individual account
   C. $250 per individual account
   D. $0 because contributions to IRAs are no longer allowed

2. Premature distribution from an IRA is subject to a

   A. 5% penalty plus tax
   B. 6% penalty plus tax
   C. 10% penalty plus tax
   D. 50% penalty plus tax

3. Money can be rolled over from a qualified plan to an IRA

   A. every 60 days
   B. once a year
   C. at no time
   D. as directed by the customer

4. An individual with an IRA subsequently joins a corporation that covers the employee with a pension plan. What actions are taken regarding the IRA?

   A. The IRA must be made part of the pension plan.
   B. The IRA must be closed.
   C. The employee may continue to contribute to the IRA.
   D. The IRA is frozen.

5. What is the maximum permissible contribution to an IRA by an individual?

   A. $2,000
   B. $2,250
   C. $4,000
   D. 25% of one's earnings or $30,000, whichever is less

6. Your client, who is 50 years of age, wants to withdraw funds from her IRA. He asks you about the tax implications of early withdrawal. You should tell him the withdrawal will be taxed as

   A. ordinary income
   B. ordinary income plus a 10% penalty
   C. capital gains
   D. capital gains plus a 10% penalty

7. An individual who is less than age 70 1/2 is qualified to contribute to an IRA

   A. if he has earned income
   B. provided he is not covered by a pension plan through an employer
   C. provided he does not own a Keogh plan
   D. provided his income is between $40,000 and $50,000 if married and $25,000 and $35,000 if single

8. A client has just started her IRA. She will be vested

   A. immediately
   B. in two years
   C. in five years
   D. at age 70 1/2

9. Which of the following statements regarding IRAs is NOT true?

   A. IRA rollovers must be completed within 60 days of receipt of the distribution.
   B. Cash-value life insurance is a permissible IRA investment, but term insurance is not.
   C. The investor must be under 70 1/2 years of age to open and contribute to an IRA.
   D. Distributions may begin at age 59 1/2 and must begin by the year after the year in which the investor turns 70 1/2.

10. A client and his wife are going to make their annual contribution to their IRA. This year he earned $40,000 and his wife earned $45,000. How much may they contribute?

    A. $2,000
    B. $2,250
    C. $4,000
    D. $5,000

11. Under the Tax Reform Act of 1986, all of the following investments offer either full or partially tax-deductible contributions to individuals who meet eligibility requirements EXCEPT

    A. IRAs
    B. Keogh plans
    C. variable annuities
    D. none of the above

12. Which of the following individuals will NOT incur a penalty on an IRA withdrawal?

    A. Man who has just become disabled
    B. Woman who turned 59 a month before the withdrawal
    C. Person, age 50, who decides on early retirement
    D. Man in his early 40s who uses the money to buy a house

Answers

1. B. Maximum contributions to an individual account are $2,000. Maximum contributions to a spousal account are $2,250.

2. C. The penalty for premature withdrawals from an IRA or a Keogh account is 10% plus normal income tax. Excess contribution penalty is 6%, while the 50% penalty applies after age 70 1/2.

3. B. A rollover is permitted once a year. Customers must accomplish this within 60 days after receipt of the distribution from a qualified plan.

4. C. Any individual who has earned income may continue to make contributions to his IRA even when covered by another pension plan.

5. A. Maximum contributions to an individual IRA account are $2,000 per year. Maximum contributions to a spousal account (where there is a nonworking spouse) are $2,250. Maximum contributions for a working couple are $4,000 ($2,000 each). Maximum contribution to a Keogh plan is 25% of annual income, up to a maximum of $30,000.

6. B. All withdrawals from IRAs are taxed at the individual's ordinary income tax rate at the time of withdrawal. Distributions taken before age 59 1/2 will incur an additional 10% penalty.

7. A. Any individual with earned income who is under the age of 70 1/2 may contribute up to $2,000 to an IRA. The deductibility of those contributions will be determined by that person's coverage under other qualified plans and by his level of income.

8. A. An account owner is *always* 100% vested in the value of her IRA.

9. B. Cash-value life insurance, term insurance and collectibles are not permissible investments in an IRA.

10. C. Because both the client and his wife had earned income, both are entitled to contribute 100% of that earned income, up to $2,000, to separate IRAs.

11. C. Contributions to variable annuities are made with aftertax dollars.

12. A. Early withdrawals, without penalty, are permitted only in the case of death or disability.

Keogh (HR-10) Plans

Keogh Plan Eligibility

Keogh plans are intended for self-employed individuals and owner-employees of nonincorporated business concerns or professional practices.

Income must be earned. Income must be earned income from personal services, not passive income.

Plan must be nondiscriminatory. Owner-employees who have hired employees on their payrolls must provide for these people's retirement security under a Keogh plan in the same manner and to the same extent that the owner-employee's retirement security is provided.

Contributions

Tax-deductible

equiv. to 20% before contribution

The Keogh planholder is permitted to make tax-deductible *cash* contributions of up to 25% of earned (after-contribution) income or $30,000, whichever is less. As with IRAs, a person may make contributions to a Keogh until he has reached age 70 1/2.

Employee coverage. If the owner of a sole proprietorship or the partners in a partnership have common law employees, these people must be covered under the employer's Keogh plan at the same rate of annual contribution as the owner.

Nontax-deductible

Individuals with Keogh plans may make nondeductible contributions of up to 10% of their income.

Top-heavy Keoghs

$200,000 maximum salary base. The maximum salary level on which Keogh contributions may be based is $200,000.

Keogh Plan Employee Vesting Requirements

ERISA/IRS minimum employee vesting requirements will be met if one of the following plans is set forth in a Keogh plan:

- Plan 1: Five-year vesting
- Plan 2: Three- to seven-year vesting

Comparison of Qualified Retirement Plans

Similarities Between Keoghs and IRAs

The principal similarities between Keoghs and IRAs are as follows:

- age limits
- tax deferral of income contributed to plans
- tax-sheltered
- cash-only contributions
- distributions
- penalties for premature withdrawal
- rollovers and transfers
- available payout options
- beneficiary(ies)

Differences Between Keoghs and IRAs

The differences between Keoghs and IRAs are shown in Table 1.

Table 1. Differences between Keoghs and IRAs

Characteristic	Keogh Plan	IRA
Permissible investments	Most equity and debt securities, U.S.-minted precious-metal coins, annuities and cash-value life insurance	Most equity and debt securities, U.S.-minted precious-metal coins and annuities
Nonpermissible investments	Term insurance and collectibles	Term insurance, collectibles and cash-value life insurance
Change of employer	Lump-sum distribution can be rolled over into an IRA within 60 days	Does not apply
Penalty for excess contribution	Excess is not deductible	6% penalty
Taxation of distributions	Taxed as ordinary income	Taxed as ordinary income

Questions

1. Which of the following may participate in a Keogh plan?

   I.   Self-employed doctor
   II. Analyst who makes money giving speeches outside regular working hours
   III. Individual with a full-time job who has income from freelancing
   IV. Corporate executive who receives $5,000 in stock options from his corporation

   A. I only
   B. I and II only
   C. I, II and III only
   D. I, II, III and IV

2. Lump-sum withdrawals from a Keogh plan allow for

   A. a long-term tax rate
   B. 10-year income averaging
   C. 5-year income averaging
   D. taxes only on capital gains

3. Guido Vitro has a salaried, full-time position, but his employer does not offer a company retirement plan. He also has his own clock repair business, which earns less than his salaried position. He wants to invest for his retirement. Which of the following investments is an option for Guido?

   A. An IRA if he does not have a Keogh plan
   B. A Keogh plan if he does not own an IRA
   C. Both an IRA and a Keogh plan
   D. An IRA, but not a Keogh because his self-employment is not his main source of income

4. Which of the following are characteristics of a Keogh plan?

   I. Dividends, interest and capital gains are tax deferred.
   II. Distributions after age 70 1/2 are tax free.
   III. Contributions are allowed for a nonworking spouse.
   IV. Lump-sum distributions are allowed.

   A. I and II
   B. I and III
   C. I and IV
   D. II and III

5. All of the following factors influence the amount of money that can be contributed to a Keogh plan in one year EXCEPT

   A. the rules regarding maximum contributions
   B. whether the plan is qualified or nonqualified
   C. the amount of self-employment income
   D. whether the plan is defined benefit or defined contribution

6. Which of the following would disqualify a person from participation in a Keogh plan?

   A. She turned 70 eight months ago.
   B. She has a salaried position in addition to her self-employment.
   C. Her spouse has company-sponsored retirement benefits.
   D. She has an IRA.

Answers

1. **C.** A person with self-employment income may deduct contributions to a Keogh plan.

2. **C.** The Tax Reform Act of 1986 permits income averaging of five years on lump-sum withdrawals from a Keogh plan.

3. **C.** Because Guido has earned income, he is eligible to contribute to an IRA; and because he has self-employment income, he is also eligible to open and contribute to a Keogh plan.

4. **C.** All interest, dividends and capital gains accumulated in a Keogh are tax deferred until their withdrawal (which must begin between age 59 1/2 and the year after the year in which the account owner turns 70 1/2). The account owner may choose to take distributions in the form of regular income payments or as a single, lump-sum distribution.

5. **B.** Keogh plans, as defined by ERISA, are all qualified plans.

6. **A.** Keogh contributions can only be made *prior to* the date on which an individual turns 70 1/2.

Corporate Pension Plans

All corporate pension and profit-sharing plans must be established under a trust agreement.

Defined Contribution vs. Defined Benefit

Defined contribution plans. In a defined contribution plan, the provisions cover amounts going into the plan currently or the plan's current allocation. The future final accumulation or account balance depends on the total of the amounts contributed, interest and dividends earned and increase in value.

Defined benefit plans. Defined benefit plans are designed to provide a specified benefit for their participants. These plans use actuarial assumptions including mortality, turnover and interest to derive the appropriate current outlay necessary to fund the future benefits.

Defined Contribution Plan Limitations

Employers sponsoring defined contribution plans are limited to the *lesser* of:

- 25% percent of the compensation of plan participants; or
- $30,000 for annual contribution deductions to the plan.

Defined Benefit Plan Limitations

To define a plan's benefit:

- The retirement benefit may be expressed as a flat or fixed dollar amount paid monthly.
- The benefit may be provided based on a percentage of compensation.

Benefit limitations take three forms:

1. replacement of earnings
2. dollar amount
3. dollars considered

The "normal retirement age" under a defined benefit plan must correlate with the applicable retirement age for Social Security purposes.

Normal Retirement Provisions

The latest date that an employer can provide for normal retirement under a qualified plan is the *later* of:

- the participant's reaching age 65; or
- the tenth anniversary of commencement of participation in the plan.

Taxation of Distributions

Earnings attributable to employee contributions as well as employer-contributed money will be taxed at the employee's ordinary income rate at the time of distribution.

Profit-sharing Plan

A profit-sharing plan does not have to entail a definite predetermined contribution formula. Profit-sharing plans that do include a definite contribution formula generally express contributions as a fixed percentage of profits. A profit-sharing plan must have "substantial and recurring" contributions according to the IRC.

Annuity Plans

Tax Advantages of Tax-deferred Annuities

Contributions excluded from gross income. If an eligible employee elects to make annual contributions to a TDA, those contributions are excluded from the employee's gross income for that year.

Tax-free accumulation. Interest earnings in a TDA accumulate tax free and do not increase the participant's taxable income until the total dollars are withdrawn at retirement.

Types of Annuity Contracts

Fixed Annuities

Guaranteed return. A fixed annuity has a guaranteed rate of return. Payment from a fixed annuity remains constant throughout the annuitant's life.

Risks. An investor with a fixed annuity risks loss of purchasing power because of inflation.

Variable Annuities

The money deposited in a variable annuity is invested primarily in a portfolio of equity securities. The annuitant participates in both the greater potential gain and the greater potential risk associated with equity securities. Payouts may vary considerably as the value of the annuity units fluctuates with the value of those securities.

Separate account. Variable annuity contributions are kept in a separate account from the insurance company's investment account.

Variable annuity payments. Variable annuity payments are not fixed at a certain amount, but are determined by mortality tables and the value of the annuitant's portfolio.

Purchasing Annuities

The pay-in period for an annuity is also known as the **accumulation stage**.

Deferred annuities. An annuity purchased with a lump-sum investment with payment of benefits deferred until the annuitant elects to receive them is referred to as a **single-premium (-payment) deferred annuity**. An annuity purchased by making several smaller payments over a period of time is known as a **periodic-payment annuity**. An investor who elects to join a contractual plan, the annuity is referred to as a **periodic-payment deferred annuity**.

Immediate annuities. In an immediate annuity contract, an investor purchases the annuity by depositing a single lump sum.

Sales Charges on Variable Annuities

Periodic-payment annuities. For periodic-payment annuities, the maximum sales charge is 8.5% of the total payments made to the contract for the lesser of the payment period or twelve years.

Single-payment annuities. For single-payment annuities, the maximum sales charge must be related to the amount of the purchase payment:

- first $25,000, 8.5% of payment
- next $25,000, 7.5% of payment
- over $50,000, 6.5% of payment

Annuity Payout Options

The annuity options available to the annuitant are:

- life annuity/straight life
- life annuity with period certain
- joint life with last survivor
- unit refund annuity

Annuity Accounting

Accumulation Unit

An accumulation unit is an accounting measure that represents the investor's share of ownership in the separate account.

Annuity Unit

An annuity unit is an accounting measure that determines the amount of each payment to the annuitant.

Assumed Interest Rate

The AIR provides an earnings target for the separate account and is usually conservatively estimated. An AIR is used to project the value of an account through the annuitant's age at death, as forecasted by mortality tables.

The AIR does not guarantee a rate of return. The annuitant always receives a payment equal to the value of one annuity unit times the number of units in the annuitant's account.

Taxation of Annuities

Contributions to annuities are made with after-tax dollars. Tax on interest received or capital growth of the contract is deferred until the owner withdraws money from the contract. On withdrawal, the amount in excess of the investor's cost base is taxed as ordinary income.

The following summarizes the taxation of annuity distributions:

- **Lump-sum distributions.** If the benefits are received in one sum, the employee will have the entire amount reported as income and that lump sum will be taxed at ordinary income rates.
- **Installment/annuity distributions.** Any lump sum, installment or annuity payment will be subject to ordinary income rates in the year it is received.

Taxation of premature distributions. Any premature distribution is subject to:

- ordinary income tax rates to the amount distributed; and
- a 10% penalty tax on the amount distributed.

Eligibility Requirements

To be eligible for a TDA, an employer must qualify under one of the following classifications:

- public educational institution
- tax-exempt 501c organization
- church organization

All TDAs, whether employer contribution or employee elective deferral, must be made available to each employee who has:

- reached age 21; and
- completed one year of service.

An employee must meet *both* of these requirements to be eligible to participate in a TDA.

Contribution Limits

Employer contribution plans. Employer contributions to a TDA can be made solely on behalf of the covered employee or in conjunction with an employee deferral.

Personal contributions. Elective employee deferrals to a TDA cannot exceed $9,500 per year.

Employer contributions. Employer contributions to a TDA are subject to the same maximums that apply to all defined-contribution plans: the lesser of 25% of the participant's compensation or $30,000 per year.

Distributions from a TDA

Distributions from a TDA must follow the same rules as all qualified plans.

Questions

1. In a variable annuity, total accumulation units are equal to

   A. the annuity's bookkeeping value
   B. the annuity owner's percentage of ownership of the separate account
   C. that portion of reinvested dividends
   D. the offering price

2. What has the greatest effect on the value of annuity units in a variable annuity?

   A. Changes in the Standard & Poor's index
   B. Cost-of-living index
   C. Fluctuations in the securities held in the portfolio
   D. Changes in stock market prices

3. Variable annuity salespeople must register with the

   I. SEC
   II. state banking commission
   III. NASD
   IV. state insurance commission

   A. I, II and III
   B. I and III
   C. I, III and IV
   D. II and IV

4. Holders of variable annuities receive the largest monthly payments under which of the following payout options?

   A. Life annuity
   B. Life annuity with period certain
   C. Joint and last survivor annuity
   D. All of the above

5. Changes in payments on a variable annuity will correspond most closely to fluctuations in the

   A. cost of living
   B. Dow Jones Industrial Average
   C. value of the underlying securities held in the separate account
   D. prime rate

6. The greatest effect on the value of the annuity unit in a variable annuity is caused by fluctuations in the

   A. prime rate
   B. Dow Jones Industrial Average
   C. value of the underlying securities in the portfolio
   D. actuarial rates

7. If Ms. Bullwether wants to sell variable annuities, she must be registered with the

   I. state banking commission
   II. NASD
   III. state annuity board
   IV. state insurance commission

   A. I and III
   B. I and IV
   C. II and III
   D. II and IV

8. Mr. Grizzly reaches age 65 and decides to retire. He wants to annuitize his annuity so that it will provide him with the maximum monthly income. You should recommend a

   A. joint and last survivor annuity
   B. life annuity with period certain
   C. life annuity
   D. unit refund annuity

9. Which of the following statements about an accumulation unit in a variable annuity is NOT true?

   A. An accumulation unit may also be called an annuity unit.
   B. An accumulation unit is the accounting measure that determines the owner's share of the separate account during the accumulation phase of a variable annuity.
   C. The current value of an accumulation unit determines the number of units each net payment purchases.
   D. Accumulation units are equal to the investor's percentage interest in the separate account times the number of accumulation units outstanding.

10. Mary Jones wants to purchase an annuity. She is concerned about protecting her purchasing power during her retirement. Her registered representative should recommend

   A. Series HH bonds
   B. fixed annuities
   C. variable annuities
   D. face-amount certificates

11. Which of the following statements regarding variable annuities are true?

   I. Variable annuities are classified as insurance products.
   II. Insurance companies keep variable annuity funds in separate accounts from other insurance products.
   III. Variable annuities can be purchased with a lump sum but are more commonly purchased with periodic payments.
   IV. Variable annuities offer the investor protection against capital loss.

   A. I and II
   B. I, II and III
   C. I and III
   D. II and IV

Answers

1. **B.** Accumulation units in a plan are the owner's percentage interest in the separate account, similar to shares of a mutual fund.

2. **C.** Annuity unit price changes are based on changes of value of securities held in the separate account. This price change is a risk that is passed on to the investor in a variable annuity.

3. **C.** Variable annuity salespeople must be registered with the NASD and the state insurance commission. Registration with the NASD is *de facto* registration with the SEC. No registration is required with the state banking commission.

4. **A.** A life annuity guarantees payment for life to the contract holder. The period certain and survivor annuity have additional benefits that reduce monthly payments.

5. **C.** Variable annuities are based on investments held in the portfolio, which the insurance company segregates into the *separate account*. The value of the units will correspond to the changes in this account.

6. **C.** The performance of an annuity unit of a variable annuity is based on the fluctuating performance of the separate account of the insurance company. This separate account is composed of a portfolio of securities (stocks or bonds). The person who buys a variable annuity hopes that the value of that portfolio will increase so that the annuity payments can increase correspondingly.

7. **D.** A variable annuity is both a security and an insurance product. For this reason, a salesperson who wants to sell variable annuities must become licensed with both the NASD (to sell the security) and the state insurance commission (to sell the insurance product).

8. **C.** In a life annuity, clients receive monthly income checks until their death, at which time payments cease. This type of annuity provides

the maximum monthly payment because there are no added options or benefits that reduce payouts.

9.   **A.**   An accumulation unit, as described in answers B, C and D, is not the same as an annuity unit. An annuity unit is the accounting measure that determines the amount of each payment during the payout period.

10.   **C.**   Variable annuities invest the separate fund in equities, so payout depends on the equities' performance. This provides some protection of purchasing power because equities generally increase more than the cost of living. The other three answers—Series HH bonds, fixed annuities and face-amount certificates—are fixed-income investments with no protection of purchasing power.

11.   **B.**   A variable annuity is both an insurance and a securities product. Choice IV is incorrect because the annuitant assumes the investment risk of a variable annuity and is not protected by the insurance company from capital losses.

ERISA

Titles

The four parts of ERISA legislation, referred to as *titles,* are:

- **Title 1.** Deals with the protection of employee benefit rights.
- **Title 2.** Composed of amendments to the Internal Revenue Code's pension and benefits sections.
- **Title 3.** Deals primarily with the division of responsibilities among the agencies administering the pension laws.
- **Title 4.** Concerns itself with pension plan termination insurance provisions and established the Pension Benefit Guaranty Corporation.

Standards

ERISA standards dictate that:

- employees are not required to satisfy unreasonable age and service requirements before becoming eligible for plan participation;
- persons who work for a specified minimum period of time under a pension plan are assured of at least some benefits at retirement age;
- adequate money will be there to pay all employee-earned pension benefits when they are due;
- plan sponsors meet their duties and responsibilities by handling their plan's funds prudently;

- employees and their beneficiaries know both their rights and their obligations under the plan;
- spouses of pensioners are afforded better coverage and protection;
- the benefits of workers in certain defined benefit pension plans are protected in the event of plan termination; and
- tax laws relevant to pensions and their distribution are made more equitable.

Tax Advantages

Corporations that choose to organize their plans under the standards set forth by ERISA receive favorable tax treatment for both the employer sponsors and employee plan participants.

Tax advantages for ERISA-qualified pension plans include:

- The employer is entitled to take a current income tax deduction for contributions made to the plan.
- The employees do not have to include in their current year's gross income any of their employer's contributions to their retirement plan. All contributions to the plan are tax deferred until they are distributed.
- Any income earned (or capital gains achieved) by the investments in the participant's account are not taxed to the plan participant until they are distributed or withdrawn.
- Distributions from the retirement plan may be eligible for special income and estate tax treatment at the time of withdrawal.

E

19 Direct Participation Programs

Characteristics of Limited Partnerships

Forms of Business Organization

Partnership

A partnership offers investors limited liability. Should the partnership default on its loans, investors could lose their entire investment but they are not personally liable for other partnership debts.

Limited Partnership

A limited partnership is a DPP that offers investors direct participation in the economic consequences of the business. Limited partnerships pass income, gains, losses, deductions and credits directly to investors.

Syndication and underwriting of limited partnerships. The syndicator's duties include preparing the paperwork needed to register the limited partnership with the SEC; organizing and overseeing the selling syndicate and selling group; and promoting the partnership generally.

Tax reporting. Limited partnerships pass through to investors the economic benefits and tax consequences of the business.

Maintaining partnership status. Limited partnerships may have no more than four of these six

characteristics and still qualify for the special tax treatment afforded partnerships:

1. continuity of life   *Set a date of dissolve*
2. limited liability
3. free transferability of interests ✓
4. centralization of management
5. intent to do business and divide profits among investors
6. business associates

Forming a Limited Partnership

Documentation

Registration statement. Federal regulations require a new partnership to file a registration statement and prospectus with the SEC. A registration statement contains complete information and supporting documents that describe the partnership.

Prospectus. The prospectus provides material information about the partnership and the GP.

Subscription agreement. An investor interested in purchasing a limited partnership unit signs a subscription agreement, which includes a statement of the investor's net worth and annual income and a power of attorney appointing the GP as the agent of the partnership.

Certificate of limited partnership. The certificate of limited partnership includes the following information:

- partnership's name;
- partnership's business;

- principal place of business, often the GP's address;
- amount of time the partnership expects to be in business;
- size of each LP's investment and any additional investment expected;
- when each investor's contribution will be returned;
- each LP's share of the profits or other compensation;
- whether and under what conditions an LP can assign an interest;
- whether LPs may admit additional LPs;
- whether some LPs will have priority over others in contributions or compensation;
- whether upon the death or incapacity of a GP, remaining GPs may continue the business; and
- if granted, the right of an LP to request compensation in property instead of cash.

Agreement of limited partnership. The partnership agreement is a contract that provides guidelines for operation and describes rights and responsibilities of the general and limited partners.

Dissolving a Limited Partnership

When a partnership dissolves, the GP must cancel the certificate of limited partnership and settle accounts in the following order:

1. secured lenders;
2. other creditors;
3. limited partners, first for their claims to a share of profits and second for their claims to a return of contributed capital; and
4. GPs, first for fees and other claims not involving profits or capital, second for a share of profits, and third for capital return.

Advantages and Disadvantages of the Limited Partnership

The DPP investor enjoys several advantages:

- management of the investment by others
- flow-through of income and expenses
- limited liability

The greatest disadvantage to the investor is lack of liquidity.

Investors in a Limited Partnership

A limited partnership must have at least one general partner and one limited partner.

General Partner

The GPs are the active investors in a limited partnership, and assume responsibility for all aspects of the partnership's operations. The GP will:

- make decisions that bind the partnership;
- buy and sell property for the partnership;
- manage the partnership property and money;
- supervise all aspects of the partnership's business; and
- maintain a 1% financial interest in the partnership.

GPs have unlimited liability and are, therefore, personally liable for all partnership business losses and debts. The partnership's creditors may seek repayment from the GP and may go after the GP's personal assets. The GP has a fiduciary relationship to the LPs.

Limitations on the GP. The GP may not prevent the ordinary flow of partnership business, assign or possess a partnership property for purposes other than those in the best interest of the partnership, or compete with the partnership for personal gain.

Unless specifically authorized to do so by the partnership agreement, the GP may not admit a new general or limited partner to the partnership, or continue the business of the partnership if a GP dies, retires or becomes otherwise incapacitated.

Conflicts of interest for the GP. To avoid the appearance of conflicts of interest, the GP:

- must use the utmost good faith in managing the business in the partnership's best interest;
- must not engage in an improper use of partnership assets;
- must not commingle the funds of various partnerships;
- must not commingle partnership funds with his personal funds; and
- may lend money or property to the partnership, but may not borrow from the partnership.

Limited Partner

LPs are passive investors who assume no part of the management responsibilities or decision making and are, therefore, usually not held personally and individually liable for the general indebtedness of the partnership. Under current tax law, LPs are classified as passive investors: any income they receive from a partnership is passive income, and any loss passed through to them is a passive loss.

Rights and responsibilities of the LP. The LP has the right to:

- vote on the admission of a new GP;
- sue the GP;
- vote on the sale or refinancing of partnership property; and
- inspect partnership books and records.

Questions

1. "DPP" stands for which of the following?

   A. Direct placement program
   B. Directed profits program
   C. Direct participation program
   D. Directors' and principals' program

2. Which of the following forms of business involves the greatest risk to the owner?

   A. Sole proprietorship
   B. General partnership
   C. Corporation
   D. Limited partnership

3. Which of the following is subject to double taxation?

   A. Sole proprietorship
   B. General partnership
   C. Corporation
   D. Limited partnership

4. A limited partnership may avoid all of the following corporate characteristics EXCEPT

   A. centralization of management
   B. associates
   C. limited liability
   D. free transferability of interests

5. A general partner is all of the following EXCEPT

   A. a key executive
   B. one who buys and sells the program's properties
   C. one who appoints the property manager
   D. one who has a limited liability status

6. Who of the following has the greatest liability?

   A. General partner
   B. Limited partner
   C. Corporate stockholder
   D. Trustee

7. The person who organizes and registers a partnership is known as a(n)

    A. syndicator
    B. property manager
    C. program manager
    D. underwriter

8. The maximum underwriting compensation allowed a DPP offering is

    A. 5%
    B. 7%
    C. 10%
    D. 15%

9. A subscription for a limited partnership is accepted when the

    A. limited partner signs the subscription
    B. limited partner's check clears
    C. general partner signs the subscription
    D. certificate is filed with the state

10. When a partnership dissolves, what is the proper order for settling accounts with the following groups?

    I. General partners
    II. Limited partners
    III. General creditors
    IV. Secured lenders

    A. II, III, IV, I
    B. III, IV, II, I
    C. IV, III, I, II
    D. IV, III, II, I

11. Which of the following are advantages of a limited partnership?

    I. Direct flow-through of gains and losses
    II. Opportunity to manage the investment
    III. Liquidity
    IV. Limited liability

    A. I and III
    B. I and IV
    C. II and III
    D. II and IV

12. Which type of business organization offers the highest degree of liability?

    A. Corporation
    B. Limited partnership
    C. Real estate investment trust
    D. General partnership

13. A conflict of interest exists if the general partner

    I. receives compensation from the partnership
    II. borrows from the partnership
    III. owns or leases property adjacent to property of the partnership
    IV. is involved in more than one program

    A. I and II
    B. I and III
    C. II and III
    D. III and IV

14. All of the following are characteristics of a limited partner EXCEPT

    A. losses are limited to the extent of the initial investment
    B. personal liability for the default of loans
    C. no control over management
    D. pass-through of partnership's tax advantages

15. All of the following are disadvantages of direct participation programs EXCEPT that there is

    A. no secondary market
    B. a potential change in tax laws
    C. no right to sue the general partner
    D. a possible conflict of interest between general partners and limited partners

16. Which of the following phrases describe the agreement of limited partnership?

   I. Contract between the limited and general partners
   II. Public document
   III. Concludes the sale of a partnership interest
   IV. Includes the rights, responsibilities and limits of general and limited partners

   A. I and II
   B. I and III
   C. I and IV
   D. II and IV

17. The general partner does which of the following?

   A. Manages the direct participation program
   B. Shares fiduciary responsibility with the limited partners
   C. Admits new partners
   D. All of the above

18. The general partner has a conflict of interest if it

   A. sells its own property to the partnership
   B. pays an affiliate for providing management services
   C. accepts compensation from the partnership for management services
   D. participates in several DPPs within one year

19. Who has unlimited liability for the limited partnership's debts?

   A. Limited partners
   B. General partner
   C. Both A and B
   D. Neither A nor B

20. When the general partner signs the subscription agreement, this indicates

   A. agreement to the contract between the general partner and the limited partners
   B. acceptance of fiduciary responsibility
   C. acceptance of the limited partner as a member of the partnership
   D. that there are no existing conflicts of interest

21. All of the following are reasons for purchasing interests in limited partnerships EXCEPT

   A. limited liability
   B. input into decisions affecting the investment
   C. tax write-offs
   D. growth potential

Answers

1. **C.** DPP stands for "direct participation program." The partners participate directly in the economic consequences of the business.

2. **A.** A sole proprietor is personally responsible for all debts of the business. Also, if the sole proprietor cannot continue working, the business folds.

3. **C.** A corporation's earnings are taxed before they are sent to stockholders in the form of dividends. The earnings are taxed again when they are received as dividends by stockholders. In sole proprietorships and partnerships, income is passed through to the owners, and they pay taxes on it. Thus, partnership and proprietorship income are taxed only once.

4. **B.** Partnerships have associates because there must be at least one general and one limited partner. The rest of the corporate characteristics listed can be avoided. Free transferability is easy to avoid; in most partnerships, in fact, interests are difficult to transfer (a fact your clients should take into consideration before investing). Centralization of management is hard to avoid; the limited partners are forbidden to participate in management. Though limited partners benefit from limited liability, the partnership as a whole can avoid this corporate characteristic if the general partner has substantial outside assets available to creditors.

5. **D.** The general partner manages the partnership and assumes unlimited liability.

6. **A.** A general partner has unlimited liability. All others have limited liability.

7. **A.** The syndicator is the organizer and promoter.

8. **C.** The NASD limits sales compensation in limited partnership underwritings to 10%.

9. **C.** A subscription is legally accepted when signed by the general partner. The general partner is required to reject the subscription if the limited partner doesn't meet the suitability requirements.

10. **D.** The order in which the partnership settles accounts is: secured creditors, general creditors, limited partners, general partners.

11. **B.** The advantages of a limited partnership are a direct flow-through of gains and losses as well as limited liability. In a limited partnership, the investor is not permitted a voice in management, and these investments offer very little liquidity.

12. **D.** In a general partnership, each of the general partners has unlimited liability. This means that a general partner is liable to lose not only everything he invested in this particular business, but also his personal assets. All of the other organizations offer some type of limited liability.

13. **C.** To avoid a conflict of interest, the general partner should not borrow from the partnership or own or lease adjacent property. The general partner is compensated by the partnership for managing the program, and this compensation does not present a conflict of interest. Although there is potential for conflict of interest when the general partner is involved in more than one program, this is not necessarily the case.

14. **B.** The limited partner's liability for the partnership's loans is limited. The LP's losses are limited to the initial investment; there is no voice in management; and tax advantages are passed through to the LP.

15. **C.** The limited partner can sue the general partner for violating the terms of the agreement or failing to exercise fiduciary responsibility. Answers A, B and D are disadvantages.

16. **C.** The agreement of limited partnership is a contract between the general and limited partners that defines rights, responsibilities and limits. It is not a public document, but the certificate of

limited partnership is. The subscription agreement concludes the sale of a partnership interest, but the agreement of limited partnership does not.

17.   **A.**   The general partner is the manager of the direct participation program. The GP has fiduciary responsibility to the LPs but does not share that responsibility with them. GPs are not permitted to admit new partners without the consent of the LPs.

18.   **A.**   The general partner should not engage in transactions with the partnership it is responsible for managing. The general partner can pay an affiliate for a service, be compensated for managing the partnership and participate in more than one program.

19.   **B.**   Only the general partner has unlimited liability.

20.   **C.**   The subscription agreement indicates that the general partner accepts the limited partner as a member. Both the general and limited partners sign the agreement.

21.   **B.**   Limited partners have limited input into how the partnership is managed. Limited liability, tax write-offs and growth are frequent reasons for purchasing interests in DPPs.

Types of Limited Partnership Programs

Real Estate Limited Partnerships

Real estate limited partnerships can provide:

- strong growth potential through appreciation of property;
- income; and
- cash distributions sheltered from taxes by deductions for mortgage interest and depreciation.

Types

There are three types of real estate program:

- **New construction.** A new construction program builds new property. The principal advantage of such a program is the potential for appreciation. Disadvantages to new construction are possible cost or time overruns, no established track record for new property the difficulty of finding permanent financing and an inability to deduct current expenses during the construction period. Investments in new construction are more speculative than investments in existing property.
- **Existing property.** Programs based on existing property with a track record are generally safer and more conservative than new construction programs. Disadvantages include greater maintenance or repair expenses than for new construction, expiring leases that may not be renewed and existing low-rent arrangements that may bring less revenue than desired.
- **Raw land.** Raw land offers appreciation potential. Undeveloped is not a tax shelter. All of the benefits of owning raw land are delayed until the sale of the property.

Oil and Gas Limited Partnerships

Types

There are three types of oil and gas program:

- **Exploratory drilling.** The principal objective of exploratory drilling programs is to locate undiscovered reserves of oil and gas. Exploratory drilling programs offer high risk and high reward. The principal tax advantage of exploratory drilling programs is the write-off of intangible drilling costs (IDCs).
- **Developmental drilling.** Developmental drilling programs target areas of proven reserves and plan new well drilling near existing fields. IDCs are somewhat lower. In general, there is less risk and less reward potential in developmental programs than there is in exploratory programs. Cash distributions are unlikely during the early stages of a developmental program.
- **Income programs.** In an income program, the partnership buys the value of the oil in the ground, with the expectation that the partnership can sell it and receive income that is sheltered by depletion allowances. Income programs do not explore or develop, nor do they pass on write-offs from IDCs.

Cost depletion is based on the amount of reserves sold and is limited to the original cost of the reserves. Percentage depletion is a fixed percentage (currently 15%) of income from the well and is not limited by the investor's basis in the property. An LP may well claim percentage depletion deductions in excess of the cost of the reserves.

Sharing Arrangements

- **Overriding royalty interest.** A person with a royalty interest takes no risks, but gets a share of the revenues. The GP who holds an overriding royalty interest incurs no costs (the LP bears all deductible and nondeductible costs), but receives a specified percentage of oil revenue.
- **Reversionary working interest.** The GP bears none of the program's costs, but does

not receive his share of revenues until the LPs have recovered their capital.

- **Net operating profits interest.** The GP bears none of the program's costs, but is entitled to a percentage of net profits.
- **Disproportionate sharing.** The GP bears a relatively small percentage of expenses and is entitled to a relatively large percentage of revenues.
- **Carried interest.** The GP shares tangible drilling costs with the LPs but pays no part of the IDCs.
- **Functional allocation.** The GP bears tangible costs, and the LPs bear IDCs. Revenues are shared.

Equipment-leasing Limited Partnerships

An equipment-leasing partnership purchases equipment that is then leased to other businesses on a long-term basis. Each investor receives a share of the income from the lease payments and a proportional share of operating expenses, interest expense and depreciation.

Questions

1. Raw land is what type of investment?

   A. Speculative
   B. Conservative
   C. Balanced
   D. Income producing

2. All of the following could be benefits of a long-term equipment-leasing direct participation program EXCEPT

   A. steady income from rental payments
   B. operating expenses to offset revenues
   C. cost recovery deductions
   D. capital appreciation

3. Which of the following generates deductions for oil and gas programs but not for real estate programs?

   A. Depreciation
   B. Depletion
   C. Interest expense deductions
   D. Operating expenses

4. Which of the following direct participation programs offer the greatest initial write-offs?

   A. New construction
   B. Raw land
   C. Equipment leasing
   D. Oil and gas drilling

5. All of the following are advantages of exploratory oil and gas programs EXCEPT

   A. low risk compared with real estate programs
   B. substantial initial deductions
   C. growth
   D. potential long-term cash distributions

6. Which of the following describe a raw land program?

    I. Depreciable
    II. Speculative
    III. Growth potential
    IV. Low risk

    A. I and II
    B. II and III
    C. II and IV
    D. III and IV

7. Which of the following advantages apply to income-producing real estate limited partnerships?

    I. Substantial depreciation deductions
    II. Investment tax credits
    III. Growth potential
    IV. Low risk

    A. I and II
    B. I and III
    C. I, III and IV
    D. II and III

8. Which of the following real estate programs is the LEAST advantageous in terms of depreciation deductions?

    A. Raw land
    B. Government-assisted housing
    C. Existing properties
    D. Sale-leaseback

Answers

1. **A.** Raw land is a speculative investment because an investor hopes to make a profit solely from appreciation in the value of the land. During the holding period, the land generates no income; however, there are expenses, such as taxes.

2. **D.** Leased equipment will generate revenue during the period of any lease. Operating expenses are deductible (against passive income). Recovery deductions (e.g., depreciation) are expenses that can be used to reduce taxable income. In most cases, leased equipment is not likely to show much appreciation.

3. **B.** Depreciation applies to both real estate and oil and gas programs (buildings in real estate, tangible property in oil and gas programs), as do deductions for interest expense. Depletion applies only to nonreplenishable natural resources, such as minerals or standing timber, and is a deduction that reflects the *using up* (depleting) of the primary assets of a natural resource investment program.

4. **D.** The intangible drilling costs (IDCs) of oil and gas drilling programs offer substantial initial write-offs. Initial write-offs are not the primary objective of participation in new construction, raw land or equipment-leasing programs.

5. **A.** Oil and gas programs are generally considered to involve greater risk than real estate programs. Answers B, C and D are generally accepted as advantages of oil and gas programs.

6. **B.** A raw land program is a speculative investment offering growth potential. However, raw land is not depreciable and is a fairly high-risk investment.

7.   **C.**   Income-producing real estate limited partnerships offer depreciation benefits and growth potential. They are also considered low risk relative to oil and gas, raw land or new construction programs. There is no investment tax credit on real estate.

8.   **A.**   Raw land is not depreciable. Answers B, C and D all offer depreciation as a tax advantage.

Limited Partnership Tax Accounting

Passive Gains and Losses

If the partnership shows a loss, a share of that amount will be passed along to each investor. This loss may benefit the investor if it qualifies as a tax deduction. For tax purposes, losses passed along to LPs are called passive losses because LPs are passive investors who do not take an active role in the business. Passive losses may be deducted from passive income only.

Tax Basis

Tax basis, which begins as the cash paid for a partnership interest, is a record of the amount a partner has invested in the partnership. After the initial payment, any economic benefit passed through to the investor decreases that original basis. Any economic disadvantage increases the basis.

An investor's tax basis determines how much loss the investor can write off in a year and how much taxable gain will be assigned the investor when the partnership sells its assets.

Partnership Tax Reporting

Every year, the partnership's accountant must fill out two tax forms: Form 1065 and Schedule K-1. Form 1065 provides the IRS with a thorough record of the financial consequences of the partnership's business for the year. Schedule K-1 is a component of Form 1065. Included on the schedule are all relevant items, including the LP's share of the partnership's ordinary income or loss.

Partnership losses reduce taxable income only to the extent that they reduce passive income.

Expenses

For accounting purposes, the following items are expensed:

- operating expenses
- annual interest expenses
- management fees
- state, local and payroll taxes
- IDCs

The cost of any of these items is used in full as a deduction when calculating taxable income.

Intangible Drilling Costs

Partnerships generally expense IDCs in the first year or two of operation.

Capitalized Expenses

Capitalized expenses include major assets such as buildings, land, machinery, certain fees and minerals. Capital costs cannot be deducted fully in the year they are incurred. Capital expenses can be deducted over a period of years.

In theory, businesses are allowed to deduct from their income an amount that represents the depreciation in value of tangible assets or the depletion of a mineral resource. In fact, depreciation and depletion deductions are usually based on a formula, not on the specific amount by which an item's value has decreased during the year.

Depreciation

In general, depreciation deductions are spread over an item's useful life in one of two ways—either **straight line** or **accelerated**. For accounting purposes, depreciation is an annual expense.

Accelerated depreciation allows a partnership to deduct the maximum amount as quickly as possible, thus accelerating deductions. Under MACRS, the IRS provides tables that specify the allowable deduction for each year of an asset's life. The IRS defines the life span of different categories of tangible assets as follows:

- **real property**—capitalized and depreciated over 27 1/2 years; and

- **personal property**—capitalized and recovered through depreciation over a time period determined by the IRS.

Each depreciable asset has a cost basis, which is its value for purposes of depreciation. Cost basis includes the purchase price, real estate commissions, title search fees, attorney's fees and certain other costs. Cost basis does not include the value of the land or any building bought only to be demolished, expense deductions that reduce depreciation or the amortized costs of rehabilitated low-income housing.

Adjusted Basis

Cost basis may be adjusted for certain capital expenditures related to the asset. Improvements that make a partnership's assets more valuable are included in cost basis. Routine maintenance expenses are not.

Depletion

Mineral resources are allowed a *depletion deduction* to compensate the partnership for the disappearance of the source of its profits. Depletion deductions are passed directly to the partners. Each LP receives a depletion deduction reflecting his share in the well or mine.

Cost depletion compensates the investor for the original purchase price of the amount of oil sold during the year. Percentage depletion is the percentage of income from the well.

Cost depletion. Cost depletion is very much like depreciation or any other expense. The deduction is a straightforward reimbursement for money spent on the purchase of the asset. The LP spends $10,000 purchasing oil reserves and, if the partnership sells the entire supply of oil, receives $10,000 in cost depletion deductions.

Percentage depletion. The percentage depletion is a percentage of annual income from the well. Percentage depletion is not limited by the investor's basis in the oil reserves. In reality, percentage deductions usually exceed cost deductions because of adjustments to the basis used to calculate cost depletion and, in some cases, percentage depletion

deductions taken over the life of a partnership may actually exceed the amount of money the investor paid for a share of the reserves.

Limits on percentage depletion. The tax code limits percentage depletion deductions in four ways:

1. Only new drilling qualifies for percentage depletion.
2. Only small, independent producers can use percentage depletion.
3. Organizations substantially involved in refining or marketing petroleum, as well as in drilling, cannot use percentage depletion.
4. Percentage depletion deductions cannot exceed 50% of income from the well or 65% of income from all sources.

Amortization

Certain expenses incurred during the early life of a partnership are amortized over a period of time rather than expensed in the first year. In later years income is offset by these amortization expenses.

Prepaid interest must be amortized over the life of the loan, not deducted in the year paid. Prepaid fees must be amortized over the life of the service purchased, not deducted in the year of payment.

Brokerage fees and commissions paid when acquiring a mortgage are treated as capital costs to be amortized during the life of the loan. Fees paid to a rental agent are amortized and deducted over the rent-up period.

Expenses incurred in organizing a partnership must be amortized over at least 60 months.

Expenses Not Recovered

Syndication expenses are not deductible. Distributions of profits to the GP are not deductible by LPs. The builder's profits are not deductible because they are considered to be a share of partnership profits.

Tax Credits

Tax credits are available on certain types of real estate, including low-income housing and certified historical structures. They are also available on some types of energy conservation equipment and on the costs of research and development.

Deferral

Depreciation puts off a tax liability to a later date; it does not necessarily eliminate the liability altogether. Depreciation deductions reduce the adjusted basis, thus increasing gain on sale.

Recapture

Recapture of accelerated depreciation. Recapture applies to excess depreciation, which is accelerated depreciation that is greater than straight-line depreciation. Excess depreciation occurs if the property is disposed of prematurely.

Recapture of IDCs. If a partnership sells an oil well before the normal amortization period ends, the IRS will recapture any previously expensed IDC. If the gain exceeds IDC deductions, an amount equal to the deductions will be treated as ordinary income; the rest will be capital gain.

Tax Reporting for Limited Partners

Distributive Shares of Revenues and Expenses

Partnerships allocate to each investor a percentage of their revenues for the year. Similarly, investors are apportioned a certain amount of the partnership's expenses.

Passive Income and Loss

If the total expenses listed on an investor's K-1 (including depreciation) exceed her share of revenues, for tax purposes that is the amount of her passive losses.

Cash Flow

The depreciation allowed by the IRC is not tied to an actual cash outlay by the partnership. It is a loss only on paper. Therefore, the investor's share of revenue is reduced only by the operating and interest expenses. This can result in a positive cash flow. The partnership may, therefore, distribute part or all of this cash flow to the LPs as a return of capital.

Tax Basis

Establishing the Basis

The investor's initial basis includes cash contributions, recourse debt and nonrecourse debt.

Recourse debt. This is debt for which the LP is liable in the event that the partnership defaults. The lender has recourse to the LP's cash and other assets. Recourse debt is always included in basis because the LP is always at risk for the entire amount.

Nonrecourse debt. This is debt secured only by the investor's assets in the partnership. In bankruptcy, therefore, the lender has no recourse to the LP's personal, nonpartnership assets. Only the GP may be assessed for repayment of the loan.

The LP's tax basis may change yearly according to the performance of the partnership.

Increasing the Basis

New contributions of cash or property, assumed recourse debt and undistributed shares in partnership income increase the risk of loss and, therefore, tax basis.

Decreasing the Basis

Basis is decreased by any distribution of cash or property, release of debt and distribution of partnership loss. Distributions of cash or property from the partnership are considered a return of the capital initially contributed. Similarly, any release or repayment of debt also lowers the partner's risk and, therefore, tax basis.

Phantom Income and the Crossover Point

When a partnership experiences little or no cash flow, but is declaring taxable income, the taxable income not backed by a positive cash flow is referred to as **phantom income**. The point at which the partnership begins to show a negative cash flow with a taxable income, rather than positive cash and tax deductions, is called the **crossover point**.

Questions

1. Mrs. Forbes invests in a limited partnership that generates $9,000 in passive losses. She is permitted to deduct these losses against

   A. passive income only
   B. either passive income or investment income
   C. any type of taxable income
   D. passive losses only

2. Your client invested $175,000 in a limited partnership that later liquidated, leaving $400,000 in unpaid debt. What is your client's maximum loss potential?

   A. $0
   B. $175,000
   C. $225,000
   D. $400,000

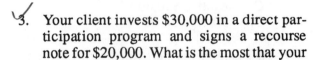 3. Your client invests $30,000 in a direct participation program and signs a recourse note for $20,000. What is the most that your client can lose from this investment?

   A. $10,000
   B. $20,000
   C. $30,000
   D. $50,000

4. A customer invests $10,000 in a real estate limited partnership and signs a $40,000 nonrecourse note. Which two of the following statements are true?

   I. The customer has established a $10,000 tax basis.
   II. The customer has established a $50,000 tax basis.
   III. The maximum loss that the customer can experience is $10,000.
   IV. The maximum loss that the customer can experience is $50,000.

   A. I and III
   B. I and IV
   C. II and III
   D. II and IV

Use the following information to answer questions 5 and 6.

An investor in the 28% tax bracket invests $200,000 in a limited partnership direct participation program. That year her share of revenue is $300,000, her share of operating expenses is $200,000, her share of interest expense is $95,000 and her share of depreciation is $55,000.

5. What does she report as taxable income or loss?

    A. Income of $5,000
    B. Income of $45,000
    C. Loss of $50,000
    D. Loss of $5,000

6. What is the cash flow?

    A. Negative $5,000
    B. Positive $5,000
    C. Negative $50,000
    D. Positive $50,000

7. In a limited partnership, the crossover point occurs when

    A. the program begins reporting tax losses while maintaining positive cash flow
    B. income exceeds expenses for tax purposes
    C. cash flow is sufficient for distributions to the limited partners
    D. the program becomes economically viable

8. An investor in a limited partnership has established a basis, for tax purposes, of $20,000. During the year, his distributed share of the partnership losses is $18,000 and he receives a cash distribution of $15,000. What amount of loss can he carry forward?

    A. $2,000
    B. $3,000
    C. $5,000
    D. $13,000

9. Which of the following would NOT generate IDCs in an oil drilling program?

    A. Labor costs
    B. Cost of casing the well
    C. Fuel costs
    D. Geologist's fees

Answers

1. A. As a result of the new rules in the Tax Reform Act of 1986, passive losses generated by a direct participation program may be deducted only against passive income; this is income that is also generated by a direct participation program or other investments the individual does not manage. Passive losses may not be deducted against investment income such as dividends, interest or capital gains generated by securities investments.

2. B. Your client's maximum loss is limited to the amount of the initial investment, which is $175,000.

3. D. Your client could lose the entire $30,000 investment and be liable for the $20,000 loan, for a total of $50,000.

4. C. The customer has invested $10,000 cash. In most cases, a nonrecourse loan could not be included in tax basis. Real estate is an exception to that rule. The customer has a tax basis of $50,000, which is the cash invested plus the share in the nonrecourse loan. However, because the loan is nonrecourse, the customer has at risk only the $10,000 cash contribution.

5. C.

Revenue		$300,000
Operating expenses	200,000	
Interest expense	95,000	
Depreciation	55,000	
Total expenses		−$350,000
Net loss		($50,000)

6. B.

Revenue		$300,000
Operating expenses	200,000	
Interest expense	95,000	
Total cash expenses		−$295,000
Cash flow		$5,000

7. B. At the crossover point, the partnership begins generating taxable income for the partners. This occurs when revenues earned by the partnership exceed deductible expenses. Ideally, the partnership can have cash flow while showing a loss for tax purposes because of deductible noncash expenses (e.g., depreciation). This can allow cash distributions, which themselves do not affect the taxable income or loss from the partnership investment. The investment should be economically viable from the inception of the program.

8. D. When the limited partner receives a cash distribution of $15,000, it is considered a return of capital and decreases the basis to $5,000. Therefore, only $5,000 of the $18,000 loss may be deducted. The remaining $13,000 of tax loss is carried forward until the basis increases and the deduction may be taken.

9. B. IDCs are intangible drilling costs. They include expenses for labor, services such as geological analysis, and items with no salvage value, such as fuel to run machinery. Partnerships can elect to treat IDCs as current expenses. (Fuel is entirely consumed as it is used.) Casing is a tangible item, something one can see and touch. Tangible costs can be depreciated but not treated as current expenses.

20 Key Facts and Figures

How Many *Business* Days?

Same Business Day

- The settlement date on cash transactions.

One Business Day

- Regular way settlement on U.S. government securities.
- OCC settlement by broker-dealers for options transactions.
- Ex-dividend date for cash transactions (from the record date).

Two Business Days

- The minimum period for seller's option contracts on U.S. government securities.

Four Business Days

- The relationship of the normal ex-dividend date to the record date.

Five Business Days

- Regular way settlement for securities other than U.S. governments.

Six Business Days

- The minimum period for seller's option contracts on securities other than U.S. governments.

Seven Business Days

- The time within which cash account (nonmargin) purchases must be paid in full.
- The time within which Regulation T margin calls must be satisfied.

Ten Business Days

- The maximum time allowed the seller to deliver certificates.
- The time within which the beneficial owner's shares will be represented if he has not responded prior to the meeting.

Twenty Business Days

- The time period respondents may take to answer an arbitration claim.

How Many *Calendar* Days?

Seven Calendar Days

- The maximum time period for mutual funds to redeem shares tendered.

Twenty Calendar Days

- The minimum time period between the filing date and the effective date (cooling-off period) of a security registration.

Thirty Calendar Days

- The time that must elapse before termination as a registered rep is effective with the NASD unless accepted earlier by the Board of Governors.
- The number of days in any month when computing interest on debt securities other than U.S. governments.
- The IRS time period restriction on purchases to avoid wash sale designation (30 days before and 30 days after).

Thirty-five Calendar Days

- The maximum time period for delivery on COD orders.

Forty-five Calendar Days

- The maximum time period within which one can receive a 100% refund of sales charges on investment company contractual plans.

Sixty Calendar Days

- The maximum length of a seller's option contract in a security.

Sixty-one Calendar Days

- The IRS total time period restriction on purchases to avoid a wash sale designation.

Ninety Calendar Days

- The length of time a cash account must be frozen for nonpayment.

How Many *Months*?

One Month

- The frequency with which statements must be mailed to active customers.

Two Months

- The maximum time a registered rep can hold the mail of a customer who is traveling within the United States.

Three Months

- The maximum time a registered rep can hold the mail of a customer who is out of the country.
- The length of time that a letter of intent can be backdated.

Six Months

- The frequency with which investment companies must send reports to shareholders (semiannually).

Twelve Months

- The frequency with which every publicly held firm and NYSE firm must be audited by an independent public accountant (annually).

Thirteen Months

- The length of life of a letter of intent.

Eighteen Months

- The time after which refunds of sales charges in excess of 15% on front-end plans expire.

How Many *Years*?

Two Years

- The time fully paid restricted stock must be owned before selling under Rule 144.

Three Years

- The length of time nonaffiliated persons must own fully paid for restricted stock before selling out under Rule 144 and be exempt from filing Form 144 and from the volume limits and current financial information requirements.

Color Code that Paperwork!

Match the following color-coded terms with the definitions in questions 1 through 6.

A. Blue chip
B. *The Blue List*
C. Blue-sky
D. *Pink Sheets*
E. Red herring
F. Yellow Sheets

1. ___ Daily publication showing current offerings of municipal bond dealers

2. ___ Preliminary prospectus

3. ___ Nickname for state laws that regulate the securities industry

4. ___ Quote sheets that carry the wholesale prices between dealers for corporate bonds

5. ___ Well-established companies that have demonstrated the ability to pay dividends in both good times and bad

6. ___ Daily publication that shows wholesale quotations for over-the-counter stocks

Answers: 1. B; 2. E; 3. C; 4. F; 5. A; 6. D.

Take a Letter!

Match the following securities regulations with the definitions in questions 1 through 3.

A. Reg A
B. Reg T
C. Reg U

1. ___ The securities regulation that exempts public offerings valued at less than $1.5 million from registration requirements

2. ___ The Federal Reserve Board regulation governing the amount of credit extended to clients by brokerage firms and dealers

3. ___ The Federal Reserve Board regulation governing the credit extended by banks for the purpose of securities transactions

Answers: 1. A; 2. B; 3. C

Common Abbreviations

ADR	American depositary receipt		GO	general obligation bond
AMBAC	AMBAC Indemnity Corporation		GTC	good till canceled
AMEX	American Stock Exchange		IADB	Inter-American Development Bank
AON	all or none		IDB	industrial development bond
BA	banker's acceptance		IDR	industrial revenue bond
BAN	bond anticipation note		IOC	immediate or cancel
BD	broker-dealer		IRA	individual retirement account
CAES	Computer Assisted Execution System		IRC	Internal Revenue Code
CBOE	Chicago Board Options Exchange		IRS	Internal Revenue Service
CD	certificate of deposit		ITC	investment tax credit
CMV	current market value		JTIC	joint tenants in common
COD	cash on delivery		JTWROS	joint tenants with right of survivorship
CPI	Consumer Price Index		LIFO	last in, first out
CQS	Consolidated Quotation System		MSRB	Municipal Securities Rulemaking Board
CR	credit record		MV	market value
CROP	Compliance Registered Options Principal		NASD	National Association of Securities Dealers
CUSIP	Committee on Uniform Securities Identification Procedures		NASDAQ	National Association of Securities Dealers Automated Quotation System
DBCC	District Business Conduct Committee		NAV	net asset value
DJIA	Dow Jones Industrial Average		NMS	National Market System
DK	don't know		NYSE	New York Stock Exchange
DNR	do not reduce		OTC	over the counter
DOT	Designated Order Turnaround System		POP	public offering price
DPP	direct participation program		RAN	revenue anticipation note
DR	debit record		RR	registered representative
ERISA	Employee Retirement Income Security Act		SEC	Securities and Exchange Commission
FDIC	Federal Deposit Insurance Corporation		SEP	simplified employee pension plan
FED	Federal Reserve Board		SIA	Securities Industry Association
FHA	Federal Housing Administration		SIPC	Securities Investor Protection Corporation
FIFO	first in, first out		SMA	special memorandum account
FNMA	Federal National Mortgage Association		SOES	Small Order Execution System
FOK	fill or kill		SRO	self-regulatory organization
FRB	Federal Reserve Board		TAN	tax anticipation note
GNMA	Government National Mortgage Association		TRAN	tax and revenue anticipation note
GNP	gross national product		WD	when distributed
			WI	when issued
			YTC	yield to call
			YTM	yield to maturity